D1600989

Endorsements for *The Struggle is Real*

"Reading this collection of thoughtful, practical articles prompted this reflection: We are never more like Jesus than when we are caring for the hurting and lonely. This timely resource is a reminder to the church that living and loving like Jesus is not optional. In fact, it is crucial to our witness. May we learn to better love the "least of these" and live out our testimony as people who are friends of sinners. Churches of any size and in any location can benefit from these valuable insights and solutions."

—**David Ferguson**, D.Phil., D.Litt., Executive Director,
The Great Commandment Network

"As a pastor for many years, I know we constantly face people with overwhelming mental and relational health needs. A local pastor cannot be a proficient clinician, but every pastor can have an adequate understanding of the problems and issues he or she encounters. First we must break the silence, remove the shame, and erase the stigma surrounding mental and relational issues in the church and provide life-transforming ministry by the power of the Holy Spirit!

"In this book, Tim Clinton and Jared Pingleton provide a solid guide to better understanding the issues and dynamics of troubled people and more effectively ministering to them. Written by national leaders and renowned specialists in various areas of Christian mental and relational health, each chapter expertly addresses in a compelling yet compassionate manner a crucial area of need extant within the local church."

—**George O. Wood**, P.Th.D., J.D., former General Superintendent,
The General Council of the Assemblies of God

"With churches serving as the number one place people go for help with mental and relational health, leaders must equip themselves for effective ministry. We have long needed this important resource to help us do just that. With expert, professional, and unapologetically Christian perspectives, this book will help your church better support the spiritual, emotional, and relational health of all who seek to follow Christ."

—**Amy Simpson**, M.B.A., author, *Troubled Minds: Mental Illness and the Church's Mission* and *Anxious: Choosing Faith in a World of Worry*

"This is a lineup of experienced healers and caring writers. It will be a valuable resource for the field of mental and emotional health for years to come."

—**John Ortberg**, Ph.D., Senior Pastor, *Menlo Church*, Menlo Park, California, Clinical Psychologist and best-selling author

"Within the minority communities, specifically the African-American culture, the church is typically the counseling office and the pastor is the counselor. *The Struggle is Real* offers a simple yet powerful bridge between the church and counseling. Thank you, Tim Clinton and Jared Pingleton, for producing a much-needed blueprint that connects faith, the church, and the mental health profession."

—**Mark Clear**, Ph.D., author, speaker, Christian Counselor/Consultant/ Coach, Executive Director, *The Multicultural Division of the American Association of Christian Counselors* (*AACC*)

"Research pervasively reveals that individuals experiencing psychological distress are more likely to first seek help from clergy before going to any other professional group. Therefore, I heartily recommend *The Struggle is Real*, especially for church discipleship initiatives and seminary curriculum programs. Not only is this insightful book practical and accessible; it provides the essential biblical framework to address the most sensitive mental pressure-points while supplying the keys to bring hope, healing, and restoration. Clinton and Pingleton have provided exactly what the church needs."

—**Jeremiah J. Johnston**, Ph.D., President, *Christian Thinkers Society*, Professor, *Houston Baptist University*

"People everywhere are hurting, including those inside the church. Written by a team of experts, this important resource is designed to shine the wonderful and liberating light of the gospel into the dark and difficult areas of people's lives. What's here will heal. You need this book, and the people you love need it too."

—**Johnnie Moore**, Founder, *The KAIROS Company*

"Social media has made all of us experts at convincing everyone else that we're fine. But the pictures we post don't match the reality we live with. We are not fine; the people we serve are not fine—we all struggle! This book is an invaluable resource for helping us minister to people who need our understanding."

—**Greg Surratt**, Founding Pastor, *Seacoast Church*, Mount Pleasant, South Carolina, President, *Association of Related Churches (ARC)*

"As a pastor serving in ministry for over 20 years, I have seen first-hand the devastation that has taken place in families as a result of ignoring and/or dismissing mental health issues. I have witnessed families disintegrating, marriages crumbling, and even lives ending through tragic circumstances. It is incumbent upon all in ministry that we preach the whole counsel of God, including dealing head-on with these issues. I appreciate Tim Clinton and Jared Pingleton putting this great resource together for those of us on the frontline. I pray their passion in this area, and this book, will serve as a catalyst for us all to begin the healing process in our churches and in our society. I believe the answer to these problems is ultimately found in Christ alone, and I know that Tim and Jared concur."

—**Jonathan Falwell**, Senior Pastor, *Thomas Road Baptist Church*, Lynchburg, Virginia

"Often, it's pastors and church leaders who are on the frontline responding to the challenges of mental health in our society. In this book, Drs. Tim Clinton and Jared Pingleton have done a masterful job bringing together experts from a wide variety of disciplines to give sound theological and practical help. People today are struggling in ways that only the church can help. '*The Struggle is Real*' is an excellent resource for equipping ministry leaders and counselors alike to meet this most pressing need."

—**Rev. Samuel Rodriguez**, President of the *National Hispanic Christian Leadership Conference*

THE
STRUGGLE
IS REAL

HOW TO CARE FOR MENTAL AND RELATIONAL
HEALTH NEEDS IN THE CHURCH

TIM CLINTON, Ed.D., *EXECUTIVE EDITOR*

JARED PINGLETON, Psy.D., *GENERAL EDITOR*

WESTBOW
P R E S S®
A DIVISION OF THOMAS NELSON
& ZONDERVAN

WestBow Press books may be ordered through booksellers or by contacting:

WestBow Press
A Division of Thomas Nelson & Zondervan
1663 Liberty Drive
Bloomington, IN 47403
www.westbowpress.com
1 (866) 928-1240

ISBN: 978-1-5127-9299-7 (sc)
ISBN: 978-1-5127-9300-0 (hc)
ISBN: 978-1-5127-9298-0 (e)

Library of Congress Control Number: 2017910683

Print information available on the last page.

WestBow Press rev. date: 09/19/2019

CONTENTS

Foreword: H. B. London, D.D. xiii

Introduction: Tim Clinton, Ed.D. and Jared Pingleton, Psy.D. xv

Acknowledgements...xvii

1. How to Assess the Mental and Relational
   Health Needs in Your Church
   Ed Stetzer, Ph.D., D.Min. 1

2. How to Prepare Pastors for Mental and Relational Health Ministry
   Mark Dance, D.Min. 15

3. How to Understand Major Mental Health Disorders
   Paul Meier, M.D.. 27

4. How to Understand Basic Bio-Physiological
   Issues in Mental and Relational Health
   Michael Lyles, M.D. 45

5. How to Develop a Suffering-Sensitive Ministry
   Gary J. Oliver, Th.M., Ph.D... 59

6. How to Develop and Maintain Personal and
   Professional Boundaries in Ministry
   Timothy Clinton, Ed.D. and Dina Jones, M.A...................... 73

7. How to Develop an Effective Regimen of
   Selfcare in People-Helping Ministries
   Eric Scalise, Ph.D. 93

8. How to Develop the Art of Making an Effective Referral
   Jared Pingleton, Psy.D. 109

9. How to Develop an Effective Lay Counseling Ministry
   Siang-Yang Tan, Ph.D..121

10. How to Develop an Effective Multicultural Ministry
    Fernando Garzon, Psy.D., Jichan Kim, Ph.D.,
    Melvin Pride, Ph.D., Dwight Rice, Ph.D............................ 143

11. How to Develop an Effective Substance Abuse Recovery Ministry
    Mac Owen and Mary Owen......................................163

12. How to Develop an Effective Opioid Crisis Ministry
    David E. Jenkins, Psy.D...................................... 177

13. How to Develop an Effective Eating Disorders Recovery Ministry
    Margaret Nagib, Psy.D. 195

14. How to Develop an Effective Grief Recovery Ministry
    Robert Shaw, D.Min. 213

15. How to Develop an Effective Reproductive Loss Recovery Ministry
    Kay Lyn Carlson, LSW.. 229

16. How to Develop an Effective Military Family Support Ministry
    David Mikkelson, Ph.D., M.Div. and
    Suzanne Mikkelson, Ph.D. 251

17. How to Develop an Effective Trauma Recovery Ministry
    Diane Langberg, Ph.D... 273

18. How to Develop an Effective Suicide Awareness
    and Crisis Response Ministry
    Jennifer Cisney Ellers, M.A. and Kevin Ellers, D.Min.......... 289

19. How to Develop an Effective Sexual Integrity Ministry
    Doug Rosenau, Ed.D.. 303

20. How to Develop an Effective Marriage Mentoring Ministry
    Les Parrott, Ph.D. and Leslie Parrot, Ed.D. 323

21. How to Develop an Effective Blended Family Support Ministry
    Ron Deal, M.MFT. 335

22. How to Develop an Effective Divorce Recovery Ministry
    Robert Burns, Ph.D., D.Min. 353

23. How to Develop an Effective Women's Mentoring Ministry
    Joneal Kirby, Ph.D.. 371

24. How to Develop an Effective Men's Mentoring Ministry
    Roy Smith, Ph.D., M.Div. 385

25. How to Develop an Effective Support Ministry for
    Parents of Autistic and Special Needs Children
    Stephanie Holmes, M.A. 401

26. How to Develop an Effective Support Ministry
    for Adoptive and Foster Parents
    Daniel Nehrbass, Ph.D. 419

27. How to Develop Effective Connections with
    Community Mental Health Resources
    Matthew Stanford, Ph.D. 437

28. How to Develop an Effective Church-Based Wellness Ministry
    Gregory Jantz, Ph.D. 449

About the Editors.. 465

Foreword

H. B. London, D.D.

I began pastoring in 1963, and along the way I learned many things that I wish I had been taught before I started. Unfortunately, I learned many of those lessons quite painfully and at considerable cost to me, my family, and my flocks. How I wish the kind of resource you are now holding had been available then! Like me, I'm sure you've had a few nightmarish stories of hurting people and stressful situations you have encountered in your ministry.

There have always been people with mental and relational health problems in the church—historically we just haven't been properly trained and equipped to know how to minister effectively to their needs. Current research verifies what I learned the hard way from my own personal experience: the pastor is typically the first person someone with a mental and/or relational health problem turns to for help. As do most pastors, I know how scary, lonely, and often overwhelming it feels to be in over my head with a suicidal crisis, a chronic alcoholic, or an abusive family situation.

Bible schools and seminaries do a good job of teaching us hermeneutics, exegetics, and homiletics. But the day in, day out demands of practical ministry to hurting people and relationships are rarely, if ever, addressed thoroughly in our training. Many pastors have had to scramble to learn on the fly or go by the seat of their pants about how to care for and cope with people who are in the throes of a serious depression, controlled by an addictive substance or behavior, or headed to a divorce lawyer.

This innovative ministry resource is designed to educate, equip, empower, and encourage you as pastors and other church leaders. It will help you compassionately yet competently care for your congregants in a Christ-honoring way. It's time to come alongside hurting people and erase their silence, shame, and stigma. They desperately need the hope, health, and healing of the gospel applied in practical ways to their very real struggles.

I believe the church should literally and figuratively be a sanctuary for hurting people. Even though the lives of people with problems and conflicted relationships are messy, stressful, and complicated, the church needs to be the proverbial hospital where their wounds are cared for with love, grace, and mercy. Christ still calls us to embrace the brokenhearted, emancipate those in captivity, and enlighten those in darkness.

What follows is an outstanding primer on how to do this important shepherding work with dignity, honor, and excellence. Written by a world-class team of experts in both ministry and Christian mental health fields, this book is a comprehensive 'tool box' designed to help you and your leaders understand and implement specialized ministries to hurting people and relationships in a practical way. Fulfilling this mission will revitalize and revolutionize your entire church. Furthermore, your own emotional load will be lightened as you see how to better care not only for those sheep who give you chronic headaches, but also for the ones for whom your heart aches. Read this powerful book with an ear to listen to the Holy Spirit's guidance about how you can increase the effectiveness of your ministry to those hurting people who are already in your church, and with an eye to see how you can better reach out with a renewed sense of purpose and mission to be Jesus to those with mental and relational health needs. Their struggles are real indeed.

H. B. London was a fourth generation minister who served as a senior pastor for thirty-one years. He was promoted to heaven shortly after writing this foreword. He authored thirteen books and was the Pastor to Pastors Emeritus for Focus on the Family.

Introduction

Divorce. Suicide. Childhood sexual abuse. Depression. Pornography. Anxiety and panic disorders. Cohabitation. Bi-polar disorder. Alcoholism. Domestic violence. Abortion. Drug and prescription medication abuse. Adultery. Gambling. Single parent families. Trauma and grief. Eating disorders. The pace, pain, and pressure of modern life have taken over countless people's lives.

The struggle is real. People are hurting in unprecedented ways and in virtually epidemic numbers. These problems exist not only "out there" in society at large; they are very much present in our churches, and we must minister to them directly and effectively. Yet in most congregations, these overwhelming human needs are typically and historically cloaked in an insidious and destructive combination of silence, secrecy, shame, and stigma.

While it seems in many ways to be the worst of times, people are also searching for answers, and research consistently verifies that when hurting people do reach out for help, the vast majority turn first to a pastor, priest, or other church leader. However, the horrible irony is that most pastors simply do not have the time or training to adequately minister to these serious and specialized needs. At the same time, the cumulative population of persons experiencing significant mental and relational health problems is astronomical, and the aggregate toll of human suffering they are enduring is overwhelming.

Churches are filled with real people who have real needs and need real help. But has the church largely abdicated its historic leadership role in providing healthcare and ministering to human needs? Worldwide, hospitals and medical clinics were typically founded and operated by Christian ministries and organizations. Yet what about mental and relational health care?

Research proves that faith-based social service delivery systems and initiatives are more efficient and effective than bureaucratic governmental programs. However, in order to maximize the church's healing potentials, we must strive to become actual sanctuaries, truly safe harbors for hurting persons and relationships. Tragically, many people shy away from the potential healing ministry of the church due to fears of being judged, criticized, and rejected if they are vulnerable to share their pain, addiction, or issues. That large room where the congregation has traditionally met for worship needs to become more than a literal sanctuary. The bottom line is that the church must become a trusted and emotional safe haven for broken hearts, a refuge for problem-filled lives, and a shelter for damaged relationships.

As we all know, mental and relational problems can be messy. And complicated. And costly. They often require major, labor-intensive investments of time, effort, and energy that consume disproportionate shares of precious and limited church resources. So how do we as the church adequately answer God's call?

First we must end the silence, expose the secrecy, eliminate the shame, and erase the stigma surrounding mental and relational health issues in the church. Contrary to much implicit—and some explicit—teaching and preaching, just because we are Christians does not mean we are immune to or exempt from experiencing adversity, anguish, and afflictions. Here in our fallen world, we are never promised a life without such difficulties. Rather, Jesus assured us that we will have struggles when he declared: "...In this world you will have trouble..." Thankfully he also promised, "...But take heart! I have overcome the world" (John 16:33, NIV).

Our earnest hope, heartfelt prayer, and ministry goal at the American Association of Christian Counselors is that this groundbreaking book will speak truth, shine light, and spread salt into our deluded, darkened, and decaying world. Written by national leaders and renowned specialists in various areas of Christian mental and relational health, each chapter expertly addresses in a compelling yet compassionate manner a crucial area of need extant within the local church. This veritable ministry toolbox is solidly biblical, eminently practical, and readily applicable. It offers a smorgasbord of strategies, structures, and solutions for how to serve suffering, sinful saints.

Written with a heart for effective ministry and a mission for redemptive transformation, this unique and powerful resource will help educate, encourage, equip, and empower pastors and other church leaders to do the work of ministry in practical and tangible ways for which Bible school and seminary typically did not prepare them. Through this vessel, we pray the Father's love and mercy, the peace and comfort of the Holy Spirit, and the grace and forgiveness of Jesus Christ will pour out help, healing, and hope to the hurting.

We commend you for your courageous leadership in reaching out to people struggling with mental and relational health issues. We pray the Lord will help you—and richly bless you—as you serve him through your ministry to the throngs of hurting people whom many marginalize as "the least."

Tim Clinton and Jared Pingleton

Acknowledgements

Our special thanks go to:

Patty Roberts for the herculean job of editing and integrating 36 different writers' styles into a cohesive and coherent ministry treatise. Her dedication to excellence is a wonderful blessing and is deeply appreciated. Masterful, if not miraculous job!

Amy Cole for designing the creative and graphically compelling cover. Symbolically effective and eye-catching at the same time!

The publishing team at Westbow for their helpfulness, guidance, and support throughout the process. Your ministry-mindedness and servanthood made this ministry tool a blessing to produce!

We want to express our deepest gratitude to the countless clients, parishioners, students, churches, ministry organizations, conference/seminar/retreat attendees, and others in God's kingdom we both have been privileged to serve over the years. The Lord has truly used you to help and teach us the most.

Thanks to the entire team at AACC who have helped out in many ways—you are wonderful colleagues!

Finally, we are most appreciative of our wonderful families, who are undoubtedly God's greatest and richest blessings to us both.

Jared: to my precious wife Linda, our four awesome sons, Jordan, Josh, Joel, and Joseph, our four delightful daughters-in-law, and our five adorable grandchildren – thanks so much for your consistent love and faithful support. I love you all dearly and deeply.

Tim: to my wife Julie, our daughter Megan and her husband Ben, and our son Zach – thanks for your love and daily prayers. You make life a beautiful ride... let's make sure we don't miss a moment... love ya.

To God Be the Glory!
Tim Clinton and Jared Pingleton

Ed Stetzer, Ph.D., D.Min.

Dr. Ed Stetzer holds the Billy Graham Distinguished Chair for Church, Mission, and Evangelism at Wheaton College. He also serves as the Executive Director of the Billy Graham Center for Evangelism at Wheaton, and as chair of the Evangelism and Leadership Program in the Graduate School. Ed is a prolific author and well-known conference speaker. He has planted, revitalized, and pastored churches, trained pastors and church planters on six continents, holds two masters degrees and two doctorates, and has written more than a dozen books and hundreds of articles.

Stetzer is a contributing editor for *Christianity Today,* a columnist for *Outreach Magazine,* and is frequently cited or interviewed in news outlets such as USAToday and CNN. He is also the Executive Editor of The Gospel Project, which is used by over a million individuals each week. Stetzer is Executive Editor of *Facts & Trends Magazine,* a Christian leadership magazine with a circulation of 70,000 readers.

As of fall 2015, Ed co-hosts *BreakPoint This Week,* a radio broadcast that airs on over 400 media outlets. He also serves as the teaching pastor at Christ Fellowship, a multi-cultural gigachurch in Miami, Florida.

CHAPTER 1

How to Assess the Mental and Relational Health Needs in Your Church

Ed Stetzer, Ph.D., D.Min.

According to the National Institute of Mental Health (NIMH), every year more than one out of every five people in America suffers from a diagnosable mental illness. And on average, one out of every five children, as well as one out of every 25 adults, suffers from a seriously debilitating mental illness; not a run-of-the-mill case of the blues or the normal, day-to-day anxieties of life, but a mental illness—like serious depression or bipolar disorder—that functionally disrupts their lives. In some cases, like that of Matthew Warren, the son of my friends Rick and Kay Warren, the pain and suffering is too much to bear, and their lives are cut short through the tragedy of suicide. Every year in America, more than 42,000 people (more than the number who die from breast cancer or prostate cancer) tragically take their own lives.

The pain and struggle of mental illness is real.

So is the pain and struggle from relational problems. Adultery, domestic violence, divorce, child abuse and neglect, drug and prescription medication abuse, alcohol addiction, pornography and other sexual addictions (simply epidemic), abortion, and other challenges like the current scourge of cohabitation are reaching historic highs in our society and causing unprecedented levels of pain and suffering.

Breaking the Stigma

As a pastor, I've seen these impersonal statistics come alive in the lives of my church members and in the lives of family and friends. Chances are you have, too. You may have even prayed for someone affected by mental illness or talked with them about their struggles. We know Jesus came

1

to comfort us in all our afflictions. But in the church, it seems we just don't talk much about mental illness. So people suffer in silence. They feel abandoned by God at times and blame their illness on some kind of spiritual failing. Worst of all, they suffer alone, without the comfort that other believers can offer them. It's time for that to change. The time has come for the church to recognize and admit that acute mental illness and severe relationship problems exist within the body of Christ—and minister accordingly.

In an effort to address these needs and minister to mental illness issues, in 2014 LifeWay Research partnered with Focus on the Family and the family of a man who endured schizophrenia to conduct a landmark investigation called "A Study of Acute Mental Illness and Christian Faith." We found that acute mental illness is just as common in the church as it is in the rest of society. We also found that churches want to help those affected by mental illness.

But pastors need more guidance and preparation for dealing with mental health crises. They often don't have a plan to help families affected by mental illness or to provide ongoing spiritual care to church members who have mental illness. Most troubling, though people in faith communities are generally seen as more psychologically healthy, in the church the stigma of mental illness is disproportionately prevalent.

In other words, in relation to mental illness, there is often greater shame in the church than outside the church—and the church is called to be a place of grace, not a place of shame. But our research also found that when people suffer from mental illness, they often turn to pastors for help. Actually, pastors and the police are often the first responders in mental health crises. Those crises give the church the opportunity to be the church—to demonstrate the love of God to families and fellow believers in their time of need. And to the extent that the church understands acute mental illness to be one example of how Christians can struggle, those crises can help every one of us better understand our own weaknesses.

This study's parameters defined acute mental illness as moderate depression, severe depression, bipolar disorder, or schizophrenia. Protestant adults responding to our telephone and online surveys during the spring and summer of 2014 included pastors, people with acute mental illness, and their family members. We used the best methods available to reach these three quantitative audiences. Further, the study used LifeWay's ProTheo theological research service to deal exegetically with sensitive issues including spiritual commitments and spiritual growth among those with acute mental illness. We also interviewed 15 Christian clinical experts on mental illness about how mental illness affects their patients and how churches can better minister to those struggling with mental illness.

While we will deal with related statistics in more detail below, it's important to start by understanding that most pastors say they know people who have been diagnosed with mental illness, including clinical depression (74%) and bipolar disorder (76%). Fewer than half of pastors know someone with schizophrenia. More than 20% of pastors say they've personally struggled with mental illness. Still, there are challenges that need to be identified and overcome.

Based on the statistics discussed below, almost one in four pastors say they are reluctant to get involved with people with acute mental illness because of the challenges involved—and there are challenges. The study also found that most of those who suffer from mental illness still believe they can thrive spiritually, as do their families. Still, one in five people with acute mental illness say no, they can't grow or thrive spiritually. So while there are some for whom the diagnosis is particularly difficult, most think spiritual growth and mental illness are not incompatible. Yet believers will likely struggle if their mental illness is left untreated and help is not sought.

So pastors have to walk a fine line between challenging people to grow while also giving them grace during their struggles. As one of the experts interviewed by LifeWay Research put it, people can't give themselves away to Christ if they don't know who they are. Someone who isn't stable in the midst of their mental illness may not be able to grow or show much progress in their Christian life.

Sin, Spiritual Struggle, Weakness, and Mental Illness

Christians should seek to understand and differentiate between sin, spiritual struggle, personal weakness, and mental illness. Sometimes the difficulty an individual experiences is caused by sin, but in some cases, it's simply a spiritual struggle. In others, it is a personal struggle or weakness, and thankfully, the Bible reminds us in Hebrews 4:15 that Jesus is able to sympathize with our weaknesses. And sometimes people face a mental illness that they can't break out of, even after a period of addressing their other issues with the Word, in the power of the Spirit, and among the Christian community. But each of these challenges—sin, spiritual struggle, weakness, and mental illness—is a place for God's all-embracing grace to shine. We can and must help people to deal with sin in their lives, to grow through their spiritual struggles, to receive comfort and encouragement in their weaknesses, and to address mental illnesses and major relational problems.

Pastoral Self Care

One factor that complicates the discussion is that in our survey, nearly 25% of pastors admitted that they struggle with some form of mental illness, diagnosed or un-diagnosed. Many more struggle with significant relational turmoil and/or dysfunction. Who's talking about that difficult reality and ministering to them and their needs? Pastors with acute mental illness don't find their condition easy to discuss.

Our churches need healthy leaders—physically, mentally, relationally, and spiritually. One positive outcome we would like to see from this study is for churches to begin to create healthy environments in which their pastor(s) can be transparent with such issues. The church appears not to be a safe place for pastoral staff to live authentically and exercise the care that's essential in order for them to flourish—both as individuals and as ministry leaders. When we're not talking about how God helps in weakness, we're withholding some of his glory. It is sinful for congregations to expect perfection out of their pastors while tolerating sin in the lives of their laity. How can the church thrive while hiding its light under a bushel?

Family's Perspective

There may be only one person in a family with an acute mental illness, but the entire family shares in the experience on both good days and bad. Those individuals' caregivers deserve much affirmation and encouragement, and their perspective is important in this issue. God designed the family to be the safest place for any of us. For those with acute mental illness, God's design is particularly meaningful and important. People with mental illness need their family, and the family needs the church! 75% of family members say the church has been supportive, and 53% of people with acute mental illness agree. That's an interesting and important difference. It tells us we are making progress, but there is still work to do.

Breaking the Stigma Through Openness and Conversation

What appears to be missing in most church responses is an open forum for discussion and intervention that could help remove the stigma associated with acute mental illness. For example—and please let this sink in—67% of family members and 60% of those personally affected by mental illness want their churches to have an open discussion about mental illness. They want to feel that their struggles are normal and that God loves them in the midst of their illness. Churches talk openly about cancer, diabetes, heart attacks, and other health conditions—they should do the same for mental illness and relationship issues, in order to reduce the sense of stigma. Thankfully, we found that relatively few people are leaving churches because of a bad reaction to their diagnosis. According to our research, only about 10% of individuals with acute mental illness "have changed churches based on church response to their mental illness."

Churches Provide Support?

Perhaps one of the study's most encouraging outcomes is agreement between pastors and family members—with pastors rated highest—that the church has a responsibility "to provide resources and support," but a disconnect occurs when asked how churches render that support. 68% of pastors say their church provides help by maintaining referral lists for local mental health professionals. Yet only 28% of family members agree that this is happening. That's an important distinction, and it reveals one of the immeasurably negative consequences of the Christian community's stigmatization of mental illness: If no one talks about it, those in need don't know the church has resources to help them.

5

Perhaps one reason pastors are reluctant to bring mental illness to the forefront is their own insecurity or lack of knowledge. There has been a de-emphasis on pastoral preparation for these kinds of issues in the past few years, particularly in evangelical schools that are more focused on preaching or theology alone. As mentioned earlier, pastors and police are often the first responders in mental health crises. Yet police often receive significantly more training than pastors on how to de-escalate some of these crises. Seminaries need to reconsider their treatment of topics like individual, marriage, and family counseling.

Meanwhile, let's not forget that we don't have to be experts in order to care. However reluctant pastors might be, individuals and family members of the mentally ill are anxious to recognize the elephant in the room and remove the taboo status. If a church is going to be transformational in society, it has to address needs, and a church that only talks about certain needs is no better than a church that only preaches about certain topics. In the same way that all of the Bible is inspired and deserves to be preached, all of the maladies of humanity deserve to be brought to light under the gospel of Jesus, where healing can be found and encouragement received.

Pastors' Experience With Mental Illness

At the beginning of this chapter, we demonstrated that most pastors indicate they personally know people who have been diagnosed with clinical depression and/or bipolar disorder. However, most pastors have only known a handful of people with each of these diagnoses. Nearly 50% know someone with schizophrenia, but the actual number of individuals with these illnesses that pastors say they know is relatively small given their frequent contact with family, friends, and church members. And yet 60% of pastors have counseled someone who was eventually diagnosed with an acute mental illness. Lower percentages of pastors have taken courses in counseling or care for the mentally ill. The most frequently used learning resources for pastors have been reading books on counseling (66%) and personal experience with friends or family members (60%). More than 75% of pastors say they are "not reluctant" to get involved with people with acute mental illness, and more than 20% of pastors have personally struggled with mental illness of some kind. Let's examine some important statistics that emerged from the LifeWay Research study on the nature and scope of mental and relational health issues that have an impact upon church life.

- 74% of pastors indicate they personally know one or more people who have been diagnosed with clinical depression.
- 76% of pastors indicate they personally know one or more people who have been diagnosed with bipolar disorder. Family members of people with bipolar disorder are among those who most want churches to talk openly about mental illness to remove the stigma.
- 50% of pastors indicate they don't personally know anyone who has been diagnosed with schizophrenia.
- 59% of pastors have counseled one or more people who were eventually diagnosed with an acute mental illness.
- 41% of pastors strongly disagree that they are reluctant to get involved with those with acute mental illness because previous experiences strained time and resources.
- 66% of pastors have read several books on counseling people with acute mental illness. Since many pastors provide counseling and all pastors shepherd a flock that functions as a social network, they may see and hear symptoms of acute mental illness. While 80% of pastors feel somewhat equipped to identify when a medical professional may be required to help someone with an acute mental illness, less than half of those feel completely prepared.
- 38% of pastors strongly agree that they feel equipped to identify a person dealing with acute mental illness that may require a referral to a medical professional.
- 23% of pastors indicate they have personally struggled with mental illness of some kind.

How Well Churches are Caring for Those With Acute Mental Illness

The majority of individuals with acute mental illness and their family members describe the local church as supportive. Among individuals who have attended church regularly as an adult, the perceptions of support are higher (67% vs. 53%). However, the response of church members to the individual caused 18% of those with acute mental illness to break ties with a church and 5% of them to fail to find a church to attend. Assessing the statistics from respondents we learn that:

- 10% of individuals with acute mental illness have changed churches based on church response to their mental illness.
- 17% of family members in a household of someone with acute mental illness say their family member's mental illness impacted which church their family chose to attend.
- 53% of individuals with acute mental illness say their church has been supportive.
- 75% of family members in a household of someone with acute mental illness say their church has been supportive.
- 39% of individuals with acute mental illness agree that their local church has specifically helped them think through and live out their faith in the context of their mental illness.

The Church's Role in Caring for Those with Acute Mental Illness

Strong majorities of pastors, family members, and those with acute mental illness agree that local churches have a responsibility to provide resources and support for individuals with mental illness and their families. Overall, family members and individuals who have attended church regularly as adults indicate that churches have been supportive. In terms of resources, individuals and families want churches to connect them to local resources, create openness about the topic by discussing it, and make people aware of and educate them about mental illness.

- 56% of pastors, 46% of family members in a household of someone with acute mental illness, and 39% of individuals with acute mental illness strongly agree that local churches have a responsibility to provide resources and support to individuals with mental illness and their families.
- 69% of individuals with acute mental illness indicate that churches should help families find local resources for support.

- 68% of pastors but only 28% of family members in a household of someone with acute mental illness indicate that their church provides care for the mentally ill or their families by maintaining lists of experts to refer people to.
- 65% of family members in a household of someone with acute mental illness believe local churches should openly talk more about mental illness so that the topic is not so taboo.
- 49% of pastors rarely or never speak to their church in sermons or large group messages about acute mental illness.
- 70% of individuals with acute mental illness would prefer to have relationships with individual people in a local church who get to know them as a friend.

These research findings are serious and sobering. But we must speak into the silence, heal the shame, and transform the stigma. Indeed, such is the mission—and calling—of the church. The following chapters contain helpful resources and useful tools to help you and your church fulfill that crucial ministry. May the Lord encourage and edify you as you are equipped and empowered to do so.

Action Steps for Churches and Pastors

This section is not a comprehensive guide to assessing mental and relational health issues in churches, but it may provide a helpful framework to empower churches with a transformational ethos to be more proactive in understanding, loving, and caring for the growing number of individuals and families who need help in this area. Here are some important action steps that can be used as a catalyst for congregational care. These action steps can be broadly classified in three categories: axioms of care, discerning praxis, and informed practice.

Axioms of care. We are not engaging with and loving our community if we are not addressing prevalent societal needs including mental illness, addictions, and relationship problems. Living out our gospel mandate within a broken world leads to healing and wholeness. Clearly, this cultural and ministry shift in the church is essential for the wholeness of many families that are struggling through real challenges when it comes to mental and relational health issues.

As Christians, it's important that gospel congruence is maintained throughout the process of caring at the local church level for individuals and families with mental and relational health challenges. At no point can we say, "Well, I am turning this over to someone else." Pastoral care and congregational support are essential building blocks to holistic health. The fact is, the scriptures are sufficient, the Christian community is necessary, and the gospel matters—at every moment. Working with others does not mean turning over the mentally ill to secular establishment(s) that are better equipped to deal with these issues. These people are our friends, family members, and church community—and the gospel, the scriptures, the indwelling of the Spirit, and the Christian community are all essential to those struggling with mental illness and to the families who love them. We need to see our role as partners in the process of restoration, and we need to synchronize our efforts as a community of faith with those of Christian counselors who are able to incorporate biblical teaching within a sound, psychological framework to help Christians rightly understand their mental illness(es) and how to overcome their mental or emotional challenges. The primary axiom of care is a profound commitment to living out the gospel practically in the care of those in our midst who are vulnerable and struggling.

Informed Practice. Many Christians need to pause and learn about mental illness. Such knowledge will shape our love, care, and support of the many families who are working through challenges related to mental and relational health issues. Ministry without the correct information, knowledge, and skills is redundant and ineffective. Our knowledge should inform our ministry as we seek to live out the gospel and restore individuals, families, and society at large. The challenge of knowledge is further compounded by the fact that although the majority of pastors recognize their need for it, they have not had (adequate) formal training related to mental illness intervention. The good news is that 66% of pastors have read books on counseling, but learning should neither begin nor end with the pastor. This information should permeate the church. Yet pastors can and should learn more—and ThrivingPastor.com/MentalHealth is a good place to start. Additionally, talking about acute mental illness, addictions, and universal relationship problems is good practice for breaking down barriers of stigma and isolation. Accept the reality that these conditions exist within the church and that they deserve attention, love, and grace.

Related to the above point, there is a need to create better training for pastors in this particular area of need. Seminary education is packed with theological courses, most of which an aspiring pastor will need, but the deficit of counseling education creates a hardship for the pastor. Pastors certainly need to realize the Word of God is sufficient to give the kind of spiritual guidance and discernment believers need. Our call is not away from biblical authority. But there are real mental illnesses with physiological components, and pastors need to know to whom they can refer congregants in the counseling and medical fields. Our survey indicates pastors favor medication and therapy when those resources are available for those who are acute mentally ill.

Discerning Praxis. Along with the foundation of a robust, gospel-centered axiom and the commitment to informed practice, churches need to be prayerful about how they can create safe environments where the needs of those struggling with mental and relational health issues are marginalized nor stigmatized, but are instead effectively addressed. Each church needs to be prayerful and open about ways in which it can partner with others to facilitate healthier homes and individuals within its community.

A helpful starting point for many churches is to begin a recovery ministry. This is usually easier in larger churches with more resources, however smaller churches can—and should—partner with other community churches to sponsor a recovery ministry for those grappling with issues beyond "normal" spiritual struggles. Such a ministry could also become the local support group for caregivers. Our survey respondents said they want open forums in which education and support can address the stigma of mental illness, addictions, and other major life problems.

In addition to forming recovery ministries to assist those individuals and families dealing with mental illness and related issues, it is essential to create a network of referrals. Referring congregants to professionals outside the church can become uncomfortable for pastors because of trust issues, so within your community, pastors need to know who is licensed, experienced, and able to assist. When building your referral network, it's generally wise to begin with professional Christian psychotherapists, and then refer to psychiatrists and others who can consider medical issues as well. An excellent resource is the Christian Care Connect of the American Association of Christian Counselors (aacc.net or 800-5COUNSEL), a nationwide network of carefully vetted Christian mental health professionals. And while there can be beneficial information in the purview of secular psychology/psychiatry, much of its perspective is different from the Christian worldview. Thus, as evangelical Christians, we approach these issues with the attitude that "all truth is God's truth," always aware that the Bible is our ultimate standard.

Put another way, we start with the gospel and we end with the gospel. At no point do we say, "I'm done with the Christian stuff; let's turn this over to the real experts." Quite the contrary, the scriptures are sufficient, the Christian community called "the church" is necessary, and the Spirit is at work throughout any proper Christian engagement with mental illness. Partnering with others does not mean abandoning the struggling person or our beliefs.

The Church and Mental Illness

As mentioned before, the church must increase its engagement in this important issue while remaining true to its calling and to the centrality of the gospel. It is past time for the church to recognize and admit that acute mental illness exists within the body of Christ and to minister accordingly. Our research found that people who suffer from mental illness often turn to pastors for help, but that pastors need more guidance and preparation for dealing with mental health crises. They often don't have a plan to help individuals or families affected by mental illness and so miss opportunities to lovingly shepherd certain members of their flock in their time of need. The entire family of a person with mental illness shares in the experience, and those caregivers deserve affirmation and encouragement. Family members want their churches to provide resources and support and to have ongoing open discussions about mental illness. If we are to "Carry one another's burdens; in this way you will fulfill the law of Christ" (Galatians 6:2, HCSB), that includes those individuals who struggle with mental illness and their families.

Mark Dance, D.Min.

Mark Dance, D.Min., pastored churches for 27 years before becoming the Director of LifeWay Pastors in 2014. In this role, he serves pastors and their spouses by helping them win at home and at church. He earned a bachelor's degree from Howard Payne University, an M.Div. at Southwestern Baptist Theological Seminary, and a D.Min. from the Southern Baptist Theological Seminary.

Dr. Dance's love of missions has led him to minister in more than two dozen countries. He is a national conference speaker, writer, and avid bowhunter. Mark and his wife, Janet, live in Nashville and have two grown children.

CHAPTER 2

How to Prepare Pastors for Mental and Relational Health Ministry

Mark Dance, D.Min.

I learned the hard way how intrinsically connected the health of a pastor is to the health of the local church. As a graduate of three Southern Baptist schools, I was surprised at how unprepared I was to address and assess my own mental health, much less that of the churches and communities I served. In this chapter I will share with you how I learned to find mental health in my life as well as in my ministry.

My Mental Health Journey

My initial ministry vision as a younger pastor was to build a Great Commission church. That vision fueled two decades of uninterrupted church growth, if you measure growth in terms of baptisms, buildings, and budgets. The problem was that I was not personally growing at the same rate as my ministry. I unknowingly and unintentionally let the work of God around me smother the work of God within me. I was about twenty years into my ministry when my internal flame started to flicker. Thinking I could build tall buildings in a single bound, I eventually realized that I was a man of flesh, not steel. I was having fun "turning the world upside down" until my world turned upside down through a four-year season of clinical depression.

That temporary trip through that dark tunnel was not only painful for me, but also for those who lived and worked around me. When my e-light came on, I did what most terminally driven people do when they run out of gas: Drive faster! I paid the price for that stupidity—and so did my family, staff, and church. Although there were no scandalous train wrecks, suicidal thoughts, or immoral actions, a slow erosion had clearly set in to my relationships, especially at the church I pastored.

I suspect that every pastor goes through temporary seasons of burnout and discouragement. Of course, we are prepared to preach "in season and out of season," so tough days are a given. However, when this mental fog didn't lift, I reached out for help, first to my MD, who diagnosed me with clinical depression. Just over a week later, a licensed therapist in our church basically diagnosed me from her pew. Her only questions to me were, "Do you know you are clinically depressed? Are you getting any help for it?" Prior to that week, no one had ever even suggested the possibility of mental illness.

I subsequently asked these two professionals, along with a few trusted church leaders, to become a support team to help me through that painful season. The awkwardness of asking my own church members for help was very real. Such discomfort is so real that it prevents countless pastors from reaching out to anyone at all. I knew there was a better way to live and serve, but I did not know how to get healthy again without the help of this group, which I affectionately called my "Dance Team." They shepherded their shepherd back into health, and I have enjoyed almost a decade of life and fruitful ministry since then.

Fortunately, my depression was temporary and treatable, as most depressions are if diagnosed early. That church became healthier as I did, which is no surprise since a pastor's personal health is so intrinsically connected to the health of his or her flock.

My depression was also altogether avoidable. In my zeal to build a Great Commission church, I neglected my *own* heart, soul, mind, and strength. Before leading the church to become a safe place to find lasting mental health and healing, I had to become a Great Commandment pastor who was consistently loving Jesus and others with all my heart, soul, mind, and strength. We simply cannot give that which we do not have, nor can we love anyone better than we love ourselves.

Mental health had to become a priority in my life before it became a real priority in my ministry.

Mental Health in Your Ministry

Do you want to better understand and even welcome individuals and families with mental and relational health struggles? What better place to find hope and healing than the local church? No longer do we need to outsource all of our members' mental and relationship health challenges to secular individuals or institutions, because the Body of Christ is the healing hands of Jesus.

Sadly, most Bible schools and seminaries don't teach us how to effectively help ourselves and others. As essential as hermeneutics, homiletics, and Hebrew are to successful sermon preparation and delivery, we are rarely trained well in how to effectively address the common conflicts and concerns our flock typically struggles with Monday through Saturday.

Here are four ways you can help on both the prevention and intervention sides of mental and relational health.

1. Educate Yourself

Most pastors do not know what we do not know about mental and relational health. For those of us fortunate enough to go to graduate school (seminary), we took an obligatory counseling class. That class did not qualify us to become counselors any more than our obligatory music class qualified us to be worship pastors. Yet the challenge of dealing effectively with mental health issues comes into our offices and computers on a weekly and sometimes daily basis. Sometimes we realize there is a clinical problem and encourage people to seek professional help. Other times we just practice pastoral care as well as we can and pray for the best.

I realize that the mere sight of the heading "Educate Yourself" can elicit an overwhelmed sigh from pastors who already have piles of unread books, posts, and articles. "Why add another homework assignment?" you may ask. I'm feeling your pain, friend. More importantly, we are called to feel the pain of our members. When one part of the body suffers, we all suffer (1 Corinthians 12:26). Understanding that suffering on a basic level will help you to help one-fourth of your members and staff.

We pastors are problem solvers, so we are reluctant to admit to ourselves or others when we are winging it. But we need to stop trying to diagnose mental health and/or relationship challenges because we are no more qualified to assess them than we are qualified to assess physical health challenges. As pastors, we don't care much for "Google theologians." Why then would we attempt to do the same with issues of mental, emotional, and physical health?

In dealing with my depression, my first conversation was with my medical doctor, and my second was with a licensed Christian therapist. Working with them was a humbling but rewarding experience for me. I still have much to learn, but I won't let what I don't know rob me or others of what I do know about mental health and relational functioning. Now is a great time in the history of the church for pastors to take the lead in initiating mental health and healthy relationship conversations and solutions in our churches.

2. Equip Your Church

I am not a mental health professional, so this chapter is not an attempt to explain burnout or depression. My desire is to help pastors and church leaders address mental and relational health challenges head-on. The first step is taking away the stigma and confusion about universal human problems in the local church.

According to Ephesians 4:11-12, our job is to equip our members for ministry. Since the average pastor and church member don't understand most clinical illnesses, I would encourage you to recruit a trusted voice to come and lead a training session. For two consecutive years, our church invited a therapist to lead a periodic one-day seminar called "Think on These Things." Approximately 400 adults showed up to hear about mental health on a Sunday afternoon!

Additionally, you can preach a sermon (or sermon series) on mental and/or relational health yourself. You don't have to look too hard to find material in the Bible on how important a healthy, transformed mind is, but be forewarned: Mental and relational health is about as popular a topic as physical health. It's much easier for us to stick to spiritual health and skip all of those pesky passages about the mind and heart. Also, keep in mind that you are an equipper, not an expert. No one expects you to be an expert on this topic, so try not to come across as one.

A few years ago, LifeWay Research and Focus on the Family partnered in a robust mental illness study (LifeWay Research, 2014) which found that most pastors (66%) are reluctant to talk about mental illness/health to their congregations. Meanwhile, 65% of family members and 59% of those with mental illness want their church to talk openly about mental illness, so the topic will not be taboo. Another way to address mental health in your church is to let someone give a testimony about how God has helped them with a mental illness. Young people are craving authenticity in our worship services. Many of them seem to have grown sick of the superficial, sanctimonious smiles that betray our real lives outside of church. I shared my depression testimony at a pastors conference in West Virginia recently and just got this response from a pastor:

Mark, I am thankful for what you taught us at the pastors' conference. I felt greatly encouraged to enter counseling. I have done just that and man I am beginning to see God's love and grace for me more than ever!

An important caveat to add is that each testimony will be unique, and results will vary widely. For example, my clinical depression was temporary, treatable, and even preventable. Most of those with more severely stigmatized mental illnesses (schizophrenia, bipolar disorder, etc.) very often require medication and therapy for the rest of their lives. Mental illness has many faces, just like cancer does.

Pastors are messengers of hope, health, and healing. When people limp into our churches, we need to make sure they know that they do not have to walk through their dark valley of mental illness alone. Jesus and his beautiful Bride desire to help those hurting people live abundant and eternal lives.

3. Provide Practical Solutions

The last church I served provides an on-campus office for a licensed therapist who has clients inside and outside that church. She collects fees, pays rent, and often sees church members for free or at a fraction of her regular fee. Most importantly, her presence underscores the church's desire to help broken people in a biblical way. That wonderful church is not afraid to help those to whom most churches pay little attention. Your church can help them too. The LifeWay study also found that although pastors and churches want to help those who experience mental illness, those good intentions don't always lead to action.

Here is the unfortunate reality and sad current state of many churches across the country:

- Few churches have plans to assist families affected by mental illness.
- Few churches are staffed with a counselor skilled in addressing and treating mental illness.
- There is a lack of training for leaders in how to recognize mental illness.
- There is a need for churches to communicate to congregations about local mental health resources.
- There is a persistent stigma and culture of silence that leads to shame.

You don't have to have an on-campus counselor to provide mental and relationship health services. You just need to take the lead by finding out who the trusted voices in your area are and utilizing them to help your people.

4. Vet a Referral List

I learned how to build bridges to the mental health community by simply talking to people who work in it. A great referral source is the American Association of Christian Counselors (aacc.net or 1-800-5COUNSEL). Their Christian Care Connect is a nationwide network of counseling professionals that have been stringently vetted both Christianly and clinically.

I have also learned when to burn bridges that do not advance the agenda of God's kingdom. I learned early on in my ministry that not all counselors give wise counsel. In my first church in San Antonio, Texas, a very broken young man named "Danny" came to me seeking counsel about how to get out of the trap of his struggle with a deeply shameful personal sin. He apparently had additional issues as well that needed more help than I was qualified to give. I was a whopping 23 years of age and had no idea what to tell him, so I reached out to the only counselor I knew, a fellow pastor nearby. This church leader just down the street fancied himself a "Christian Counselor." His collar was all the credentials I needed, but I was shocked when he enthusiastically applauded Danny's self-destructive lifestyle and unhealthy personal choices and told him he was doing just fine.

A vetted referral list takes time, but it is worth the effort to ensure that those to whom we are referring our wounded sheep are trusted, safe, and solid. Not that referrals are the end of our ministry to those we refer. On the contrary, a referral is just the beginning. In the words of Dr. Ed Stetzer (2015):

> Churches tend to either abdicate their role in mental health to outside medical professionals or to isolate themselves from the medical community. Neither response is helpful. Even those in secular branches of psychology and psychiatry say psychological health is better when people are connected with a faith community, and that should drive churches to healthy partnerships with trained medical professionals.

We need to follow up a referral with prayer, accountability, and support. When we do, a church member will be less likely to feel rejected, abandoned, and shunned.

The Mentally Healthy Pastor

Since coming out of that fog of clinical depression, God has used my testimony to encourage thousands of pastors across North America. That LifeWay study revealed that one in four Americans suffers from some kind of mental illness in a given year. What may surprise you is that this statistic also applies to pastors. If you suspect you are pastoring in a fog of depression or in the midst of some other personal struggle or private relationship problem, please resist the temptation to self-diagnose or self-medicate. Instead, reach out to your doctor or a mental health professional for help. When I host pastoral events across the country, I encourage pastors to anonymously text in questions about their lives, families, and ministries. This question came up at a recent Pastor Date Night: "Where can pastors and their wives turn when they suffer from mental illness such as bipolar, major depression, etc?" If you are not sure where to start, call the Focus on the Family Pastoral Care Line for a free and confidential consultation: 844-4PASTOR. They are connected to over 2000 vetted Christian counselors across the country. Reach out to the AACC Christian Care Connect as well. If you are personally struggling with persistently negative thoughts or are experiencing individual or relational problems, please reach out. Admittedly, talking to your medical doctor or to a mental health professional takes courage, but fortunately you have a fantastic intercessor praying for you right now!

"Simon, Simon, Satan has asked to sift all of you as wheat. But I have prayed for you, Simon, that your faith may not fail" (Luke 22:31-32, NIV). Satan has plans for your life, but so does God! Although I don't believe it was God's will for Peter to fail, he obviously knew about—and allowed Peter to go through—the sifting and refining process through which he could grow in strength and humility. He would need both later.

We know in retrospect that God had big plans for Peter, but we also know that God has plans for our ministries too. Jesus is still praying for our good and his glory, interceding at the right hand of the Father. He is praying that our faith would not fail, even when we do.

Over the years I have served with several staff members who struggled with mental illness and relationship problems on different levels. During my season of clinical depression as a lead pastor, I had two younger staff members who were struggling even more than I was. One was bipolar and ended her life. The other one ended his marriage and ministry. Although our church leaders worked very hard to help them both through their respective battles, there were never any obvious solutions or easy answers. I still have so much to learn, but I do not feel pressured to know all there is to know about the subject. I simply know that I need to care enough to get the help I need for myself and for others with whom I live and serve.

As pastors, we are often the first responders to mental health challenges in our church and community. The research shows that most people who are in need of professional counseling for a mental or relationship problem reach out to a pastor first. How we handle that hurting person is crucial to their health and to the health of those around them.

"Think On These Things"

Our minds are working all the time. Donna Seal is the licensed therapist who had the challenge of having me as both her pastor and patient during my season of depression. I met with her monthly for five years after I was diagnosed. Donna helped me to understand my thoughts by organizing them into these three categories.

Thoughts that are Truthful

Some thoughts are NOT TRUE. These thoughts need to be replaced by God's Word, which is always truthful. "They exchanged the truth of God for a lie" (Romans 1:25, HCSB).

We can love God with all our minds by consistently downloading the truth of God's Word. We can also intentionally replace his truth for the lies of the world, the flesh, and the devil. Approximately 50,000 thoughts go through our heads each day, and not all of them are true. "We take captive every thought to make it obedient to Christ" (2 Corinthians 10:5, NIV).

Thoughts that are Helpful

Helpful thoughts are both good and true. Loving God with all of our minds is more than popular or secular psychology; it is clear, foundational biblical theology. In Philippians 4:8 we are reminded that God will guard the minds of those who dwell (think) on whatever is honorable, just, pure, lovely, commendable, or morally excellent. Paul David Tripp wisely reminds us that "No one is more influential in your life than you are, because no one talks to you more than you do" (Tripp, 2012).

Thoughts that are Hopeful

Hopeful thinking is not the same as wishful thinking. Hopeful thoughts are true, but also hard; for instance, "I'm not doing okay" (hard truth), "BUT I can get better with God's help" (hopeful truth). Some of our thoughts are true but just plain hard to take, especially when the truth stings. "Faithful are the wounds of a friend, but the kisses of an enemy are deceitful" (Proverbs 27:6, NKJV).

We have to trust what God says in his Word or we will never be spiritually and emotionally healthy.

A Personal Invitation

Jesus invites us all to find rest and healing in him. Humans alone are not the final answer to life's problems. Although God uses people to help people, these helpers are merely enablers if they are not pointing people to the Great Physician. His clarion call is:

> Come to Me, all of you who are weary and burdened, and
> I will give you rest. All of you, take up My yoke and learn
> from Me, because I am gentle and humble in heart, and
> you will find rest for yourselves. For My yoke is easy and
> My burden is light" (Matthew 11:28-30, HCSB).

The Greek word Jesus used for "rest" is "anapausis," which means "intermission; to stop." You can see that this is where we get our English word "pause." How much and how well do you rest? No, I mean, *really* rest? Sabbath is one of the most challenging and ironic "occupational hazards" most of us pastors privately struggle to practice. And by practice, I mean regularly, consistently, and faithfully. I wonder how much of our stress and consequent mental and relational struggles could be prevented, or at least reduced, if we took Jesus's command seriously and religiously. Prevention is easier than cure—every time.

Jesus is inviting us into the yoke of his presence. Knowing full well when we are tired and overwhelmed, he simply desires to be a part of our lives. His yoke of grace not only lightens our load, but also carries it. Jesus is not really offering to *share* our loads as an equal partner; he is offering to completely *take* them from us. Each day I attempt to humbly bring my "weary" self and "burdened" to-do list and put them into his capable hands. "Do not be conformed to this age, but be transformed by the renewing of your mind, so that you may discern what is the good, pleasing, and perfect will of God" (Romans 12:2, HCSB).

May the Lord bless you and your ministry abundantly.

References

LifeWay Research (2014). New study of acute mental illness and Christian faith. Retrieved January 12, 2017 from: http://lifewayresearch.com/mentalillnessstudy/

Stetzer, E. (2015). Isn't it time we talked about mental health? *Facts and Trends, Winter 2015,* 51. Retrieved from: http://factsandtrends.net/files/2014/11/FTWinter2015-smaller.pdf

Tripp, David. (2012). *Dangerous Calling: Confronting the Unique Challenges of Pastoral Ministry.* Wheaton, IL: Crossway.

Paul Meier, M.D.

Paul Meier, M.D., is the author or co-author of more than 90 books that have sold more than seven million copies in over twenty languages. Most of Dr. Meier's books are in the field of Christian psychology or psychiatry, but four of them are Bible prophecy novels.

Dr. Meier is also the founder of the national chain of non-profit Meier Clinics, which are all staffed by Christian psychiatrists, psychologists, and therapists. Paul has an M.S. in Cardiovascular Physiology from Michigan State University and an M.D. from the University of Arkansas Medical School. He completed his Psychiatry Residency at Duke University. He also both attended and taught at Trinity Evangelical Divinity School in Deerfield, Illinois and at Dallas Theological Seminary, where he earned his seminary degree and became an ordained minister.

For more than 20 years, he was the co-host of a national Christian talk-radio show heard by two million people a day on over 400 stations. He also taught Christian psychology on numerous mission trips all over the world, traveling to various countries in Europe and South America, Russia, Cuba, and Israel. In 1989, Dr. Meier served as the team physician for a mountain climbing expedition with astronaut Jim Irwin, in search of Noah's Ark on Mount Ararat in Turkey. Their team was threatened and chased away by terrorists on the mountain and so never completed their journey.

CHAPTER 3

How to Understand Major Mental Health Disorders

Paul Meier, M.D.

Three things determine how we will turn out; genes, environment and choices – the genes we inherit when we are "designed in our mothers' wombs" according to Psalm 139, the environment we grow up in or put ourselves into as we grow up, and the choices we make in our lives, including both good and evil choices. The choice to trust Jesus as our personal Lord and Savior is the most important choice anyone could possibly make.

Every day throughout the world, evangelical pastors counsel millions of human beings who come to them seeking health for a wide variety of problems. Most of the problems are spiritual or emotional in nature, but about one out of five are caused primarily by biochemical imbalances that are either inherited or caused by medical problems. These need to be referred to an M.D. psychiatrist for proper diagnosis and treatment.

The Meier Clinics are a national, non-profit chain of Christian psychiatric and counseling clinics, and we see about a thousand cases every day. I will share with you some of the major things we have learned about mental disorders throughout the past forty years of practice. About twenty percent of the population have one or more disorders related to brain chemistry that are primarily genetic, so those persons typically cannot improve significantly without medication, no matter how long they stay in quality counseling.

Healthy families and churches provide great environments for people to mature and grow emotionally and spiritually and to make better choices throughout their lives, but we are born with the genes God designed for us to have. Psalm 139 says so, as we are fearfully and wonderfully made by God.

The purpose of this chapter is to explain the genetic factors that most of us have—as do most of our clients—and also to explain the genetic factors that cause symptoms that can be severe and sometimes even dangerous. Some clients need psychiatric medications temporarily to get them through a crisis and keep them functioning so they don't have to drop out of school or work. After several months to a year of happiness and success, and hopefully pastoral or outpatient Christian counseling to help the client resolve and handle their crisis, most psychiatrists would gradually wean their client off the antidepressant or other medications, and in most cases, the client will do just fine without the meds since the brain chemicals are back where God intended them to be.

Others with inherited tendencies toward depression, bipolar, social phobia, psychoses, or other brain chemistry deficiencies will need lifelong medications to function normally. Almost every time such a client is weaned off his or her meds, he or she will eventually (and sometimes right away) go back downhill, and the inherited abnormal level of their particular brain chemical composition will recur, causing the depression, social phobia, bipolar, or whatever it was that was inherited.

If someone inherits low thyroid hormones, for example, they will eventually develop hypothyroidism. When that happens, the person will become more and more depressed and sluggish; experience drier skin, possible hair loss, and/or constipation; feel colder than her peers, have more trouble concentrating, and experience weight gain. She may not know she has hypothyroidism, and she may come to her pastor for counseling for her depression, yet she will not improve in spite of the pastor's excellent counseling. She may even go to a psychiatrist, but if that doctor is not thorough enough and merely prescribes antidepressants, she may still not improve, or at least not as much as would be expected. It takes someone asking her questions about dry skin, hair loss, constipation, and feeling colder than others to pick up on her hypothyroidism. When her family doctor puts her on thyroid medication (like Armour Thyroid or Synthroid), all those symptoms, including depression, go away within weeks. But she will almost certainly need to stay on thyroid hormones the rest of her life to prevent those inherited symptoms from coming back.

Someone who inherits diabetes must have insulin daily or they will die. God is easily able to heal any disease, but he does NOT promise that becoming a Christian will give you perfect health and eternal life here on earth without dying first. Everyone Jesus ever healed during his three-year ministry on earth died of something else later. "Many are the afflictions of the righteous," according to Psalm 34:19 (ESV).

Why wouldn't the same God allow some of us, as humans in fallen bodies, to inherit brain chemical deficiencies just like he allows some of us to inherit other chemical deficiencies, like thyroid hormone or insulin? Legalistic Christians usually feel just fine about a medical illness, but think all mental illnesses are the result of sin. It is true that many mental illnesses are the result of a variety of sins (like holding in bitterness, for example), childhood conflicts, or other emotional and spiritual problems, but remember that about twenty percent of mental illnesses are either inherited or have a strong genetic tendency. *Blue Genes,* a book I coauthored in 2005 (Tyndale), is all about these brain chemicals that can make you feel "blue" or have other mental illnesses. I strongly urge every pastor, counselor, physician, and psychiatrist to read this so people won't suffer needlessly because of ignorance about these factors.

Before I go further into the genetic factors involved in mental illness, I must first take a moment to give you some information about the importance of proper nutrition. For a more thorough understanding of how nutrition affects our mental health, please read chapter ten of *Blue Genes.*

Thousands of chemicals and enzymes are involved in our mental health, but the main four are serotonin, norepinephrine, GABA (gamma-aminobutyric acid), and dopamine. Serotonin is necessary for us to have the fruit of the Spirit—love, joy, peace, and patience, as well as good sleep. Norepinephrine is necessary for joy, but also for focus, concentration, motivation, and energy. GABA is necessary to put the brakes on our worries, relieve our anxieties, help us be less shy, and overcome other phobias. It also helps people with bipolar disorders function normally, as long as they stay on their GABA medicine for the rest of their lives. Quitting the medicine will cause the GABA deficiency to return along with whatever mental illness is related to it.

Dopamine is needed to prevent all forms of psychosis, including delusions of grandeur, delusions of persecution, hearing voices that are not there, etc. In my forty-year practice of psychiatry, I have probably had hundreds of patients who thought they heard demon voices telling them to do nasty things. In every single case, when I put them on a dopamine medication, the voices went away, often within one or two weeks. I still believe in demons because I believe the Bible and have seen evil powers at work, but when someone tells me they hear demons talking to them out loud, the voices have always gone away when the patient takes a dopamine medicine. Either those demons are allergic to Abilify or they aren't really demons, but a biochemical deficiency.

As a brief illustration of how nutrition impacts mental health, please remember this example: a banana is one of the best mental health foods a person can eat. Bananas contain tryptophan, an essential amino acid, and they also contain Vitamin B6. Vitamin B6 carries the tryptophan across the blood-brain barrier, where the brain, using hundreds of other chemicals, turns the tryptophan into serotonin, bringing love, joy, and peace to that person. You never see a depressed monkey, do you? They eat lots of bananas.

We each have about a hundred billion brain cells with little spaces in between them called synapses. In these synapses, there are reuptake sites that suck up the old serotonin and replace it with new serotonin, keeping it in balance. But about 15-20% of the population have inherited reuptake sites that work overtime and suck up too much serotonin, so their serotonin level gets low, causing depression and often also OCD (obsessive-compulsive disorder). If this genetic tendency to suck up too much serotonin is mild, then proper nutrition (including eating more tryptophan and Vitamin B6) may solve the problem, but if nutrition is not sufficient, then a lifelong antidepressant becomes necessary. In scientific terms, an antidepressant is called a "serotonin-reuptake inhibitor." To put it simply, the antidepressant does not make anybody falsely happy. It just helps that person become their normal self again by blocking some of the reuptake sites so that less serotonin is sucked up, allowing their serotonin level to return to normal, so that they are happy and at peace. They are also sleeping better, since serotonin helps provide good sleep.

Without proper nutrition, antidepressants and other psychiatric medications for other mental illnesses will not work correctly. I personally urge all my clients to go to www.mytoyourhealth.com, or to call 1-800-758-2801 and order a bottle of To Your Health Liquid Vitamins. This mental health product is derived entirely from natural foods. I helped invent its mental health components, but just to be up front, I do not own any part of this product and get no commissions on it. Liquid vitamins are 98% absorbed by the body, compared to 25-50% of most vitamins in tablet form. TYH contains more than sixty vitamins, antioxidants, etc., but unlike almost any other vitamin, it also contains tryptophan, Vitamin B6, phenylalanine, tyrosine, choline, and other essential chemicals that are found foods. Our bodies process these into most of our normal brain chemicals which in turn promote mental health. In mild cases of genetic disorders, these vitamins alone are sometimes sufficient, but usually medications are also required. Many of my clients who require antidepressants for mild cases of depression like mild chronic dysthymia are able to get well using only the vitamins I recommend, and they no longer need to see me. So even though the vitamins actually cause me to lose some patients, I still encourage everyone—including myself—to take them daily.

Specific Genetic Mental Disorders

ADHD

ADHD stands for Attention-Deficit Hyperactivity Disorder. Individuals who inherit some (still not completely understood) brain chemical deficiencies, such as in norepinephrine, dopamine, and others, will develop ADHD that shows up in early childhood and lasts for life. This includes lifelong traits like making careless mistakes while doing boring projects, misplacing things often, having trouble organizing, putting things off to do later, being easily distracted, not listening well to others, fidgeting when sitting still for a long time, having difficulty unwinding, talking too much, finishing the sentences of others, interrupting others due to impatience, and hating to wait at restaurants or get stuck in traffic. There are many other examples. We usually start a patient like this on an ADHD medication like Ritalin, Adderall or Vyvanse. Often a C average student becomes an A average student overnight. I have had clients who came to me on the verge of losing their jobs, and after I put them on ADHD meds, they literally come back to see me three months later having received a promotion. The meds greatly reduce most of these traits within ten minutes and last anywhere from 4 to 12 hours per dose.

Perfectionism

Most people who are perfectionists are that way due to environmental factors, like being the oldest child of their sex in their family. There is a tendency for the parent of the same sex to expect too much out of that child or to project his own unconscious insecurities onto that child who unknowingly reminds him of himself. In biblical terms this constitutes seeing the speck of sawdust in your brother's eye rather than the log in your own eye (Matthew 7:3-5). As adults, these perfectionists become overly self-critical, causing themselves to become more depressed, since depression is often called "anger turned inward." I tell these clients that the job of demons, according to the Bible, is to be "accusers of the brethren," to get us to become overly self-critical, for example. Don't be your own demon. I encourage these clients to open their Bibles when they get home and write on a blank page today's date, followed by a personal pledge to become your own best friend, and to make an attempt to never tell yourself anything negative that you would not tell your best friend under the same circumstances. Then sign it and date it. For example, if your best friend locked his keys in the car while you were going somewhere together, you would not yell at your best friend, "You stupid idiot!" You are a sociopathic jerk if you would. You would tell your friend the truth: "Welcome to the human race. We all make mistakes. We will figure it out." But you would probably lie to yourself if you did it, calling yourself a stupid idiot. Life is hard enough based on the truth. Why make your life more difficult and depressing by lying to yourself? Tell yourself what you would tell your best friend, and you will live in truth rather than in lies.

But some people inherit perfectionism and even severe perfectionism in the form of OCD, usually related to low serotonin levels. Perfectionists are often more successful but also enjoy life less than others. Children who grow up being repeatedly abused often become paranoid, thinking later in life that even the nice people in their environment don't like them or want to take advantage of them or hurt them. The greater the amount of buried anger a person has, the more paranoid he or she usually becomes. But some people inherit enough of a dopamine problem that although they are not quite delusional, they are still somewhat paranoid, seeing life negatively. They tend to become arrogant, controlling, critical, micro-managing, and seeing evil motives in others even when no evil motives are present. Other personality traits can also be inherited. A wise counselor will try to differentiate to the best of his or her abilities how much of a client's personality traits are treatable through therapy and how much of those traits are genetic, requiring medications to overcome the genetic portion.

OCD

OCD stands for Obsessive Compulsive Disorder, which is characterized by extreme perfectionism accompanied by compulsive habits. The obsessions can be about anything, but are often about religious things like losing one's salvation or germs or guilt or a variety of other things. Obsessives often have songs that will not leave their head, which can be relieved with almost any of the serotonin antidepressants at about double the normal dose. In fact, all of the symptoms of OCD can be either reduced or eliminated in this manner, or by adding a small dose of a dopamine medication to a serotonin medication. Common examples of compulsions include counting things, rechecking doors four or five times, having to do things in twos or in even numbers or in some other number combination, having to touch certain things, cleaning everything before touching it, etc. I treat many OCD clients and enjoy them very much, especially when I see their symptoms disappear or at least diminish greatly. But people with OCD who are not treated correctly are more likely than most to end up committing suicide. There are three types of OCD.

Trauma-induced OCD. Some people do not inherit OCD and do not have OCD symptoms their entire lives, but have had a traumatic experience, like our dear soldiers in the Middle East who have fought against terrorists and seen people killed. Or they may have a severe car accident, or be raped, or have some other severe trauma. As a result of that trauma, the person can develop various symptoms of Post-Traumatic Stress Disorder (PTSD), such as panic attacks, nightmares, flashbacks, sensitivity to sounds, or even temporary OCD. With intensive therapy, these symptoms will eventually go away, even without medications. However, meds may help relieve them more quickly, saving lots of unnecessary pain.

Nuture-induced OCD. This type of OCD is also not inherited, but is caused by an overly perfectionistic or abusive upbringing. If you had a parent who criticized you no matter how well you did, then you will likely get so used to that criticism that when you grow up and get out on your own—and even after that parent dies—you will tend to keep that parent in your brain by being too hard on yourself. As we discussed earlier, deciding to become your own best friend and to not say things to yourself that you would not say to your best friend under the same circumstances can help a great deal. Professional counseling is also very important.

Genetic OCD. Most of the cases of OCD that I treat as a psychiatrist are the genetic kind. Lots of people are just born with it, and it is usually related to low serotonin levels. These folks have the symptoms listed above no matter how nice their parents were and even without having suffered any dramatic trauma. Almost any antidepressant, like Prozac, Zoloft, Lexapro, Cymbalta, Prestiq, or others, when given in double the normal dose required to get rid of most depressions, will either dramatically reduce the OCD symptoms or eliminate them entirely. If such an antidepressant helps some but not enough, prescribing an additional, lower than normal dose of any of the dopamine medications is usually effective.

CASE STUDY: Rachel was a 32 year-old Israeli citizen who many years ago flew all the way to Dallas to see me to treat her OCD. Some of my books have been translated into more than 20 languages, including Hebrew. She was a committed Christian who believed in Yeshua (what Jews call Jesus). She had lifelong OCD and it was severe. She spent her whole life being very self-critical, in spite of having very loving parents. She obsessed about having committed the unpardonable sin, a common OCD symptom, and about being unworthy of God's love. She was suicidal for most of her life but was afraid to commit the sin of suicide. She had a host of compulsions similar to the ones listed above.

At our Dallas, Texas clinic, we have a Day Program (our Catalyst program) where people come from around the world and stay in a nearby hotel (local clients stay at their homes at night) and come for six or more hours a day of intensive Christian therapy, five days a week, for an average of three weeks, but sometimes longer. We pack six months to a year of counseling into those three weeks, and people have dramatic recoveries. We use meds on the ones who need it, my nurse practitioner seeing them daily if they are on meds and me supervising the entire process.

Rachel primarily needed meds, but the counseling helped, too. By the end of three weeks on a serotonin medication and with the counseling she received, Rachel was totally normal and happy for the first time in her life, and she was free from her lifelong OCD. However, Rachel attended a Messianic synagogue that was still very legalistic. Most Messianic synagogues in America and throughout the world are fantastic and teach God's love and grace. The people at her church were good people—just misinformed. They thought every emotional problem, including genetic OCD, could be and should be cured using only the Bible and prayer. So when Rachel returned completely healed, the people at her church told her she had to quit taking the medications and rely only on their Bible teachings and prayers. She did, and a few weeks later, she hanged herself and died.

Some time later, a member of their church read my book, *Blue Genes,* that explains in great detail the things which I have described briefly in this chapter. She encouraged others in their church to read it, and after a while their whole attitude changed; now they encourage people with OCD or other genetic brain chemistry problems to see a local psychiatrist and get on the right meds.

Everyone also drastically needs the Lord, Bible study, prayer, and fellowship. Our relationship with God is the most important thing in our lives, but sometimes God also helps people, whether diabetic or bipolar or with OCD, with new scientific discoveries about how the brain works and the medications that make it work normally again.

Psychoses

One out of 33 people in the world will become psychotic at some time in their lives, either having grandiose delusions or paranoid delusions. They will often hear audible voices in the middle of the day (nighttime does not count) that sound completely audible, but when they look around, nobody is in the room. This is caused by a dopamine deficiency. Some people become so severely depressed, such as with a severe post-partum depression, that their dopamine doesn't function properly, they become psychotic, and they may even be dangerous to themselves or others.

Treating severe depression with an antidepressant and a dopamine medication (called an atypical antipsychotic agent) will nearly always bring the client back to normal within a month or so. If this only happens once in a person's life, he or she may or may not need medications in the future. But they may want to stay on the meds just to be sure it never happens again. If it happens more than once, then staying on the meds for life is urged to prevent such an episode from ever coming back.

Some people inherit schizophrenia—about 1% of the population, actually—in which the person becomes permanently delusional and/or has hallucinations that are usually audible but can also be visual. Visual hallucinations are usually caused by drug abuse, but auditory ones are usually caused by psychoses. Schizophrenia can develop in childhood, but usually develops in a very normal young man or woman in his or her late teens or twenties, occurring less often after age 30. If a parent is schizophrenic, about one out of six offspring will also become schizophrenic at some time. Schizophrenics are treated with dopamine meds (atypical antipsychotics) and usually improve significantly on them. They may or may not ever seem totally normal, but they can improve dramatically as long as they stay on their meds. However, if they later quit taking their meds, even twenty years later, for example, they will become psychotic again very soon.

Before a person becomes psychotic, he or she usually will have two or more of the following five symptoms. They all start with the letter A to remember them more easily:

1. **Affective disorder.** Flat affect usually, or a blank stare.
2. **Associative disorder.** Loose associations (wandering thoughts).
3. **Ambivalence.** Being nice one minute and disproportionately angry for no apparent reason the next minute, out of the blue.
4. **Autism.** Seeming to be in a world of his or her own. You call their name and they may not even notice that you are doing so.
5. **Anhedonia.** The inability to have fun. Trouble laughing or crying.

Bipolar Spectrum Disorders

There is a wide range of types of bipolar disorders, so we will discuss here what they all have in common and what makes each type somewhat different from the others. From mildest to most severe, they are Cyclothymia, Bipolar II, Bipolar I and Schizoaffective Disorder. Cyclothymia is the mildest form, milder than Bipolar II, and people with Cyclothymia usually don't even miss work when they are going through a cycle. They just get less sleep, and are more energetic, more chatty, and more impulsive. Then, after a few days, they slip into a mild depression for a week or two.

Bipolar II is more a more severe form than Cyclothemia, but the person is not psychotic and exhibits no extremely bizarre behaviors.

Bipolar I is characterized by bizarre behaviors and/or psychosis.

Schizoaffective Disorder is a combination of both Schizophrenia and Bipolar I in the same person; it is the most severe disorder on the bipolar spectrum.

Some clients who have mild and atypical bipolar symptoms that are hard to fit into any of these patterns may be diagnosed as having an Atypical Bipolar Disorder.

In each of the bipolar spectrum disorders, there is a period of time that usually lasts a few days (but can continue as long as one or two weeks) during which the person is either manic or hypomanic. Manic means psychotic (as discussed above) or bizarre behaviors, like running down Main Street naked, or other extreme behaviors. Hypomanic means less severely manic, which we will describe below. After a few days (or one to two weeks) of being either manic or hypomanic, the person has a rather sudden crash into a period of depression for a period of time that is usually longer than the manic or hypomanic phase. Typically three or four days of mania or hypomania are followed by eight or nine days of depression, with the degree of depression varying from mild to suicidal.

About 20% of bipolar individuals end up committing suicide, but those treated with proper medications usually do very well and live normal lives. After a depressive period of anywhere from three to twenty-one days, the person returns to his or her normal level of happiness or depression, usually for three or four months, before beginning another cycle. The length of time between cycles for various bipolar disorders can vary from a cycle every few weeks to a cycle every few years. The most common cycle for bipolar patients is three days hypomanic, six days depressed, and three months normal (or dysthymic). The cycles can occur every three months so regularly that the client can predict them ahead of time on their calendar.

The best medication for bipolar disorders is Lamictal (generic is lamotrigine), which is also used as an anti-seizure medicine by neurologists. When used to treat bipolar disorders, it almost always works and seldom has any side effects. Additionally, it reduces physical pain if someone has chronic pain from arthritis or back problems or whatever. It gets rid of anxiety and panic attacks. It also helps depression somewhat, but not as much as an antidepressant would. It decreases irritability, shyness, and cravings for alcohol or illegal drugs.

70% of bipolar clients abuse alcohol or drugs to pull themselves out of the mania or to numb themselves emotionally during their depressive dip. On a medicine like Lamictal, they typically feel so normal and good that it is often quite easy for them to quit drinking or doing drugs, unlike a normal alcoholic who does not have a bipolar disorder. Lamictal works through several mechanisms that we do not yet understand, but one of them is through the GABA system, so I consider it a GABA medication generally. Another good GABA medication for bipolar is Trileptal. Several dopamine medications (atypical antipsychotics) also make excellent mood stabilizers and keep bipolar clients normal, such as Abilify, Seroquel, Zyprexa, Geodon, and others.

If the client has Bipolar I and has been psychotic, it is best to use one of the above, because they will not only prevent bipolar, but will also prevent the psychosis from coming back. Lamictal by itself, although effective in treating bipolar, may not prevent the recurrence of future psychosis. Lithium has been used for decades in the treatment of bipolar illnesses, but it is not used nearly as much anymore because it tends to have many more side effects than the more modern medications for bipolar.

Antidepressants that work great in most people will not work well in bipolar clients unless they take a mood stabilizer with it. An antidepressant, given alone, can actually cause mania in someone who has an inherited bipolar disorder. In fact, if a person who needs an antidepressant has a first degree relative (father, mother, brother, sister, or child) who has bipolar, even if this person does not have any bipolar themselves, they should take a mood stabilizer along with the antidepressant. Generally, antidepressants do not work very well in first degree relatives of people with bipolar unless a mood stabilizer like Lamictal or one of the others is prescribed with it, but when given with such a mood stabilizer, the antidepressant will probably work very well.

If you have any client, friend, or relative who has one of the genetic disorders described in this chapter, be sure to love that person enough to refer him or her to a good psychiatrist who knows what they are doing when it comes to medications. A psychiatrist usually does almost no counseling—just medication management—so he or she does not need to be just like you spiritually. However, if your psychiatrist does do your counseling, having one that is likeminded is very important. If you can find a likeminded psychiatrist with a good bedside manner to do your medication management, that makes it much easier, but in many cities and towns no one like that available, so choose your psychiatrist based more on their intelligence than on their bedside manner.

The Meier Clinics (www.meierclinics.org) are a national chain of non-profit Christian counseling clinics, many of which also have one or more psychiatrists, physician assistants, or nurse practitioners, all of whom are capable of good medicine decisions. Anyone can call 1-888-7-CLINIC and we will try to help you find a psychiatrist nearby if we do not have a clinic in your area. The Christian Medical Society, The American Association of Christian Counselors, and Focus on the Family are also great referral resources. It may also be a good idea to talk to the main secretary of the largest evangelical church in your area to learn which psychiatrist they normally refer people to.

Five Symptoms of Mania or Hypomania that Start with the Letter "S"

1. **Sleep disorder.** The most important symptom required to diagnose a bipolar spectrum disorder is several days of significant insomnia (anywhere from no sleep to four to five hours a night in someone who normally sleeps seven to eight hours a night), but with SIGNIFICANTLY INCREASED ENERGY and activity. Lots of people miss a few nights of sleep when going through stress, etc., but they are very tired the next day, especially after

the second night in a row of poor sleep. A bipolar person will have significantly less sleep or even no sleep for several days (or longer) in a row with significantly more energy and activity.

2. **Speech disorder.** During the hypomanic or manic stage, the bipolar client nearly always has what we call "pressure of speech." It is like they have so many words to get out that they can't stop talking. They will talk fast and also dominate the conversation, noticeably more than normal (when they are not in a cycle).

3. **Spending sprees.** When they are hypomanic, bipolar clients do a variety of impulsive things, one after the other, but it is very common for them to spend much more money than usual. Some have run up their credit cards dramatically during a three or four-day hypomanic cycle. Some Bipolar I clients spend their entire life's savings in a day, spending (or gambling) themselves into bankruptcy.

4. **Superspirituality.** During the manic or hypomanic stage, the bipolar patient becomes more grandiose and usually feels very happy, very powerful, and smarter than anyone, but they can get irritable and angry at anyone who is foolish enough to disagree with them. For Bipolar II clients, while they also have some of these tendencies, they are not as severe. Some Bipolar II clients have cycles that are mild enough that they can still go to work and function reasonably well; well enough that their peers just think they are pretty wound up and a little grandiose and chatty. Manic Bipolar I patients, however, may think they are God, or that they have special spiritual gifts that they do not have, or that they have found the key to the universe. They may think God is speaking to them through an animal or object, or even that God wants them to start a new religion. I wonder how many sects or cults were started by Bipolar I human beings who were going through a manic episode.

5. **Sexual acting out.** During a manic episode, people with a bipolar disorder (Bipolar I usually) who are normally sexually pure, spiritually mature, and who would never have sex outside of marriage, may have sex with whomever is in the elevator with them. They often become very sexual and have little or no control

over their behavior, but when they get over their mania and realize what they have done, they feel horrible about it and may even become suicidal. Many marriages have unfortunately ended over a one-night stand someone had during a manic episode that he or she never would have had, had they been in their right mind. Sometimes my bipolar clients do so well for years in a row that they convince themselves they no longer need their meds. I warn all of them that if they get off their bipolar meds, they will become manic again the next time their cycle is due. One of my clients, a top executive in Houston, was a very spiritual and moral man. But years ago, he quit his meds without telling me, and when he became manic, he went to a topless bar in Houston, dished out thousands of dollars to prostitutes there, and also tried to buy the bar. In the hospital, we put him on meds that would rapidly pull him back down to reality, and he felt absolutely horrible about it all. Needless to say, he has never gotten off his meds since then.

Summary

Now that you have read this chapter, I hope you have a better understanding of the complexity of the human mind. Most people's problems ARE spiritual and emotional in nature; they can benefit greatly from wise pastoral or professional counseling, and usually no medications are needed. But some people have medical problems, like hypothyroidism, sleep apnea, chronic pain (causing continued repressed anger which leads to depression), or other medical conditions that cause their mental health symptoms. For others, poor nutrition may be the primary cause, especially if they have low Vitamin D, low Vitamin B, or even low iron. Still others abuse alcohol, marijuana, or illegal drugs, almost all of which lower the serotonin level in the brain and eventually cause depression, often to the point of becoming suicidal. Many suicides have been caused by drinking too much alcohol or smoking pot. And about 20% of all humans inherit one or more brain chemical deficiencies, which cause such conditions as ADHD, OCD, social phobia, schizophrenia, various kinds of depression and anxiety syndromes, bipolar spectrum disorders, abnormal personality traits, childhood autism, and many others. Many of these people suffer their entire lives and never find relief in spite of extensive counseling, prayer, and other efforts, simply because they have never been referred to a psychiatrist who can make their negative symptoms go away within hours, days, or sometimes weeks. I absolutely love being a Christian psychiatrist. I love to see people who have been suffering find out what it feels like to be happy and normal because they let me put them on meds that make their brains normal. I don't ever plan to retire because I enjoy it so much!

Michael Lyles, M.D.

Dr. Lyles is a graduate of the University of Michigan Six Year Premedical Medical Program. He completed his psychiatric residency and APA/NIMH Minority Fellowship at Duke University Medical Center where he was the recipient of the North Carolina Neuropsychiatric Association Resident of the Year Award. He was an Assistant Professor of Psychiatry and Associate Director of Outpatient Services at the University of Kentucky College of Medicine. He moved to Atlanta in 1986 to enter private practice, and has served as the medical director of a partial hospitalization program, an outpatient chemical dependency program, and inpatient psychiatric units at three different facilities. Michael has worked in the private sector in a community mental health center, state psychiatric hospital, and county, state and federal prisons.

Dr. Lyles is committed to raising the standard of care in the community by teaching gatekeepers such as clergy and primary care doctors, along with lay groups. He is board certified in Adult Psychiatry by the American Board of Psychiatry and Neurology. His major areas of clinical activity are mood disorders, anxiety disorders, and ADHD. Michael has produced over 60 publications and videos and serves on the speaking and advisory boards for several pharmaceutical companies. He is an executive board member of the American Association of Christian Counselors.

CHAPTER 4

How to Understand Basic Bio-Physiological Issues in Mental and Relational Health

Michael Lyles, M.D.

I feel so alone at church. I invite people over for meals and try to make friends. But when they find out that I am bipolar, they either preach to me about sin and healing or ignore me. I refuse to be invisible about my illness. However I long for true friendships and community. I don't need a sermon. I need a friend that will see me as a person. I need a hug… and perhaps someone who will try new recipes with me.

~Mary, a patient with bipolar disorder who was searching for a church to join

An esteemed mentor once told me that the character of a country can be determined by how it treats women, children, and the elderly. After more than three decades of psychiatric practice, I believe that the true measure of a local church's character can be found in how it treats people with mental illnesses. My office is crowded with Christians who are afraid to disclose their struggles with mental trauma to anyone in their local congregations. For the most part, they fear some sort of rejection or judgment if they are authentic in describing their struggles. I routinely ask my patients who are members of local churches if they have shared their struggles with their pastor, small group leader, or anyone in a discipleship role. The patient who is quoted above (Mary) is an exception, as she felt that she could not grow properly in a faith community that did not know her struggles. I agree with her and actively encourage my patients to find safe people to whom they can disclose their experiences. However, Mary stated that her bipolar illness represented a trauma in her life, and the behavior of her local church

45

re-traumatized her in a different manner. She tragically concluded, "I now feel spiritually defective to go along with my defective mind."

Many people of faith feel too ashamed, guilty, or embarrassed to take the risk that Mary did in revealing their struggles with mental illness. My average patient is much more comfortable asking for prayer for cancer than mentioning a mental or "emotional" issue to their faith community. Most of my patients struggle in silence as they hear mental illness described as being a function of spiritual weakness, a personality deficit, a salvation issue, a lack of properly applied faith, or a consequence of demonic influence. They have tried to pray it away, claim appropriate scriptures, get over it, or plead for or claim a miracle or deliverance. When the immediate miracle does not transpire, some become so frustrated and hopeless that they curse the day they were born (Job 3).

In contrast, some of my patients have experienced tremendous emotional healing because of their experience with their local church. One middle-aged man had suffered with depression since his college years. He struggled through a successful business career while actively serving as a Bible study leader. He felt like a fraud as he taught others about the Bible, while struggling with deep hopelessness and depression in his private life. He eventually took the risk of sharing his story with his pastor, who referred him for a psychiatric evaluation while spiritually supporting him. The evaluation revealed several significant medical and genetic problems that caused his brain to function very abnormally. In fact, the tests suggested that he should have barely graduated high school and should be on disability from severe depression, but he had earned a graduate degree and had a thirty-year business career! When confronted with this paradox, he was quick to give the following response:

> I am overwhelmed with the information that you shared with me. I am extremely grateful to God and a small, select group of people who tried to understand me. They supported me and stood by me - even when my behavior was not understandable or pleasant to be around.

The focus of this chapter is to understand why some churches are absolutely redemptive to psychiatric patients and their families, while some leave such patients feeling alienated and angry. This is an important question, as 20% of Americans will suffer with a significant mental illness in their lifetime. Many of these individuals seek help first in local churches which are not always prepared to minister to them. In many cases, some churches do not even recognize that this is an issue that needs attention. A large church in Atlanta sponsored a leadership training session on ministry to the mentally ill. At the conclusion of the meeting, one of the pastors in attendance stated that he was happy to learn some skills in this area that could help him if someone with mental illness joined his church. One of his pastor colleagues leaned over to him and said, "They are already there." He was correct; I knew of thirty of my patients who already attended his church. The challenge is to "see" them, and the parable of the Good Samaritan (Luke 10:30-35) is instructive in providing a paradigmatic framework for churches to recognize and effectively minister to those with mental illness.

"A Certain Man"

The man in this story is not known to us by name. He was not asking to be robbed. He was going about his life and was robbed and left half-dead. He now became defined by his trauma, not his personhood. We do not know if he had a family, whether he was rich or poor, what his occupation was, or if he was a Jew or a Gentile. We only know that he was robbed and left "half-dead." This is very descriptive of my psychiatric patients. They were going about their lives and were traumatized by life experiences that robbed them. Some cannot even identify what robbed them. They just know that they were robbed—robbed of relationships, jobs, education, health, finances, hope, dignity, and a future. As a result, they are off the beaten path of life, isolated, alone, and in a type of pain that is hard to describe. They are truly "half-dead" because they are alive enough to still experience their pain. They are alive enough to notice the people who are walking by and actively avoiding them. They are still alive enough to fear that emotional/spiritual and perhaps physical death is just a matter of time. They are alive enough to realize that they are vulnerable to being re-victimized. They are alive enough to fear that they have lost everything of value in life. They are alive enough to hear a prayer or scripture quoted to them "from across the street." Mostly, they are alive enough to know that they are alone.

"Passing By" Myths

The churches that my patients complain about to me share some of the characteristics of the religious (and secular) people who passed by on the other side. In the story, perhaps they passed by because they were too busy doing God's work. Perhaps they feared harm to their reputations if they stopped. After all, this could have been some nameless nobody who may have had a bad reputation. [Jesus faced similar discrimination and disparagement with a different Samaritan at a well (John 4:5-27). The disciples were tempted to remind him that there are some people that you just don't associate with if you are respectable.] Someone helping this man could risk being robbed by those same robbers who could still be in the area. Someone might mistake a helper as being the robber of the man. Taking care of this "certain man" could be upsetting, as he was probably a physical and emotional mess. They would certainly risk getting bloody, which would make them ceremonially unclean. Or they could just pass by because someone else who was better trained could help him more effectively. And maybe he wasn't all that badly injured; he probably ought to just help himself. After all, half dead is also half alive, and if he had more faith, he wouldn't need to depend on someone else.

The churches that "pass by" may have a warped view of the Christian experience. In those churches it is falsely believed that people only end up in this condition because of something they did to invite – or even cause – their situation. Maybe this was a consequence or punishment for sin, because Christians who are living "right" should never get beaten up mentally or robbed emotionally. One of my Christian mentors was embarrassed when I went into psychiatry. He told me that only "unsaved" people experienced mental illness and that I was casting my medical pearls before swine. Another pastor told me that he could empty the psychiatric ward of Duke Hospital (where I worked at the time) if everyone on that unit got saved. He found it inconceivable that nearly a third of the patients in that ward at that time self-identified as evangelical Christians. He exclaimed, "There is no such thing as a mentally ill Christian!"

Mentally Ill Christians?

There are at least two basic problems with the inherent thesis that Christians should be immune to mental illness. First is the assumption that it is inconsistent with a biblical worldview for a person of faith to deal with emotional issues. From this position, the abundant life of John 10:10 does not include seasons of despair and emotional agony. This position states that depression, anxiety, fear, and confusion are not fruits of the Spirit and thus are not part of the victorious Christian life. However this position can only be properly defended if one omits most of the psalms, Job, many of the personal experiences of the prophets, most of Isaiah 53, and the entire books of Lamentations and Acts. Jesus would have healed everyone the same way and instantaneously, without multiple variations in how he touched people's eyes when healing physical blindness. Words such as "suffering" and "heaviness" would be deleted from the Bible, and Paul would not have a "thorn in the flesh" that he could not pray away. In fact, in reviewing my Bible's concordance, words like affliction, afraid, agony, alone, anger, anguish, anxious, and ashamed would have to be deleted – just from the "A" section alone! And there would be no need for a community of faith to comfort each other (1 Thessalonians 5:11), listen to and pray for each other (James 5:16), and support each other through all manner of trauma and pain (Galatians 6:2; Acts 20:35; 1 Thessalonians 5:14).

Secondly, this position assumes that emotional symptoms consistently indicate a specific emotional or spiritual causation, leaving no room for medical intervention. This is not defendable biblically as Nehemiah, David, Jeremiah, Job, Peter, Judas, Ezekiel, and Elijah were all depressed at some point in their lives, and for very different, not uniform, reasons. One size does not fit all diagnostically. In one clinical day recently, I saw people dealing with symptoms of depression due to diabetes, anemia, medication side effects, thyroid disease, sleep apnea, traumatic brain injury, vitamin D deficiency, and menopausal hormonal problems. Please understand that behavior does not prove causation. People can have psychiatric symptoms such as anxiety from dieting problems, thyroid disease, blood sugar issues, clinical depression, a medication side effect, or a spiritual causation. Sometimes psychiatric symptoms can be triggered by the strangest things.

One of my patients had gastric bypass surgery that resulted in his not absorbing iron from his diet. This iron deficiency caused leg pains that disrupted his sleep, and the sleep disruption triggered depression. I tell my patients that Humpty Dumpty does not always fall spontaneously off the wall. Sometimes he is pushed! This gastric bypass patient's condition was an example of multiple variables combining to push him into a depression that could have easily been confused with a concurrent spiritual issue. My professional life would be much easier if each specific psychiatric symptom could be explained accurately and consistently by one diagnosis (a specific spiritual defect).

The viewpoint that Christians don't (or can't) experience mental illness also leaves no room for the impact of the central nervous system, especially the brain, as a mediator of emotional issues. In fact, this perspective doesn't treat the brain as an organ but relegates it to a hybrid status of being part physical and part spiritual. But in reality, the brain is an organ that impacts emotional perception and mood, along with a myriad of other functions such as motor movement, cognition, and basic body drives including breathing, sleep/wake cycles, memory, sensory perceptions such as hearing/sight/taste, and many others. As an organ, the health of the brain can be affected by toxins, infections, hormonal imbalances, vitamin deficiencies, sleep deprivation, head injuries, insulin resistance, and genetic mutations that impact brain chemical physiology. This simplistic theology treats the human body like a grocery store where the different departments (dairy, bakery, meats, canned goods, and paper products) can exist separately from each other without any networking or interdependency. The human body is actually the opposite of this; our various systems (circulatory, endocrine, skeletal, and neurological) are very dependent on and interdependent with each other. For example, dysfunctions in brain health can affect the function of the thyroid, ovaries, heart, and bones. Therefore the types of problems that cause severe depression may also correlate with an increased risk for diabetes, stroke, heart attacks, osteoporosis, infertility, and dementia. The brain does not function in isolation but is one part of a larger interconnected whole called human physiology.

Theodicy: The Theology of Suffering

This type of unrealistic and inaccurate theology selectively omits Bible passages that talk about tribulation or suffering. This theology cannot explain the psalms that were written by an innocent man (David) who had been hunted without cause by a mentally unstable king (Saul). To reconcile this mindset with the totality of Scripture, we would have to leave out Lamentations, most of the book of Acts, and all of Job and Nehemiah, as mentioned earlier. And apparently Jeremiah just needed to shape up and stop all that sadness and crying!

The reality is that the Bible is a "book of trauma" that describes many lives that were punctuated with pain and suffering. Churches that minister well to my patients do not run from this fact but instead embrace it. People talk honestly about their struggles and do not claim to have all the answers about their life circumstances (1 Corinthians 13:12). They know that the message of the Bible is that God cares and has provided help for us to respond appropriately to the pain we experience. A mature theodicy or theology of suffering gives meaning to the inevitable trials of life and includes the following points of emphasis:

1. Suffering is common to the Christian experience (Psalm 34:19, 37:23-24).
2. Suffering is seldom welcome. Paul prayed repeatedly for his "thorn in the flesh" to go away (2 Corinthians 12:7-9).
3. Suffering is not logical. Job did not understand his suffering (Job 5:6-7).
4. Suffering is not always easy to comprehend (Ecclesiastes 1:8).
5. Suffering properly is part of being Christ-like (Isaiah 53).
6. Suffering is understood by Jesus who is empathetic, having walked through similar experiences (Hebrews 4:15-16).
7. Suffering is monitored by God who will provide us with options for addressing our suffering (1 Corinthians 10:13).
8. Suffering is a vitamin for our growth (1 Peter 1:6-7, 4:1-2).
9. Suffering is a daily challenge (Lamentations 3:21-24).
10. Suffering is not to be endured alone (Romans 8:26-27; Hebrews 13:5).

11. Suffering gives reasons to support each other (1 Corinthians 12:26).
12. Suffering provides opportunity to get closer to God (Psalm 119:67).
13. Suffering teaches us to wait on God (Lamentations 3:25-26; Isaiah 40:31).
14. Suffering well is the key factor (1 Peter 4:19).
15. Suffering provides opportunity to know that God is still in control (John 16:33).

Seeing the Man

The Good Samaritan did not jump to any preconceived conclusion. He saw the man where he was and ministered to him as he was. He began by seeing the man. I believe that the Good Samaritan could "see" the man because perhaps the Good Samaritan had been through some things himself. Perhaps he had been victimized and left on the side of a lonely road. Perhaps someone in his family had been helped by someone who refused to pass by on the other side. Many people in churches are reluctant to help others because although they themselves (or their families) have been through issues, they were treated with shame or stigma. On the other hand, if such experiences were handled in a healthy way, they may have better prepared and motivated a person to minister to someone else in need. Coming from a place of pain or dysfunction can sharpen our vision for those who are hurting on the roadside if we have allowed God to help us through our pain.

Helpful churches that make an effort to compassionately see and respond to patients who suffer with bio-physiological problems are at least minimally knowledgeable about mental illness. They know that clinical depression involves physical symptoms such as appetite variances, sleep problems, lack of interest in pleasurable activities, social isolation, spontaneous crying spells, and sometimes physical symptoms such as pain. They know that depressed people may be quiet and may isolate themselves at church; that they may disappear from small groups or Bible studies; that they assume no one will miss them or come looking for them; that they believe the promises in the Bible do not apply to them and that prayer is an act of futility—at least for them.

These churches know that bipolar disorder is characterized by periods of elevated mood, grandiosity, spending sprees, sexual impulsivity, driving fast, and irritability; that these symptoms are referred to as manic symptoms; that these people can be the life of the fellowship group initially and then go over the lines of appropriate behavior; that they may flirt or try to take on responsibilities for which they are not gifted; that they may be moody and get their feelings hurt easily; and that when they 'crash,' they can be prone to periods of extreme depression that can be a complete and intense contrast to their mania. Some people have speculated that King Saul in 1 Samuel may have had bipolar disorder.

These churches know that the "bad child" at church may have attention deficit disorder which can masquerade in kids as behavior problems including impulsivity, hyperactivity, and the inability to focus and concentrate on non-interesting topics. They realize that these kids know right from wrong and are repentant for their mistakes, but just can't seem to help themselves, in part because of medical problems with how their dopamine systems are functioning in their frontal lobes.

These helpful and accepting churches have learned to "see the man" by educating their members about these and other problems and by helping them get more training regarding what to look for.

Innkeepers and Churches

The Good Samaritan was a safe person who did not rob the traumatized man of whatever dignity and half-life he still had left. He assessed the man's situation and gave him what he was able to give at the time. He was not paralyzed into inaction by his fear of the unknown. He did what he could and partnered with someone who could provide what he was not trained to provide (i.e., the innkeeper).

Mental health professionals serve in the innkeeper role for many churches, helping with problems that are more than primarily spiritual issues. In this story, we do not see a focus on the personal beliefs or practices of the innkeeper. He simply does his job in partnership with the Good Samaritan. But notice this important point: the Good Samaritan never abandons the trauma victim. He takes ownership of his situation and comes back for him. The churches that my patients adore never leave them or forsake them (Hebrews 13:5).

"Innkeepers" are varied. Sometimes they are psychiatrists but most psychiatric medications for mood and anxiety problems are written by OB-GYNs and primary care doctors. Some innkeepers are devout believers; others are not (just like all medical specialists). The Bible is not anti-doctor; if it were, Jesus would have expressed that when he was touched by the woman with the issue of blood (Luke 8:43-48). In this passage, Jesus did not criticize the woman for trying to get some help medically. The Bible says that she had spent all of her money on co-pays, and it speaks of the limits of medicine compared to Jesus's miraculous power, power that was documented by a disciple who was himself a physician: Luke.

Some churches "preach" against medications for psychiatric problems. One pastor told me that a friend criticized him for taking an antidepressant. A pastor patient of mine was told that the only pill that a Christian needed was the "GosPill" (a.k.a. gospel). This perspective commits the same error already stated: believing that the brain is not an organ that can get medically sick. It assumes that all psychiatric medications are addictive, although most are not. Some people fear that medication will impact a person's ability to fully experience God because they will have fake feelings from the medications. They may incorrectly think that the fruit of antidepressants will blur the fruit of the Spirit. People who believe this have too large a view of psychotropic medications and too small a view of God! An antidepressant may help someone to not have suicidal thoughts, but it will not give the person a reason or purpose to live. An anti-anxiety medication may quiet nervousness and fear, but it will not provide a peace that exceeds logical understanding. A mood stabilizer may help someone to be less irritable, but it will not make the person kind. An antipsychotic medication may decrease a person's paranoid fears of others, but it will not make someone loving or patient. There is sometimes a role for medications, but that role should not be blown out of proportion in either direction—by giving it too much emphasis or none at all. Incidentally, Paul's exhortation to Timothy to take some wine for his stomach problems was standard medical practice in that day (1 Timothy 5:23).

Elements of a Plan

Churches that effectively minister to those in emotional distress have a plan and serve hurting people accordingly. They own that these are "our" people and family, not "those" people. They promote a culture of authenticity and mutual accountability where people talk safely about their struggles. They do not gossip or violate confidential communications. They develop relationships with their local mental health community – before they need them. (We can assume that the Good Samaritan already had a relationship with the innkeeper because the innkeeper extended him a line of credit). These churches identify the mental health resources in their community and meet with and minister to them. They take food to the staff at psychiatric hospitals during holidays. They send cards of encouragement to mental health professionals when there is not a holiday. They "love on" their mental health resources, simply because Jesus said that this is who we are and how we are to be (John 13:35). They encourage enough dialogue to be able to ascertain how the mental health professional would approach a person of faith. They do not exclusively engage in the (usually fruitless) exercise of trying to find a "Christian psychiatrist;" those are few and far between and may not be competent just because they market themselves as Christian. It is much more fruitful to find and develop relationships with good, knowledgeable clinicians who can do excellent evaluations.

The church can and should continue to shepherd the spiritual status of the hurting person through their growth and healing process, with assistance from a Christian counselor (much more widely available) as needed. Effective churches encourage their members to get complete assessments and do not make assumptions. They serve their members, even if that means cutting grass, applying nail polish, or preparing a meal. They focus on the whole family system that is involved, not just the individual. Finally, they treat mentally ill people as people, not as diagnoses, and they do not neglect those persons' spiritual and other needs in the process.

The plan also needs to include a strategy for answering some of the common questions that patients ask of their churches:

1. Is it safe to be honest here?
2. Will I face rejection and blame?

3. Will anyone listen to me... I mean really hear me out?
4. Will I just get preached to or talked at... not with?
5. Will anyone walk with me through my pain?
6. Will I be abandoned?
7. Can I find hope?
8. How is Jesus relevant to my situation?

It was pointed out earlier that many of my patients feel that in their churches they only have a diagnosis and not a name. However, a mental illness is an adjective, not a noun. These are people who do have a name and a personal identity before God... and it is not "bipolar" or some other diagnostic label! Their struggle is real *and so is their God* who wants to express his love through his people in local churches (Isaiah 61:1-3). His very names are supportive of this:

Jehovah Jireh, My Provider – because we are all needy;
El Shaddai, The Almighty – because we are all weak sometimes;
Jehovah Rapha, My Healer – because we are all sick in some way sometimes;
Jehovah Shalom, My Peace – because we are all troubled sometimes;
Jehovah Salah, My Forgiver – because we all make mistakes; and
Jehovah Nissi, My Banner – because we are all vulnerable and need covering sometimes.

In closing, churches need to become "Christian firefighters," running toward those dealing with the fire of mental illness when everyone else is running away. Mental illness is very common in the communities that our churches reflect. A healthy church will first see the people in need, create a safe environment, and listen to them because they are our brothers and sisters (James 1:19). Then the healthy church will minister to them with the trifecta of truth: hope based on God's love, appropriately applied science, and the ultimate truth of the Word.

References

Carter, R. (2010). *Within our reach: Ending the mental health crisis.* Emmaus, PA: Rodale, Inc.

Depression and Bipolar Support Alliance: www.dbsalliance.org

Langberg, D. (2015). *Suffering and the heart of God: How trauma destroys and Christ restores.* Greensboro, NC: New Growth Press.

National Alliance on Mental Illness: www.nami.org

Winter, R. (2012). *When life goes dark: Finding hope in the midst of depression.* Downers Grove, IL: InterVarsity Press.

Gary J. Oliver, Th.M., Ph.D.

Gary Oliver is a husband, father, university and seminary professor, psychologist, and author who serves as the Executive Director of The Center for Healthy Relationships and Professor of Psychology and Practical Theology at John Brown University in Siloam Springs, Arkansas.

He received his B.A. from Biola University, an M.Div. from Talbot Theological Seminary, a Th.M. from Fuller Theological Seminary, and an M.A. and a Ph.D. in psychology from the University of Nebraska in Lincoln. He is a licensed clinical psychologist in both Arkansas and Colorado. Dr. Oliver is a Clinical Fellow and Approved Supervisor of the American Association for Marriage and Family Therapy (AAMFT). He has earned the Certified Family Life Educator (C.F.L.E.) diploma from The National Council on Family Relations.

Dr. Oliver has over 40 years' experience in individual, premarital, marital, and family counseling. For over 10 years Dr. Oliver served on the Board of Directors and the National Speaking Team for Promise Keepers and spoke to over one million men in live venues throughout the country. He serves on the Executive Board and the national speaking team of the American Association of Christian Counselors.

In addition to his clinical experience, Dr. Oliver has over ten years' experience serving on the staff of churches in California, Nebraska, and Colorado. For 18 years he was also Associate Professor, Program Director, and founder of the D. Min. in Marriage and Family Counseling Program at Denver Seminary.

He is the author of *It's All About Relationships* (with David H. L. Olson), *It's Okay To Be Angry* (with H. Norman Wright), *Mad About Us: Moving from Anger to Intimacy with Your Spouse* (with Carrie Oliver), *Made Perfect in Weakness: The Amazing Things God Can Do With Failure*, and *Real Men Have Feelings Too,* as well as the co-author of ten other books with H. Norman Wright, including *Raising Emotionally Healthy Kids, Hip-Hop and His Famous Face,* and *Bruce Moose and the What Ifs.*

CHAPTER 5

How to Develop a Suffering-Sensitive Ministry

Gary J. Oliver, Th.M., Ph.D.

Editor's Note:

Suffering is universal; it is endemic to the human condition. Yet suffering hurts. Perhaps nothing in all of human existence causes us to ponder the adversities of life and confronts us with our vulnerability as creatures like the cruel agony of suffering. In over four decades of professional clinical experience, nothing I (Jared) have ever seen causes people to become disillusioned with God, leave the church, and even abandon their faith more than their inability to successfully make sense of their sufferings and grappling with questions of evil.

In many ways Christians have failed to adequately address the problems posed and exposed by suffering and develop a practical theology of theodicy— defending God's goodness in the face of evil and suffering or what C. S. Lewis poignantly termed "the problem of pain." We have not equipped people to suffer well—with strength, meaning, dignity, purpose, and hope. We have not effectively taught people the reality that in this life Jesus promised we will have many troubles (John 16:33). As Viktor Frankl put it: "Suffering is an ineradicable part of life, even as fate and death. Without suffering and death human life cannot be complete" (2006, p. 19).

Distressing as that is to realize, Lewis famously explained that "God whispers to us in our pleasures, speaks in our conscience, but shouts in our pain—it is His megaphone to rouse a deaf world" (2015, p. 15). Further understandings of suffering include Carl Jung's belief that neurosis is always a substitute for legitimate suffering, William Shakespeare's observation that someone who jests at scars has never felt a wound, and Benjamin Franklin's wise counsel that those things which hurt, instruct.

However, like Job, we cannot always understand why God allows us to suffer—although we try. James Dobson declared, "It is an incorrect view of scripture to say that we will always comprehend what God is doing and how our suffering and disappointment fall into his plan" (2012, p. 156). Accordingly, Philip Yancey pointed out that "Knowledge is passive, intellectual; suffering is active, personal. No intellectual answer will solve suffering" (2002, p. 9). Yet Corrie Ten Boom assured us that however deep the pit, God's love is deeper still, Dietrich Bonhoeffer noted that only the suffering God can help us in our despair, Leo Tolstoy concluded that it is by those who have suffered that the world has been advanced, and the apostle Paul reminded us in 2 Corinthians 12:9 of one of Jesus' paradoxical statements—and then challenged us with his own response to it: "… He has said to me, 'My grace is sufficient for you, for power is perfected in weakness.' Most gladly, therefore, I will rather boast about my weaknesses, so that the power of Christ may dwell in me" (NASB).

While Gary's personal story which follows has a powerfully redemptive and God-glorifying outcome, not all people's situations do… but they can.

> [From Gary: Actually in one way my outcome massively stunk. In the past two months I've dealt with the anniversaries of a dead son and a dead wife… my journey took years of both wet and dry tears, moanings that couldn't be uttered, depths of loneliness I couldn't imagine. My hope is that people who read this WON'T think that Gary Oliver is just one of those super-strong spiritual guys who can handle anything… so not true. I'm a very weak man who over time learned that I could trust my promise-keeping God… and that it was always worth pressing on.]

In this chapter Gary shares a number of valuable "gifts" which he allowed God to teach him (albeit very painfully) through his journey. He courageously testifies to the profound emotional, relational, and spiritual lessons he learned—along with the resultant growth he gained—through his experiences of ongoing horrible suffering and multiple traumatic losses. His progressively deepening faith and indefatigable attitude are both impressive and inspiring. Notice how his insightful paradigmatic shift regarding his tragic experiences produced more psycho-social-spiritual maturity in, and now through, him.

*Let the same be true of us and of those we serve as we take seriously people's suffering. With God's help **we CAN** learn how to healthfully manage our own pain so that we can be present for others. Then we can develop useful and effective ways to minister to hurting people at the point of their greatest need. With God's help **we CAN** create safe places for people to be able to dump their pain as we non-judgmentally bear their burdens with them. With God's help **we CAN** understand that proof-texting, pious preaching, and pontifical platitudes rarely furnish the support, help, and compassion for which hurting people are so desperate. With God's help **we CAN** learn to not be afraid to let hurting people figuratively vomit, spew, and rant in the midst of their outrage. God can handle all of that, but many times Christians feel threatened and defensive when suffering people simply need to be lovingly listened to.*

Allow the Holy Spirit to speak through Gary's story to penetrate your heart. Then think about how you and those you serve can become catalysts for his compassion and conduits for his comfort toward those who are suffering.

Imagine going to the doctor for what you think is a routine check-up and being told you have two rapidly growing, inoperable tumors… and apart from an experimental chemotherapy treatment, you may only have three months to live. Three months…

What emotions might you feel? What thoughts would immediately flood your mind? What questions would you have for the doctor? For God? What specific worries and fears might you experience? Who is the first person you would call? What would you say? Where would you start the process of organizing the final three months of your life?

Well, that is exactly what happened to me, and those are some of the very questions I had to ask myself. By God's grace, and over time, everything turned out to be a growth opportunity—even a sovereign opportunity—for me. Once again, God turned what Satan had designed for discouragement and destruction into a chance to continue demonstrating, and even showcasing, his faithfulness by providing some life lessons that I hope God will use to encourage you or someone you know.

In order to understand those lessons, I need to start about twenty-five years ago when I was told that what doctors thought was just a benign growth on my tongue was actually cancer, and that they were going to operate in two days. I stood there holding the phone while staring out the window. These things don't happen to me! These are the kinds of things I help others deal with. Me… have cancer? No way! As it turned out, this was to be the first of eight occasions on which I would be told I had cancer, and the first of seven surgeries for that dreaded disease.

Several years ago, and just a few months after doing the funeral service for my father, I sat in a doctor's office and heard him give the same diagnosis to my late wife, Carrie, except that her condition was inoperable metastatic pancreatic cancer with a prognosis of just three to six months to live. It was infinitely more painful for me to hear her diagnosis than it was to hear my own. In his goodness and grace God gave Carrie two more years. Little did I know that within a four year period, I would bury my dad; my wife of twenty-seven years; my twenty-three year-old son, Matt; and my only sibling, Marsha… and in the process go through four more cancer surgeries.

Just a few years later, in 2010 I received my sixth diagnosis of cancer, and on May 6, just one day after the 3rd anniversary of the death of my son, Matt, I underwent a 10-hour surgery that was followed by a long recuperation, the first month of which I was confined to my bed. A surgical team had removed 80% of my tongue and replaced it with muscle from my legs. I was in ICU and on a ventilator for two days.

When I awoke for the first time, I was told about the extent of my surgery. Doctors said that at some point my friends *might* be able to understand a few of my words, but I would probably never be able to speak in public again, I wouldn't be able to chew, I would have a hard time even swallowing, I wouldn't have any ability to taste, and I would probably live with a feeding tube for the rest of my life. That isn't good news for anyone, but it's especially devastating for someone whose life and ministry has been teaching, preaching, speaking, counseling, coaching, and consulting.

At that point I decided to not accept the idea that I would never be able to speak again. I began the painstaking, wearisome, and remarkably discouraging journey of teaching myself how to speak—hours and weeks and many months of sitting in front of the mirror, trying over and over and over again just to say my ABC's. At first they were unintelligible... I couldn't even understand myself. I often had to end my practice "sessions" early, depressed and in tears. I felt overwhelmed by hopelessness and helplessness. However, after about seven months my friends were able to understand a few of my words, and I slowly began to sound like an intoxicated Elmer Fudd. That was progress.

In November of that same year, as I was finally making headway in my recovery, I went back to MD Anderson Cancer Center in Houston for another "routine" check-up and was shocked to receive my seventh diagnosis of cancer. I was told that they'd found two rapidly-growing inoperable tumors in my neck, that it was advanced Stage 4, and that I might have less than three more months to live. Three months? Really? Bummer. They said there was a new "butt-kicking chemo cocktail" that had just been approved to "try" on this kind of cancer, but they had no idea if the new cocktail would help. It was my only viable treatment option, so thus began a new emotional roller-coaster ride—and a new growth opportunity.

I thought my chemo regimen back in 2003 had been nasty, but this time I felt like I had been hit by a Mack˙ truck. The effects included major fatigue (just walking up a set of stairs exhausted me), nausea, the loss of fingernails and toenails, sores and rashes on my skin, inflammation around my eyes that secreted a substance making it difficult to open them on my own (some mornings I actually had to pry my eyes open), a swollen tongue, a cognitive "fog" that impacted my ability to focus, decreased creativity, neuropathy (a numbness in the tips of my fingers and toes), difficulty concentrating, and decreased appetite. However, there was one positive aspect: I was still able to laugh at myself and my own jokes even if no one else was laughing.

What I had already been through had in some ways prepared me for this new dark valley. Somehow I knew that I wasn't alone, that God's promises were still in effect, and that these circumstances didn't change the reality of the faithful God I'd served for most of my life. After several months of treatment, my amazed physicians told me that the tumors had disappeared, and that's when I finally began the year-long healing process.

So why did I take the time to tell you my story in such detail? First of all, it is a testimony to the goodness and power of God. Furthermore, I want you to know that what I am about to share is not merely abstract theory, pop psychology, or trite spiritualization of painful and challenging realities. I have lived through extended seasons of darkness, discouragement, and agonizing emotional and physical pain, and I've faced the news that I may only have a few more months to live. Through it all, by God's grace and mercy, he has allowed me to learn some invaluable life lessons. He has given me certain gifts along the journey and allowed me to grow in ways I never anticipated, and I want to share those with you.

Emotional Growth

God used these horribly traumatic events to allow me to experience significant emotional growth. I was raised in Long Beach, California, and when I was a child, The Pike (an amusement park on the beach) boasted the world's largest wooden roller-coaster. It was known as the Cyclone Racer, and when I was in middle school, it only cost 50 cents a ride. I still remember the day when I had saved enough money to ride it ten times in a row. What great joy!

A roller-coaster is fun to ride, but it would not be very enjoyable to live on. Burying four family members in four years, dealing with seven cancer surgeries, and being told you may only have three months to live can put you—and those you love—on an emotional roller-coaster ride. But it can also provide a greater opportunity to learn when you can trust your emotions and when you cannot. Fear, discouragement, depression, anger, and anxiety are just a few of the emotions you will face, and sometimes they can seem to block your awareness of everything else... including God.

I have spent most of my life helping people work through difficult and debilitating emotions. In dealing with cancer, I had to personally face these emotions head-on and decide if I was going to believe some of their lies and let them determine my reality or take them captive to what I knew to be true. I remember many days when I would have to remind myself that "feelings don't always equal facts," especially when success meant just getting out of bed (it wasn't always easy) and putting one foot in front of the other.

Also, I have come face-to-face with thoughts and feelings that at one time would have seemed overwhelming and impossible to cope with. I engaged in hand-to-hand combat with feelings of hopelessness, helplessness, loneliness, deep loss, disorientation, futility, and irrelevance, and through it all, I rediscovered that emotions are a gift from God with a message that, in God's hands, can provide potential learning opportunities. However, I had to learn to slow down and stop; to look and listen for what God was saying.

Relational Growth

Another gift from wrestling with cancer has been learning to understand the healing power of friends in a new way and at a new level. Some of my friends have "taken me to school" on how to provide love and support at a time when I had no idea what I needed and was just hoping to be able to make it through another day—and on occasion not being sure if I even wanted to see a new day.

Appreciating the power of presence is another area where I have grown—just being there sometimes for a person without any rehearsed statements except, "I don't know what to say, but I love you and am here with you." This speaks to the power of a voicemail, e-mail, or text message sent with no expectation of a response, the often-repeated reassurance that I was being prayed for, or a verse or a poem. I was amazed by the number of notes I received from people I had never met. Any expression of concern or prayer is encouraging, but to receive one- and two-page handwritten notes from total strangers was astonishing and a profound source of encouragement and validation of God's faithfulness.

Spiritual Growth

In the spiritual dimension, dealing with cancer, dying, and death has given me the opportunity to better understand the power of perspective and praise. When it comes to perspective, most people go through life with a problem-focus. Their cup is always half-empty, and they are experts on what could be better, what others have that they do not, who is better off than they are, and how they would be happier "if only" their circumstances were different.

Cancer helped me develop more of a promise-focus. This simply means that the reality of the day-in and day-out struggle of confronting cancer in my own life and in the lives of those I love has given me the opportunity to see the promises in God's word from a whole new perspective. When I look at my life in light of what God has promised **and experience Him as the ultimate promise keeper,** it becomes much easier to move from a fear-focus to a faith-focus.

Another "gift" God has given me is a whole new understanding of the power of praise. The phrase "Count your blessings; name them one-by-one" is no longer just part of a song so common it had lost much of its meaning. There were many days when giving thanks was my life preserver. I began each day by counting my blessings—for six months in words that only God could understand.

Dealing with the diagnosis compelled me to pursue God and dig deeply into his word. I was led to study the word "joy" and came up with some amazing discoveries. Did you know that a primary objective in Jesus' teaching was for his disciples to experience *JOY*? Did you know that the words *joy, joyous*, and/or *joyful* are found more than 200 times in Scripture? Did you know that the verb *rejoice* also appears well over 200 times? Look at these verses (emphases added):

> *"… In Your presence is fullness of JOY; In Your right hand there are pleasures forever"* (Psalm 16:11, NASB).

> *"For His anger is but for a moment, His favor is for a lifetime; Weeping may last for the night, but a shout of JOY comes in the morning"* (Psalm 30:5, NASB).

> *"These things I have spoken to you so that My joy may be in you, and that your JOY may be made full"* (John 15:11, NASB).

> *"Truly, truly I say to you, that you will weep and lament… but your grief will be turned into JOY…. if you ask the Father for anything in my name, He will give it to you. Until now you have asked for nothing in My name; ask and you will receive, so that your JOY may be made full"* (John 16:20, 23-24, NASB).

The Bottom Line

Here's the bottom line: in my life, *God used bad news to help me focus on the good news,* and in the process get everything back into perspective. I have learned that success in life is not primarily how *long* I live, but how *well* I live. I hate cancer. Every nasty thing anyone has ever said about cancer is true. At the same time, God can use cancer to help a person surrender the illusion of control. I cannot control *how long* I live but, with God's help, I can control *how well* I choose to live, for whatever time God chooses to give me.

As I write this, I have been told that while my tumors are gone, I am not entirely cancer-free and must still take medication every morning to keep the cancer at bay. There is a high probability that the cancer will figure out what the medication is doing and try to spread despite it. If that happens, either there will be a new treatment available or it will be my time to "finish the course" and move on. Please know that I do not say that glibly or without painful emotion, but with confidence and peace.

I am blessed that I don't dread each day, and I'm very aware of how well I'm doing, especially given the nature of what I have been through. However, while counting my blessings is a very effective and legitimate way to maintain perspective by fighting the assaults of the evil one and warding off the almost constant emotional, psychological, and spiritual warfare confronting me, I also know that it does not change for one second the new realities I have to learn to live with throughout each and every day. This can be very difficult, but God continues to prove himself faithful regardless of my circumstances, and throughout every situation, I am able to experience sovereign joy.

During my adventures with cancer and in grieving other tragic life losses over the past twenty-five years, I have been given eyes that see things I had never noticed before, ears that hear with a new acuity and clarity, and a heart that is much more tender. I have grown emotionally, relationally, and spiritually. I have discovered that there is a big difference between surviving and thriving; I know Christ did not die and rise again for us to merely survive. Mere survival is not the "exceedingly abundantly above all that we ask or think" which Paul discusses in Ephesians 3:20. Just treading water is not what he meant by "becoming more than conquerors."

If I am told yet again that I may have only three months to live, how will I respond? After prayerfully reflecting on what God has lovingly taught me through the adventures of the past several years, I have realized that the most important considerations are not:

- IF I'm going to die… it's going happen.
- HOW I'm going to die… I can't control that one.
- WHEN I'm going to die… I can't control that one either.
- IF it's going to be hard or painful… it probably will be.

When I finally come face-to-face with death, when it becomes my turn to cross that river, the most significant bottom-line consideration will be HOW I can reflect and manifest the goodness, grace, and mercy of my precious Lord—that I so abundantly experienced throughout my life—in such a way that people will be able to see the difference Christ makes in every chapter of life… especially the final chapter. My hope and prayer is to draw on, and drink from, the reservoir of resources God has given me and, with his grace, to respond in a manner that will cause people to say, "How great is our God!"

In the meantime, every day is a gift of grace with new opportunities to "count our blessings" and give testimony to a quality of life that refuses to be defined by our circumstances, but is instead defined by God's completed work for us on the cross as we serve a risen savior. **To God be the glory!**

The struggle is real . . . indeed it is.

The pain of each surgery was real—and so was God's *faithfulness.*
The massive loss of each loved-one was, and still is, very real—and so was God's *comfort.*
The nausea and exhaustion of each chemo treatment was real—and so was God's *presence.*
The fear of facing a life of never being able to speak, taste, chew, or swallow… of never being able to do or say what I'd spent of lifetime of saying and doing was very real—and so were God's *promises.*

The sense of God's presence, the power of his promises, and the love and encouragement of good friends… *in the midst of the storm…* were also real. The fact that I still carry the wounds of profound losses is real, but so is the fact that I didn't have to allow those losses to define me. Likewise, the fact that he "supplied all of my needs," that he "didn't leave me or forsake me," that he was a "promise-keeper" and not just a promise-maker... and the fact that our circumstances, no matter how tragic or horrific, don't have to define our reality and determine our future; now that's good news.

Here's the deal. Joy doesn't just happen. Happy endings don't just happen. They come from choosing to *understand*, *listen* to, *learn* from, *grow* through, and *press* into the ultimate reality of the promises, power, and presence of our Lord Jesus Christ.

References

Dobson, J. (2012). *When God doesn't make sense.* Carol Stream, IL: Tyndale.

Frankl, V. (2006). *Man's search for meaning.* Boston: Beacon Press.

Lewis, C. S. (2015). *The problem of pain.* New York: HarperOne.

Yancey, P. (2002). *Where is God when it hurts?* Grand Rapids, MI: Zondervan.

Tim Clinton, Ed.D.

Tim Clinton, Ed.D., LPC, LMFT (The College of William & Mary), is the President of the American Association of Christian Counselors (AACC), the largest and most diverse Christian counseling association in the world. Dr. Clinton also serves as the Executive Director of the James Dobson Family Institute and recurring co-host of "Dr. James Dobson's Family Talk," heard on nearly 1,300 radio outlets daily. Licensed as both a Professional Counselor and Marriage and Family Therapist, Dr. Clinton is recognized as a world leader in mental health and relationship issues. He has authored and edited nearly 30 books.

Dr. Clinton is founder of the biennial AACC World Conference (which consistently hosts nearly 7,000 leaders representing all 50 states and nearly 40 countries) in Nashville, Tennessee. He is also founder of Light University—a global leader in certificate, diploma, and mental health continuing education—enrolling nearly 300,000 students since its inception. He served at Liberty University for over 30 years in numerous academic roles, including Vice Provost, Professor of Counseling, and Executive Director of the James C. Dobson Center for Child Development, Marriage, and Family Studies.

Dr. Clinton has been married 38 years to his wife, Julie, and together they have two children, Megan and Zach. In his free time, you'll find him outdoors or at a game with his family and friends.

Dina Jones, M.A.

Dina Jones serves as the Director for Professional and Public Relations for the American Association of Christian Counselors. Dina holds an M.A. degree from Liberty University in Professional Counseling. She has worked in church counseling, career counseling, and life coaching with a career emphasis. Dina is a member of the Mid-Atlantic Career Counseling Association and has served as a board member for two years, with one year as the Hospitality Chair. Additionally, she teaches both residentially and online for the College of General Studies at Liberty University. Dina serves on meal teams and is involved with the women's ministry program at Lynchburg First Church of the Nazarene. She is a loving wife and mother of three.

CHAPTER 6

How to Develop and Maintain Personal and Professional Boundaries in Ministry

Timothy Clinton, Ed.D. and
Dina Jones, M.A.

Pastoral ministry is one of the most demanding jobs on the planet. It requires a blend of three biblical roles: prophet (speaking and proclaiming God's truth), priest (caring for the hurting and equipping the eager), and king (administrating plans and systems). All pastors need to be at least functionally proficient in all three, but they probably excel in only one. A pastor may be a brilliant and inspiring speaker, but interpersonal skills and administration may be a strain. Or a pastor may be known for kindness and availability to those in need, but speaking and administration may suffer. A few pastors are gifted administrators, but their messages are often rather flat and they'd rather create plans and systems than meet with hurting people.

More, More, Faster, Faster

When pastors and other church leaders don't understand their natural "bent," – their strength, the role that gives them energy and joy – they can be easily overwhelmed by trying to do everything for everyone. A realistic appraisal of one's gifts and talents is the first step in creating a workable and enjoyable career in ministry.

Internal pressures caused by operating too much out of our strengths is a problem, but external pressures are often much more immediate... and much more stressful. The Fuller Institute, George Barna, and Pastoral Care, Inc. conducted research of pastors, and they found that:

- 40 percent of pastors report serious conflict with a parishioner at least once a month.
- 66 percent of church members expect their pastors to live by a higher moral standard than themselves.
- The role of pastor ranks near the bottom of most-respected professions, just above car salesman (Fuller, Barna, & Pastoral Care, 2014).

These problems aren't easily resolved. Richard Krejcir's study of pastors found 78 percent had been forced to resign at least once, and 63 percent had been fired twice. More than half reported that the cause of termination was unresolved conflict with an elder, key lay person, or a faction in the church (Krejcir, 2007).

Pastors almost invariably begin their careers with idealistic hopes, but the drain of endless pressures can erode if not destroy their dreams. All too soon they realize they will continually face the demand to be everywhere all the time, the pressures of keeping their staff and key volunteers happy and effective, the endless worry about funding, the struggle to grow past the next target, the demands of their families, and the desperate need to stay fresh spiritually so they will have something new to offer those they lead. To make life work, pastors need to establish boundaries.

Boundaries Defined

Boundaries are reasonable limits on a pastor's time and energy. These limits need to be communicated clearly and often in order to protect the pastor's mental, emotional, and relational health so he or she can perform at the highest level. A leader who lacks good boundaries may appear to be a selfless servant, but clear limits and realistic expectations are necessary for the success of the pastor, the health of those who relate to him or her, and the growth of the church. Boundaries define "what is you" and "what is not you"—what you will and will not accept, engage, entertain, and invest in. Boundaries are fences that draw the invisible lines that define your responsibilities.

If pastors don't establish realistic expectations and clear limits, they will soon be "running on empty" with no margin, living with resentment toward those who oppose them or drag their feet, and creating (instead of correcting) a toxic culture.

For pastors, setting good boundaries isn't optional; it's essential. Strong boundaries can protect your physical wellbeing, family connections, and spiritual health, as well as the integrity of your ministry. Weak boundaries endanger your marriage and kids, your leadership, your reputation, and your physical health and joy.

Without healthy boundaries, you will do more and accomplish less, you'll talk more and connect less, you'll try harder and exhaust yourself more—and you'll only fall further behind. Everyone's problem will feel like *your* problem.

We often ascribe noble motives to poor boundaries: We want to be viewed as kind and compassionate, we want to be heroes who step in to care, we want others to admire our dedication, and we never want to be labeled as "irresponsible." Our compulsive working and helping (whether our primary strength is prophet, priest, or king) give us short-term benefits of applause, control, or power, but inevitably cause us long-term suffering in the form of exhaustion, resentment, and burnout. Without boundaries, we will eventually spin out, become depleted, and find ourselves battling the twin problems of loneliness and lower productivity—no matter how busy we are.

Quite often, those who struggle with boundary issues draw wrong conclusions. When they experience disapproval, they resolve to be even more available and helpful. When they suffer from conflict, they determine to "show them" and do everything perfectly. When they fail to meet a deadline, they choose to stay even later and work even harder. No matter who calls or for what reason, they assume they have to drop what they're doing and be there. Certainly, there are a few leaders who are irresponsible, but they're probably not the ones reading this chapter. We're addressing those who are *overly* responsible, those who feel compelled to never say "no" to anyone about anything. The underlying problem is security and identity. Like King Saul, they "feel small in [their] own eyes" (1 Samuel 15:17, NIV), so they are driven to compensate by succeeding where others have failed and pleasing even those who are incredibly difficult to please. They have an underlying fear that no one truly appreciates or respects them.

Boundaries are the limits you set on yourself. Your boundaries determine how you will respond to the never-ending demands, requests, and expectations that seem to confront all pastors.

A common misunderstanding is that you can put a boundary on another person; you cannot. For example, a client told me defiantly, "My boundary is that my brother, who is an addict, can't make demands on me any longer." Granted, the brother shouldn't talk to anyone in a demanding or demeaning way, but my client can't control how her brother speaks to her. Her boundary, instead, must be how she will respond to her brother. When he speaks to her in a derogatory way, she has options: She can refuse his request, and if he still insists, she can leave the room or hang up the phone. Her boundary can't be that her brother can't ask her for money—that's not under her control. Her boundary is that if he asks, she will say "no."

According to Lee and Balswick in their excellent book, Life in a Glass House,

> It is easy to forget that the term 'boundary' is largely metaphoric. Whenever we give a phenomenon a name, there is the temptation to view it as a 'thing' in its own right. What we are talking about, however, is patterns of relationships, not things. The term 'boundary' is meant as shorthand for interactions that occur where two social systems meet (Lee & Balswick, 1989, p. 80).

Healthy boundaries clarify identities, roles, and relationships.

Because boundaries are about *our own behavior*, they require us to be *honest* with ourselves. We have to look reality squarely in the eye, recognize our tendency to let people control us, and then take control of our role in our interactions.

This topic is important for every person, but for pastors the issue of boundaries can be electrically charged. Leading a congregation without clearly established boundaries is hazardous for you, your family, your staff and volunteers, and your congregation. Your lack of healthy and appropriate boundaries inevitably trickles down and leads to frustration, insecurity, resentment, and distrust. As a leader, your boundaries (or lack thereof) deeply impact the attitudes of those around you.

One of my favorite movies is *Remember the Titans,* which is the true story of a team of African-American and white high school football players during the days of integration. In a particularly dramatic scene, Gerry Bertier, the captain of the Titans, yells at teammate Big Ju, "See man, that's the worst attitude I ever heard."

Big Ju immediately answers, "Attitude reflects leadership, captain."

As you lead your congregation and your home, the attitudes of those around you reflect your leadership. If you find yourself constantly frustrated by their resistance or apathy, it's wise to stop and evaluate how your behavior might be creating a tense and toxic environment. You may be doing too much for them, creating unhealthy dependence. Or you may be neglecting them by doing too much for others, resulting in their resentment. Either way, the root cause is your poor, inconsistent, and/or inadequate boundaries.

As a pastor, you need boundaries on several levels. You need to carve out undistracted time to prepare to do your best in speaking, caring, or administration. You need guarded time with your family, so you tell your staff not to call during those times except in rare emergencies. You need specific time to exercise, spend time with friends and mentors, and recharge your spiritual engines. And practically, you tell your staff that no one will meet with congregants of the opposite sex after hours without another person in the building.

Healthy boundaries require you to sometimes say "no" and become less popular with a well-loved church member in order to say "yes" to times of preparation and planning. In so doing, you gradually learn to live with realistic expectations: To be your best, love your best, and do your best, you can't do everything. Though perhaps personally painful, you may even have to shelve a great idea or delegate something you really love to do.

Healthy boundaries render very positive results, but they don't always come easily or naturally. Some leaders may have a head start because they are following the example of a strong and wise mentor, but most pastors are on a steep learning curve. As responsibilities increase, they feel more driven, more anxious, and less able to say "no" to anyone.

Jesus and Boundaries

We typically think of Jesus as the epitome of a selfless servant, one who gave himself to the point of death. However, if we look more closely at the gospels, we find that Jesus had very clear and strong boundaries. While he came not to be served but to serve, he still had no problem letting others make their own decisions, saying "no" when it was appropriate, and investing in his own spiritual, emotional, mental, and relational health. Let's look at a few examples.

The rich young ruler. Matthew tells us about a wealthy young man who took the initiative to meet Jesus. He obviously had heard Jesus, or at least had heard about him. He asked, "Teacher, what good thing must I do to get eternal life?"

Jesus told him to obey the commandments. The man asked, "Which ones?"

Jesus then rattled off about half of the Ten Commandments and added, "Love your neighbor as yourself" (these six concerning our human relationships are referred to by some as the "second table" of the Ten Commandments; the first four, or "first table" pertain to our relationship with God).

The man must have been either arrogant or lacking in self-awareness, because he answered, "All these I have kept."

Jesus then challenged his self-sufficiency and put his finger on the young man's true source of security: his money. Jesus told him, "If you want to be perfect, go, sell your possessions and give to the poor, and you will have treasure in heaven. Then come, follow me."

When he heard this, the man became very discouraged. He wanted Jesus's affirmation, but he wasn't willing to part with his money. He walked away.

How would most pastors respond to a rich person like this in their congregation? Jesus didn't soften the demands of discipleship, and he didn't run after the man to convince him to come back. Jesus let the man make his own decision—without manipulating him or begging him to change his mind.

This was a training school for the disciples. They couldn't imagine the religious leaders offending this rich young man, so they were shocked that Jesus had been so blunt. They asked him, "Who then can be saved?"

Jesus explained, "I tell you the truth, it is hard for a rich man to enter the kingdom of heaven. Again I tell you, it is easier for a camel to go through the eye of a needle than for a rich man to enter the kingdom of God" (Matthew 19:16-24, NIV).

Jesus had clear boundaries. Because he wanted others to make their own decisions about following him, he let the man walk away.

The crowd. At the height of his popularity, a massive crowd followed Jesus. John tells us that Jesus miraculously fed 5000 men (and the total was probably up to 20,000 people including women and children), using a boy's sack lunch. The people wanted to crown him king then and there, but Jesus slipped away to a mountain to be alone.

That night, the disciples left in a boat for the other side of the lake, and when a strong wind stopped their progress, Jesus appeared to them walking on the water. The next day, the crowd was confused. They wondered how Jesus had gotten to the other side of the lake without a boat. A massive crowd walked around the lake to find him. There they demanded that he give them more bread to eat. Jesus explained that the physical bread was a symbol of a far greater gift: himself, the bread of life. They argued with him, and in a crescendo of intensity, he never gave in to their demands. Finally he told them, "Unless you eat the flesh of the Son of Man and drink his blood, you have no life in you."

The people were stunned and enraged. This wasn't the kind of king they expected! They wanted something different than what Jesus offered, so they left him. After those thousands of people had gone, only the twelve disciples were left standing with Jesus. Still, Jesus respected each person's decision. He asked them, "You do not want to leave too, do you?"

Peter answered for them, "Lord, to whom shall we go? You have the words of eternal life" (John 6:1-69, NIV).

Jesus spoke the truth without fear. He didn't mind challenging others' expectations, disappointing their demands, or letting them choose whether or not to follow him.

Rest and re-creation. One of the recurring themes of Jesus's ministry was that he often retreated by himself or with his closest friends to rest, reflect, and replenish his perspective. For instance, he withdrew to pray (Luke 5:16), he took three of them to a mountain to experience his transfiguration (Luke 9:28-36), and in his darkest hours before his arrest, he asked those three to join him in Gethsemane for support (Matthew 26:36-45).

Practical Steps

A pastor leads and serves. A pastor is an example, a culture builder, a pace-setter, a trailblazer, and the one who establishes priorities for the congregation. His or her plate is always full of personal, family, and church responsibilities. In Boundaries for Leaders, Henry Cloud observes,

> Leaders can motivate or demotivate their people. They can propel them down a runway to great results, or confuse them so that they cannot clearly get from A to Z. They can bring a team or group together to achieve shared, extraordinary goals, or they can cause division and fragmentation. They can create a culture that augments high performance, accountability, results, and thriving, or cause a culture to exist in which people become less than who they are or could be. And most of the time, these issues have little to do with the leader's business acumen at all… but more to do with how they lead people and build cultures (Cloud, 2013).

Pastors are wise to examine several important areas where boundaries are essential for personal and professional growth.

1. Set boundaries over your work time to protect your physical, mental, and emotional health.

One of the biggest occupational hazards for pastors is an out-of-control schedule filled with never-ending tasks and demands. As we've seen, the vocation of pastor typically begins with a deep and enthusiastic love for God and his people, but additional responsibilities often increase stress, anxiety, depression, and despair. Too many pastors suffer from burnout, which is "a gradual process of loss during which the mismatch between the needs of the person and the demands of the job grows even greater" (Maslach & Leiter, 1997).

Pastors report an alarming level of pressure and stress:

> 84 percent say they're on call 24 hours a day.
> 80 percent expect conflict in their church.
> 54 percent find the role of pastor frequently overwhelming.
> 53 percent are often concerned about their family's financial security.
> 48 percent often feel the demands of ministry are more than they can handle.
> 21 percent say their church has unrealistic expectations of them (Green, 2015).

Almost half of pastors feel that they are unable to meet their ministry's demands. Far too many ministry leaders respond to unrealistic expectations by trying harder and harder in an endless cycle of too much activity and too little fulfillment.

Ironically, success doesn't lower stress levels. If your ministry is growing and you find your time in higher demand, the pressures multiply. Then it becomes even more important to get sufficient sleep, nourish yourself (but not to excess!), carve out time to relax and be with friends, spend time in real worship to experience God's love and strength, and get enough exercise. Research supports the fact that when healthy routines are in place, you will get more done in less time due to increased energy, decreased illness, and the power of focus. But stress often leads to counterproductive choices, which soon become self-defeating habits. It is not selfish to take good care of oneself. If our batteries are low, we can't jumpstart someone else's. We simply cannot give what we do not have.

Be intentional in taking good care of yourself so you have the energy and focus to serve. Remember, Jesus slept. Jesus ate. Jesus went fishing and hiking.

2. Set boundaries to protect your investment in spiritual growth.

In *The New Christian Counselor,* Dr. Ron Hawkins comments,

> To stay centered and healthy, we need to drink deeply of
> spiritual waters. We need regular, daily soul care, and we
> need periods of prolonged relaxation. It's not wrong to get
> tired in doing good work for God and for people, but we
> drift into pathology when we can't stop and take care of
> ourselves (Hawkins & Clinton, 2015).

Pastors serve in a spiritually rich vocation, but their role carries with it the inherent danger of producing spiritual dryness and emotional barrenness. Our faith is—and should be—a crucial part of our identity, yet our jobs are not our faith.

Have you ever totally zoned out of worship because you were rehearsing your sermon delivery? Have you ever planned to read a book or scripture for your own quiet time but found yourself outlining your sermon instead of listening for the Lord's voice? It can be all too easy to slip out of soul care and into work. Your work may be caring for other people's souls, but if you do so at the cost of your own, everyone loses.

Popular Christian author and adult pastor's kid Jon Acuff says, "Hustle has seasons," meaning that hard work toward an honorable goal is sometimes required of us, but periods of rest and relaxation must be interwoven with that hard work. Acuff explains on his podcasts that if you hustle at the same rate every day, you'll eventually burn out—and your goals aren't served by burnout. Maybe you're launching a new ministry for foster parents, your church has adopted a village in Guatemala, or your first full-time pastoral assignment comes with four months left in seminary. In times like these, you might walk through a season of long days—or "hustle"—but even then, don't forget to carve out time to rest, spend time with your family, and worship the Lord deeply.

We are stewards of our souls. In order to lead others to grow spiritually, we must continue growing—not only through additional academic knowledge, but by becoming more intimate with Christ.

3. Set boundaries to protect your relationships: Don't miss the best moments with your family.

It's heartbreaking to counsel a pastor's spouse or child through resentment toward their mate or parent who gave their heart and time to ministry and had too little left for the family. I wish I could say that this scenario is rare, but in many years in professional counseling, I've sat across from a myriad of family members wrestling with the pain of "losing" a loved one to the church (or to some form of ministry).

My wife, Julie, likes to remind young mothers, "The days are long but the years are short." This same insight applies to pastors. The urgency of ministry can become all-consuming until one day you wake up and your children are out of car seats, asking for the car keys, or moving into a college dorm. By then, you may be emotionally distant from your children and your spouse.

Don't miss your moments. Your family needs your presence, and time spent with those you love is priceless. This is your first calling. Consider carefully which circumstances you will allow to interrupt your family time, then share your commitments with a trusted friend and your spouse, and allow both to hold you accountable.

Many pastors know cognitively that they are balancing several roles, but do not always know when and how to transition between their roles (Lee & Balswick, 1989). Being the spouse or child of a pastor comes with unique challenges and stressors that can impact both the individual and the family. It is of utmost importance to remember that sometimes, even in church, your child might need you to be a parent more than a pastor. Your availability to the congregation has the potential to impact your availability to your family, which in turn can stir confusing negative emotions toward the ministry (and even toward God) in the hearts of your loved ones. You can— and must—protect and guide your family through these challenges by your willingness to truly listen to and address their needs and concerns. Ask your family what they think about your new boundaries and your commitment to ministry—and be ready to listen nondefensively.

Paul wrote a stern warning to Timothy, "But if anyone does not provide for his own, and especially for those of his household, he has denied the faith and is worse than an unbeliever" (1 Timothy 5:8, NKJV).

Providing for the family means more than just food and clothing. Families need emotional presence and support as much as they need material things. Pastors must make sure that they are not missing the critical moments with their families.

4. Give your team clear direction and guidance.

No matter the size of the church, pastors set the tone for their teams (paid staff and/or key volunteers), select and place people where they can be effective, oversee decisions and plans, and shape the organizational culture. Team members need clear answers to fundamental questions, such as:

- What are their roles?
- What should they be working on, and what should they not be working on?
- Who should be included in communication on what types of issues?
- Who should each person go to if they have a problem?
- How do you define success and failure?
- How available should each staff person be to requests from the congregation?

Some leaders believe giving their teams "freedom from constrictions" is a loving and trusting approach, but clouded expectations lead to poor communication, misunderstanding, conflict, distractions, and poor performance. We can trust people and still provide plenty of direction, support, and guidance.

By default, the pastor sets the example for all the staff of a church, but that example may not be an appropriate one to emulate; many pastors work well beyond what is considered a "healthy" number of hours. One study found that 43% of pastors work between 51 and 70 hours per week (Vaccarino & Gerritsen, 2013). When work hours increase, the time that can be spent with family or in self-care decreases. Additionally, when the pastor is unable or unwilling to set boundaries in his own life, it sets a poor example for those with whom he works. And effective boundaries are never merely stated; they always lead to action, and repeated actions become healthy habits.

Take time to carefully construct and articulate your expectations for your team. Explain what is desired and what isn't acceptable. Encourage your staff to set boundaries, and most importantly, lead by example. If you don't set good boundaries, your staff may have difficulty setting boundaries. Tony Gaskins writes, "You teach people how to treat you by what you allow, what you stop, and what you reinforce" (Gaskins, 2013).

5. For your congregation, set accurate expectations of your role as their pastor and of the culture you will create in your church.

One influential pastor who had a consistently refreshing spirit and never seemed exhausted preached a sermon at a church he hoped to pastor. His message went something like this:

> Thanks for having me here. I know that after my sermon you're going to be having a potluck and then voting on whether or not you would like to have me come be your pastor. If you should choose to elect me, I want you to know three things: My first priority will be to do everything I know to do to walk with God. My second priority will be to do everything I know to do to make sure that pretty lady over there [his wife] walks with God. Third, I'm going to do everything I know to do to make sure those two young boys [his sons] join us on the journey of faith. If I have any time or energy left after that, I'll devote that to being your pastor.

The church board voted unanimously to invite him, and the church continued to thrive under his wise counsel for many years. And by the way, he got a lot fewer 2:00 a.m. phone calls than some of my other friends who are pastors.

When your congregation knows what they can ask of you, they can ask more freely. Don't be afraid to communicate to your congregation when you are available, how they should reach you during those times, and the limits of your availability. Be definite and direct without being demanding. Everyone will be happier and more effective if boundaries are clear.

It may feel unnatural to you—even unspiritual—to communicate limits on your time and energy, but it will equip your congregation to respect your boundaries and set their own.

6. Protect your reputation and your ministry's integrity.

As a leader, you live in a fish bowl, or what Lee and Balswick call a "glass house." For better or worse, people hold you to a higher standard, and some will be tempted to use your real or perceived failures as ammunition against you or perhaps as an excuse to give in to their own temptations.

Clear boundaries, especially in counseling people of the opposite sex and in money matters, are essential to protect your reputation and safeguard your integrity. In addition, your choices set the tone for your entire congregation in valuing each individual, no matter their race, socioeconomic status, or role in the church. Human nature is competitive and it thrives on comparison. People naturally put others down so they can feel superior, but that isn't the way the kingdom of God works.

God's kingdom is upside down: the way to true greatness is to humbly serve; the source of true riches is to generously give; the way to have power is to give it away. We love only to the extent we've experienced God's radical love, we forgive only to the degree we're convinced God has forgiven us, and we accept others only because God has graciously embraced outsiders like us. This means we treat others with the ultimate respect: no gossip, no bitterness, no manipulation, and no jockeying for positions of power. No one is a second-class citizen—not singles, not widows, not teenagers with alternative dress, not individuals struggling with mental health issues, not the elderly, and not women. No one is treated as "less-than." As a pastor, you have tremendous influence, and you can create a warm, welcoming culture.

Far too many church leaders have fallen because they weren't careful to adhere to boundaries regarding people of the opposite sex. Problems at home can make a pastor vulnerable to the attentions of others, and then a simple act of kindness can lead to foolish choices. Some of us use touch to communicate support, but even this gesture can be dangerous.

One expert warns, "In deciding whether to use touch, it is important to consider the level of trust between you and the client, whether the *client* may perceive the touch as sexual, the client's past history associated with touch (occasionally a client will associate touch with punishment or abuse and will say "I can't stand to be touched"), and the client's cultural group (whether touch is respectful and valued) (Cormier, 2013).

7. Empower your family and your ministry team members to understand boundaries.

In my experience with many pastors and their families, I've seen far too many spouses and kids who felt violated by church members but powerless to do anything about it. Pastors need to set boundaries for themselves, but they also need to train and support their family members as they establish clear expectations. For instance, a pastor's spouse is not automatically a full-time volunteer, and the kids don't have to be at every event.

Encourage your family members to identify, develop, and pursue their spiritual gifts and talents—even if this means that your spouse is living out their calling as a public school educator when the church would rather them be the coordinator of the nursery or Sunday School program, and even if it means your son feels called to participate in a summer theater team instead of joining you on a mission trip.

If pastors don't maintain boundaries, their family members often feel like they don't have permission to set boundaries. A pastor's spouse who is made to feel like their mate, home, and time all belong to the congregation will feel deeply wounded and resentful—of the church, of their partner, and perhaps of God. Quite often, the message preached is that "This is a broken church for broken people." However, many pastors and their families feel excluded from this warm embrace. Like others, they feel broken, but they also feel constantly pressured by the church to be perfect.

For pastors and their families, transparency is a forerunner to setting good boundaries. You may believe that it will make others think you're weak, but transparency and accountability are actually signs of strength, not weakness (remember the powerful paradoxical principle of 2 Corinthians 12:9)!

8. Consider your emotional impact on others.

Good boundaries not only protect us, they protect others from us. When we're stressed, we become anxious and demanding. Our words become harsh, and we withhold our affirmation from people until we're convinced they deserve it. But when we're taking care of ourselves, we have more insight and compassion to care for those around us, and our words bring life instead of death, hope instead of discouragement, and joy instead of shame.

We aren't responsible to make every person happy. We're responsible *to* people but not *for* them. This means we are to treat people with a blend of truth and grace, but their response is up to them, not us. When we say "no," we say it with kindness and strength. Even when people don't like what they hear from us, we can still have peace, knowing that we've spoken truth with grace.

Conclusion: The Heart of a Leader

Of course, we're all in the process of figuring out how to set healthy boundaries, and as we learn, we sometimes make mistakes. This skill, like all others, is acquired by careful analysis, consistent practice, and constructive feedback from those who are a little further down the road.

Unfortunately, some people around us aren't really interested in our being healthy; they just don't want us to say "no" to them. When we try to set good boundaries and communicate realistic expectations, some will applaud, many will be confused, and a few will accuse us of being selfish. Those few expect their pastors to be married to their jobs, to be on call all the time, and to spend every ounce of energy to fulfill the desires of every person in the congregation.

If we feel compelled to jump through all those hoops (or feel terribly guilty when we can't), we're showing that our security is in the wrong place. We're trusting in the approval of others instead of trusting in the love, forgiveness, and acceptance of God. When we're secure in God's affection and approval, we have the strength to say "yes" when it's appropriate and to say "no" when it's necessary—and the wisdom to know the difference.

The process of change, however, is often awkward and difficult. Before we establish clear boundaries and realistic expectations, we live with a strange blend of hope and fear: a renewed hope that this time we really can live up to everyone's expectations and our own lofty goals… and a nagging fear that we can't. Change requires us to be honest about these powerful emotions. Then, with the encouragement of a mentor or friend, we can make new choices. As we learn new habits of the heart, our hopes change—from being a hero and always meeting everyone's standards to walking with God in wisdom, strength, and joy… and not just for a day, but for the rest of our lives. This kind of change takes enormous courage, but it's worth it.

Setting and maintaining healthy boundaries isn't negotiable. Without them, we can serve passionately for a while, but sooner or later, we'll feel pressured and exhausted, and we'll despise the sheep instead of loving them. It's impossible to be a great leader without establishing effective boundaries. The process is both academic and practical. While we can certainly learn by reading, thinking, praying, and talking to friends and mentors, we don't make real progress until we take action. At first, we miss the mark as often as we hit it: our boundaries are too soft or too rigid. But we learn from our successes and failures, and soon a new pattern emerges. As we take better care of ourselves, we become better leaders—more compassionate, more creative, more dedicated, and more effective—and we become better spouses and parents, too. Establishing and maintaining healthy boundaries takes real work. For most of us, it feels odd and unnatural at first, but its benefits multiply into every aspect of our lives.

References

Cloud, H. (2013). *Boundaries for leaders: Results, relationships, and being ridiculously in charge.* New York: HarperCollins.

Cormier, S., Nurius, P. S., and Osborn, C. J. (2013). *Interviewing and change strategies for helpers* (7th ed). Belmont, CA: Cengage Learning. 96.

Fuller Institute, George Barna, and Pastoral Care, Inc. (2014). Why pastors leave the ministry. Retrieved March 11, 2017 from http://www.feic. org/wp-content/uploads/2014/10/Why-pastors-leave-the-ministry.pdf

Gaskins, T. (2013) *Single is not a curse.* Soul Writers.

Green, L. C. (2015). Research finds few pastors give up on ministry. Retrieved March 15, 2017 from http://www.lifeway.com/pastors/2015/09/01/research-finds-few-pastors-give-up-on-ministry/

Hawkins, R. and Clinton, T. (2015). *The new Christian counselor.* Eugene, OR: Harvest House Publishers. 227.

Krejcir, R. (2007). Statistics on Pastors. Francis A. Schaeffer Institute of Church Leadership Development.

Lee, C. and Balswick, J. (1989). *Life in a glass house: The minister's family in its unique social context.* Grand Rapids, MI: Zondervan. 80.

Maslach, C. and Leiter, M.P. (1997). *The truth about burnout.* New York: Jossey-Bass. 24.

Vaccarino, F., and Gerritsen, T. (2013). Exploring clergy self-care: A New Zealand study. *International Journal of Religion & Spirituality in Society, 3*(2), 69-80.

Eric Scalise, Ph.D.

Eric Scalise is the Senior Vice President and Chief Strategy Officer (CSO) at Hope for the Heart in Plano, Texas. He is also the President of LIV Enterprises & Consulting, LLC, a Licensed Professional Counselor, and a Licensed Marriage and Family Therapist with nearly 40 years of clinical and professional experience in the mental health field. Dr. Scalise's specialty areas include professional/pastoral stress and burnout, combat trauma and PTSD, marriage and family issues, leadership development, addictions, and lay counselor training. Eric is an author and a national and international conference speaker who frequently consults with organizations, clinicians, ministry leaders, and churches on a variety of issues.

CHAPTER 7

How to Develop an Effective Regimen of Selfcare in People-Helping Ministries

Eric Scalise, Ph.D.

Pastors, ministry leaders, counselors, and those who are seen as caregivers and people helpers are often thought of as being compassionate people. Indeed, many of us who feel called into the ministry readily identify with the compassion of Christ as he related to those around him. Webster's Collegiate Dictionary defines the term compassion as a "sympathetic consciousness of others' distress, together with a desire to alleviate it." It comes from the Latin word, *compat*, which means to "suffer with." Much of the research on this subject underscores the critical importance of both the helping relationship and the caregivers who are frequently in close proximity to the emotional suffering and resulting grief of those with whom they work and counsel. Herein lies both a potential problem (increased stress and burnout), as well as a wonderful opportunity to function as God's ambassadors of reconciliation. May God grant us the mindset of Paul when he said, "I have fought the good fight, I have *finished* the race, I have kept the faith" (2 Timothy 4:7, NKJV, emphasis added).

How do you sustain joy along the way? When an unexplainable, unpredictable, or traumatic event takes place, theological rulebooks are often inadequate when a response of compassion is required. This is because to be effective, compassion must be visible. The teaching of Scripture is to "Let your light so shine before men, that they may see your good works and glorify your Father in heaven" (Matthew 5:16, NKJV). Yet, the goal is to remain "salt" and "light" in the face of alcoholism, drug use, trauma, grief and loss, depression, marital discord, separation and divorce, child abuse, sexual addiction, parenting struggles, unemployment, financial stress—and the list could go on.

These are the day-to-day issues people bring when seeking guidance and help. Sometimes, the impact and sheer level of pain that confronts us can overwhelm even the most capable and mature ministry caregivers. A primary challenge for those of us those who live and function in these roles is to recognize that self-care is something we tend to focus on when it pertains to those we serve, and not necessarily to ourselves. The question then becomes not only how do we finish the race God has ordained for us, but how do we finish well?

The Lord gave me a helpful life lesson a number of years ago while flying overseas to speak with nearly a thousand pastors on, of all things, stress and burnout. The week leading up to my departure had been particularly chaotic and hurried. On top of that, making difficult connections in multiple airports due to adverse weather conditions was not what I had in mind. When I finally boarded my last international flight, I managed to buy a newspaper and was ready to sit down and relax. If you travel frequently as I do, you may tend to politely ignore the flight crew as they go over airplane rules, seatbelts, emergency exits, and the like.

So there I was, perfectly content in "tuning out," when the voice of the flight attendant came across the loudspeaker and said, "Ladies and gentlemen, I know many of you have already had a long day and that you are tired, but if you would be so kind as to set aside your reading materials and give us your attention for a few brief moments, we would like to cover some important safety information with you."

This at least prompted me to pull the corner of the newspaper back a few inches and glance up into the aisle. To my surprise, a flight attendant was standing just a few feet away, smiling at me with that "look." I was on my way to teach on ministry-oriented stress and here I was, "drowning" in it at the moment. Of course, I put down the paper, sighed, and smiled back. And in the middle of the preflight announcements, I heard the following—which I have heard many times before, but am not always "listening."

"If we should experience the sudden loss of cabin pressure, oxygen masks will deploy from the ceiling above you. If you are traveling with small children, *please put the mask on yourself first* and then assist the child."

The Holy Spirit immediately began to stir me regarding this profound truth. Why should parents put on their own masks first? One would tend to think it would be more humane, loving, and compassionate to help the child first. However, because children are probably more vulnerable and less able to take care of themselves in the moment, the most responsible course of action is for parents to make sure they are in a position to help and facilitate care. To do that, they need to be stable and breathing in the oxygen themselves. The same is true for us as pastors, caregivers, and ministry leaders. When people bring to us their hurts or are in the middle of a crisis, they are typically less mobile, less resourced, more incapacitated and anxious, and perhaps less able to discern the voice of the Lord at the moment than we are (at least in theory). If we want to ensure that we are "available" to the Lord and to others, *we must take care of ourselves first*—appropriately and in a balanced way—or we risk becoming ineffective and at times even a hindrance to what God is trying to accomplish.

When you entered into a ministry/caregiving role, you probably expected to be successful. Most people do not feel passionately called by God to something, only to fail. One common distortion is that many of us define success primarily by quantitative measures (e.g., for pastors… bodies, buildings, baptisms, and budgets) and not by qualitative measures such as those that make a difference in someone's life by helping him/her become more Christ-like. There can be a strong temptation to develop a comparative mindset. We can set increasingly unrealistic standards that have less to do with trusting God and walking in faith, and more to do with how we think we compare to the leader or ministry next to us. In fact, if we evaluated Christ using this paradigm as our sole criterion, we might deem his ministry to have been an abject failure!

Too many caregivers and ministry leaders accept very difficult job descriptions, and few other vocations have such a broad range of "high expectation" demands. Here is an important principle when it comes to caregiving: the individual expectations might be legitimate, but the composite expectations can be all-encompassing and at times destructive. It may feel nice to be affirmed by those we help, but we cannot allow this to become our primary motivation for service or our sense of identity. Otherwise, we may end up seeking the applause of people, and allow others to define our calling and purpose.

Paul identified himself to the Corinthians as a "bondservant," but note that it was for "Jesus's sake" (2 Corinthians 4:5, NKJV). In other words, while he was certainly there to serve the church, it was not primarily for their sakes—but for and to his Lord. If we do not recognize this dynamic, it may subtly and surreptitiously catch us off guard such that we accept the false narrative that we are not allowed to fail, hurt, or in essence, be human. The result can be a crisis of faith at both a personal level and within the ministry, because we have either not learned how to set reasonable boundaries with the people we serve, or we have chosen not to. The truth is that if we become overly responsible for the wellbeing of others, we will become exhausted and they will never learn or grow. In time, we may become desperate for relief and experience burn out.

In my work with caregivers and ministry leaders over the years, I have found several common outcomes that are frequently set into motion once they realize they may not be able to live up to the expectations that are set by others:

1. **Developing a preoccupation with stress-producing people or situations.** We remain in the intensity of the stress-filled environment and seek after adrenaline-infused experiences— always moving, always busy, with the appearance of human *doings* rather than human *beings*.

2. **Indulging in escape behaviors** for many of the same reasons our congregants do—we are tired of being discouraged, lonely, or in pain, and our chosen path is a way to "self-medicate" via certain substances or behaviors, although usually in an unhealthy manner.

3. **Avoiding intimate relationships with one's spouse or close friends and substituting fantasy for reality.** True relational intimacy requires time and effort, and when we are emotionally and spiritually drained, we are less able to make the necessary investment. Sexual addiction is now a worldwide epidemic. It can be tempting to engage an image on a computer screen, because it is easy, there is an immediate emotional/physical reward, and there is little risk of failing or being rejected by that image.

4. **Seeking to control everything and everyone as a means of coping.** Control is frequently utilized as a survival tool that is embraced rather than understood as a characterological disorder. If we come to believe that we are powerless—perhaps from being hurt from repeated traumatic experiences—we may embrace the false notion

that if we can simply control our environments and the people in them, we will somehow be safer. Unfortunately, this is rarely the case, as most people do not respond well to excessive control.

5. **Justifying actions by blaming other things and/or other people.** Blame shifting is an attempt, albeit with unintended negative consequences, to avoid responsibility and accountability. If we can make the issue(s) primarily about someone or something else, then we can more easily separate ourselves from the emotional and practical aftermath.

6. **Choosing to simply quit or leave the profession/ministry.** The enemy of our souls would like nothing better than to see us fail and give up. Sadly, the Body of Christ too often "shoots its own wounded," and this grieves the Holy Spirit deeply. Pastoral attrition is tragically commonplace.

So what are the consequences of stress overload? Dr. Hans Selye, a Canadian endocrinologist who is considered the "father" of stress research, began to define the phenomenon during the mid-1930s in terms of what he called the *General Adaptation Syndrome*. The normal pattern is for the body to cycle through a three-step process: alarm, resistance, and exhaustion. He went on to define stress as the "non-specific response of the body to any demand" (Selye, 1956). Think about that statement for a moment. The implication here is that almost any demand placed on the body (including the mind, emotions, and spirit), has the potential to create a stress response.

Stress can have both a psychosocial (within the environment) and a biogenic (within the body) orientation. *Eustress*, which is a normal part of everyday life, is necessary for keeping us alert and active. It enables us to be productive and creative and assists with decision-making activities. However, a chronically high level of stress becomes *distress* and results in a rapidly developing downward spiral for day-to-day functioning. The two primary stress hormones that begin this process are adrenaline and cortisol, both of which are powerful, naturally occurring stimulants.

The stress cycle starts in the brain. When a stressor is detected as a threat, the amygdala, hypothalamus, and pituitary glands trigger the fight-or-freeze-or-flight stress response. The sympathetic nervous system activates several different physical responses to mobilize for action. The adrenal glands increase the output of adrenaline (also called epinephrine), cortisol and other glucocorticoids, which tightens and contracts the muscles and sharpens the senses. Five main systems respond to stress and can be compromised by prolonged stress: the cardiovascular system, immune system, nervous system, endocrine or glandular system, and metabolic system. The body also forms free radicals that are associated with degenerative diseases, illnesses, and an acceleration of the aging process (Hart & Weber, 2005).

While the fight-or-freeze-or-flight response is instinctive, it tends to compromise rational and balanced thinking. This is because adrenaline signals the body to move blood out of the brain and into the major muscle groups where it may be needed more (to prompt swift action and/or reaction). What happens is that a small almond-shaped section of nervous tissue, called the amygdala, hijacks the messages from the neo-cortex (the thinking part of the brain), directs them into the limbic system (the feeling part of the brain), and makes calm responses vastly more difficult—think of road rage when someone cuts you off in traffic after an already demanding day at the office. As you contemplate the myriad of situations, decisions, and stressors most caregivers and ministry leaders constantly face, is it any wonder that making wise, healthy, and balanced decisions can become a challenge after one's resources (emotionally, cognitively, physically, and spiritually) are pushed to their very limits?

When excessive amounts of adrenaline and cortisol enter the bloodstream, the cumulative effects over time can be harmful. These include:

- a narrowing of the capillaries and other blood vessels leading into and out of the heart;
- a decrease in the flexibility and dilation properties of blood vessels and their linings;

- a decrease in the body's ability to flush harmful (LDL) cholesterol out of its system;
- an increase in the overall production of blood cholesterol;
- an increase in the blood's tendency to clot; and
- an increase in deposits of plaque on arterial walls.

And although the research is still emerging, there is also some evidence that increased cortisol levels result in unwanted weight gain and the accumulation of fat cells around one's midsection. This is why a number of currently available dietary and weight control supplements are designed to reduce these levels (e.g., CortiSlim, CortiStress, Cortistat-PS, Cort-Aid, etc.).

According to the American Institute on Stress, 80-90% of all doctor's visits today are stress-related.[1] The American Heart Association further states that more than 50 million Americans suffer from high blood pressure, and nearly 60 million suffer from some form of cardiovascular disease, resulting in over one million deaths each year (two out of every five who die; one every 32 seconds).[2] Heart disease has been the leading cause of death each year since 1900 and crosses all racial, gender, socioeconomic, and age barriers. Finally, the U.S. Department of Health and Human Services recently reported that 25% of all prescriptions written in the United States are for tranquilizers, sleep aides, antidepressants, and anti-anxiety medications.[3]

We have seen that pastors, counselors, and ministry leaders are not only susceptible to increased levels of stress, but when combined with a call to love and serve others, the result is what is commonly referred to as *compassion fatigue*. Compassion fatigue can be understood as a comprehensive exhaustion that takes place over time when one is constantly in the "giving" position and, as a result, loses his/her ability and motivation to experience joy and satisfaction or to feel and care for others (Figley, 2002). Caregivers (e.g., doctors, nurses, counselors, social workers, teachers, disaster relief workers, crisis responders, pastors, etc.) are among the most vulnerable of groups in this regard. Compassion fatigue is

---

[1] American Institute on Stress: www.stress.org/
[2] American Heart Association: www.americanheart.org
[3] U.S. Department of Health and Human Services: www.hhs.gov/

sometimes referred to as secondary or vicarious traumatic stress associated with the emotional residue related to the cause of caring. The traumatic event or crisis did not happen to the pastor or counselor directly, but he/she was close enough to those whom it did impact that its detrimental effects now have a causal effect.

We must consider a proactive strategy in addressing the realities of being caregivers and ministry leaders. Before doing so, it is essential that we likewise understand the two primary categories of stress. First, there is the inherent stress *of* the profession/ministry. Many would agree that just working and being around people is stressful. Second, there is the internal stress *we bring* into the profession/ministry (e.g., unresolved hurts of our own, patterns of besetting sin, unhealthy relationships, unforgiveness, an insecure leadership style, extreme control needs, etc.). Pastors and ministry leaders who have successfully addressed the second category of stress (what we bring), will do a much better job of handling the first category.

Here is a potentially difficult, but important question we must all ask ourselves from time to time: Is my ministry *causing* the problems in my life; or, is my ministry *revealing* the problems in my life? Stress and pressure have a way of squeezing things out of us. The good news is that cause-and-effect dynamics can be improved or resolved, and revelation can be used by the Holy Spirit to promote needed adjustments and change. Our role is to have "ears to hear," "eyes to see," and a heart that is willing and open before the Lord.

You might wonder, what goes into a good stress prevention or self-care plan? The following are a number of principles you may find helpful in your own journey. Consider them and prayerfully develop a personalized approach tailored to your own needs and/or situation. Write the plan down and review it at least once every month or so. Start by being honest with yourself and open to what the Holy Spirit is speaking.

1. **Learn how to recognize the stress-producing areas in your life that require attention, and take ownership of what needs to be done**. "Let us search out and examine our ways, and turn back to the Lord" (Lamentations 3:40, NKJV). You cannot *extinguish* a problem until you can first *distinguish* a problem. Things that remain a secret usually continue to have power over us and may

be sources of fear, guilt, and shame. Here is my definition of fear: it is the "darkroom" that develops all our negatives. Fear is a dark place where negative thoughts, emotions, and behaviors emerge. The only thing I know of that will stop a developing photograph is light. This is because light penetrates and darkness does not. Ephesians 5:13 (NKJV) says, "But all things that are exposed are made manifest by the light, for whatever makes manifest is light."

2. **Learn how to renew your mind.** We need to reject the lies of Satan and replace them with the truth of Scripture. It is like taking an antibiotic to fight off an infection; but the "medicine" will never do us any good unless and until we take it in. So too with God's Word. The process is like weeding in a garden. If the ground is dry and hard, it can be very difficult to remove the weeds. The Word washes our minds and softens our "heart ground," thereby allowing God to root out the things in our lives that have become detrimental to spiritual, emotional, and relational health. Paul encourages us in Romans 12:2 (NKJV) to "not be conformed to this world, but be transformed by the renewing of your mind, that you may prove what is that good and acceptable and perfect will of God."

3. **Learn to depersonalize some of what you do in the ministry and limit your time around negative people.** Clients frequently bring a host of complaints and problems to caregivers and ministry leaders; such persons are unlikely to be encouraged, positive in their outlook, or full of faith in the midst of their pain. This can be draining for the minister after a while. Remember Jethro's observation of Moses in the wilderness, that he was "wearing himself out" while trying to counsel everyone (Exodus 18). Criticism from a congregant is a frequent companion of any caregiver or ministry leader, but sometimes it is an adult form of crying or throwing a tantrum. Because of our title or position, we can become "lightning rods" for criticism simply because we are in an authority position at the moment. This can be especially true if a person has unresolved issues arising from their family of origin, so it is important to remember that strong negative reactions may not really be about you or your leadership. Your parishioner's struggle is real, too.

4. **Learn to not lose sight of your first love because "you" are not your ministry.** Before our identities as pastors or ministry leaders, before our identities as husbands, wives, fathers, mothers, or any number of other roles, we are first and foremost the adopted sons and daughters of our heavenly Father. We must not allow the "ministry" to become the "mistress" in our walk with God; to do so becomes like chasing the wind and is a formula for discouragement and burnout. When Jesus prayed in selecting his apostles, the scripture says, "Then he appointed twelve, that they might be with Him and that He might send them out to preach, and to have power to heal sicknesses and to cast out demons" (Mark 3:14-15, NKJV). It is a blessing and privilege to be given opportunities to preach the gospel, move in the miraculous, and engage in frontline spiritual warfare, but this is not the first reason that God has called or appointed us. It is that you and I "might be with Him," our first love.

5. **Learn to rest because the nature of God has much to do with rest.** Rest, true God-given rest, does not necessarily imply inactivity, but rather trust and dependency. God has so ordained our bodies that about every sixteen hours, they need to shut down for a while. If you live to a normal life expectancy, you will sleep approximately 25 years of your life. Speaker/author Steven Covey tells a story about two men who chopped wood side-by-side all day together. One man stopped every hour and rested, while the other worked straight through the day. When they finished, the man who rested actually chopped more wood. Why? Because when he stopped, he also sharpened his axe. Resting allows us to stay sharp. We sharpen our physical axes, our emotional and relational axes, and especially our spiritual axes. Ecclesiastes 10:10 says, "If the axe is dull and he does not sharpen its edge, then he must exert more strength" (AMP).

6. **Learn to be silent and learn to be still.** What is it about the ministry that often compels us to try to accomplish more than Jesus did? I cannot imagine anyone busier and more in demand than Christ was during his life on the earth. Yet he clearly understood the value of being alone with the Father. Luke records, "However,

the report went around concerning Him all the more; and great multitudes came together to hear, and to be healed by Him of their infirmities. So He Himself *often* withdrew into the wilderness and prayed" (5:15-16, NIV, emphasis added). The busier we are, the more we need to strategically withdraw, wait on the Lord, and allow the Holy Spirit to "renew [our] strength" so that we can "mount up with wings like eagles... run and not be weary... walk and not faint" (Isaiah 40:31, NKJV).

7. **Learn to give your burdens to God each day.** We were not designed to be ministry pack mules. We are sheep. The only burden sheep carry is their wool, and they lose that twice a year. In Matthew 11, Jesus admonishes us by saying, "Come to Me, all you who labor and are heavy laden, and I will give you rest. Take My yoke upon you and learn from Me, for I am gentle and lowly in heart, and you will find rest for your souls. For my yoke is easy and My burden is light" (vs. 28-30, ESV). Oxen are often paired together, and sometimes during their training one ox is a wise, seasoned animal and the other is new, young, and inexperienced. Whenever a new ox is brought in, a special training yoke is often used. The neck hole for the wise, seasoned old ox fits his neck almost perfectly, but the yoke for the young ox is much larger. The reason—the young ox is not supposed to feel the "burden" of the load, but only to learn what it means to walk alongside the other. It is an easier yoke. Jesus told us his yoke is easy, yet it remains a yoke, which means that we cannot simply go anywhere we choose. However, God does want us to learn to walk alongside Him. If you are constantly feeling the burden of the caregiving yoke, it may mean that you—and not the Lord—are in the lead.

8. **Learn to triage your daily and life events.** Emergency personnel have been trained to come into a situation, assess the genuine priorities, and begin making decisions regarding the most critical things first. Sometimes this can literally make the difference between life and death. The same is true in caregiving. Spiritual triage—discerning what God is doing in the moment, having the wisdom to know how to respond, and being led by the Holy Spirit—is a critical, stress-reducing ministry skill. Not everything

that is important is necessarily urgent and not everything that is urgent is necessarily important. David cried out to God, saying, "Show me Your ways, O LORD; Teach me Your paths. Lead me in Your truth and teach me, For You *are* the God of my salvation; On You I wait all the day." (Psalm 25:4-5, NKJV).

9. **Learn to resolve those things that can be attended to easily and quickly.** I frequently talk with caregivers who spend 90% of their time, energy, and resources on the 10% that they may be able to do very little about. Reversing those numbers could help immensely in how we address our personal and ministry lives. Have you ever had a pebble in your shoe? A splinter in your finger? An eyelash in your eye? These are not life threatening events, but they can still be extremely irritating and distracting—in other words the "little foxes that spoil the vine" (Song of Solomon 2:15, NKJV). A simple adjustment (i.e., taking the shoe off and shaking it out) can provide immediate relief. Ask God to show you the things in your life that represent pebbles, splinters, and eyelashes; things from which, with a little attention, you might experience relief and even freedom. Perhaps it means getting one more hour of sleep each night, or actually taking a day off and relaxing. It could be any number of minor adjustments that have significant payoffs. We only have to be off course on a journey by a little to miss the destination by a lot.

10. **Learn to manage your time by saying "No," or else your time will control you.** Time does not manage us; it tends to take over us. We must be active—and at times determined in our self-examination and intentional in our correction—when it comes to this issue. I have learned than cemeteries are full of indispensable people. The fact of the matter is that life usually goes on with or without us. If the Lord was to literally call you home today, would someone still preach the sermon or teach the lesson? Finish the project that was started? Visit the hospital? Finalize the budget? The answer is a resounding "Yes." Caregivers and ministry leaders too often move their spouses, families, and their own self-care out of their schedules when something else comes up and crowds the

calendar. We rationalize that we will make it up later, and yet we never seem to have the time.

11. **Learn to delegate to others whenever, wherever, and however it is appropriate.** Some of the most secure leaders I know are the ones who can let their ministry go and who are comfortable having strong, anointed people around them. Moses heeded his father-in-law's advice (Exodus 18) and surrounded himself with able leaders. Does it really matter if someone else can give a better presentation, teach a better class, write a better article or book, do a better job counseling a parishioner? Hopefully not! Good leaders produce followers. Great leaders produce other leaders. However, the greatest of leaders understand what it means to become a follower again. The important thing, what truly matters, is that the Kingdom of God is advanced.

12. **Learn the value of authentic relationship, and find one or two key people in your life to whom you are willing to be accountable.** Someone once told me that accountability is the "breakfast of champions," but that too many people skip the most important meal of the day. Isolation and the lack of accountability is, in my opinion, the primary strategy that Satan uses to take down any leader—"[walking] about like a roaring lion, seeking whom he may devour" (1 Peter 5:8, NKJV). Whenever we are alone (in reality or perception) and cut off from supportive relationships, we are the most vulnerable. We do not necessarily need more "yes" men. Most leaders already have their share of them—good people, prayer warriors, faithful and loyal, to be sure—but we also need "truth-tellers" in our lives. These are individuals who also love us, are safe, and whom we can count on to give us honest, direct, and transparent feedback. However, we must give these individuals permission and an open invitation to do so. The spiritual landscape is littered with caregivers and ministry leaders who have failed to embrace this truth. Look at the foresight of the wisest man who lived. In 1 Kings 4:1-19, we see a wide-ranging list of Solomon's officials (priests, scribes, recorders, military commanders, project managers, governors, and the like). Yet imbedded in this list is a priest named Zabud, who is also described as "the king's friend"

Dr. Tim Clinton and Dr. Jared Pingleton

(vs. 5). Solomon apparently had the wisdom to have at least one person on his staff who also served in the capacity of friend. Who is your Zabud? If you do not have one, may I encourage you to find one? Better yet, consider being a Zabud to another caregiver or ministry leader.

Christian leadership is a high and sacred calling to humbly, yet transparently represent Christ as his ambassadors to a lost and hurting world. This is the ministry of reconciliation, and from the perspective of the Apostle Paul, "… as though God were pleading *through us* [emphasis added]: we implore you on Christ's behalf, be reconciled to God" (2 Corinthians 5:20, NKJV). In order to "run with endurance the race that is set before us" (Hebrews 12:1, NKJV), we must be deliberate when it comes to our own self-care. Only then can we put on the compassion of Christ and consistently manifest his grace, truth, and love to all who so desperately need his touch. May you have true joy in the journey.

References

American Heart Association: www.americanheart.org

American Institute on Stress: www.stress.org/

Figley, C. (2002). *Treating compassion fatigue.* New York: Brunner-Routledge.

Hart, A. and Weber, C.H. (2005). *Caring for people God's way: Stress and anxiety* (pp. 164-165). Nashville, TN: Thomas Nelson Publishers.

Selye, H. (1956). *The stress of life.* New York: McGraw-Hill.

U.S. Department of Health and Human Services: www.hhs.gov/

106

Jared Pingleton, Psy.D.

Jared Pingleton is a respected leader in the Christian mental health field and serves as the Director of Mental Health Care and Ministry for the American Association of Christian Counselors. Jared is a credentialed minister and a licensed clinical psychologist who is dually trained in both psychology and theology and specializes in the theoretical and practical integration of the two disciplines. In professional practice since 1977, Jared has enjoyed the privilege of working with thousands of individuals, couples, and families to offer help, hope, and healing to the hurting.

Dr. Pingleton earned his Psy.D. and M.A. degrees in Clinical Psychology from Rosemead School of Psychology, Biola University; an M.A. in Counseling Psychology from the University of Missouri-Kansas City, and a B.S. in Psychology and Biblical Studies from Evangel University. He did additional graduate work at the University of Kansas and at the Assemblies of God, Talbot, and Fuller Theological Seminaries. In addition to clinical practice, he has served on the pastoral staff of two large churches and has taught at numerous Christian colleges and theological seminaries. Jared has published several professional journal articles and authored or co-authored numerous books, including *Making Magnificent Marriages; Be Strong and Surrender: A 30 Day Recovery Guide; Praying With Jesus: Reset My Prayer Life; Marriage: Its Foundation, Theology, and Mission in a Changing World; Christian Perspectives on Human Development;* and is the Consulting Editor of *The Care and Counsel Bible* by Thomas Nelson Press.

Formerly Director of Counseling Services at Focus on the Family, Jared has extensive national and international media experience, appearing as a guest, co-host, or host of hundreds of television and radio programs and in leading print publications. Dr. Pingleton maintains several professional affiliations, has received five "Who's Who" awards along with several other national recognitions, and is a popular speaker, preacher, and conference leader. Jared and his wife, Linda, have four sons, four daughters-in-law, and five adorable grandchildren. He is a lifelong, passionate Kansas City Chiefs and Royals fan and enjoys sports of all kinds, travel, hiking, rappelling and mountain climbing, architecture, classical music, antiques, vintage automobiles, and landscaping. For more about him, including contact information, go to www.drpingleton.com.

CHAPTER 8

How to Develop the Art of Making an Effective Referral

Jared Pingleton, Psy.D.

Life is relational. We were designed by the Creator in relationship, through relationship, and for relationship. Without the reality and reciprocity of relationships, life itself would not exist or continue. But like life, healthy relationships are rarely simple or easy.

Sometimes life throws difficult things our way. For all of us, there is often hurt and heartache. Distance and disappointment. Crisis and conflict. Pain and pathos. The results of life's trials, temptations, and tragedies can leave us filled with agony, doubt, resentment, and unforgiveness. We wonder why God permits our suffering, sadness, and sorrow. Questions of theodicy abound. We may feel hurt, alone, confused, hopeless, and scared to reach out for help. Consequently, mental and relationship health issues find their way home. To everyone's home.

The statistics are absolutely overwhelming – the scope of the struggle is enormous. As was detailed in Chapter 1, it is currently estimated that roughly 20-25% of adults in the U.S. suffer from mental illness in any given year, and that between 14 and 20% of young people have experienced a mental, emotional, or behavioral disorder. Of the ten leading causes of disability identified in the United States and in other developed countries, four are brain and behavioral disorders: major depression, bipolar disorder, schizophrenia, and obsessive-compulsive disorder.

The economic impact of serious mental illnesses in America approaches $200 million in lost wages per year. They also create significant, but difficult to calculate, associated "soft" costs and losses such as hospitalizations, increases in suicide, heightened stress on families and loved ones, and many misdiagnosed and/or untreated disorders. And relational problems such as divorce, domestic violence, child abuse and neglect, blended family concerns, and other interpersonal issues are equally prevalent, prominent, and painful. Most major mental illnesses have a fairly gradual onset and rarely appear "out of the blue." Generally, family members and friends will recognize that something about the individual is unusual, odd, or "not quite right" about their thinking, speech, behavior, or social interactions, often well before the diagnosable indicators of severe mental illness are fully manifested. Being informed about early warning signs and developing symptoms can lead to appropriate intervention and treatment which can often help to greatly reduce the severity and stress of an illness to both the individual and their loved ones. Consequently, early intervention can delay or even prevent the onset of a chronic course for a number of disorders.

As with many medical conditions, early detection and treatment can not only minister to the person's suffering more effectively, but many times the pain and subsequent course of treatment can be reduced accordingly. Being educated about and alert to key early warning symptoms may even prevent more severe distress and dysfunction. Here are some common signs and symptoms that you as a pastor or church leader can identify which are potentially indicative of mental illness:

- Recent social withdrawal and loss of interest in relationships with others;
- Intensified conflict and difficulty relating normally with others;
- Unusual reduction in functioning at work, school, church, and/or community activities;
- Problems with concentration, memory, confusion, and cognitive processing;
- Loss of initiative or desire to participate in normal and/or pleasurable activities;
- Marked changes in sleep and/or appetite;
- Rapid or dramatic shifts in emotions or "mood swings;"
- Deterioration in personal hygiene;
- Excessive and/or unexplained fears, suspicions, worries, and anxieties;
- Numerous vague or ambiguous physical ailments and complaints;
- Intense and prolonged feelings of sadness, nervousness, irritability, or anger;

- Progressive inability to cope with everyday stress and strain;
- Heightened sensitivity to sensory stimuli such as sights, sounds, smells, or touch;
- Uncharacteristic, bizarre, or peculiar behavior, thoughts, and/or beliefs; and/or
- Vague or specific mentions of hopelessness, apathy, despair, and/or suicidality.

Please know that these symptoms in and of themselves cannot clearly or conclusively predict mental illness. In fact, symptoms of mental illness may be the result of a medical condition (for example, hypothyroidism typically manifests or mimics symptoms of depression). A person displaying signs of mental illness should be screened by a physician to determine if there are any underlying medical issues, concerns, or problems. Each person's situation must be carefully assessed and their treatment individualized.

Barring any medical causes, persons exhibiting even a few of these symptoms are likely to be experiencing significant psychological problems which may be impairing or interfering with their ability to love and work well, and thus are candidates to be screened by a trained mental health professional. Supportively and compassionately encouraging persons who are displaying several of these symptoms to seek help may prove difficult but is essential.

One thing that should be considered is the role of pharmacologic assistance in the treatment of certain mental or emotional problems. There is still a persistent stigma in our culture (and particularly in some realms of our Christian subculture) attached to the use of medication to treat mental illnesses including depression, anxiety disorders, and even more serious issues. Fortunately, that shame and stigma has diminished somewhat in recent years, but it is still alive and well in many places, including in many churches.

As followers of Christ we may falsely believe that our emotional and/or relationship problems should miraculously, if not magically, go away if we simply have more faith or trust in God. Yet ironically, we would certainly never tell someone with diabetes to just cavalierly go off their insulin, someone with myopia to throw away their eyeglasses or contact lenses, or someone with cancer to not take their chemo due to their perceived or judged deficient faith. Somehow, those with mental and relational health challenges don't always receive the same grace—which then consolidates, exacerbates, and perpetuates their shame and stigma. Consequently, suffering and dysfunction continue, and thus the adversary of our souls is deliriously and diabolically delighted.

While faith and trust may be at the root of many of our difficulties, there are some issues that aren't caused by deficiencies in our relationship with God. We live in a fallen world where things go wrong with our physical bodies, including one of the largest organs, our brains. For many whose disordered behaviors or thoughts are caused by chemical imbalances in the brain (verified progressively more by recent brain science discoveries), the correct medication can allow these individuals to regain their neurochemical equilibrium, along with an increased capacity to deal with personal issues, problematic beliefs, and dysfunctional ways of thinking. You can do your parishioners an invaluable service by supporting them in their appropriate use of medication when indicated and prescribed.

To be sure, far from being overlooked in this discussion, spiritual tools, resources, and disciplines have been proven helpful in reducing the symptom severity and relapse rate of mental and relational problems. They can activate and speed up the recovery process, as well as render distress and suffering easier for the person to endure. Providing hope, health, and healing to the hurting in an informed and capable manner is a valuable and specialized form of ministry no less important than any other way in which you serve your congregation. Abundant research has demonstrated that strong spiritual supports and beliefs are not only instrumental in preventing some mental and emotional difficulties in the first place, but are also highly effective in their treatment and recovery.

As ministry leaders, we are neither immune to nor exempt from these "growth opportunities" ourselves. Whether addressing these issues personally, or on behalf of members of our flock professionally, the quintessential question becomes: "To whom can I turn for help?" This is a crucial concern which must be considered carefully and cogently. In this chapter, we will now address the need for making an effective referral, the "art" of making an effective referral, and the "science" of making an effective referral.

The Need for Making an Effective Referral

Like it or not, research studies about persons seeking help for their personal issues consistently verify that the vast majority of Americans needing help reach out first to a pastor. Although you probably didn't sign up for this honor (and colossal responsibility), it has been said that pastors and other church leaders are "first responders" for most people seeking help or guidance regarding a mental health concern, a suicidal crisis, a severe relationship problem, or a major life trauma. Yet most pastors are not trained in Bible school or seminary to know how to adequately, much less expertly, help navigate their sheep safely through the proverbial rocks and reefs in the storm-tossed waves of their seas of despair and despondency.

Most persons who enter professional ministry do so with altruistic motives. They possess a genuine care and concern for lost souls. They love people. Yet they often feel completely unprepared and unequipped for the often overwhelming depth and degree of human suffering they encounter on a regular basis in their congregations. And because they aren't properly trained to minister to those needs, many feel inadequate, stressed, and guilty. And even for those who have the know-how, few have the time and logistical capacity to deal in-depth with an entire flock of hurting souls and relationships. Tragically, this huge burden of not being able to help everyone ends up creating intrinsically high levels of stress, job dissatisfaction, and burnout for the average pastor.

So how do we help those whom we can't help? The truth is that all of us are gifted in some areas but no one is gifted in every area. While it is a fact of psychology that everyone can help someone, it is a reality of ecclesiology that no one possesses all the gifts and therefore can help everyone. Thus, we were given the interdependent illustration of the Body to describe the distribution of spiritual gifts to the Church (Romans 12; 1 Corinthians 12; Ephesians 4). Hey, no one can do it all! Nor should we feel as though we have to. That is a burden far too complex and cumbersome for any human to bear.

But in many ministerial quarters, a subtle and surreptitious type of oxymoronic "Lone Ranger Christianity" has implicitly become sort of a glorified ideal to which leaders should strive to aspire. However, even the great Masked Man had his faithful friend Tonto for support, feedback, accountability, and assistance. We just need to take off the mask, become honest and transparent, and quit trying to be the superhero.

For me as a clinical psychologist, often the best way I can help someone is to refer them to another mental health professional who can help them better than I can. It not only provides great personal relief at times to recommend someone else more highly trained, experienced, or specialized in a certain area but great professional satisfaction to know that suggesting the client see Dr. Smith down the hall or Dr. Jones down the street is the best way I can help them. That is truly a win-win for all concerned. It is not only good old fashioned common sense; it displays the best clinical practice along with the highest professional ethics. Again, no one can help everyone.

The "Art" of Making an Effective Referral

Your aid in facilitating a parishioner's understanding of the various forms of professional assistance available can be valuable and encouraging at a time when people often feel highly vulnerable, confused as to where or to whom to turn, and how to access those services. It's a big, scary world out there.

Once you have established a strong collegial working alliance with a good, solid, spiritually and emotionally mature therapist [more about that later], often the tricky part becomes how to successfully hand off your church member to them. Many times your sheep may feel abandoned or rejected by thinking you don't care for them or don't want to help them yourself. In this scenario, it is essential to emphasize to the person/family that often the best way you can care for them is to recommend someone else—a trained specialist in their particular area of need—who has the time, talent, and training to help them better than you can. This "artful" skill requires you to be definite, delicate, and diplomatic.

Make the need for referral clear; explain why you believe it to be in their best interests, and make sure to follow up with them later to see if they contacted the clinician and how the process is going. A good referral is crucial to good counseling. Many times, it is also important to reduce the silence, shame, and stigma that many in the church still have regarding counseling or psychotherapy and mental illness and relational problems. That applies to the appropriate use of antidepressants and other medications, too. Many Christians still believe they just need to have more faith, get the sin out of their lives (as if they can!?), or somehow get tougher and pull themselves up by their bootstraps (which, if you actually think about it, defies the nature of gravity!).

Please use the utmost in discretion in discussing the need for a referral. The church can feel like a notoriously public and exposed place, particularly to someone beset and burdened by shame. Hurting people already feel exposed, vulnerable, and as though everyone else can look through them to see the embarrassing problems with which they are struggling. Your discussion about the need for a referral should be done in private and with the utmost respect for the person or family's dignity, worth, and self-respect.

Before that conversation – and having done your homework on both the best available resources in the community which can be of support to the hurting person(s) involved, and the most workable strategies for anticipating and responding to their potentially resistant attitude or mindset toward receiving help – prayerfully consider how to be the most sensitive to their unique concern(s). Keep in mind that it's not that people don't want relief from their suffering (unless they are very masochistic!); it's that change is hard, scary, uncertain, and generally requires a lot of difficult work. Furthermore, asking for help may not only feel humbling and humiliating to the hurting person(s), it may activate deep-seated feelings of guilt, inadequacy, failure, and ineffectualness, all of which are hard to face in the best of circumstances.

In asking the Holy Spirit for discernment and direction on how you can wisely steer the conversation, consider enlisting the wise and caring support of another trusted, mature church leader, deacon, or elder, while at the same time being careful not to make the person(s) feel ganged up on. And always, if there is an imminent danger or threat of suicide and/ or harm to others, please call 911. Don't risk a tragedy or another statistic; this is where the old adage of being safe rather than sorry holds true.

Please be mindful that our culture is still in some respects confused and/or ignorant about the nature and dynamics of emotional, mental, and relational dysfunction; in other ways it humiliates those who suffer with these (e.g., media/sitcom depictions and labels of "crazy," "wacko," "nutcase," or "funny farms," "psycho wards," etc. to disparage persons with such pain). Your role is both instrumental and invaluable in helping to sensitively and compassionately normalize the incidence and universality of typical human struggles. Everyone hurts. All relationships experience conflict. Most people's resistance to receiving help is based on fear, pride, shame, stigma, or some combination thereof. Be gentle, understanding, accepting, and kind.

Remind yourself, and them, that nearly 44 million U.S. adults suffer from a diagnosable mental illness each year… that's one out of every four or five people! Address it. Communicate about it with your congregation. Don't over spiritualize it. There is much ministry to do. Keep shepherding! And concerning those parishioners you have referred for help, set and maintain healthy boundaries regarding their treatment by asking them in general ways how the counseling process is going. It may also be helpful to ask their permission to consult with their clinician and have them sign the requisite release of information form to do so.

Many clinicians find that working together with a referring pastor makes each of their respective roles easier and more productive. Feedback from the clinician about the therapy is very important to help you stay alongside persons whom you refer for help, not only to offer them ongoing quality pastoral care, prayer, and support, but to ensure that they do not feel discarded or forgotten. Likewise, feedback from you about medication compliance, social interaction and relational functioning, supportive structures, and other pastoral observations can be vital information for a clinician to better help your sheep. If you do not live in an area that has mental health professionals who meet all the above criteria, please refer to the AACC's *Christian Care Connect,* either on our website at aacc.net or at 1-800-5COUNSEL.

The *Christian Care Connect* (CCC) is a carefully selected nationwide network of coaches, clinicians, and clinics along a continuum of care ranging from "coffee cup" coaches for support to deal with common concerns to state-of-the-art inpatient treatment facilities which address and treat the most complex clinical challenges – all from a Christian perspective based on a biblical worldview. Significantly— and unlike most other referral networks—individuals and facilities on the CCC have been carefully and comprehensively vetted both Christianly and clinically.

The CCC search engine can be activated in multiple ways, ranging from specialization and training level to geographic proximity to scheduling availability.

The "Science" of Making an Effective Referral

Several factors are important in prayerfully selecting a person, agency, clinic, treatment facility, or other resource from which we seek guidance and assistance for ourselves, our family members, or our parishioners when their problems transcend the scope of our expertise or training. Among other things, we wonder if the therapist will be safe, trustworthy, and respectful of our congregant's issues. Will they treat these concerns with care, compassion, and confidentiality? Will they be nonjudgmental, accepting, and sensitive? Can I trust them as an uplifting ally to my ministry, or will they be an undermining adversary to it? And most importantly, are they doctrinally orthodox and do they know what they're doing theologically as well as psychologically—i.e., will they lead a client astray or to the path of life?

Consequently, it is imperative that you first make a concerted effort to develop a close and healthy working relationship with one or more reputable Christian counselors in your area in order for you to make referrals with confidence and assurance. Take them out for breakfast or lunch. Get to know them personally so you may say with confidence and integrity to a parishioner that you would not hesitate to refer a friend or loved one to this particular clinician. Here are some key "fruit" to look for in selecting a good referral for Christian counseling:

- Does the therapist possess and manifest a personal and growing relationship with Jesus Christ?
- Does the therapist possess and demonstrate a genuine sense of caring, compassion, and concern for people who are hurting?
- Does the therapist base their work on a biblical worldview and value system?
- Does the therapist express a desire to be seen by you as a trusted colleague in ministry, and are they open to consulting with you on the client's behalf provided the appropriate (legally required per

HIPAA regulations) release forms are signed to maintain a healthy confidentiality boundary?

- Does the therapist have the appropriate professional training, credentials, experience and state licensure as a certified mental health professional?

Once we realize the need to make a referral and have convinced our church member of that, the question then becomes: "What sort of mental health professional is best suited for their need?" There are several types of professional credentials reflecting various levels of training and expertise, ranging from masters level professional counselors, marriage and family therapists, and social workers, to doctoral-level psychologists and psychiatrists. It isn't unusual to find the mental health care field somewhat confusing. So for clarity, what follows are the fundamental differences between various kinds and levels of clinicians:

- **Counselors** (individuals with a minimum masters level training in child, individual, and/or marriage counseling);
- **Social Workers** (persons with masters level training in counseling along with specialized emphasis on incorporating community resources in their assistance to hurting persons and families);
- **Psychologists** (individuals with doctoral level education who specialize in diagnosing, assessing, and treating mental health disorders by means of psychological assessment, counseling, and psychotherapy); and
- **Psychiatrists** (medical doctors with specialized training in the diagnosis and treatment, including primarily pharmacologic treatment, of mental disorders).

Despite all of this awareness and your best efforts, do not be surprised if your congregant misperceives your well-facilitated referral as pejorative and rejecting. Be sensitive to the likelihood that the swirling currents of shame and stigma run deep, and parishioners who are facing mental and/ or relational challenges are probably used to feeling criticized, judged, and abandoned. Gently but firmly normalize the universality of people's pain and problems, and assure them they are loved, accepted, and cared for by you and their church family.

One practical way to practice what is preached is to listen to suggestions from the person or family as to how they can best be helped. After appropriate resources are sought out and referral(s) are made, there may be other obstacles preventing or precluding the hurting person from getting the care they need.

Many hurting people lack the financial resources to receive the treatment they need and so will benefit from a benevolence fund or financial assistance. Others may need child care during appointments, regular meals, or transportation to appointments. Pray for provision. Enlist help from others. Utilize community resources. Start ministries to serve those needs. Evaluate how your church can make a bigger contribution to persons with similar problems. Tailor programming to target those issues. Dedicate a trained volunteer or team of volunteers to serve faithfully and consistently alongside a hurting person, couple, or family to ensure structural support, follow-through, and continuity of care. Seek out and appropriate relevant community resources and connect hurting people to them. Preach, practice, and teach compassion and empathy; in your sermons come down hard on gossip, judgement, and rejection.

Be committed to ongoing shepherding and pastoral care. Making a referral doesn't mean you wash your hands of the person(s). Quite the opposite; in some respects that's when the hardest work begins! It is essential that after resources are sought out and referrals are made a pastor or other church leader continues to regularly reach out to, meet with, and personally serve the individual, couple, or family. Many hurting people avoid relationships, so it's fairly common (and sadly easy) for those persons to fall through the proverbial cracks.

Please continue to lovingly pastor persons as they work through their challenges; such is a crucial element of the high and holy calling of a minister of the liberating gospel of Jesus Christ. He lived and died for everyone; Scripture never hides or whitewashes our brokenness. All of us are *imago Dei* and are of equal worth and value at the foot of the cross, regardless of our psychiatric diagnoses! Because at the end of the day, as well as at the end of our lives, whatever we have done to the "least" of these...

Siang-Yang Tan, Ph.D.

Rev. Dr. Siang-Yang Tan, Ph.D., (McGill University) is Professor of Psychology at Fuller Theological Seminary in Pasadena, California and Senior Pastor of First Evangelical Church Glendale. He is a licensed psychologist and Fellow of the American Psychological Association. He has published numerous articles and books, including a major text, *Counseling and Psychotherapy: A Christian Perspective* (Baker Academic, 2011), *Full Service* (Baker, 2006), *Coping with Depression* (2nd ed., with John Ortberg, Baker, 2004), *Rest* (Regent College Publishing, 2003), *Disciplines of the Holy Spirit* (with Douglas Gregg, Zondervan, 1997), and *Lay Counseling* (2nd ed., with Eric Scalise, Zondervan, 2016). Siang-Yang is married to Angela, and they live in Pasadena, California. They have two grown children, Carolyn and Andrew.

CHAPTER 9

How to Develop an Effective Lay Counseling Ministry*

Siang-Yang Tan, Ph.D.

The "nonprofessional revolution in mental health" described by Sobey (1970) many decades ago has developed even further in recent years. For many reasons—including the sheer need for mental health services, the effort to cut healthcare costs internationally, and the reduction of mental health benefits by health insurance plans in the United States—the role of paraprofessional or lay counseling in the provision of mental health services has grown tremendously in the United States and abroad (Garzon & Tilley, 2009; Tan, 1997). Lay counselors or paraprofessional helpers are "those who lack the formal training, experience, or credentials to be professional psychotherapists, but who are nevertheless involved in helping people cope with personal problems" (Tan, 1997, p. 368).

They have provided much-needed but increasingly ill-afforded mental health services in various ways, such as through telephone hotlines, suicide-prevention programs, church-based lay counseling services, national caregiving ministries, and peer-helping programs in many schools, colleges, businesses, prisons, religious institutions, and other community agencies (Tan, 1992). A major example of paraprofessional or nonprofessional helping is lay Christian counseling for general psychological or emotional

---

* [adapted and updated from chapter 3, pp. 40-58, by Dr. Tan called "Lay Christian Counseling for General Psychological Problems" in *Evidence-Based Practices for Christian Counseling and Psychotherapy*, edited by Everett L. Worthington, Jr., Eric L. Johnson, Joshua N. Hook and Jamie D. Aten. Copyright © 2013, Everett L. Worthington, Jr., Eric L. Johnson, Joshua N. Hook and Jamie D. Aten. Used by permission of InterVarsity Press, P. O. Box 1400, Downers Grove, IL, 60515, USA, www.ivpress.com. For a more expansive and comprehensive treatment of this topic, please see *Lay Counseling, Revised and Updated: Equipping Christians for a Helping Ministry*, by Drs. Siang-Yang Tan and Eric Scalise (2016), Zondervan.]

problems, usually in a local church context, but also in other parachurch (e.g., Youth for Christ) or Christian ministry (e.g., missionary) contexts (Tan, 1991, 2002; see latest update in Tan & Scalise, 2016).

Pastors and church leaders are progressively considering lay Christian counseling as a legitimate Christian ministry based on biblical teaching as well as overwhelming congregational needs. The biblical basis for lay helping, as well as building a deeply connected and loving Christian community, is found in texts such as Romans 15:14, Galatians 6:1-2, John 13:34-35, 1 Thessalonians 5:14, and James 5:16. Furthermore, 1 Peter 2:5-9 emphasizes the priesthood of all believers, indicating that every Christian should be involved in appropriate ministries in the church and beyond, including lay helping and pastoral care, according to the spiritual gifts he or she has been graciously given by the Holy Spirit (Romans 12; 1 Corinthians 12; Ephesians 4; 1 Peter 4:8-11). In addition to biblical support for lay Christian counseling ministries, there is also some limited empirical support for the efficacy and effectiveness of lay Christian counseling, although more and better controlled outcome studies are needed before more definitive conclusions can be made (Garzon & Tilley, 2009; Tan, 1991, 2002).

Empirical Support for Lay Counseling

The empirical support for the effectiveness of lay counseling or nonprofessional or paraprofessional helping is quite extensive. Earlier reviews of the research literature with forty-two studies on the comparative effectiveness of paraprofessional and professional helpers (Durlak, 1979,1981; Nietzel & Fisher, 1981), as well as subsequent meta-analyses (Berman & Norton, 1985; Hattie, Sharpley & Rogers, 1984), have similarly concluded that lay counselors are generally as effective as professional therapists for most common problems such as anxiety, stress, and depression (Atkins & Christensen, 2001; Bickman, 1999; Christensen & Jacobson, 1994; Lambert & Bergin, 1994; see also Ali, Rahbar, Naeem & Gul, 2003; Neuner et al., 2008).

However, for some severe situations and problems, there may be a greater level of effectiveness with professional therapists compared to paraprofessional helpers (Barlow, 2004). For example, professionals' specialized and extensive training, especially in diagnosing and treating persons with severe psychopathology, makes them the referral of choice in more difficult, protracted, and/or serious situations. However, that does not negate the previously cited empirical evidence supporting the overall effectiveness of lay counselors. Lay or paraprofessional counselors have generally been found to be effective helpers (Tan, 2011; Tan & Scalise, 2016).

Description of Lay Christian Counseling

Lay Christian counseling is not a unitary or uniform approach to helping people with general psychological or emotional problems. As Garzon and Tilley (2009) have noted, there are at least four major categories of lay Christian counseling approaches, mainly from a more conservative, evangelical perspective: active listening, cognitive and solution-focused, inner healing, and mixed (see also Garzon et al., 2009). A brief treatment description of each of these four major categories will now be provided, following Garzon and Tilley (2009).

Active listening approaches. Active listening approaches to lay Christian counseling include empathy, positive regard, and basic listening skills, combined with the use of spiritual resources such as prayer and the scriptures. A major example of this approach is Stephen Ministry, a Christian caregiving program developed by Kenneth Haugk (1984) beginning in 1975. It has experienced tremendous growth so that more than 10,000 congregations from over 150 denominations and 21 countries are now using Stephen Ministry in their lay caregiving. Churches first enroll in the Stephen Series program of training, provision of resources, and continuing support from the main organization, Stephen Ministries, in St. Louis, Missouri. They then send their pastor(s) or selected lay leaders to attend a week-long leadership course that trains them in the Stephen Ministry model of lay caregiving and how to implement it in a local church context. The leader(s) of this ministry will subsequently select lay members of the congregation to become Stephen ministers by providing them with fifty hours of lay care training on topics such as active listening; feelings; assertiveness; confidentiality; setting boundaries for helping; ministering to people with specific struggles such as grief, depression, divorce, crisis, or childbirth; ministering to the dying, the suicidal, shut-in persons, older persons and inactive members; making referrals to mental health professionals and other resources; and the appropriate use of prayer and scripture. The trained lay members are then commissioned in church as Stephen ministers who will meet with a "care-receiver," assigned by a Stephen leader, once a week for an hour. These Stephen ministers will also meet with Stephen leaders for peer supervision twice a month.

Cognitive and solution-focused approaches. The cognitive or cognitive behavioral approaches to lay Christian counseling emphasize the crucial role of dysfunctional or unbiblical automatic thoughts, self-talk, basic assumptions, or core beliefs and schemas in the development of emotional distress or psychological problems (e.g., Backus, 1985; Crabb, 1977). They also include the use of prayer and scripture in cognitively restructuring or changing such distorted and unbiblical thinking into more realistic and biblical thinking (see Tan, 1991, 2007). Solution-focused approaches to lay Christian counseling have recently been used in the context of lay pastoral care (Holland, 2007). Such approaches focus on helping clients to use their unique strengths and resources in working toward problem resolution, as they imagine their futures without the problem.

A specific example of a biblically-based, integrated cognitive-behavioral approach to lay Christian counseling has been developed by Tan (1991; Tan, 2007). It incorporates an inner healing prayer component with seven steps (Tan & Ortberg, 2004) and uses biblical cognitive restructuring (e.g., Crabb's biblical counseling and Backus's misbelief therapy), which replaces unbiblical thinking with scriptural truths. His approach can be taught to lay Christian counseling trainees in a twelve-session training program with three-hour sessions (Tan & Scalise, 2016).

Inner healing approaches. Another category of lay Christian counseling consists of inner healing prayer approaches (also known as healing of memories) that focus on helping clients to journey back to their past under the guidance of the Holy Spirit to uncover painful experiences or memories that may be contributing to their troubled present (Hurding, 1995, p. 297) and to pray for the presence of Christ or God to minister to them in the context of those painful memories (Garzon & Burkett, 2002, p. 42). Inner healing approaches include Francis MacNutt's Christian Healing Ministries and Ed Smith's Theophostic Prayer Ministry (Smith, 2002, 2007). Smith's approach focuses on identifying lies associated with painful memories and praying for the Lord Jesus to reveal the truth to the client about such lies, leading eventually to peace (Garzon & Tilley, 2009). Also in this category is John and Paula Sandford's Elijah House Ministry (1982; also J. Sandford & M. Sandford, 1992; for a review, Garzon, E.Worthington, Tan & R. Worthington, 2009). All of these methods require training the lay Christian counselor in the particular inner healing prayer approach. For further details on these approaches and their training programs, see Garzon and Tilley (2009) and Garzon et al. (2009).

Mixed approaches. This final category of lay Christian counseling consists of mixed approaches, which include either several psychological theoretical perspectives or more focused examination of theological dimensions, such as the role of the sinful nature and the demonic in the development of emotional distress, or both. Two examples of mixed approaches are eclectic with an integrated cognitive behavioral component and Neil Anderson's Freedom in Christ Ministries (Anderson, 2000a, 2000b, 2003, 2004). Anderson's approach focuses on unbiblical lies, which often cause emotional and spiritual distress and the need to take "the steps to freedom" in seven key areas involving confession and renunciation of certain sinful attitudes and behaviors, and forgiveness (Garzon et al., 2009).

There is one randomized waiting list control group outcome study on the effectiveness of an eclectic with an integrated cognitive-behavioral component approach to lay Christian counseling (Toh & Tan, 1997). This study evaluated the effectiveness of lay Christian counseling provided in a local church context (First Evangelical Free Church of Fullerton, California, which had over five thousand attendees at the time the study was conducted). Toh and Tan provide the following details of this lay Christian counseling program for the treatment of general psychological or emotional problems. The characteristics of this program include: (a) lay counseling services to those within and outside the church; (b) a formal selection process for lay counselors involving the use of clinical instruments and in-depth interviews; (c) a year-long counselor training program conducted by professionals; (d) post-training supervision provided by licensed mental health professionals; (e) screening and referral of counselees to avoid too severe symptomatology (e.g., applicants with a history of suicidal ideation or attempts, psychotropic medication, severe or chronic psychological dysfunction, and suggested diagnosis of character disorders from the MMPI [Minnesota Multiphasic Personality Inventory, which is the most widely respected clinical psychology assessment device] are referred to mental health professionals); (f) a commitment to a brief, solution-focused therapy (limited to ten sessions) designed for counselees with "temporary adjustment disorders"; and (g) provision of services to adults, adolescents, and couples only (i.e., no services to children) (Toh & Tan, 1997, pp. 260-61).

The year-long training curriculum used to train the lay Christian counselors in this study consists of the following three phases: The first phase is a 22 two-hour lecture series covering such single-session topics as the nature of persons; integration and the use of scriptures; personality and counseling theory; developmental psychology of the individual and family; narcissistic and borderline personalities; children and adolescents as well as child and adolescent therapy; marital and family therapy; divorce, step-parenting and blended families; psychopathology; anxiety and phobic reactions; depression, grief, and loss; incest rape; addictive/compulsive disorders; eating disorders, anorexia, and bulimia; suicide ideation and intervention; stress reduction and biofeedback; and psychotropic medications, hospitalizations, and forensic psychiatry. The second phase involves testing of the potential counselors. The third phase, over the last four months of training, focuses on empathic listening skills, role play, identifying and handling resistances, and termination. These skills are taught in conjunction with Mann and Goldman's (1982) approach to time-limited psychotherapy. (Toh & Tan, 1997, p. 261)

The category of lay Christian counseling used in this study is therefore an eclectic one with some integration of a cognitive-behavioral component. A similar eclectic approach focusing more on active listening skills as well as some biblically-based cognitive-behavioral components and marital and family counseling—based on Egan (1990a, 1990b), Haugk (1984), Satir and Baldwin (1983) and Tan (1991)—has been used in the lay Christian counseling program at another local church, La Canada Presbyterian Church in La Canada, California. The twenty-six-week training program is conducted every year, usually from March to August (Tan, 1991).

There are many other lay Christian counseling services and training programs available (Tan, 1991, 2002; Tan & Scalise, 2016), but only one eclectic with an integrated cognitive-behavioral component approach has been evaluated with a randomized waiting list control group design. This study had significant positive findings leading to the present conclusion that lay Christian counseling for general psychological problems can be considered a possibly efficacious treatment (Hook et al., 2010). More and better controlled outcome research is definitely needed on the effectiveness of lay Christian counseling (Garzon & Tilley, 2009).

The Role of the Professional Counselor in Lay Christian Counseling

Professional counselors and psychologists can have an important role in lay Christian counseling. They can help in the following ways (Tan, 1997): training and supervising lay counselors; serving on boards of directors of lay counseling ministries or organizations; educating the public, including churches, about the positive contributions of psychological or mental health services; consulting with churches or parachurch organizations interested in setting up lay counseling services; serving as a referral source when professional counseling or therapy is needed (but avoiding any conflict of interest); conducting outcomes research and evaluating the effectiveness of lay counseling; and educating other mental health professionals about the significant role they can have in the development of lay counselors and lay counseling ministries.

Implementation of Lay Christian Counseling in the Church

Five steps for starting a lay counseling ministry. In order to implement lay Christian counseling, especially in a local church context, the following five steps for starting a lay counseling ministry are recommended (Tan, 1991, 1995, 2002; Tan & Scalise, 2016).

1. An appropriate model of lay Christian counseling ministry for a particular church should be chosen. Besides the *spontaneous, informal model* of lay Christian counseling or people-helping that typically occurs in settings such as homes and restaurants or wherever people meet and share their problems with each other with no formal selection, training, or supervision of lay counselors, there are really only two primary models of lay Christian counseling or caregiving. The first is the *informal, organized* model in which lay counselors or helpers are carefully selected, trained, and supervised in an organized ministry of lay Christian counseling or caregiving that occurs in informal settings such as restaurants, homes, hospitals, and nursing homes. The second is the *formal, organized* model in which lay counselors are also carefully selected, trained, and supervised in an organized ministry of lay Christian counseling or caregiving that takes place in more formal settings such as a lay counseling center in a local church, where appointments are made for the lay counselor to meet at a specific time with a client, couple, or family. The first step then is to choose which of these two models is best for a particular local church or parachurch ministry. However, some larger churches may actually choose to use both models to provide different levels of help to those in need. For example, a church with several hundred or several thousand people may implement Stephen Ministry, which fits the informal, organized model, as well as having trained lay Christian counselors provide counseling services through a formal lay counseling center at the church.

2. Full support for the lay Christian counseling ministry and model(s) adopted should be obtained from the local church pastors, pastoral staff, and church board, so that the church leadership is one hundred percent behind the lay Christian counseling service as a crucial part of the overall church ministries and outreach. Lay Christian counseling is therefore viewed by the church leadership as a biblically based extension of pastoral care and counseling ministry in the church and beyond.

3. Appropriately gifted and qualified lay Christian counselors from the congregation should be screened and carefully selected, using

criteria such as spiritual maturity, psychological and emotional stability, love for and interest in people (demonstrated, e.g., by empathy, genuineness and warmth, or respect); appropriate spiritual gifts for helping others (e.g., encouragement); some life experience; previous training or experience in people-helping (helpful but not essential); age, gender, socioeconomic, and ethnic/cultural background relevant to the needs of the congregation and the people needing help; availability; teachability; and ability to maintain confidentiality. Usually an interview is conducted with potential lay counselors before selection is made. The selection process can also be open (i.e., anyone can apply to be a lay counselor) or closed (i.e., based on nominations or recommendations by pastors or church leaders). Psychological testing of potential lay counselors should be avoided or only conducted with great caution and with attention to appropriate ethical guidelines (Tan, 1997).

4. An adequate training program for lay Christian counselors should be provided. Many lay Christian counselor training programs are now available, some of which have been mentioned earlier in this chapter. They vary in length from several hours of basic training in listening and helping skills, to fifty or more hours of training often spread over several weeks, months, or a year. Limitations on the number of lay counselors trained at one time vary from just a few to twenty-five or thirty. Training sessions of two to three hours each are typically held on a weekly or biweekly basis. A training program should include the following (Collins, 1980): basic Bible knowledge relevant to lay helping; counseling or helping skills with opportunities to practice such skills (e.g., through role-playing); understanding common psychological or emotional problems such as depression, anxiety, stress, and spiritual dryness; understanding law and ethics as they apply to lay counseling and awareness of the dangers inherent to helping people; and importance and techniques of referral. Lay Christian counselors need to know their limits and limitations and when and how to make good referrals of clients to professionals. Limits to confidentiality should also be discussed with clients and informed consent be obtained from them before starting lay counseling. Such limits usually include situations

involving danger to the client or to others, or child or elder abuse. A good training program for lay Christian counselors will also include the following components: clear and practically oriented lectures; reading assignments; observation of good counseling skills as modeled or demonstrated by the trainer or professional counselor or through watching a videotape; and experiential practice of counseling skills, especially through role-playing.

5. Programs or ministries in which the trained lay Christian counselors can serve should be developed, organized, and implemented. The specific lay Christian counseling programs or ministries that are eventually implemented will depend on the model(s) of lay counseling services chosen for a particular church. Ongoing training and supervision of the active lay Christian counselors should be provided, preferably by a licensed mental health professional, but at least by a pastor or church leader with some experience in people-helping ministries. Weekly or biweekly supervision of the lay counselors, usually in dyads or small groups, should be conducted, with individual supervision available as needed.

Legal advice should be obtained regarding whether malpractice insurance is needed by the lay counselors (see Sandy, 2009) and whether or not they should be called "lay counselors" and the ministry they do "lay counseling," since in some U.S. states licensing laws limit the use of terms such as *counselor* and *counseling* to licensed professional counselors. It may therefore be necessary in such states to use alternative terms such as *lay helping* and *lay helpers* or *lay caregivers.*

Ten guidelines for setting up a lay counseling center. If a formal, organized model for providing lay Christian counseling services is selected for a particular local church, the following ten guidelines for setting up a lay Christian counseling center should prove helpful (adapted from Partridge, 1983):

1. Determine clear objectives for the lay counseling center.
2. Establish the "ethos" or distinctive character of the center by giving it an appropriate name.

3. Carefully select, train, and supervise the lay counselors.
4. Arrange for suitable facilities and office space or rooms for the center.
5. Establish the operating hours of the center.
6. Set up a structure within which the center will function, including having a director and a board of reference.
7. Publicize the services of the center.
8. Clarify what services the center will offer, and what it will *not* offer.
9. Carefully consider the financing or funding for the center, and include it in the annual church budget.
10. Determine the affiliation of the center to the church (Tan, 1995, p. 57).

It is usually advisable to start a church lay counseling center modestly. For example, it can initially be open on two or three evenings a week, rather than five days a week. The range of services and times offered can be expanded over time. However, such gradual growth or expansion of a lay counseling center may not be necessary in a large church where staff, finances, and facilities are already available and there is great need for lay counseling services. In this case the center might immediately begin functioning on a full-scale basis (Tan, 2002).

Tips for Practical Application

The previous section on treatment implementation already offered many practical tips for starting a lay Christian counseling ministry to help people with general psychological problems such as anxiety, depression, and marital and family struggles. Here are a few other suggestions for practical application.

First, some church lay Christian counseling programs limit the number of sessions they offer to clients. For example, First Evangelical Free Church in Fullerton, California, follows a time-limited therapy framework with a ten-session limit. Clients are referred to other professional therapists if they need more than ten sessions. La Canada Presbyterian Church in La Canada, California, also initially offers clients ten sessions of lay

Christian counseling in their program, but clients can negotiate with their lay counselors to extend for another ten sessions at a time in appropriate situations. Other church lay counseling programs do not have such limits, although they still often use a relatively short-term counseling model. Flexibility in limits to the number of sessions provided for clients is recommended, because some clients may need more long-term support (including prayer support). Such clients may need to be seen over a year or two, but sessions can be gradually reduced to once a month.

Second, while ethical guidelines are necessary and should be followed for lay Christian counseling to be conducted in an ethical, efficient, and effective way, ethical guidelines for professional practice should not be indiscriminately applied to lay counseling (Tan, 1991, 2002). This is especially true in the case of peer counseling, which is a particular example of lay counseling with peers involving a certain degree of friendship counseling. Hence, professional caution about avoiding dual-role relationships with clients does not fully apply to such peer or lay counseling situations.

Finally, while lay Christian counseling is usually provided through a formal, organized model such as a church lay counseling center, or through an informal, organized model such as Stephen Ministry, it can also be made more widely available through informal and more spontaneous channels. Such channels include small groups and fellowships, men's and women's ministries, and youth ministries, where leaders informally and spontaneously provide lay Christian counseling or caregiving on a regular basis. Their informal people-helping ministries can be strengthened and encouraged by providing these leaders with some basic training in lay Christian counseling skills, even if they do not serve officially as lay counselors in their church's lay counseling program.

Conclusion

Lay Christian counseling for general psychological, emotional, and relational problems is an important ministry in the local church and other parachurch contexts. As needs significantly increase for mental health services worldwide and as cost-cutting measures in healthcare and benefits drastically reduce mental health coverage in insurance plans in the United

States, lay counseling services and ministries will continue to mushroom. Lay Christian counseling will be a crucial answer to such needs and therefore warrants further development as well as more and better outcome research to strengthen the empirical base supporting its effectiveness or efficacy. It is presently considered a probably efficacious treatment for general psychological problems (Hook et al., 2010). It is hoped that it will become an empirically supported treatment or an evidence-based intervention in the years to come as more controlled-outcome studies on its efficacy are conducted, especially focusing on specific lay Christian counseling approaches.

Pastors and professional Christian therapists need to know more about lay Christian counseling approaches. Many of their parishioners and clients may have been exposed to such lay Christian counseling that can significantly impact their expectations for integration of Christian faith in professional therapy (Garzon et al, 2009). The time has come for Christian lay counseling to be a viable option for many persons with mental and relational health needs.

References

Ali, B. S., Rahbar, M. H., Naeem, S., & Gul, A. (2003). The effectiveness of counseling on anxiety and depression by minimally trained counselors: A randomized controlled trial. *American Journal of Psychotherapy, 57,* 324-36.

Anderson, N. T. (2000a). *Victory over the darkness: Realizing the power of your identity in Christ* (2nd ed.). Ventura, CA: Regal Books.

Anderson, N. T. (2000b). *The bondage breaker* (2nd ed.). Ventura, CA: Regal Books.

Anderson, N. T. (2003). *Discipleship counseling: The complete guide to helping others walk in freedom and grow in Christ.* Ventura, CA: Regal Books.

Anderson, N. T. (2004). *The steps to freedom in Christ.* Ventura, CA: Gospel Light.

Atkins, D. C., & Christensen, A. (2001). Is professional training worth the bother? A review of the impact of psychological training on client outcome. *Australian Psychologist, 36*(2), 1-9.

Backus, W. (1985). *Telling the truth to troubled people.* Minneapolis, MN: Bethany.

Barlow, D. H. (2004). Psychological treatments. *American Psychologist, 59,* 869-78.

Berman, J. S., & Norton, N. C. (1985). Does professional training make a therapist more effective? *Psychological Bulletin, 98,* 4017.

Bickman, L. (1999). Practice makes perfect and other myths about mental health services. *American Psychologist, 54,* 965-78.

Christensen, A., & Jacobson, N. S. (1994). Who (or what) can do psychotherapy: The status and challenge of nonprofessional therapies. *Psychological Science, 5,* 814.

Collins, G. R. (1980). Lay counseling within the local church. *Leadership, 7*(4), 78-86.

Crabb, L. J., Jr. (1977*). Effective biblical counseling.* Grand Rapids, MI: Zondervan.

Durlak, J. A. (1979). Comparative effectiveness of paraprofessional and professional helpers. *Psychological Bulletin, 86,* 8092.

Durlak, J. A. (1981). Evaluating comparative studies of paraprofessional and professional helpers: A reply to Nietzel and Fisher. *Psychological Bulletin, 89,* 56669.

Egan, G. (1990a). *Exercises in helping skills* (4ᵗʰ ed.). Monterey, CA: Brooks/Cole.

Egan, G. (1990b). *The skilled helper* (4ᵗʰ ed.). Monterey, CA: Brooks/Cole.

Garzon, F., & Burkett, L. (2002). Healing of memories: Models, research, future directions. *Journal of Psychology and Christianity, 21,* 42-49.

Garzon, F., & Tilley, K. (2009). Do lay Christian counseling approaches work? What we currently know. *Journal of Psychology and Christianity, 28,* 130-40.

Garzon, F., Worthington, E. L., Jr., Tan, S.-Y., & Worthington, R. K. (2009). Lay Christian counseling and client expectations for integration in therapy. *Journal of Psychology and Christianity, 28,* 113-20.

Hattie, J. A., Sharpley, C. F., & Rogers, H. J. (1984). Comparative effectiveness of professional and paraprofessional helpers. *Psychological Bulletin, 95,* 53441.

Haugk, K. (1984). *Christian caregiving: A way of life.* Minneapolis, MN: Augsburg.

Holland, J. (2007). Solution-focused lay pastoral care. *Journal of Family and Community Ministries, 21,* 22-30.

Hook, J. N., Worthington, E. L., Jr., Davis, D. E., Jennings, D. J., II., Gartner, A. L., &

Hook, J. P. (2010). Empirically supported religious and spiritual therapies. *Journal of Clinical Psychology, 66,* 46-72.

Huppert, J. D., Bufka, L. F., Barlow, D. H., Gorman, J. M., Shear, M. K., & Woods, S. W. (2001). Therapists, therapist variables, and cognitive-behavioral therapy outcome in a multicenter trial for panic disorder. *Journal of Consulting and Clinical Psychology, 69,* 747-55.

Hurding, R. F. (1995). Pathways to wholeness: Christian journeying in a postmodern age. *Journal of Psychology and Christianity, 14,* 293-305.

Lambert, M. J., & Bergin, A. E. (1994). The effectiveness of psychotherapy. In A. E. Bergin & S. L. Garfield (Eds.), *Handbook of psychotherapy and behavior change* (4th ed., pp. 143- 89). New York: Wiley.

Mann, J., & Goldman, R. (1982). *A casebook of time-limited psychotherapy.* New York: McGraw-Hill.

Neuner, F., Onyut, P. L., Ertl, V., Odenwald, M., Schauer, E., & Elbert, T. (2008). Treatment of posttraumatic stress disorder by trained lay counselors in an African refugee settlement: A randomized controlled trial. *Journal of Consulting and Clinical Psychology, 76,* 686- 94.

Nietzel, N. T., & Fisher, S. G. (1981). Effectiveness of professional and paraprofessional helpers: A comment on Durlak. *Psychological Bulletin, 89,* 55565

Partridge, T. J. (1983). Ten considerations in establishing a Christian counseling centre. *The Christian Counsellor's Journal, 4*(4), 31-33.

Sandford, J. L., & Sandford, M. (1992). *A comprehensive guide to deliverance and inner healing.* Grand Rapids, MI: Chosen Books.

Sandford, J., & Sandford, P. (1982). *The transformation of the inner man.* Tulsa, OK: Victory House.

Sandy, J. L. (2009). *Church lay counseling risk management guidebook.* Fort Wayne, IN: Brotherhood Mutual Insurance Company.

Satir, V. M., & Baldwin, M. (1983). *Satir step by step.* Palo Alto, CA: Science and Behavior Books.

Smith, E. M. (2002). *Healing life's deepest hurts.* Ann Arbor, MI: Vine Books.

Smith, E. M. (2007). *Theophostic prayer ministry: Basic training seminar manual.* Campbellsville, KY: New Creation Publishing.

Sobey, F. (1970). *The nonprofessional revolution in mental health.* New York: Columbia University Press.

Tan, S.-Y. (1991). *Lay counseling: Equipping Christians for a helping ministry.* Grand Rapids, MI: Zondervan.

Tan, S.-Y. (1992). Development and supervision of paraprofessional counselors. In L. VandeCreek, S. Knapp, & T. L. Jackson (Eds.), *Innovations in clinical practice: A sourcebook* (Vol. 11, pp. 431-40). Sarasota, FL: Professional Resource Press.

Tan, S.-Y. (1995). Starting a lay counseling ministry. *Christian Counseling Today 3*(1), 56-57.

Tan, S.-Y. (1997). The role of the psychologist in paraprofessional helping. *Professional Psychology: Research and Practice, 28,* 368-72.

Tan, S.-Y. (2002). Lay helping: The whole church in soul care ministry. In T. Clinton & G. Ohlschlager (Eds.), *Competent Christian counseling* (Vol. 1, pp. 424-36, 759- 62). Colorado Springs, CO: WaterBrook Press.

Tan, S.-Y. (2007). Use of prayer and scripture in cognitive-behavioral therapy. *Journal of Psychology and Christianity, 26,* 101-11.

Tan, S.-Y. (2011). *Counseling and psychotherapy: A Christian perspective.* Grand Rapid, MI: Baker Academic.

Tan, S.-Y. (2013). Lay Christian counseling for general psychological problems. In E. L. Worthington, Jr., E. L. Johnson, J. N. Hook & J. D. Aten (Eds.), *Evidence based practices for Christian counseling and psychotherapy* (40-58). Downers Grove, IL: InterVarsity Press.

Tan, S.-Y., & Ortberg, J. (2004). *Coping with depression* (2nd ed.). Grand Rapids, MI: Baker.

Tan, S.-Y., & Scalise, E. T. (2016). *Lay counseling, revised and updated: Equipping Christians for a helping ministry.* Grand Rapids, MI: Zondervan.

Toh, Y. M., & Tan, S.-Y. (1997). The effectiveness of church-based lay counselors: A controlled outcome study. *Journal of Psychology and Christianity, 16,* 260-67.

Toh, Y. M., Tan, S.-Y., Osburn, C. D., & Faber, D. E. (1994). The evaluation of a church-based lay counseling program: Some preliminary data. *Journal of Psychology and Christianity, 13,* 270-75.

Fernando Garzon, Psy.D.

Fernando Garzon is a professor and the Assistant Dean for Academics in the School of Psychology and Counseling at Regent University. His research interests and publications focus on spiritual interventions in counseling, such as Christian meditation, adapting mindfulness for Christians, applying grace in acceptance-based therapies (ACT, etc.), and inner healing prayer. Dr. Garzon also researches lay Christian counseling approaches (Freedom in Christ, Theophostic Ministry, etc.), Christian integration pedagogy, and multicultural issues. His clinical experience encompasses outpatient practice, managed care, and hospital and church settings. Many of Dr. Garzon's articles are catalogued and can be accessed at http://works.bepress.com/fernando_garzon/.

Jichan J. Kim, Ph.D

Jichan Kim is an assistant professor in the Department of Psychology at Liberty University. He earned his B.A. from City College of New York, an M.A. and M.Div. from Gordon-Conwell Theological Seminary, an Ed.M. from Harvard University, and his Ph.D. from the University of Wisconsin-Madison. Dr. Kim's published research focuses on forgiveness psychology and immigrant communities. Jichan is an ordained pastor and has served in Korean immigrant churches in New York City, near Boston, and in Madison, WI in various capacities for over a decade.

Melvin E. Pride, Ph.D.

Melvin Pride is an Associate Professor of Counseling and the Director of Clinical Training at Liberty University, where he also serves on the counseling remediation committee. With over 15 years of counseling experience as a Licensed Professional Counselor, Dr. Pride has a passion for student improvement and for bridging relational obstacles among different people groups. He is a member of the American Association of Christian Counselors, the American Counseling Association, and the Association for Spiritual, Ethical, and Religious Values in Counseling.

Dwight Rice, Ph.D.

Dwight Rice is an assistant professor, instructional mentor, and director of the Masters in Pastoral Counseling in the Department of Community Care and Counseling at Liberty University. Dr. Rice's research interests include growing in favor with God and others, behavioral assessments, and the skillful use of hobbies in self-care.

CHAPTER 10

How to Develop an Effective Multicultural Ministry

Fernando Garzon, Psy.D., Jichan Kim, Ph.D.,
Melvin Pride, Ph.D., Dwight Rice, Ph.D.

The Word of God equips us for every good work (2 Timothy 3:16-17, NIV), yet only with cultural knowledge can we convey scriptural truths in a form in which they can be heard and understood (1 Corinthians 9:19-23). Ministries in the U.S. today clearly face more complicated challenges than in previous decades. The struggle to navigate today's unique social climate and build an effective multicultural ministry requires a multidimensional skillset. We realize also that the appearance and outworking of multicultural ministry will differ depending on each ministry's context for and model of such ministry. However, regardless of the context and model, a holistic understanding of personhood and relationship is essential. Ministers have the opportunity to reflect Christ's love in every multicultural relational encounter. Indeed, our influence moves those we relate to either toward or away from Christ (Lawrenz, 2012). If we assume that every relational difficulty or struggle with culturally diverse people is rooted in a spiritual problem, we may neglect important cultural differences that are contributing to the issue. Unintentionally, we may impede the power of the gospel message through lack of awareness of these differences.

The purpose of this chapter is to empower persons interested in developing an effective multicultural ministry to reach various cultural groups more effectually. We will do this in several ways. First, we will examine three of the most populous cultural groups in the United States: African Americans, Latino Americans, and Asian Americans. (Unfortunately, chapter length constraints prevent exploration of Native Americans, Whites, and multi-racial individuals.) We will consider these three groups by using two brief case scenarios at the beginning of each section and then connecting those cases to key demographics, values, and issues related to that particular group. Of course, we proceed with the caveat that the two cases and information in each section are not meant to stereotype. Rather than a gross oversimplification, we hope each section highlights a few of the many unique journeys of individuals in these groups. We also desire each section to highlight useful adjustments that can be made in ministry to make it more multiculturally effective.

African Americans

African Americans in the U.S. have always faced "contemporary" racial issues. From times of slavery to segregation to obtaining civil rights until now, they have always addressed such challenges and overcome them. However, the tendencies of society at large to avoid discussing this group's historical experiences, to inadequately understand its struggle to deal with racism, and to fail to grasp the consequent implications of these experiences have added to the difficulty in dealing with each challenge. Therefore, the first recommendation for ministries is apparent: it is critical that ministries be ready to address such issues head on. We believe that no organization, institution, or people group is better equipped to handle authentic race relationships and to act as a healing force in our society than is the church.

As was noted in the introduction to this chapter, there are numerous subcultures within every group, so it is a big mistake to assume that all African Americans are like the two case scenarios given below. We will address the areas of demographics, culture, diversity and implications for ministry.

Case Scenarios

Jim, a "baby boomer" by generation, was born in 1960 and grew up in a farming community. His parents both dropped out of school in the sixth grade, but Jim completed high school and then college (obtaining a business degree) through his military service. While successful, he believes that he has not been allowed the same opportunities as his White counterparts. He remembers the times of segregation and turbulence in

American society and personally experienced the fight for integration. His parents' Christian faith and the values they instilled in him helped him through this time. He is married and has three children. Jim continues to receive encouragement and emotional support from his church and his family, and he values these relationships.

Bruce is 26 years old and grew up in the inner city in a single parent home. He has been in trouble with the law on several occasions and has had difficulty maintaining a decent paying job. He has three children, but is estranged from his wife. He works two jobs to try to provide for himself and pay support to his wife for his children. Although exposed to the church, Bruce is not a committed Christian. He does not rely on the church as a resource, though he sometimes attends church on special occasions.

African American Demographics, Diversity, and Implications for Ministry

According to the United States' census bureau, the African American culture has grown from 12.6% of the population in 2010 to 13.6% in 2015. This people group is considered to be a very religious group. The Pew Research Center (2009) observes that 87% of African Americans describe themselves as belonging to one religious group or another. Jim and Bruce represent two people from different eras and different life experiences; however, they have in common an exposure to spiritual things, such as church, prayer, songs of praise, and the power of faith. This characteristic is often overlooked by both churches and other ministry groups that are trying to build a relationship with African Americans. However, when this fact is approached with authenticity, it can be a natural bridge for any ministry attempting to reach this broad culture.

But what is the proper term to use to address this group? Prior to the 1960s, those in political power gave names such as Negro and Colored to African Americans (Hayes and Erford, 2010). Such terms continue to carry strong negative connotations because of their connection to historical segregation. Though originally also considered a negative term, the term Black was popularized in the 1960s as a positive identification with the slogan "Black is beautiful." Singers such as James Brown with his hit song,

"I'm Black and I'm Proud" (Boyd-Franklin, 1989) endorsed it. The self-identification as Black signified the first time that African Americans had named themselves instead of being named by the dominant culture. In the 1980s, Jesse Jackson was credited with introducing the designation African American, which was intended to connect Black Americans to Africa as a part of their heritage. Because of the times in which they were born, Jim is more apt to identify with the term Black, whereas Bruce is more inclined to identify with African American. Neither term is offensive today; however if in doubt, ask which term is preferable.

Traditional Values and Implications for Ministry

As is indicated above, faith is important to many African American people (Boyd-Franklin 2010), and the church as an institution plays a very important role in this community. Historically, the church has provided security, support, leadership opportunities, strong interpersonal relationships, and a sense of belonging. Jim experienced this sense of belonging and connectedness in his life, but Bruce, although exposed to spiritual things, did not have the same experience.

Additional values lie in collectivistic allegiance to the family and a general sense of identity and loyalty to their cultural group. Billingsley and Caldwell (1994) and Boyd-Franklin (1989) describe the African American family as a strong diverse institution in the Black community. It may be composed of "persons related by blood, marriage, formal adoption, informal adoption or by simple appropriation (p. 429)." This definition incorporates both the single family unit and other support systems for this entity. Therefore, it is important for ministries not to restrict their view of the African American family to the traditional nuclear family exclusively (Boyd-Franklin, 1989). Historical context helps this make sense. Slaves were not always allowed to remain together as a family unit, so other configurations of family structures were adapted for survival. In regard to strong cultural group identity, the powerful historical/contemporary experiences and overall societal difficulty in processing these occurrences solidified a strong group identification.

Education is also a key value for African Americans. In Jim's case, his parents had only sixth grade educations, but they instilled in Jim the value of education. He would be the first in his family to finish high school and the first to finish college, effectively placing himself and his children in a better economic position and providing a model for his other relatives. In working with Jim, acknowledging this accomplishment would be important. The example set for his children, nieces, and nephews will be meaningful to the family's future. Bruce's strength can be seen in his desire to care for his family. Although he is not in the home, he exhibits a sense of responsibility by attempting to provide support. He obviously chose crime at some points in his life; however, his exposure to the church has planted seeds for him to return to the church on special occasions. These are seeds that culturally sensitive ministries may harvest.

Common Mental Health Issues and Implications for Ministry

Common mental health issues for African Americans include depression, anxiety, anger, and PTSD (Hayes & Erford, 2010; Parham, 2002). Jim, although successful, may exhibit some forms of depression and anger influenced by the unfair racial treatment he received in his struggle to advance in the business world. A major key to ministering to Jim is an authentic acknowledgement of and help for him to verbalize the challenges he has overcome, including any experiences of implicit or overt racial discrimination. Since Jim has experienced strong relationships and connections in his life, he would likely value a genuine open relationship with someone ministering to him.

Bruce grew up in a different context (the inner city) where he may have experienced or witnessed violence. He could possibly be suffering from anxiety, anger, or even PTSD from having grown up in this setting. He, too, would value an authentic relationship with a genuine connection. However, the lack of trust embedded in his experience means that ministries must be ready to earn a relationship with him. Bruce may give subtle tests to see if he can trust those who are trying to minister to him.

African American Section Summary

We have attempted to address some of the background inherent in ministering to the African American community. Of major importance are spirituality, authenticity, and an understanding of the significance of historical events and discrimination affecting this cultural group. African Americans represent a diverse population. The number exposed to religious experiences implies a high potential for connection with caring ministry groups. Recognizing the historical climate that African Americans have endured or been influenced by can help in building an alliance of trust with the Black individual. We are not advocating a sense of guilt or shame in these matters, but rather a genuine, authentic response to the unique experiences embedded in the group's history.

Latino Americans

In this section, we will explore two case scenarios that highlight different aspects of Latino experience in the United States. Periodically, we will use them as examples as we consider this culture's demographics, values, and common mental health issues. We will also note throughout this section the implications of this information on how to build an effective ministry with the Latino population.

Case Scenarios

Rodrigo and his family are evangelical Christians originally living in a poor slum in San Salvador, El Salvador. "Poor" in his country meant that his family lived in a small, hut-like home with metal sidings, a dirt floor, no indoor plumbing, and a tin roof. The neighborhood was caught in the midst of a violent drug gang war, and his family was suffering hunger. Fearing for his family's safety, Rodrigo asked God to help him move them out of this "war zone." He constantly looked for work, and in desperation, he finally told his family he was leaving to find employment in the United States. He made the treacherous journey through Guatemala into Mexico and finally into the United States. Finding work in construction and living in a small apartment with eight other construction workers, he regularly sent money back to his family. Over several years, his family was able to move into a much better house in a safer neighborhood, and they had food and clothing. Rodrigo has remained in the same apartment located in a predominantly Latino neighborhood, and he speaks Spanish most of the time when not at his job. He praises God for answering his prayer.

Juanita is a second-generation 24-year-old whose devout Catholic parents came to the United States from Guatemala 26 years ago. Her father continues to work in a factory while her mother does housecleaning. Juanita is a U.S. citizen by birth. She became a born again Christian at 16 and speaks English fluently as a native speaker. She has many U.S. majority culture friends as well as Latino friends. She has graduated from college with a degree in accounting and has been working for a firm for the last two years. She recently married Roy, a White person. Clashes with her parents sometimes occur. They have been encouraging her to have children and have been making hints about moving in together with her and her husband. Juanita is trying to balance cultural respect for her parents with living the life she wants with Roy.

Illegal Immigration, Latino Demographics, Diversity, and Implications for Ministry

As Rodrigo's case scenario highlights, embedded in the illegal immigration issue are important personal stories that are sometimes missed in the national discussion. Missing these stories is a key mistake for any ministry desiring to work with Latinos, as it generates judgment and condemnation rather than compassion and understanding. We are not advocating for illegal immigration but rather are highlighting to ministries the importance of empathizing with the motivations for illegal immigration; such understanding is critical in order for any outreach to be effective. What would you do in a situation like Rodrigo's?

Both Rodrigo and Juanita exemplify the numerous countries Latinos come from. All Latinos are not Mexicans. Ministries must be careful to learn about participants individually regarding their country of origin and also how they like to call themselves. (Some prefer their country-of-origin name over Latino, and some react negatively to the term "Hispanic," so be careful with that term.) Now the second largest ethnic group in the United States, the Latino population is projected to be over 30% of the U.S. population by 2050 (Shrestha & Heisler, 2011). A wide diversity of lifestyles exists in this population. Juanita and Rodrigo are clearly two very different people.

Indeed, Latinos vary in many ways—racially, politically, educationally, economically, religiously, and in their reasons for immigration. Racially, for example, some Latinos retain Indian tribal identities along with their national identities. Socio-economic aspects also differ. Juanita is definitely middle class, while Rodrigo has a lower socio-economic status (SES). Though the Roman Catholic population is large in Central and South America, the evangelical church population also continues to grow. Folk religions and syncretism may be seen among both religious populations, so keep in mind that even if someone self-identifies as a Christian and is involved in your ministry, that doesn't necessarily mean that folk religions are not being practiced.

Their generation of immigration (first, second, third, etc.), language usage, and social surroundings are critical in understanding a Latino person's unique expression of culture. Juanita is second-generation and has many U.S. majority culture friends as well as Latina friends, so her values may vary substantially from the traditional values that her parents or Rodrigo are more likely to hold.

Latino Traditional Values and Implications for Ministry

When one recognizes the diversity of subcultures embedded in the Latino culture and how context variables like generation of immigration, language usage, and social context can create unique expressions of individuality, he or she is ready to consider some core traditional values that may or may not be expressed in the person participating in ministry. *Familismo, machismo, marianismo, personalismo, sympatía, respeto, confianza,* and *fatalismo* represent traditional Latino values (Moitinho, Garzon, & Davila, 2013).

Familismo involves a collectivistic and family-centered stance toward personal decisions and activities. Great emphasis is placed on how one's choices impact others—especially the family—rather than just focusing on the self. When parents are first-generation or very traditional, a patriarchal hierarchy often exists, and extended family may be living together in the same house or nearby. Traditional husbands may exhibit a *machismo* gender role which, when expressed positively, involves emphasis on being a protector, provider, and primary decision-maker; negatively it can lead to abuse. A traditional wife sometimes will take on a *marianismo* complementary role. This involves self-sacrifice for the family, long suffering, and being a nurturer of the children. As a second-generation Latina, Juanita exemplifies how differences can emerge between generations in the ways in which various aspects of these values are expressed. She cherishes her parents but also wants a life of her own with her husband. It is likely that her ideas of her proper gender roles may also vary from *marianismo*. If she and her husband have children, their kids will likely move even further away from the traditional values of Juanita's parents. This highlights how important it is for ministries to find ways to accommodate the different value systems embedded in Latino persons who are involved in ministry activities.

Personalismo reflects unhurried warm personal interactions with a sense that people are more important than projects or things. This means that persons in ministry must focus on building relationships rather than just creating lots of activities. *Sympatía* conveys a focus on harmony, avoidance of conflict, and indirect or subtle communications rather than direct confrontations. Juanita may want to navigate her concerns with her parents' desires in a way that conveys respect (*respeto*) rather than confronting them directly about their wishes.

Relationships with *confianza* imply that there is familiarity and trust in the relationship, both of which matter more than job titles or normal ministry processes. For example, if a traditional Latino person knows you well personally and needs something from your ministry, she will want to talk with you directly, rather than dealing with others in the ministry that she does not know, even though it may appear more appropriate to deal with them because of their job title. *Fatalismo* is sometimes seen in Roman Catholic contexts and conveys a sense that all of life is uncertain and that a person can do little to alter his or her fate. Of course, when it is evident that this value is present and producing harmful effects in a person, the good news of the gospel can have a positive impact on the person's heart and perspective.

Common Mental Health Issues and Implications for Ministry

Several key issues impact the Latino community. These include immigration stress, acculturation stress (the stress of adjusting to a new culture and finding one's own voice in the new context), depression, alcohol/substance abuse, domestic violence, suicide, and anxiety (Rios-Ellis, 2005). The case scenarios will be used to help understand some of these issues, although they can be produced by many different cultural life experiences.

Rodrigo misses his family, has left a very dangerous neighborhood in El Salvador, and has experienced a treacherous journey to enter the United States. He is now facing all of these immigration-related stressors along with the need to adjust to the U.S. majority culture, learn to speak English, and navigate a very foreign world. One can readily see that the combination of these challenges leaves Rodrigo vulnerable to depression. Also, there is no guarantee that his apartment-mates are godly people. If he feels isolated from positive supports, substance abuse becomes a real possibility. In addition, more than 25% of Latino marriages experience domestic violence, and the rate of suicide is higher for Latinos than for African Americans, Asians, or Whites (Rios-Ellis, 2005).

Juanita has a different experience as a second-generation Latina with many U.S. majority culture friends, although she may experience anxiety as she attempts to respond to her traditional parents and adjust to life in an intercultural marriage with her White husband. Of course, Rodrigo and Juanita are only examples of the many ways that these mental health issues can be expressed in Latinos. They are merely intended to give you an idea of the possibilities.

Ministries can play a critical role both for Rodrigo and Juanita. One of the most important initial needs for Rodrigo is to develop a healthy support network. The church and its related ministries are perfect places for him to connect with a life-giving, stabilizing spiritual community. This could greatly diminish the temptations for substance abuse or getting trapped into harmful relationships or patterns. Juanita and her parents need ministries that can adapt to the unique needs of different generations of Latinos. A "one size fits all" ministry tailored just for traditional Latinos may miss ministering to the needs of second-generation Latinas like Juanita and third-generation Latinos. As implied previously, second and third-generation children raised in the United States and immersed in U.S. culture may clash with their traditional parents, especially around dating practices. Ministries ready to identify with these situations can provide a spiritual and cultural bridge to the restoration of family unity and harmony.

Latino American Section Summary

Aside from the political debate, ministries that want to be effective with Latinos must understand the personal stories, like Rodrigo's, embedded in legal and illegal immigration into the United States. The expression of Latino culture varies with each person. It is critical to consider and take into account a Latino person's generation of immigration (first, second, third, etc.), language usage, and social surroundings. Depending on these and other aspects, the core Latino traditional values described above may or may not be expressed. Specific mental health issues impact this community, and the church can play a key role in ministering to the needs of this population.

Asian Americans

We now introduce two unique, yet hardly uncommon, cases of individuals who would be identified as Asian or Asian American. Our purpose in so doing is to stimulate a conversation around the ministry with and for such populations in the U.S. These cases are only a small sample of the many unique cultural expressions by people in this group.

Case Scenarios

Jeff is a 22-year-old Hmong American who was born in Thailand and came to the U.S. at the age of four in 1998. He lives in a suburban area near Minneapolis, MN, and as a first-generation college student in his family, he someday hopes to become an entrepreneur running an international business outside the U.S. His family came to the U.S. to escape political persecution against those who, like his father, fought on the side of the U.S.

during the Vietnam War. His family clan has two mothers (one step and one biological) through whom he has nine biological and step siblings. His father is legally divorced from his biological mother, but that was done only to get around the U.S. law that prohibits polygamy – a common practice among the Hmong people back in his home country. Jeff's family used to practice Shamanistic spiritual rituals together with other Hmong relatives and friends even after moving to the U.S. However, his family subsequently began attending a Hmong immigrant church where Jeff accepted Christ as his Savior. When he first stepped out of his ethnic community to attend elementary school, he felt isolated as an ethnic and language minority, but his desire to live a better life than his economically-disadvantaged parents motivated him to strive to achieve upward mobility through education.

Sung-hee is a 36-year-old undocumented immigrant living in New York City. She was a full-time mother of two young children in the Republic of Korea and came to the U.S. nine years ago with her husband who had had a hard time making the family's ends meet as a construction worker back in Korea. Her family of four came to the U.S. in hopes of achieving their own American Dream. She currently works as a waitress at a nearby Korean restaurant, while her husband works at a large Korean market as a stocker. They first began attending a large Korean immigrant church in Queens, NY to get social support among other Korean immigrants, but Sung-hee gradually became a fervent believer of Christ and is now actively involved in the congregation in various ways. They currently live a minimalist lifestyle by necessity; they do not own a car, they are renting a two-bedroom apartment for $1,500 a month, which is almost half of their combined monthly incomes, and they have not had a chance to travel outside the New York City metropolitan area. They often hear about other immigrants' success stories, and they hope they can have their own success story in the near future.

Asian Demographics, Diversity, and Implications for Ministry

"Asian American" or "Asian" is an umbrella term that covers people from different geographic regions in Asia and the Pacific Islands (e.g., Polynesia and Southeast Asia), as well as from different ethnic (e.g., Chinese, Hmong, Indonesian, Samoan, and Tibetan) and generational backgrounds (e.g., first-generation immigrants, and second and third-generation immigrant children). There are 20.3 million Asians in the U.S. (identifying themselves solely as Asian or as Asian in combination with another race). 6.3 million of them live in California, and 4.5 million Asians identify themselves as Chinese according to 2014 population estimates published by the U.S. Census Bureau (2016). Despite the presence of dominant subculture groups in the U.S. (e.g., Chinese), neglecting the stories of Jeff or Sung-hee will only result in marginalizing many others who also are welcome to be part of the Body of Christ in the United States

Given the diversity within and also between Asian populations, ministers should give careful thought as to why they would like to identify certain people in their congregation by their racial or ethnic identity. A rushed racial or ethnic identification might backfire because it can be seen as evidence of one's lack of awareness of individual, generational, cultural, and economical differences among the varied cultures embedded within such a broad term as "Asian." For instance, although Jeff was born in Thailand and can be easily identified as a person of Asian descent by appearance, he might not feel always comfortable being differentiated as someone who has a hyphenated identity (Asian "-"American) or is associated with a particular ethnic group. Through his schooling in the U.S., English has become his dominant language (even though he learned it as a second language), and he now identifies himself culturally as more American than as a person from a particular Asian country or ethnic group. For that reason, being sensitive to (Jeff's and) others' differences requires a deep level of humility. Listening to individuals' unique stories by creating a space where they can disclose who they are without the fear of their stories being invalidated, should be the initial step toward building trust in a multicultural ministry context.

Specific Issues Faced by Asians in the U.S. and Implications for an Effective Multicultural Ministry

First, intergenerational conflicts, which occur when children's rates of acculturation outpace that of their parents, need special attention because the tension between older and younger generations can become a source of mental health issues. For instance, intergenerational conflicts and youth acculturation issues are risk factors for Asian American youths' suicidal behaviors (Lau, Jernewall, Zane, & Myers, 2002). Despite the potential danger of categorizing diverse cultures into two simple categories, a tendency has been well-documented that while the West tends to emphasize independence, the East tends to emphasize interdependence—"I" culture vs. "we" culture (Lee & Mock, 2005)—in that in the East, one's identity is so enmeshed with that of the family or community that what one does either brings honor or shame to the community. This shame can become a source of anxiety and depression among Asian Americans, and it seems to be linked to Asian Americans' hesitation to seek outside help for life struggles in general and mental health issues in particular.

Sung-hee's life revolves around the Korean ethnic community, making her acculturation into the dominant society difficult. However, she enjoys serving the Lord in her Korean community and is grateful to have a strong ethnic identity as a Korean. Meanwhile, her children, similar to the case of Jeff, will experience their own set of difficulties as they struggle to be part of the dominant culture group while maintaining a connection with their cultural heritage. We urge ministries to consider this question: Which aspects of the cultural and generational differences should be respected or transformed? Parent-child conversations are often challenged when they are impeded by the indirect and restrained communication style, hierarchical relationships, and inhibition of emotional expression common to Asian culture (Uba, 1994). Ministers may then be able to play an important role as a liaison between generations, making constructive conversations and peaceful negotiations plausible.

Another issue needing special attention crosses class and racial lines: the model minority myth, in which Asian Americans are portrayed as "a hardworking, successful, and law-abiding ethnic minority that overcome hardship, oppression, and discrimination to achieve great success" (Chao, Chiu, & Lee, 2010, p.44). However, Wu's (2002) verdict seems correct here; the model minority myth is an oversimplification of millions of Asians in the U.S. It is also a concealed racial taunt to a group not necessarily thriving economically or emotionally given the hardships many Asian Americans face, particularly in light of the increasing interracial and/or interethnic tensions in many inner city areas. The subtle messages of this myth can take a toll on the mental health of Asian Americans who experience stress, shame, depression, and anxiety as they strive to fit into such a romanticized portrayal of who they should be (Tang, 2007). However, differences between Asian immigrants' socio-economic backgrounds in their country of origin may play a significant role in their success, since immigrants who come from more prosperous backgrounds, even if they are from the same ethnic group, tend to have a better chance at their American Dream than those from less prosperous backgrounds (Louie, 2004). Furthermore, those who need the most attention within the Asian community (Jeff's parents for instance) may continue to be neglected if others are quick to identify them as outliers or interpret their silence as doing fine.

As a college student, Jeff might easily be seen as a model minority with a bright future (as predicted by the myth); however, what others fail to see is that he cannot receive any educational support from his non-English speaking parents who lack both an understanding of the U.S. educational system and the financial resources to support his education. Regardless of others' misunderstanding, he still has to deal with the very real fact that full responsibility, along with heavy pressure, is placed on him and on him alone. Also, sooner or later Sung-hee will have to learn the reality, without losing her hope for a better future, that she is precious in God's sight apart from her own or others' evaluations of her success.

Asian American Section Summary

Intergenerational conflicts can increase tensions within the households of Asian Americans, and the model minority myth can increase tensions across different social classes and racial groups. Hope for true healing of these tensions can only be found through the message of the gospel that unites all people across all generations, classes, and races through the cross of Christ. As sensitive ministers diligently work to reduce racial prejudices and cultural stereotypes and resolve disparities where necessary, they should also be extremely diligent to present Christ's forgiving love that cures the wounds so prevalent in the hearts of Asians plagued by such tensions.

Conclusion

The harvest is plentiful, but the laborers are few (Matthew 9:37). We have presented what amounts to a wide door of opportunity (1 Corinthians 16:9) for anyone seeking to minister to these cultural groups. Our hope is that you now have a broader picture of African Americans, Latino Americans, and Asian Americans, and that you feel better equipped in your work with these wonderful children of God. May the Lord bless you in your calling.

References

Billingsley, A., & Caldwell, C. (1994). The church, the family, and the school in the African American community. *The Journal of Negro Education, 60*, 427-440.

Boyd-Franklin, N. (2010). Incorporating spirituality and religion into the treatment of African

American clients. *The Counseling Psychologist 38*(7) 976–1000. Washington, DC: Sage Publishing. doi: 10.1177/0011000010374881

Boyd-Franklin, N., & Lockwood, T. W. (2009). Spirituality and religion: Implications for psychotherapy with African American families. In F. Walsh (Ed.), *Spiritual resources in family therapy* (pp. 141-155). New York, NY: Guildford Press.

Boyd-Franklin, N. (1989). *Black families in therapy: A multisystems approach*. New York, NY: Guildford Press.

Chao, M. M., Chiu, C. & Lee, J. S. (2010). Asians as the model minority: Implications for U.S. government's policies. *Asian Journal of Social Psychology, 13*(1), 44–52.

Hayes, D. G, & Erford, B. T. (2010). *Developing multicultural counseling competence: a systems approach*. New York, NY: Pearson.

Lau, A. S., Jernewall, N. M., Zane, N., & Myers, H. F. (2002). Correlates of suicidal behaviors among Asian American outpatients youths. *Cultural Diversity & Ethnic Minority Psychology, 9*(3), 199–213.

Lawrenz, M. (2012). *Spiritual influence: The hidden power behind leadership.* Grand Rapids, MI: Zondervan.

Lee, E., & Mock, M. R. (2005). Asian families: An overview. In M. McGoldrick, J. Giordano, & N. Garcia-Preto (Eds.), *Ethnicity & family therapy* (3rd ed.) (pp.269–289). New York: The Guildford Press.

Louie V. S. (2004). *Compelled to excel: Immigration, education, and opportunity among Chinese Americans.* Stanford, CA: Stanford University Press.

Moitinho, E., Garzon, F., & Davila, Z. (2013, September). *Mi casa es su casa: Essentials for counseling Hispanic/Latino clients effectively.* Presentation at the American Association of Christian Counselors World Conference.

Parham, T. A. (2002). *Counseling persons of African descent.* Thousand Oaks, CA: Sage.

Pew Research Center (2009). A religious portrait of African Americans. Religion and Public Life. Retrieved from http://www.pewforum.org/2009/01/30/african-americans-and-religion/

Rios-Ellis, B. (2005). Critical disparities in Latino mental health: Transforming research into action. *Research National Council of La Raza, Institute for Hispanic Health White paper.*

Shrestha, L., & Heisler, E. (2011). The changing demographic profile of the United States. *Congressional Research Service, 22.*

Tang, M. (2007). Psychological effects on being perceived as a "model minority" for Asian Americans. *New Waves: Educational Research and Development, 11*(3), 11–16.

Uba, L. (1994). *Asian Americans: Personality patterns, identity, and mental health*. New York: The Guilford Press.

U.S. Census Bureau. (2016, April 21). *Profile America facts for features: CB16-FF.07. Asian/Pacific American Heritage Month: May 2016*. Retrieved from http://www.census.gov/newsroom/facts-for-features/2016/cb16-ff07.html

Wu, F. H. (2002). *Yellow: Race in America beyond black and white*. New York: Basic Books.

Mac and Mary Owen

 As a testimony to God's saving grace and power, Mac Owen was rescued from certain death (both spiritual and physical) as a result of drug and alcohol addiction on February 22, 1988. When Mac accepted God's call, the Father refused to let him stay where he was and started carrying out the work he had begun in Mac. In 1990 Mac and Mary started a recovery ministry for addicts and their loved ones.

Mac served as an elder at White's Ferry Road Church in West Monroe, LA for 17 years. In 2006 Mac became the Louisiana Celebrate Recovery State Representative. Today Mac is the Celebrate Recovery National Director, and Mary is the Celebrate Recovery National Training Coach. Mac and Mary work for Saddleback Church in Lake Forest, CA, facilitating Celebrate Recovery workshops all over the world, equipping church leaders to start this ministry in their churches and reach out to the hurting in their communities.

Mac and Mary have been married for 40 years. Their three children are all active believers who have married and blessed them with ten grandchildren. The Owens moved to Colorado in 2012 where Mac is now an elder at Impact Christian Church. They teach Bible classes and speak at church and community events and marriage retreats. Their story of redemption is told in their book, *Never Let Go,* written with Travis Thrasher.

Mac and Mary's mission, through the power of Jesus Christ, is to bind up the brokenhearted and to proclaim freedom for the captives of sin and release from darkness for the prisoners of hurts, hang-ups, and habits (Isaiah 61).

CHAPTER 11

How to Develop an Effective Substance Abuse Recovery Ministry

Mac Owen and
Mary Owen

One day my (Mary's) father woke up to find my mother sitting on the floor, holding my six-week-old brother. She had a haunting, blank stare on her face. Little Johnny was just lying in her arms, fussing and crying – yet she was unresponsive to him. This went on for two days. Doctors said she needed to be admitted to the state hospital. Once there, the medical staff wouldn't tell Dad anything about her condition or let him see her. It took several weeks to obtain a court order to see her.

Appalled to find my mother in a tiny room, crouched in a corner like a wild, caged animal, Dad immediately brought her home. He wondered if she would ever function in life again. Eventually, that state mental hospital was closed down due to its barbaric (mis)treatment of those with mental health issues.

My parents were young and hadn't been married long. They were full of love and life. But now my parents' battle with an unknown illness began. The term "paranoid schizophrenic" didn't mean anything to my father. He only knew that the woman he loved was sick, and he now had a family secret.

I met Mac when we were fifteen and sixteen years old, respectively. I became pregnant after having sex, ironically the first time for both of us. I added another silent, stigmatized, shameful secret to our family.

Rumors circulated at church about why I mysteriously vanished during the summer of '75. Nobody in our church that we knew of had ever been pregnant outside of marriage, so I planned a summer-long trip to go out of town in order to keep intact my secret of placing our baby for adoption. Mac and I married one-and-a-half years later, and we partied all the time.

We later learned that our partying lifestyle helped mask our guilt from giving up the child we would never know.

We also didn't know at the time that Mac was heading down the road to drug addiction. He often acted truly insane, and I worried, "Could Mac have mental health issues like my mother?" Our family was disintegrating before my eyes. I tried to keep the rest of the world from seeing how broken we had become. I had another shame-filled secret to keep, and my sorrows continued, but *God* knew. *God* knew everything. Psalm 56:8 (NLT) says, "… You have collected all my tears in your bottle. You have recorded each one in your book."

I now found myself a daughter, wife, and young mother facing the reality that my life wasn't going to be the white picket fence fairy tale I thought everybody else was living. My mother was schizophrenic. My husband was a drug addict. We had a son we would never know, and I was trying to shield our two young daughters from the reality of our life and give them some semblance of normalcy. Yet I couldn't do enough and control enough and say enough. I was totally powerless. Nothing was in my control.

1988 was a watershed year for our family. We began to face and deal with some of our family secrets. Like the secret of Mac's addiction, which suddenly came out in the open when he confessed before our church that he was a drug addict. Like the secret of our baby we placed for adoption, who we now knew was blessed with a good Christian home. But we continued to keep secret my mother's mental health issues because we didn't want people calling her crazy, which was society's label for people with her condition. So we kept her situation private, and my father took the brunt of the shame and weight of my mother's mental health issues.

That same year, I heard about something that might wake my mother up from a lifetime of agonizing mental torture. While watching *20/20* on TV, I heard about a new drug called "the Lazarus pill" that would figuratively wake people up from the dead. The drug was Clozaril, and the amazing thing was that people who had schizophrenia and used it were coming back to life. After some research the doctor told Dad, "Your wife is going to be the first person in Louisiana to use it."

Since my mother despised going to hospitals, they decided to give it to her at home, but the first hurdle was getting her off her current medications. Through the years doctors had put her on so many different kinds of medicine to calm down her system that her body had become addicted to them. Throughout my entire childhood, I watched my mother take a shoebox of medicine daily, and now she ended up getting off all of them… going cold turkey. It was brutal. For several days, all my mother did was crouch in the corner of the bathroom in her nightgown. I stayed there with my father to help them through the process. Mom was catatonic the whole time, she wouldn't eat, and we could barely get her to drink a little water.

After a very rough few days, one night we gave her a tiny little Clozaril pill before going to bed. The next morning she was completely dressed, smiling, and asking what we wanted for breakfast! It was as if the past few days *and the last few decades* had never happened. It *was* like Lazarus waking from the dead!

While we were dealing – privately – with all these family secrets, we thought that if we ever shared them with our church, we would be shunned and shamed and told not to come back. But that's not what happened. When we finally got up the courage to confess the truth before our church family, they were truly loving and supportive and broken-hearted with us that we had gone through this pain alone. They were there for us every step of the way as we began to deal openly with these struggles.

Our story shows how, although Satan tries his very best to tear every good thing apart, God always wins! Things weren't perfect—and never will be until we get to heaven—but through the darkness, God's church became a beacon of light and hope. The question isn't whether bad things will come your way, nor is it, "When will they arrive?" The question is, "What are you going to do when the bad times show up?" Are you going to try to muscle through alone and fail? Or will you turn to the one place meant to be the safest place on earth (and which features a *sanctuary*), God's church?

Even though Mac and I found much healing, we still have hurt in our lives. No one is fully free from hurt on this earth. But being part of God's forever family now, we don't face our struggles, shame, and stigma alone.

So as leaders in the church, what do we do with people who are showing up with drug and alcohol addictions and/or mental health issues?

Celebrate Recovery has become one of the best vehicles for bringing people to Jesus and helping hurting people find hope in the church.

Celebrate Recovery has helped millions of people find healing from their hurts, hang-ups, and habits. Over 35,000 churches are using the Celebrate Recovery curriculum, which gives churches the tools they need to reach out to those they previously didn't know how to help.

Celebrate Recovery is a non-denominational, thoroughly biblical and balanced program for helping people overcome their hurts, hang-ups, and habits. It uses eight principles based on the Beatitudes from Christ's Sermon on the Mount and twelve biblical steps of recovery. Through this program, people have been restored and have developed stronger relationships with God and with others. In this safe and accepting atmosphere, thousands of people who struggle with all kinds of life-controlling substances and behaviors have been helped along the road to recovery.

What is Celebrate Recovery?

A safe place to share.
A place to come as you are.
A refuge.
A place of belonging.
A place to care for others and be cared for.
A place where we highly regard confidentiality.
A place to learn.

What Celebrate Recovery Is Not:

Therapy.
A place for secrets.
A place to look for dating relationships.
A place to rescue or be rescued by others.
A place for perfection.
A place to judge others.
A quick fix.

How Does Celebrate Recovery Compare to Counseling Ministries?

Celebrate Recovery is not a counseling ministry nor is it a substitute for professional counseling. Celebrate Recovery is a biblical and Christ-centered ministry, taking participants through a process of restoring their relationship with God, themselves, and others. Celebrate Recovery takes place in a group setting, and participants are invited to share openly about their struggles and victories. Participants do not attempt to "fix" each other. Instead, they are offered a Christian community in which to find support, encouragement, hope, unconditional love, and acceptance.

Originally structured to provide support for those in recovery from alcohol and drug addictions, in 2016 Celebrate Recovery started a new initiative for those with mental health issues. People dealing with mental health issues are nothing new. However, with Celebrate Recovery, our approach is becoming more compassionate and accepting. We want to strive to be effective in supporting people who are living with some form of a mental and/or relational health challenge.

Celebrate Recovery Wants to Help Break the Stigma for Those Who Struggle with Mental Health Issues.

Statistics show that almost half of all human beings experience some type of mental and/or relational health issue(s) in their lifetime. It is time for us to start treating mental and relational health as a normal issue that people can talk about. This is an important step in helping those struggling with mental health issues. We want to show the world that seeking help is a positive step, and what better place than Celebrate Recovery to admit these struggles?

When Celebrate Recovery first started in 1991 with just 43 people at Saddleback Church in Lake Forest, California, few people in the church talked about sex addiction, IV drug use, and prostitution. Now we see these struggles being discussed in churches all over the world. People are being given a safe place to speak up without shame. By treating mental health issues, along with addictions, as something that can be a common part of the human condition, we can help remove the stigma that keeps people silent—and not seeking help—for fear of being judged and rejected.

As leaders in Celebrate Recovery, our role is not to clinically treat those struggling with mental health, relational, and substance abuse issues. Our position is to support them. We believe the largest factor in the effectiveness of the recovery process is removing the isolation addicts face due to their paralyzing sense of shame.

"Then the LORD God said, 'It is not good that the man should be alone; I will make him a helper fit for him'" (Genesis 2:18, ESV). Right from the beginning, God made it clear that we are not meant to be alone; we are meant to be in community. Especially when things are difficult, we need each other. This verse talks about the creation of Eve for Adam, but even Jesus—who was certainly fully capable of being by himself—wanted and needed friends when he was struggling emotionally. His disciples were more than just students getting ready to become preachers; they were Jesus's friends. They hung out, they ate together, and they shared their lives with one another.

Think back to the worst moment of your life. Were you alone? Did you have someone there with you? If so, what kind of difference did it make for you? What kind of friend did you need at that time? We can be that kind of friend for someone else. We often say in recovery, "God never wastes a hurt." A small group format like Celebrate Recovery is a chance to see our hurt become something made beautiful by God. "A new commandment I give to you, that you love one another: just as I have loved you, you also are to love one another" (John 13:34, ESV).

What Celebrate Recovery Will Not Do:

Celebrate Recovery will not diagnose. When noticing something out of the ordinary, many people may try to assign labels. Many folks are more comfortable with labels, because they are not as messy as people's real lives, and we often assume that labeling a situation means we understand it. But that is not our role in Celebrate Recovery. A diagnosis is useful within the walls of a clinician's office, but for a Celebrate Recovery meeting, a diagnosis is both unhelpful and unnecessary.

Celebrate Recovery will not fix. This is one of our basic guidelines. "We are here to support one another. We will not attempt to fix one another."

It is very possible that a person who is struggling may not want anyone's advice. They may just want to vent in a safe place. Unsolicited advice adds another brick to the wall the person has already built around themselves. We need to respect others and treat them the way that we would want to be treated. This means being sensitive to others' personal boundaries and not overstepping them.

Celebrate Recovery will not give up on someone. Helping someone with mental and relational health challenges and/or alcohol and drug abuse issues can be emotionally draining. However, we need to remember that it is even more difficult for the one who is struggling. Consider this scripture: "This is real love. It is not that we loved God, but that he loved us and sent his Son as a sacrifice to take away our sins" (1 John 4:10, NLT). God could have given up on us, but he didn't. God loved us when we were unlovable, and we need to love in the same way. We want to remember that with God, there is always hope. His love transcends and eradicates hopelessness.

When a person who is struggling with their mental health comes into Celebrate Recovery, they may not have the ability to distinguish between hurts, hang-ups, and habits and their mental and relational health issue(s). They will hear words like "recovery" and "freedom" and not understand why the 12 Steps may not quickly and easily give them the freedom they are looking for. In Celebrate Recovery, we use what we call the Mental Health Recovery Agreement, which gives a person the ability to invite someone they trust into the process of their recovery. We can then come alongside them and walk supportively through the 12 Steps with them. Here is the Mental Health Recovery Agreement used by Celebrate Recovery.

MENTAL HEALTH RECOVERY AGREEMENT

1. I will reaffirm daily that my identity comes from Jesus Christ and who He says I am. I will deny the lie that my identity is in my diagnosis.

    "So in Christ Jesus you are all children of God through faith"
    (Galatians 3:26, NIV).

2. I will submit to the will of God in my life, knowing that while I may not understand the reasons why I have a mental illness, God is in control. If I let Him work in my life, He will do what is best for me in my circumstances.

   "And we know that for those who love God all things work together for good, for those who are called according to his purpose" *(Romans 8:28, ESV).*

3. I will share my victories and my struggles with someone I trust on a consistent basis. In doing so, I refuse to live in isolation from others.

   "Two people are better off than one, for they can help each other succeed" *(Ecclesiastes 4:9, NLT).*

4. I will faithfully follow any treatment plans designed for me by my doctor and/or therapist. I will continue to take medications as prescribed by my doctor. I will meet with my doctor and/or therapist regularly to make sure the correct plan is in place.

   "The way of a fool is right in his own eyes, but a wise man is he who listens to counsel" *(Proverbs12:15, NAS).*

5. I will continue to work the Celebrate Recovery 12 Steps and 8 Principles, having as an ultimate goal to be more and more like Jesus in everything I do.

   "So all of us who have had that veil removed can see and reflect the glory of the Lord. And the Lord — who is the Spirit — makes us more and more like him as we are changed into his glorious image" *(2 Corinthians 3:18, NLT).*

Celebrate Recovery cannot promise physical healing of mental health issues, any more than it can promise physical healing of cancer. However, what we can offer is based on what we are.

Celebrate Recovery Is:

- A safe and loving place for those seeking to find support in the midst of mental illness, alcohol and/or substance abuse, and dual diagnoses (i.e., someone who struggles with both a mental health disorder and an addiction).
- Willing to support mental health through Christ-centered accountability and sponsorship.
- A safe place to work through all of life's hurts, hang-ups, and habits, believing that freedom in Christ is something that can be complete even without physical healing.

Celebrate Recovery is not a replacement for professional counseling, therapy, and medical treatment. We are here to support those efforts and encourage people as they use them. There is no denying the fact that living with mental health issues can be difficult. But living with mental and relational health issues and/or alcohol and drug abuse does not have to be a lifelong sentence of misery. People can have hope for a better tomorrow. By living one day at a time, one moment at a time, those struggling can find peace. They can live a life that is extraordinary. They can truly become overcomers.

The 8 Principles Based On the Beatitudes

Principle 1: Realize I'm not God; I admit that I am powerless to control my tendency to do the wrong thing and that my life is unmanageable. (Step 1)

> *"Happy are those who know they are spiritually poor"* *(Matthew 5:3a, TEV).*

Principle 2: Earnestly believe that God exists, that I matter to Him, and that He has the power to help me recover. (Step 2)

> *"Happy are those who mourn; God will comfort them!"* *(Matthew 5:4, TEV).*

Principle 3: Consciously choose to commit all my life and will to Christ's care and control. (Step 3)

> *"Happy are those who are humble" (Matthew 5:5a, TEV).*

Principle 4: Openly examine and confess my faults to myself, to God, and to someone I trust. (Steps 4 and 5)

> *"Happy are the pure in heart" (Matthew 5:8a, TEV).*

Principle 5: Voluntarily submit to every change God wants to make in my life and humbly ask Him to remove my character defects. (Steps 6 and 7)

> *"Happy are those whose greatest desire is to do what God requires" (*Matthew 5:6a*, TEV).*

Principle 6: Evaluate all my relationships. Offer forgiveness to those who have hurt me and make amends for harm I've done to others, except when to do so would harm them or others. (Steps 8 and 9)

> *"Happy are those who are merciful to others" (Matthew 5:7a, TEV).*

> *"Happy are those who work for peace" (Matthew 5:9, TEV).*

Principle 7: Reserve a daily time with God for self-examination, Bible reading, and prayer in order to know God and His will for my life, and to gain the power to follow His will. (Steps 10 and 11)

> *"LORD, I call to you for help; every morning I pray to you" (Psalm 88:13, TEV).*

Principle 8: Yield myself to God to be used to bring this Good News to others, both by my example and by my words. (Step 12)

> *"Happy are those who are persecuted because they do what God requires!" (Matthew 5:10a, TEV).*

The 12 Steps and Their Biblical Comparisons

Step 1: We admitted we were powerless over our addictions and compulsive behavior; that our lives had become unmanageable. I know that nothing good lives in me, that is, in my sinful nature.

> *"… For I have the desire to do what is good, but I cannot carry it out" (Romans 7:18, NIV).*

Step 2: We came to believe that a power greater than ourselves could restore us to sanity. *"For it is God who is at work in you to will and to act in order to fulfill his good purpose" (Philippians 2:23, NIV).*

Step 3: We made a decision to turn our life and our will over to the care of God.

> *"Therefore, I urge you, brothers, in view of God's mercy, to offer your bodies as living sacrifices, holy and pleasing to God—this is your spiritual act of worship" (Romans 12:1, NIV).*

Step 4: We made a searching and fearless moral inventory of ourselves.

> *"Let us examine our ways and test them, and let us return to the LORD" (Lamentations 3:40, NIV).*

Step 5: We admitted to God, to ourselves, and to another human being, the exact nature of our wrongs.

> *"Therefore, confess your sins to each other, and pray for each other so that you may be healed" (James 5:16a, NIV).*

Step 6: We were entirely ready to have God remove all these defects of character.

> *"Humble yourselves before the Lord, and he will lift you up" (James 4:10, NIV).*

Step 7: We humbly asked Him to remove all our shortcomings.

> *If we confess our sins, he is faithful and just and will forgive us our sins and purify us from all unrighteousness" (1 John 1:9, NIV).*

Step 8: We made a list of all persons we had harmed and became willing to make amends to them all.

> *"Do to others as you would have them do to you" (Luke 6:31, NIV).*

Step 9: We made direct amends to such people whenever possible, except when to do so would injure them or others.

> *"Therefore, if you are offering your gift at the altar and there remember that your brother has something against you, leave your gift there in front of the altar. First go and be reconciled to your brother; and then come and offer your gift" (Matthew 5:23–24, NIV).*

Step 10: We continued to take personal inventory and when we were wrong, promptly admitted it.

> *"So, if you think you are standing firm, be careful that you don't fall!" (1 Corinthians 10:12, NIV).*

Step 11: We sought through prayer and meditation to improve our conscious contact with God, praying only for knowledge of His will for us, and the power to carry that out.

> *"Let the word of Christ dwell in you richly" (Colossians 3:16a, NIV).*

Step 12: Having had a spiritual experience as the result of these steps, we tried to carry this message to others, and practice these principles in all our affairs.

"Brothers, if someone is caught in a sin, you who are spiritual should restore him gently. But watch yourself, or you also may be tempted" (Galatians 6:1, NIV).

For more information about Celebrate Recovery, visit www. celebraterecovery.com.

David E. Jenkins, Psy.D.

Dr. Jenkins is Professor of Counseling and the Director of the M.A. in Addiction Counseling program in the Department of Counselor Education and Family Studies at Liberty University. He has served as Clinical Director of the International Board of Christian Counselors of the American Association of Christian Counselors and is on the Executive Board of the Society for Christian Psychology. Dr. Jenkins also served on the Executive Draft Committee for the 2014 update to the AACC's *Code of Ethics for Christian Counselors*.

With over 25 years of experience as a clinical psychologist, Dr. Jenkins specializes in the integration of Christian faith and clinical practice. He has worked extensively with addictive, mood, and anxiety disorders in the context of individual, marital, group, and family therapy. Dr. Jenkins has provided education, consultation, supervision, and training for a variety of churches, ministries, and professionals. He is also an author and speaker at conferences, seminars, and retreats.

CHAPTER 12

How to Develop an Effective Opioid Crisis Ministry

David E. Jenkins, Psy.D.

The struggle with the opioid crisis is real! Individuals, families, communities, and our nation are being negatively impacted in significant ways. We must confront the realities of this struggle head-on and with conviction and hope. This chapter reviews the nature and scope of the opioid crisis, the process of addiction with its unique aspects related to opioids, Christian perspectives on addiction, and how the church can bring help, hope, and healing by responding to the opioid crisis with love and grace, but also with truth and competence.

Is the opioid problem best understood as a "crisis" or an "epidemic?" A *crisis* is a decisive moment during an unstable time in a situation which is facing a turning point. An *epidemic* is an outbreak of disease or outcome that spreads quickly and widely, affecting a large number of individuals at the same time. Our current situation related to opioids can best be thought of as a *crisis* that has reached *epidemic* proportions. It took years for us to get here; it will take years for it to change, and our response to it may need to be much like responses to recent natural disasters.

Nature and Scope of the Opioid Crisis

Several governors in the U.S. had already done so at the state level, but on October 27, 2017, President Trump declared the opioid crisis a national public health emergency. Less than a month later, the Council of Economic Advisors (CEA, 2017) report estimated the costs of the opioid crisis to be over $500 billion, a figure representing 2.8% of the nation's gross domestic product for that year. When added to the estimated $700 billion costs of alcohol, tobacco, and other drugs, substance abuse costs our nation over

$1.25 trillion per year! [Vital sources of up-to-date information include the White House website (www.whitehouse.gov/opioids) and the sites of the Substance Abuse Mental Health Services Administration (SAMHSA; www.samhsa.gov), the National Institute on Drug Abuse (NIDA; www.drugabuse.gov), and the Centers for Disease Control and Prevention (CDC; www.cdc.gov)].

A primary reason for the opioid crisis reaching epidemic proportions is the dramatic increase in the number of prescriptions for opioid medications used in non-cancer pain management, which increases the average length of time for which opioids are prescribed and leads to higher dosages and amounts per prescription. From 1999 to 2010, the number of prescriptions for opioid medications quadrupled, although there was no increase in reported pain levels during the same period of time (Guy et al., 2017), and during the same time period, opioid overdose deaths and treatment admissions rose at a similar rate. The Agency for Healthcare Research and Quality (AHRQ, 2016) estimated a 64% increase in opioid-related hospital admissions with a 99% increase in emergency department visits from 2005 to 2014.

The most shocking statistics relate to opioid overdose deaths. The CDC (2018) estimated there were 47,600 opioid overdose deaths in 2017, representing a 12% rate increase from 2016. Over 130 people per day die from opioids! Nearly 36% of those deaths involved prescription opioids, 33% involved heroin, and 60% involved synthetic opioids such as fentanyl and carfentanil (percentages total more than 100% because more than one type of opioid may be involved in an overdose death). The synthetic opioid fentanyl is 80-100 times more potent than morphine while carfentanil is 100 times more potent than fentanyl (i.e., 10,000 times more than morphine). According to the NIDA (2017), synthetic opioids were responsible for tripling the number of opioid overdose deaths from 2013 to 2015. The 28,466 deaths from synthetic opioids in 2017 represent a 48% increase from 2016. Unfortunately, deaths related to the opioid crisis of epidemic proportions are continuing to rise.

Not everyone who uses prescription opioids develops problems related to their use. Over 70% of the over 15 million people prescribed opioid medications do not misuse them (NIDA, 2017). However, between 8 and 12 percent develop an opioid use disorder, 4 to 6 percent progress to the use of heroin, and about 80% of heroin users first misused prescription opioids. SAMHSA (2017) estimates there are approximately 2.1 million people in the U.S. with an opioid use disorder (OUD).

Stage Model of the Addictive Process

One way to understand the process of addiction is to consider the progression of how addiction develops and the stages someone goes through. A four-stage model (see *Figure 1.*) includes experimentation, social, medicinal, and addictive stages as someone progresses from use to misuse to abuse to dependence to addiction. Following the description of each stage below, unique aspects related to opioids are considered.

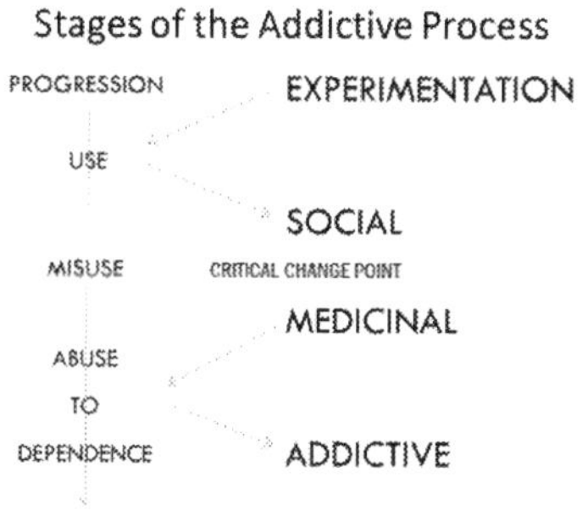

Stages of the Addictive Process

PROGRESSION   EXPERIMENTATION

USE

SOCIAL

MISUSE   CRITICAL CHANGE POINT

MEDICINAL

ABUSE

TO

DEPENDENCE   ADDICTIVE

Figure 1. Stage Model of the Addictive Process. © 2007 David E. Jenkins, Psy.D

Experimentation. The experimentation stage is characterized by infrequent use where a substance (or behavior) is tried 1-3 times. Curiosity is often the motive, and learning is typically the outcome. Usually others are present. During experimentation, there may be one-time consequences as part of "learning," for example nausea during use and/or a hangover after use. Based on the results of the "experiment," the person will decide either to not use again or to continue to use. If use continues, they typically progress to the social stage.

Social. Social use is characterized by non-patterned use on special occasions such as parties and holidays. Using alcohol as an example, most people who drink (such as a glass or two of wine with a meal) do not progress beyond this stage. The experimentation and social stages are considered as use.

Medicinal. A critical change point occurs if use progresses beyond the social stage. Use becomes something other than social when *reasons* for use begin to appear, no matter how minor or typical. For example, someone who has a drink or two a couple of nights a week to help them relax after work has attached a reason to the use, which tends to become more of an individual versus a social activity. Although the use has become a problem, the user is still not addicted. Another early reason for use is enjoyment of the using for its own sake rather than enjoyment of an occasion. As use continues, it is more likely to become a regular, customary way of coping with or escaping from life and/or relationship problems. Another indicator of medicinal use is *constriction of lifestyle;* formerly non-using activities are deferred in favor of using. Life begins to narrow around the drug/behavior. A third indicator of the medicinal stage is the appearance of *consequences* of use, however minor. When reasons for using become related to relieving consequences of using, a very serious, but often deceptively subtle cycle begins to occur. This cycle begins to increase in severity and speed, moving the person increasingly toward the addictive stage, progressing to substance misuse and abuse. Dependence is characterized by progressively intensifying tolerance (needing more of the substance or behavior to achieve the same effect) and withdrawal (unpleasant effects experienced due to not using).

Addictive. The addictive stage is characterized not only by tolerance and withdrawal, but also by *craving* and *loss of control*. The person now uses increasing amounts in an attempt to feel "normal" physically and/or mentally, and, if deprived of use, experiences withdrawal symptoms in the form of physical and/or psychological distress. Consequences of use continue to increase across several life spheres. Due to physiological changes in the body and brain caused by chronic use, the person craves the substance and increasingly loses control of the frequency and amount of their use. The cycle of binge/intoxication (loss of control), withdrawal/negative effect (withdrawal), and preoccupation/anticipation (craving) (Koob & Volkow, 2016) now enslaves the person with what is generally considered to be—thanks to recent advances in our understanding of neurobiology—the acquired disease of addiction.

Unique aspects related to opioids. This stage model presents one view of the typical progression to addiction, but it might also be helpful to consider ways addiction to opioids may progress a bit differently than addiction to other substances. For one thing, curiosity is not the motivation for those with non-cancer chronic pain who are being treated with prescription opioids. And people experimenting with substance use don't typically start with using opioids, but rather with alcohol and marijuana. For opioid users, the social stage may get by-passed. Also, most persons who have Opioid Use Disorder (OUD) began with nonmedical use of medications that were prescribed for someone else; that is, their use was illicit from the start. While this pattern characterizes many who progress in substance use, those using opioids for medically supervised pain management may be likely to develop dependence (tolerance, withdrawal), they generally do not progress to addiction (craving, loss of control). Due to illicit use and misuse, guilt and shame may be prominent for many with OUD. This may be particularly true for those who progress to addiction but began with prescribed opioid medication. There may also be higher rates of moderate and severe addiction with OUD compared to other substance use disorders.

Neurobiology of Addiction

It is important to remember that addiction involves biological changes as well as psychological, social, and spiritual changes. Our bodies were designed by God for pleasure and for responding effectively to our environment. The neurotransmitter dopamine is the main brain chemical involved in the experience of pleasure and reward. The hormone cortisol is the primary substance involved in regulation of the stress response. The effects of positive reinforcement and negative reinforcement go well beyond mere behavioral learning, reflecting effects in the brain's reward system and in our stress response.

When we have a rewarding experience, dopamine is released in several areas and structures in the brain, resulting in the experience of pleasure and an increased likelihood that the associated behavior will be repeated. Built-in processes, structures, and chemicals (e.g., endogenous opioids) facilitate this experience. This is part of God's design that enables us to be in right relationship with him, with others, with ourselves, and with our world, but because of sin's effects, certain substances and behaviors are able, through regular use and engagement, to hijack this design. As someone progresses through the addictive process, the brain increasingly adapts to changes in the reward system and relies upon the substance to produce and respond to the release of dopamine. With addiction, these changes in the brain drive the individual to seek out addictive substances and behaviors more and more, as the experience of pleasure from doing so becomes increasingly elusive. At the same time, if the person doesn't use the substance, he or she often experiences an unpleasant rebound effect. As tolerance and withdrawal continue to strengthen, craving and loss of control follow, and it is the presence of these four processes that characterizes addiction; a point at which the brain cannot function normally even when the substance is not used.

In response to stress, the brain stimulates the release of the hormone cortisol. As the stressful situation resolves, the hypothalamus and pituitary gland are signaled to stop releasing the hormones that lead to the release of cortisol by the adrenal glands. This, too, is part of God's design for us to live effectively in a world in which we are to be blessed, be fruitful, multiply, rule, and have dominion, but as substance use progresses into misuse, abuse, dependence, and addiction, stressful effects begin to occur biologically, psychologically, socially, and spiritually. Additionally, as the person becomes less effective at responding, the intensity and duration of the stress increases. With addiction, the brain becomes increasingly dependent upon the use of substances to regulate the stress response, but due to tolerance and withdrawal, both the presence and the lack of the addictive substance increasingly contribute to the stress response. The brain is now unable to have normal involvement in both positive (e.g., pleasure) and negative (e.g. reduction of stress) reinforcement. The neurobiology of addiction is now dominating and overriding the person's rational, volitional, and even spiritual functions.

Pain and Opioids

One of the factors to consider in the opioid crisis of epidemic proportions is the use of opioids in the management of non-cancer pain. Our brains are designed to respond to pain as well as pleasure; the experience of pain is affected by the same endogenous opioids involved in the normal experience of pleasure. While nearly 70% of those prescribed opioids for pain management do not misuse or abuse them, 30% do. Thankfully, there are several effective nonpharmacologic pain management options that can used in place of or along with opioid medications.

For short-term management of post-surgical pain, for example, opioid medications help modulate the perception and experience of pain through chemical effects on the opioid receptors. As healing and recovery occur, the body's capacity for managing the pain process on its own becomes sufficient as the need for the analgesic effects of the opioid medication decreases. The person stops taking the opioids, may or may not use other pain medications such as nonsteroidal anti-inflammatory drugs (NSAIDs) like ibuprofen or acetaminophen, and as healing continues can soon manage any remnants of pain without any outside assistance. When using opioids for management of chronic pain, tolerance and withdrawal (i.e., dependence) frequently develop; however, in many cases the additional aspects of craving and loss of control (i.e., addiction) do not.

The relatively recent development of newer opioid medications in the mid-1980s and 1990s led to increased numbers of prescriptions. Unfortunately, inaccurate and even deceptive information was disseminated about how addictive these medications are, and this has played a major role in the current opioid epidemic—mainly due to the increased amounts, increased availability, and decreased perception of their risk. One bright spot in the midst of the current opioid crisis is that prescribing practices have been changing, and nonpharmacologic options for pain management have been receiving greater attention. Some of these pain management options include cognitive behavioral therapy, exercise therapy, mindfulness-based stress reduction, acupuncture, and electrical stimulation.

Treatment and Recovery Options

Regardless of how an individual's opioid use disorder has developed, a number of options for treatment and recovery are available, and thankfully a number of treatment modalities for use disorders involving other substances are also helpful with OUD. The American Psychological

Association (APA, 2017) has identified Cognitive Behavioral Therapy (CBT), Motivational Interviewing (MI), Motivational Enhancement Therapy (MET), and Mindfulness-Based Stress Reduction (MBSR) as effective modalities for treating OUD. CBT helps deal with irrational and distorted thoughts, beliefs, and expectancies associated with OUD. MI is an effective counselor style of engaging those who struggle with OUD such that they strengthen their motivation and commitment to change. MET, using basic tenets of MI during an initial assessment phase, often employs a battery of questionnaires followed by several treatment sessions based on information from results of the assessment. Primary goals of MET include helping the person strengthen their motivation to change, developing an individualized plan for doing so, enhancing commitment to change by following the plan, and preparing for the management of high-risk situations. Throughout MET, progress is monitored collaboratively and strategies are adapted or added as needed or desired.

These modalities can occur across several types of treatment for OUD. Residential or inpatient treatments are available, as are partial hospitalization, intensive outpatient, and outpatient options. Group therapy is often an effective option where those who are struggling receive and give support and challenge. Within individual therapy, co-occurring mental disorders such as depression and anxiety and co-occurring substance use disorders can be treated. Additionally, individual therapy can be helpful in pain management whether or not an OUD is present.

Despite consistent evidence of its effectiveness, one of the most controversial treatment types for OUD is Medication Assisted Treatment (MAT). Understandably, there is confusion about using opioids to treat OUD, but the idea of using medication to help with substance addiction is not new. A current example is using "the patch" to help people with addiction to tobacco, and medications have been used for several decades to help those addicted to alcohol.

When it comes to OUD, three primary medications are showing efficacy: methadone, buprenorphine, and naltrexone (SAMHSA, 2016). Methadone blocks euphoric effects of opioids and reduces withdrawal symptoms. In learning terms, both positive and negative reinforcement for using opioids are reduced. By lowering the high and reducing withdrawal, those addicted to opioids have more control over the choices they make, and that combined reduction of both loss of control and craving (two key aspects that differentiate addiction from dependence) allow for greater recovery-oriented decision-making. Methadone must be managed in structured clinic settings. Because Buprenorphine can be managed in qualified physician offices, it is a more readily available treatment option. Buprenorphine has some opioid qualities but those effects are weaker than full opioids like heroin and methadone. It also has a "ceiling effect" so the high is not as high; this lowers the potential for misuse and diminishes the effects of dependency. Buprenorphine also helps increase the window for recovery-oriented decisions and choices for those with OUD. Naltrexone is used in the treatment of alcoholism and OUD and can be prescribed by any healthcare provider who is licensed to prescribe medications. Because Naltrexone blocks euphoric effects and reduces cravings by binding with and blocking (vs. activating) opioid receptors in the brain, it is not addictive. Although it works differently from methadone and buprenorphine, naltrexone also helps increase the capacity of opioid-addicted individuals to make recovery-oriented choices rather than being driven by their addiction.

Christian Perspectives

Christians think about human beings holistically. God created mankind male and female, in his image and likeness, with (1) physical bodies (including brains); (2) souls and minds that are not entirely bound by the physical world and that distinguish them from the rest of creation; (3) relationships with God, others, and self; and (4) spirits that animate and connect them to him. Thus, a biopsychosociospiritual model for thinking about addiction to opioids is highly congruent with a biblically-informed Christian worldview.

Addiction is a complex phenomenon, and the church is hindered in its efforts to rise up and overcome the scourge of opioid addiction by reductionism, the felt need to simplistically reduce addiction to either primarily biological factors or primarily spiritual factors. God will ultimately redeem all of what it means to be human, including our biological, psychological, social, and spiritual dimensions, but until then, our brains, minds, relationships, and spirits are subject to the effects of the

Fall and need remedial care. This is especially true when one or more of these four dimensions has been altered, perhaps permanently (at least in an earthly sense) by the degrading effects of sin. Reductionism is the primary reason for resistance to both MAT and spiritual approaches to recovery such as 12-step programs and Celebrate Recovery.

Because choice, willpower, and personal responsibility matter, "sin" is involved in OUD. However, we need to think more complexly about sin, recognizing that various categories of sin may lead to someone's addiction. Are we talking exclusively about the effects of personal sin? Given that over 80% of those with addiction difficulties have experienced Adverse Childhood Experiences (ACEs), are we talking about the effects of the sin of others on those who have been victimized? Or, given the genetic vulnerability to addiction, are we talking about the effects of sin in the created order that renders our bodies, including our brains, subject to death and decay? Each "category" of sin demands a different response. Restoration for personal sin involves confession, repentance, and seeking forgiveness and reconciliation. Restoration for the sin of others involves righteous anger, grief, and willingness to forgive offenders. Restoration for sin in the created order involves accepting that all of life has been tainted by sin's degrading effects, accepting our inability to restore ourselves and our world on our own, commitment to noble stewardship of our physical bodies, and gratitude to God for his loving provision of hope, now as well as in the hereafter.

It is also important for Christians to consider the biblical view of *infirmity*, which is physical, mental, moral, or spiritual weakness and vulnerability, and it may be helpful to think of addiction as an "acquired" disease. People with genetic vulnerability to addiction will not develop it if they remain abstinent from the use of addictive substances, and people without genetic vulnerability can become addicted if they choose to use and do so regularly and chronically enough that one or more of the four dimensions becomes altered and dependent. Consider individuals who develop heart disease or Type II diabetes due to sinful lifestyle and dietary choices, even knowing their genetic vulnerabilities. Even if they become aware of their sinful choices, repent, and then live a God-honoring lifestyle of healthy diet and exercise choices, they are still left with needing to manage the heart disease or Type II diabetes. Does such a person live in a perpetual state of sin as a result? Are the symptoms in their bodies an indictment of their present spiritual condition?

Now, consider individuals who become addicted to opioids because of managing post-surgical pain according to accepted medical protocol; or individuals who have a sports injury with no prior history of or inclination toward addiction of any type, much less to opioids? When the brain is altered due to the effects of opioid use, are the symptoms and effects of addiction an indictment of the person's current spiritual condition? Does that person live in a perpetual state of personal sin because they experience lingering effects of an acquired disease of addiction?

Christians must also keep in mind the biological, psychological, social, and spiritual dimensions and consider that healing and cleansing are possible even if addiction remains. Certainly miraculous complete healings and deliverances from addiction and its effects do happen… Praise God! Prisoners are released, captives are set free, the blind see, and we are grateful and humbled! But there are also equally miraculous stories of God's redemption in the lives of those who still bear the effects and burden of OUD. Both expressions of God's power and grace are real, do matter, and can help the church engage the opioid crisis. One demonstrates the immediacy of God's presence and activity; the other bears witness to his ongoing love and patient daily sustenance. Here, especially, we must guard against reductionism since God himself is the one who knows best how to love and redeem his own. The church must equally embrace and hold forth both expressions so that opioid-addicted persons can come and experience the love of God.

How the Church Can Help

The foremost way the church can help address the opioid crisis is the meaningful and effective engagement of pastoral leadership. Pastors need to lead the way in ministering to those impacted by the opioid crisis, and they are uniquely situated as leaders in their communities as well as in their churches to mobilize strategic resources to target this national public health emergency.

Pastors and the rest of the church must also step up and pray as if the life of their family, church, community, nation, and world depend upon them doing so… because it does! All types of prayer—liturgical corporate prayer, spontaneous private prayer, healing prayer (of brains as well as spirits!), delivering prayer, desperate prayer—all of it is needed. Pray for those afflicted, for those that love them, for the people and places that provide competent care, and for civic authorities and agencies tasked with oversight and regulatory responsibilities. Pray for "supply" issues such as border enforcement, confiscation efforts, and effective strategies for limiting the availability of and easy access to opioids. Pray for "demand" issues such as effective treatment options, prevention efforts, healing of persons, families, and communities, and transformation of a culture that demands immediate gratification and the complete absence of suffering. And if something has been left out of these suggestions, then pray for that! But pray!

The church is also desperately needed as a refuge for those who are grieving the loss of loved ones to the opioid crisis. The most unfortunate reality of this public health emergency is that people are dying—130 daily—from opioid overdoses. Whether those deaths are the result of "accidental overdose" by someone who took too many pain medications in combination with alcohol or the result of a fentanyl-laced heroin injection, churches have a unique opportunity to provide their congregants and communities God's presence through the journey of grief. This becomes even more important when silence, shame, stigma, and misunderstanding permeate the circumstances around the deaths. Regardless, the loss of the valued loved one is still as great, but the grief has increased potential to become complicated, actually extending the tragic consequences of this scourge. It may help to consider that grief from this crisis occurs on a number of levels; individual, familial, local, national, and global. Among other options, churches can offer grief support groups, periodic memorial services, annual community prayer vigils, outreach to families directly impacted by opioid-related deaths, and support for medical and response personnel (coroners, first responders, emergency room staff, etc.).

Additionally, the church can help by deepening its theology in areas related to the opioid crisis, starting with the theology of the body, including the brain. What was God up to when he created us with physical bodies? How have the degrading effects of sin affected the body and brain? What will be different once our bodies (including our brains) are in their glorified state? How does all of this relate to addiction and those affected by it? The church must refine her theology of suffering—both how we respond to physical and emotional pain and the ways we show love to those who suffer. Given the overwhelming connection between adverse childhood experiences and the development of addiction, not only our theology of suffering must mature, but also our theology of justice for holding accountable those who set children's lives on a trajectory of suffering and misery. Growth in these areas would help the church lead the way in raising awareness of the opioid crisis and championing effective responses.

The church is uniquely equipped to deal with the silence, shame, and stigma that pervade the opioid crisis. To help address the stigma of opioid addiction, the church can educate herself on the science of addiction, brain involvement, imaging studies, and MAT (which may be a defining issue for you and your church). In 1 Corinthians 6:11 (NASB), after the apostle Paul lists several different types of people that will not inherit the kingdom of God, he states, "Such were some of you." Interestingly, he then goes into one of the clearest teachings on the physical body. Correspondingly, in Matthew 9:12 (NASB) Jesus says, "It is not those who are healthy who need a physician, but those who are sick."

This type of openness in the church helps relieve shame as well as stigma. For most people who struggle with OUD, shame incites hiding, devaluing, and a sense of being "less than," all of which hinder recovery by preventing requests for help, demoralizing those who do seek help, and causing them to doubt their ability to beat addiction because it is so big. Shame even questions whether the lives of those recovering are worth it. But this is one area where the church can truly shine. Lovingly presenting the truth of who we are in Christ Jesus—and all that truth encompasses— is the remedy for even the objective shame stemming from sin and its degradation. Similarly, objective guilt resulting from sinful choices and resultant consequences for the offender and others is best remedied as part of the life of the church.

One of most important areas in which the church is uniquely equipped for effectively responding is the realm of prevention. A couple of decades of very robust public health and behavioral science research convincingly documents the important role that well-lived faith plays in the lives, families, and communities of believers. Several of the most important protective factors that help safeguard against problems like addiction include nurturing parenting skills, stable family relationships, caring adults outside the family as role models and mentors, and meaningful community involvement as an expression of a healthy life of faith. Healthy spirituality and religious life mitigate against the most common individual, familial, community, and societal risk factors for addiction and other problems (SAMHSA, 2018). Individual risk factors include genetic predisposition to addiction and prenatal exposure to alcohol. Family risk factors include parental substance abuse, child mistreatment, and inadequate supervision. Community risk factors include poverty and violence. Societal risk factors include permissive laws regarding substance use and lack of economic opportunity.

The church has a vital role to play in prevention by fostering protective factors and reducing risk factors. This is particularly important given that community-based approaches have been shown to be especially effective at preventing not only substance abuse and addiction, but also a number of other concerns. SAMHSA, NIDA, and CDC have existing kits and packages on their websites, available for download at no charge, for churches and individuals that decide to become involved in responding effectively to the opioid crisis. The Center for Faith and Opportunity Initiatives (https://www.hhs.gov/about/agencies/iea/partnerships/index.html) also has an Opioid Epidemic Practical Toolkit that can help churches actually take the lead in their communities while also forming diverse partnerships to cover the continuity of care for those who need treatment.

The church can be a valuable resource for those needing formal treatment for opioid addiction. Churches can help those who struggle with OUD to access treatment by maintaining directories of local, regional, and national providers. They can also help defray some of the costs of treatment, perhaps even designating specific funds for those needing treatment. Many persons with OUD also have other co-occurring addictive disorders and/or are experiencing other mental disorders such as depression or anxiety. These disorders add an additional burden to those who are suffering and intensify the need for the church to be involved in meaningful ways. Churches can open their buildings to mutual help groups such as Celebrate Recovery and 12-Step groups such as Alcoholics Anonymous. They may also be able to provide additional forms of social support such as employment and vocational training, education, recreational opportunities, and ways to be of service to others. These types of resources can be helpful both for those in active treatment and in strengthening efforts to prevent relapse.

Other practical ways churches can be involved include providing childcare during mutual help group meeting times and providing transportation to and from treatment or group meetings. As when congregants are in the hospital, churches can do visitation for those in treatment centers. Facilities or agencies providing treatment often allow local churches to conduct vesper services or Bible studies. One way all churches can help is to pray for those in the community that provide treatment and recovery services. Social support is one of the most important aspects of effective recovery from opioid and other addictions.

It might help to think of the local church as a "wellness center" for your community, particularly when considering health in biological, psychological, social, and spiritual domains. Each church may not be able to cover every domain or provide resources in each of the ways mentioned above, but each church can do *something*—and the things mentioned above have proven helpful to those struggling with opioid use and its effects.

Conclusion

The opioid crisis of epidemic proportions is a national public health emergency that demands effective responding from nearly all segments of our society. Churches can be involved in unique ways, but their involvement must be meaningful. The early church gained great favor with its culture because of how the members demonstrated love for one another. 1 Peter 2:11-12 states:

> Beloved, I urge you as aliens and strangers to abstain from fleshly lusts which wage war against the soul. Keep your behavior excellent among the Gentiles, so that in the thing in which they slander you as evildoers, they may because of your good deeds, as they observe them, glorify God in the day of visitation (NASB).

It is fascinating that this passage's context is abstaining from "fleshly lusts"… sounds a lot like addiction, doesn't it? Excellent behavior "among the Gentiles" expressed as "good deeds" is an effective way to witness to others about the love of God in Jesus Christ. The best ministry the church can engage in includes responding with loving regard for those whose lives have been adversely impacted by the opioid crisis. May God help us do so! This struggle is real, but so are the grace, mercy, and help of God—and his people—in our time of need!

References

Advokat, C.D., Comaty, J.E., & Julien, R.M. (2019). Opioid analgesics. In *Julien's primer of drug action* (pp. 333-378). New York, NY: Worth Publishers.

Agency for Healthcare Research and Quality. (2016). *Opioid-related hospitalizations up 64 percent nationwide between 2005-2014; First state-by-state analysis shows wide variations* [Press release]. Retrieved from http://www.ahrq.gov/news/ newsroom/press-releases/opioid-related-hospitalizations.html.

American Psychological Association. (2017). *Overcoming opioid abuse: How psychologists help people with opioid dependence and addiction* [Fact sheet]. Retrieved from http://www.apa.org/helpcenter/opioid-abuse.pdf.

Centers for Disease Control and Prevention. (2018). *Drug and opioid-involved overdose deaths — United States, 2013–2017.* Retrieved from https://www.cdc.gov/drugoverdose/pdf/pubs/2017cdc-drug-surveillance-report.pdf.

Council of Economic Advisers. (2017). *The underestimated cost of the opioid crisis.* Retrieved from https://www.whitehouse.gov/sites/whitehouse. gov/ files/images/ The%20Underestimated%20Cost%20of%20 the%20Opioid%20Crisis.pdf

Elman, I., & Borsook, D. (2016). Common brain mechanisms of chronic pain and addiction. *Neuron, 89,* 11-36.

Guy, G.P., Zhang, K., Bohm, M.K., Losby, J., Lewis, B., Young, R., ... Dowell, D. (2017). Vital signs: Changes in opioid prescribing in the United States, 2006–2015. *Morbidity and Mortality Weekly Report, 66*(26), 697-704. Retrieved from https://www.cdc.gov/mmwr/volumes/66/wr/pdfs/mm6626a4.pdf.

Koob, G.F., & Volkow, N.D. (2016). Neurobiology of addiction: A neurocircuitry analysis. *Lancet Psychiatry, 3,* 760-763. Retrieved from www.thelancet.com/psychiatry.

National Institute of Drug Abuse. (2017). *Research on the use and misuse of fentanyl and other synthetic opioids.* Retrieved from https://www.drugabuse.gov/about-nida/legislative-activities/testimony-to-congress/2017/research-use-misuse-fentanyl-other-synthetic-opioids.

Substance Abuse Mental Health Services Administration. (2016). *Medication-assisted treatment (MAT).* Retrieved from https://www.samhsa.gov/medication-assisted-treatment.

Substance Abuse Mental Health Services Administration. (2017). *Key substance use and mental health indicators in the United States: Results from the 2016 National Survey on Drug Use and Health* (HHS Publication No. SMA 17-5044, NSDUH Series H-52). Rockville, MD: Center for Behavioral Health Statistics and Quality, Substance Abuse and Mental Health Services Administration. Retrieved from https://www.samhsa.gov/data/.

Substance Abuse Mental Health Services Administration. (2018). *Risk and protective factors.* Retrieved from https://www.samhsa.gov/capt/practicing-effective-prevention/prevention-behavioral-health/risk-protective-factors.

Margaret Nagib, Psy.D

 Dr. Nagib is a clinical psychologist specializing in inner healing and treating eating disorders, trauma, addiction, self-injury, and mood disorders. She is the author of the book, *Souls Like Stars*. As a key faculty member of Timberline Knolls Clinical Development Institute, she travels the country providing clinical training and presentations to professionals.

Margaret earned her undergraduate degree from Pace University in New York and a Doctorate in Clinical Psychology from Wheaton College, where she also served as adjunct psychology professor. She held a similar role at Simpson University, and also attended two years at Bethel School of Supernatural Ministry.

CHAPTER 13

How to Develop an Effective Eating Disorders Recovery Ministry

Margaret Nagib, Psy.D.

Anorexia, bulimia, and binge-eating disorder are serious psychiatric disorders that devastate lives. A 2011 study estimated that eating disorders afflict roughly 30 million Americans (Wade, T. D., Keski-Rahkonen A., & Hudson J..). A common misconception is that only adolescent white females are affected by eating disorders, but eating disorders affect people of all genders, ages, races, ethnicities, body shapes and weights, sexual orientations, and socioeconomic statuses. No one is immune—and in every case, eating disorders rob individuals of their divine identity and purpose.

Eating disorders can also involve serious health consequences and in some cases even death. More people die from anorexia each year than from any other mental illness, and suicide is the primary cause of these deaths (Arcelus, Mitchell, Wales, & Nielsen, 2011). Although only about one-third of people suffering with an eating disorder actually receive treatment, the good news is that with treatment full recovery is possible (Hudson, J. I., Hiripi, E., Pope, H. G., & Kessler, R. C., 2007). With this in mind, the church can provide valuable support to a man or woman on the journey back to wholeness.

In this chapter we will discuss ways the church can help by raising awareness, reducing the stigma, referring members to treatment when appropriate, and providing community care through supportive pastoral counseling and small groups.

Raising Awareness

The saying 'knowledge is power' is especially true for anyone who wants to help someone who has an eating disorder. Like other mental illnesses, eating disorders are often gravely misunderstood. Having some basic information that is accurate and helpful is an important first step.

An Overview of the Three Main Types of Eating Disorders

Anorexia nervosa. As stated earlier, anorexia nervosa is the most lethal of the three eating disorders. This is primarily due to a high rate of suicide among anorexics as well as to the various medical complications that can accompany this disorder. Researchers have postulated that many anorexics commit suicide because the level of self-loathing they experience becomes unbearable. The more severe the symptoms, the more this disorder ravages a person's ability to see themselves as they truly are. Prolonged malnourishment affects a person's ability to think clearly. It exacerbates the distorted thoughts around identity and body-image that initially provoked the eating disorder symptoms. And it intensifies the obsessive thinking around food and weight that overtakes most of their waking thoughts. Prolonged malnutrition takes its toll on the body, mind, and self-perception. Brain shrinkage, heart attacks, and osteoporosis are just a few of the host of serious medical complications that can ensue as a result. As the disorder progresses and the individual becomes more consumed with the ritualistic eating disordered behavior that is driven by obsessive thoughts, he or she withdraws from relationships.

An eating disorder diagnosis is made by a licensed medical or behavioral health provider. The diagnosis of anorexia is characterized by several key symptoms:

Severe restriction of food intake. Eating less than needed to maintain a body weight that is at or above the minimum normal weight for the individual's age and height. This can range from a low caloric diet to full fasts.

Intense fear of gaining weight. Intense fear of gaining weight or becoming fat; persistent behavior that interferes with weight gain, such as over-exercise, vomiting, or using drugs (diuretics, laxatives, amphetamines, etc.), despite being underweight. Obsessions about food and weight dominate the majority of the individual's thinking.

Problems with body image. Denial of low body weight and the seriousness of the problem, despite statistically low body weight, medical issues, or other negative consequences; distorted body image or faulty estimation of size and shape. Because self-esteem is negatively affected by poor body image, the individual is likely to suffer with intense self-loathing.

10% of all individuals with anorexia are men.

Bulimia nervosa. Bulimia can also create serious medical complications. These include but are not limited to dehydration (which can lead to kidney failure), heart complications, heart failure, tooth decay, gum disease, and esophageal and stomach tearing. The diagnosis of bulimia is characterized by several key symptoms:

Binge eating. Recurrent episodes of eating abnormally large amounts of food in a short amount of time and feeling out of control during these episodes; unable to stop despite desiring to.

Purging or non-purging. Being driven to eliminate calories through either extreme measures such as vomiting, or non-purging methods such as times of severe calorie restriction, over-exercise, or the use of drugs (diuretics, laxatives, amphetamines).

Fear of gaining weight. Progressively obsessional and intense fear of gaining weight or becoming fat.

Problems with body image. Distorted body image or faulty estimation of size and shape. Because self-esteem is negatively affected by poor body image, the individual is likely to suffer with intense self-loathing.

10% of all individuals with bulimia are men.

Binge-Eating Disorder. Binge Eating Disorder (BED) is the most common of the three types of eating disorders. Medical complications associated with BED include but are not limited to irritable bowel syndrome, high blood pressure, heart disease, Type II diabetes, sleep apnea, kidney disease, gall bladder disease, arthritis, and infertility. The diagnosis of binge eating disorder is characterized by several key symptoms:

Binge eating. Recurrent episodes of eating abnormally large amounts of food in a short period of time. The individual will tend to eat rapidly, eat until uncomfortably full, eat large amounts when not hungry, eat alone out of embarrassment, and feel disgust, self-loathing, depression, and/or guilt after eating.

Non-purging. The individual does not use extreme methods to get rid of the calories consumed.

Up to 35% of all individuals with binge eating disorders are male.

Co-Occurring Disorders and Sub-Clinical Eating Disordered Behavior

Co-occurring disorders. Individuals who have an eating disorder commonly have a co-occurring mental illness. This is in part because eating disorders rarely occur in a vacuum. The most common illnesses that co-occur with eating disorders are depression, anxiety (obsessive compulsive disorder is common among anorexics), and substance abuse. It is very important that a thorough assessment be completed by an eating disorder professional to identify any co-occurring illness(es) that will need to be treated alongside the eating disorder.

Sub-clinical eating disordered behavior. One doesn't have to be diagnosed with a disorder to struggle with disordered eating and/or poor body image. We live in a diet-obsessed culture fueled by a $20 billion diet industry. In recent years the focus has been on "healthy eating," but the problem is that there is so much inconsistent information out there about exactly what this entails. We have taken healthy eating to disordered eating levels with black and white thinking that eliminates whole food groups. The dieting industry has capitalized on this confusion. We can now purchase a muffin labeled "gluten free, sugar free, dairy free, paleo" for our morning breakfast. This is not healthy. In the name of "healthy eating," Americans are more confused than ever. All this has served to steer us away from how God designed us to interact with food intuitively. (For more information see *Intuitive eating: A revolutionary program that works* by Evelyn Tribole and Elyse Resch.)

Orthorexia (a term that means "righteous eating") is an unhealthy obsession with eating foods that are considered healthy. Symptoms include obsessions with food quality and/or purity, avoiding specific foods, abiding by rigid eating rules, obsession with calorie count or nutritional value, fasting, and exercise addiction. "Every day is a chance to eat right, be "good," rise above others in dietary prowess, and self-punish if temptation wins (usually through stricter eating, fasts and exercise). Self-esteem becomes wrapped up in the purity of orthorexics' diets, and they sometimes feel superior to others, especially in regard to food intake" (National Eating Disorders Association website).

The truth is that eating issues lie on a continuum from disordered eating to full blown eating disorders. We live in a nation that struggles with food. According to the EatingDisorderHope.com website,

- Over 50% of teenage girls and 33% of teenage boys are using restrictive measures to lose weight at any given time.
- 46% of 9-11 year-olds are sometimes or very often on diets, and 82% of their families are sometimes or very often on diets.
- 91% of women recently surveyed on a college campus had attempted to control their weight through dieting; 22% dieted often or always.
- 95% of all dieters will regain their lost weight in one to five years.
- 35% of normal dieters progress to pathological dieting. Of those, 20-25% progress to partial or full-syndrome eating disorders.
- 25% of American men and 45% of American women are on a diet on any given day.

Reducing the Stigma

It's not what you are eating; it's what's eating you. Why are these behaviors so alluring and all-consuming? Loved ones, clergy, and even unapprised medical professionals can easily misunderstand eating disorders. Looking at the overview, you may also find it difficult to relate to or understand why anyone would want to engage in eating disordered behavior. Eating disorders are complicated illnesses caused by a conglomerate of genetic, psychological, relational, and social contributors that are unique to the sufferer. However, we can all relate to this fact that is common to all individuals who struggle with food-related issues: disordered eating can provide a strategy to cope with emotions that we don't otherwise know how to manage in healthier ways. A common saying in the eating disorder treatment world is that "It's not what you are eating; it's what's eating you." When we don't know how to deal with uncomfortable emotions and unmet needs, we tend to cling to anything that offers us relief and a sense of hope, even if it's a false hope.

To help sufferers and their loved ones understand the role that an eating disorder or other unhealthy coping mechanisms have come to play in an individual's life, I use the metaphor of a rickety, rotting raft in a stormy ocean. The raft is composed of all the behaviors we use in an attempt to numb pain, escape fear, and control the uncontrollable. Chances are that the issues underlying a person's eating disorder concerns have been present for a long time, and the individual feels stuck and powerless to change their behavior.

Consequently, the raft is tied together with substantial false beliefs about oneself, others, and God. False beliefs aren't just surface concepts; they can become woven into the deepest recesses of our hearts—they can define us. When these false beliefs define us, we hold onto them for dear life. They become the only thing keeping us afloat. Eating disorder sufferers have come to rely on the eating disorder to carry them through the storms of life, even though the eating disorder is no better than a dangerous, rickety, rotting raft. As a result, the individual will struggle to fully change their behavior because although the eating disorder is ultimately destructive, it does perform a valuable function in the person's life. It may serve to protect them, help them cope with emotions that feel unmanageable, provide them a sense of self-worth and identity, or numb the pain of loss or trauma.

Understanding and communicating this to your congregation greatly increases compassion and reduces stigma. If someone in your church has approached you with an eating disorder or eating disordered behaviors, validating the seriousness of their concerns and communicating acceptance, support, and hope for the future is paramount to reducing any stigma they may experience. Remember, we all have or have had our own versions of the rickety, rotting raft in our lives. Such a "raft" is any behavior we cling to that helps us cope with the difficulties we face, but which is actually based on a lie and is ultimately destructive. But God has a message of hope for each of us, and it's much more than something that traps us and hurts us. He has an abundant life for us, completely free from consuming thoughts and compulsive behaviors that are not in line with how he sees us or with the wonderful destiny he has prepared for us.

The process of recovery involves a "slow exchange" of releasing the pain and old, unhealthy mindsets with their accompanying behaviors, and embracing his healing joy and life-changing truth. This process begins when we recognize that although God may seem a million miles away, he really is with us in the middle of the storm. "The Lord is close to the brokenhearted; he rescues those whose spirits are crushed" (Psalm 34:18, NLT). It involves a choice to allow God and trustworthy friends, loved ones, and treatment providers to come alongside us to speak truth and to help us return to solid ground.

The following are ten truths about eating disorders that help to dispel common myths that contribute to the stigma surrounding eating disorders (adapted from the Eating Disorders Coalition website).

1. Many people with eating disorders look healthy, yet may be extremely ill. *(Myth: People with eating disorders have to be stick thin or morbidly obese.)*
2. Families are not to blame; they can be the patients' and providers' best allies in treatment. *(Myth: Eating disorders are caused by bad parenting.)*

3. An eating disorder diagnosis is a health crisis that disrupts personal and family functioning. *(Myth: She/he looks physically fine and gets straight A's at school. There is nothing wrong.)*

4. Eating disorders are not choices, but serious biologically influenced illnesses. *(Myth: Eating disorders are just about a person's vanity. He should be able to stop restricting, over-eating, purging, or over-exercising. She just needs to stop being defiant and eat.)*

5. Eating disorders affect people of all genders, ages, races, ethnicities, body shapes and weights, sexual orientations, and socioeconomic statuses. *(Myth: Eating disorders only affect young, white, affluent females.)*

6. Eating disorders carry an increased risk for both medical complications and suicide. *(Myth: Eating disorders do not have serious physical, emotional, or spiritual consequences.)*

7. Genes and environment play important roles in the development of eating disorders. *(Myth: Eating disorders are self-imposed behaviors.)*

8. Genes alone do not predict who will develop eating disorders. *(Myth: Some people are doomed to have an eating disorder because it runs in their family.)*

9. Full recovery from an eating disorder is possible, but early detection and intervention are important. *(Myth: People with eating disorders will always suffer. They cannot recover.)*

10. People who love and follow God can still struggle with eating disorder behaviors. *(Myth: Eating disorders are sins.)*

Referring to Treatment When Appropriate

It takes courage for someone to reach out. As a valued part of their community of faith, you can offer hope to those suffering with eating disorders and help them see that there is another way. You can lovingly communicate that they are not alone in their struggle and that there are those around them who will support and help them take steps toward recovery. As stated earlier, the eating disorder recovery process involves the "slow exchange" of the old for the new; from old and harmful beliefs, behaviors, and ways of coping to the abundant life God has waiting for them. In time, the "raft" of the eating disorder will become obsolete.

Eating disorders are complicated illnesses that require psychological, medical, and spiritual intervention. One of the most important things a church community can do is to help a struggling individual to find and initiate professional treatment. Eating disorders rarely occur in a vacuum. The first step in the treatment process is a thorough assessment performed by a licensed professional who specializes in treating eating disorders. This can be a psychotherapist, psychiatrist, or other medical professional versed in eating disorder treatment. The treatment provider will also assess whether or not the person has any other mental health issues. Many people who have eating disorders also suffer from an accompanying depression or anxiety disorder, and up to half of all individuals with an eating disorder also struggle with some type of substance abuse problem. Once the individual has been assessed, the professional will recommend a level of care that is appropriate for that person, based on the severity of their eating disorder symptoms, any co-occurring issues, and medical stability.

Levels of Care

Outpatient. Outpatient care includes regular sessions with a therapist, nutritionist, and medical professional on an outpatient basis.

Intensive outpatient. Intensive outpatient care involves all-day or half-day treatment three to five times per week, including nutritional support at meals, group and individual therapy on a daily basis, and medical monitoring.

Residential. Residential treatment is utilized when the individual is medically stable but unable to function on their own. Impairment is seen in the workplace or at school, there is a decline in self-care, and the individual's worsening symptoms cannot be managed on an outpatient basis. Treatment is provided in a residential setting for an average of 30 to 90 days.

Inpatient. Inpatient hospital treatment becomes necessary when the individual is medically compromised (poor vital signs, low weight, problems with electrolytes, dehydration, rapidly worsening symptoms, suicidal thoughts and intent, etc.). The goal is to restore medical stability.

Components of Care

A treatment team approach is generally the most effective in facilitating recovery for persons struggling with eating disorders. It is suggested that a database of trusted professionals and eating disorder organizations be created to which parishioners can be connected to begin the process of assessment and treatment. Eating disorders require a treatment team approach that involves the following components.

Nutrition counseling. A registered and licensed nutritionist or dietician who specializes in working with eating disorders provides nutrition counseling.

Medical management. A physician who understands the physical complications associated with eating disorders oversees the patient's medical care and orders appropriate lab work to track various aspects of the individual's health.

Psychiatric evaluation. A psychiatrist evaluates the patient to determine whether medication will be a beneficial or necessary adjunct to treatment. If so, the psychiatrist will also provide medication management.

Psychological care. A licensed counselor who specializes in treating individuals with eating disorders provides psychological care.

Family counseling and support. Family members of the patient receive specific support from a pastor or licensed counselor who has training and experience in helping the families of those with eating disorders. Family members are inevitably impacted by the patient's eating disorder.

Spiritual guidance, healing, and support. Pastors and lay leaders in the church minister grace, support, and healing to the individual and his or her family.

Psychological issues that should be addressed in eating disorder treatment include the following.

- Emotional regulation
- Self awareness and effectiveness
- Needs and boundaries
- Underlying issues (It's not what you're eating; it's what's eating you.)
- Co-occurring mental illness(es)
- Nutritional recovery: food as medicine
- Physical recovery
- Body image
- Trauma
- Shame

Providing Community Care Through Pastoral Counseling and Small Groups

Pastoral Counseling

Key spiritual issues that can be addressed in pastoral counseling include hope, true identity, desire, and destiny.

Hope. Every necessary but difficult journey begins with one of the most powerful forces on earth: hope. Hope is found in the most unlikely places, and while it seems to elude us when we're in our darkest hours, it's also in our darkest hours that the first glimmers appear. Hope gives us the strength to step into the process of working through our pain, knowing that we can come out on the other side healed and free.

Counseling your parishioner in the area of hope will help to give them courage to be honest with themselves and with the brokenness they've experienced, so they can step into the process of healing. The voice of hope echoes God's promise that he has so much more for us and that he will guide us on our healing journey. You can help your parishioner listen for and begin to recognize the voice of hope in their life. Once we partner with

God and enter the hope-filled process, it leads us to forgiveness instead of resentment, authenticity instead of hiding, and truth instead of fear.

Hope doesn't exist apart from a growing confidence in the promises of a good God who invites us to surrender our ashes so they can be transformed into beauty. Supporting your parishioner in understanding, owning, and declaring God's promises as outlined in scripture is an important part of the process. You can gently guide him or her to surrender their fear to a good Father who will replace it with strength.

Our hope in Christ is integrally tied to knowing who we are in him. When there is a loss of hope, look for disconnection with spiritual identity.

True identity. Identity theft is a crime in which an impostor obtains key pieces of personal identifying information and then uses that information for his own personal gain. In my work as a clinical psychologist at a residential treatment facility for women, I see an even more insidious type of identity theft. I see women who have, in essence, had their divine identities stolen by eating disorders. They have lost connection with the God-given glory of what it means to be a woman. This inadequacy is perpetuated by a lie that underlies our cultural over-emphasis on physical perfection: "The only thing that is truly important or valuable about your identity as a woman is your appearance." This lie begins to subtly affect us when we are insecure in our true identity and the disconnection with our true self is reinforced.

Individuals struggling with an eating disorder have forfeited key pieces of their "identifying information" to "an imposter." They forfeit the truth about their bodies, identities, and roles in the world. You can help them to identify these lies, throw them away, and replace them with God's truths that "I am fearfully and wonderfully made. I am special, holy, and chosen. I am royalty with a divine calling of which I am worthy. I am a child of the most high God" (Psalm 139:14; 1 Peter 2:9; Ephesians 4:1; Psalm 82:6). Appearance is just one lie the enemy uses to distort identity.

In my work with Christian women and adolescent girls who are fighting to take back their stolen identities, I often share with them the story of a woman who spent 18 years of her life bent over, unable to straighten up. This woman is not known for her amazing appearance or incredible talent; no, the story of this woman lives on due to her brush with greatness and instantaneous healing from a horrible infirmity. What is interesting about this story from Luke 13 is that the Pharisees criticized Jesus for wanting to heal on the Sabbath a woman they saw as very lowly. My guess is that she surely did not fit whatever the cultural ideal was for a woman in her day. Jesus very quickly corrected the Pharisees and spoke to the woman's true identity when he said, "… should not this woman, a daughter of Abraham, whom Satan has kept bound for eighteen long years be set free on the Sabbath day from what bound her?" (v. 16, NIV).

While the cultural ideals in those times may have been different from today's, the characters are the same. Jesus reminds us of who our Father is, and that makes all the difference. The "impostor" who tried to steal this woman's identity 2,000 years ago is the same one who deceives men and women today. Similarly, the Father who instills self-worth and restores her to an upright position is also the same.

Desire. Underneath every human desire is a deep and God-given desire— to be known, to be loved, to be interpersonally effective, and for a woman, to be beautiful. The irony is that many of the women I treat are incredibly physically beautiful according to current societal standards, and yet they feel deficient and grossly inadequate on many levels. The enemy distorts our God-given desires. Before we know it, we have been deceived into thinking that something or someone else is the solution. The prophet Isaiah speaks to this. "Come, all you who are thirsty, come to the waters; and you who have no money, come, buy and eat! Come, buy wine and milk without money and without cost. Why spend money on what is not bread, and your labor on what does not satisfy? Listen, listen to me, and eat what is good, and you will delight in the richest of fare. Give ear and come to me; listen, that you may live" (Isaiah 55:1-3, NIV).

Many of us are terrified of our desires – not just our deepest desires, but any desires. We run from our wants, repress our hopes, and try to escape our longings. But our desires are part of being human, of being alive. God made us "desiring people." Longing, hoping, and wanting is part of being fully human—it's not a flaw or a sin. We long for love, security, and meaning. God has made us so that he fills that void in our hearts. His love, his strength, and his guidance give us the joy and purpose for which he created us. Many of us, though, need to do some work to uncover our true desires. His promise is that as we cry out in trust and thirst for him, he comes and satisfies our needs and longings with good things.

Destiny. I teach my clients the biblical truth that we are a Spirit-filled, royal priesthood. We are sons and daughters of the king: cherished, prized, valued, accepted, and warmly received by God. We walk confidently in his authority and power because he fashioned us for "greater works" (John 14:12). As eating disorder sufferers begin to embrace this true identity, the work of learning their unique gifts and walking out their God-given purpose and destiny can also begin. Walking in our God-given destiny can only occur when we embrace the foundational truth that God is a good father. The world tells us that his promises are too good to be true and that we need to take care of ourselves, but the Scripture beckons us to no longer conform to this pattern of thinking, and instead to surrender our worldly mindsets and be transformed by the God who is even better than we imagine him to be. Help your parishioner along the path of being transformed by the renewing of their mind. Then they will know and be able to walk in what is in God's heart for their lives—his good, pleasing, and perfect desire for them.

Small Groups for Eating Disorders

Any of the above topics can lend themselves to a small group study. Related topics for small group study would include body image, healthy relationship with food, what it means to be wholly male or wholly female, etc. A church community may also want to consider establishing a support group designed specifically for individuals in recovery from an eating disorder. The following are wonderful resources for small group study or for a support group:

- *Hope for the hollow: A 30 day inside-out makeover for women recovering from anorexia, bulimia, and binge eating disorders* by Jenna Morrow.
- Findingbalance.com, a Christian eating disorder program providing digital learning libraries, online support programs, semi-annual conferences, and small group tools.

- *HEAL, Healthy eating and abundant living: Your diet-free, faith-filled guide to a fabulous life* by Allie Marie Smith and Judy Wardell Halliday.
- *Hope, help, and healing for eating disorders: A new approach to treating anorexia, bulimia, and overeating* by Gregory L. Jantz.
- *Seeing yourself in God's image: Overcoming anorexia and bulimia* by Martha Homme. This curriculum includes a group member's guide and a facilitator's guide.

Final Words

We see the dichotomy; we live in a world focused on perfection, where millions struggle with body image issues, low self-esteem, and eating disorders, yet we serve a God who created all of his children in his extraordinary image. Because we exist in this world of messages that seek to distort and confuse people's minds, it is imperative that as Christians, we friends and family members champion those in our lives who are afflicted, just as Jesus championed the woman in Luke 13. We must always remember who we are, who our father is, and what he has said about our divine identity and destiny.

If you (or someone you know and love) has an eating disorder, please get help. Please take whatever steps are required to reclaim the holy identity Satan has stolen from you. Recovery is possible. Once set free from the bondage of anorexia, bulimia, or binge eating, you can return to the life God has always intended for you. If you are in recovery from an eating disorder, stay strong, knowing that the God of the entire universe is standing alongside you in your progress forward. Every time you say "no" to the lure of your former eating disorder, and "yes" to your new life of walking in the light of truth, you shine like a star in the heavens proclaiming God's beauty for the universe to see.

References

Arcelus, J., Mitchell, A. J., Wales, J., & Nielsen, S. (2011). Mortality rates in patients with anorexia nervosa and other eating disorders. *Archives of General Psychiatry, 68(7)*, 724-731.

Eating Disorder Hope. eatingdisorderhope.com/information/statistics-studies

Grodstein, F., Levine, R., Spencer, T., Colditz, G.A., Stampfer, M. J. (1996). Three year follow up of participants in a commercial weight loss program: Can you keep it off? *Archives of Internal Medicine, 156 (12), 1302.*

Gustafson-Larson, A.M., & Terry, R.D. (1992). Weight-related behaviors and concerns of fourth-grade children. *Journal of American Dietetic Association,* 818-822.

Holm-Denoma, J. M., Witte, T. K., Gordon, K. H., et al. (2008). Death by suicide among individuals with anorexia as arbiters between competing explanations of the anorexia-suicide link. *Journal of Affective Disorders, 107(1-3),* 231-236.

Hudson, J. I., Hiripi, E., Pope, H. G., & Kessler, R. C. (2007). The prevalence and correlates of eating disorders in the national comorbidity survey replication. *Biological Psychiatry, 61(3),* 348–358.

Kaye, W. (2008). Neurobiology of anorexia and bulimia nervosa. *Physiology & Behavior, 94(1),* 121-135.

Keel, P. K., Dorer, D. J., Eddy, K. T., Franko, D., Charatan, D., & Herzog, D. B. (2003).

Predictors of mortality in eating disorders. *Archives of General Psychiatry, 60(2),* 179-183.

National Center on Addiction and Substance Abuse (CASA) at Columbia University. (2003). Food for thought: Substance abuse and eating disorders. New York: National Center on Addiction and Substance Abuse.

National Eating Disorders Association website. Statistics: Eating disorders and their precursors. Accessed Feb. 2012. http://www.nationaleatingdisorders.org/general-statistics

The National Institute of Mental Health: Eating disorders: Facts about eating disorders and the search for solutions. Pub No. 01-4901. Accessed Feb. 2002. www.nimh.nih.gov/health/publications/eating-disorders-new-trifold/index.shtml

Neumark-Sztainer, D. (2005). *I'm, Like, SO Fat!* New York: The Guilford Press. 5.

Shisslak, C.M., Crago, M., & Estes, L.S. (1995). The spectrum of eating disturbances. *International Journal of Eating Disorders, 18 (3),* 209219.

Wade, T. D., Keski-Rahkonen A., & Hudson J. (2011). Epidemiology of eating disorders. In M. Tsuang and M. Tohen (Eds.), *Textbook in Psychiatric Epidemiology (3ʳᵈ ed.),* 343-360. New York: Wiley.

Robert Shaw, D.Min.

Robert B. Shaw Jr. is a Licensed Professional Counselor, dually licensed in Virginia and North Carolina, and a National Board Certified Counselor. He is also an ordained minister and Bible teacher who has served as a youth pastor, Christian education director, adult education director, musician, and executive pastor in churches in New Jersey, Colorado, Maryland, and North Carolina for over twenty-five years.

Dr. Shaw spent several years counseling in church settings and community agencies and counseling military personnel and their families near Ft. Bragg, North Carolina. He specializes in trauma related issues: addictions, abuse, depression, anxiety disorders, life adjustment issues, loss, and grief counseling with church leaders and pastors, adolescents, and adults.

He serves as an adjunct professor for Liberty University, is a published author, and is a sought-out church and conference speaker who teaches practical applications of biblical truths for everyday life. Dr. Shaw often travels to the Philippines to teach and train local pastors, youth, Christian school teachers, seminary and university students, and local first responders regarding the practical aspects of Christian counseling, trauma and grief recovery, pastoral care, and mental health awareness. Dr. Shaw is the author of *Created for Significance* (2013), WestBow Press; *Created for Covering* (2013), WestBow Press; *Created for Purpose* (2015), WestBow Press; *Created for Understanding* (2016), WestBow Press; and *Created for Belonging* (2018), WestBow Press.

Dr. Shaw holds a bachelor's degree in religious studies from Wagner College, New York, a Master of Divinity degree from Christian International Theological School, Florida, and a Master of Arts in professional counseling from Liberty University, Virginia. He holds a Doctor of Ministry degree in formational counseling, a practical theology, from Ashland Theological Seminary, Ohio. He is a member of the American Association of Christian Counselors and serves the AACC as credentialing board director and in professional development. Bob and his wife, Lorinda, have been married since 1978, and they have five children and six grandchildren. He loves running, sports, the beach, traveling to historical sites, and spending time with family.

CHAPTER 14

How to Develop an Effective Grief Recovery Ministry

Robert Shaw, D.Min.

"The spirit of a man can endure his sickness, but as for a broken spirit who can bear it?" (Proverbs 18:14, NASB).

"My spirit is broken, my days are extinguished, the grave is ready for me… My eye has also grown dim because of grief, and all my members are as a shadow" (Job 17:1, 7, NASB).

"The Lord is near to the broken hearted, and saves those who are crushed in spirit" (Psalm 34:18, NASB).

Considering all the emotions we experience as human beings, fear, rejection, and grief, which are often interrelated, are among the feelings we most want to avoid. Human nature is such that we seek to avoid pain, normally at all costs. We will do whatever we can to avoid, stay ahead of, and/or medicate our pain. We try to stay busy, we try to control our environment and other people, or we try to isolate ourselves, all with the intent of keeping pain at bay. The problem is that as long we live on this fallen, imperfect earth, it is impossible to avoid pain. Pain and loss are universal.

So, since "Plan A" of avoiding pain is impossible, we subconsciously attempt to formulate "Plan B." Plan B usually develops into Plan C, Plan D, and so on, and varies from person to person and situation to situation. These alternative coping mechanisms include denying the pain, medicating the pain, ignoring the pain, or projecting the pain onto someone else. In like manner, we try to avoid experiences and expressions of grief because they tend to carry with them additional and secondary feelings and beliefs from which we want to run. These include a perceived sense of weakness, insecurity, uncertainty, unpredictability, loss of control, and vulnerability.

But grief is not something to avoid. Grief is a natural emotional response to loss; loss of any kind. Some of the contributors to the Diagnostic and Statistical Manual of Mental Disorders, Fifth Edition (DSM-5, which was released in May of 2013) believed at that time that grief should have been categorized as a mental health "dysfunction" or as a "disorder," but many professional mental health providers spoke out strongly against doing so because grief is not a disorder. Grief is a *natural and inevitable* reaction to loss.

Loss, which is a common life experience for all of us, naturally creates grief of varying levels. Consequently, it is not a dysfunction. The Creator so regretted his creation of humans due to their great wickedness, evil, and corruption that he was "grieved in his heart" (Genesis 6:5- 12, NASB). The Holy Spirit can be grieved (Ephesians 4:30), and it is clear that Jesus was "deeply grieved, to the point of death" (Matthew 26:38, NASB). Jesus was described prophetically in Isaiah 53:3 (NASB) as follows: "He was despised and forsaken of men, a man of sorrows, and acquainted with grief; and like one from whom men hide their face He was despised, and we did not esteem Him." God is not dysfunctional when he faces and experiences grief, so it is unrealistic and inaccurate for us to think we can avoid grief or that it is unhealthy to feel the pain of grief.

Certainly prolonged grief which is unaddressed can develop into dysfunctional situations such as depression, which *is* a mental health diagnosis. Consider how crucial it is to help someone identify losses in his or her life. We need to be aware that many people need to walk through a grieving process. A client may be holding onto or suppressing grief that they have ignored for many years. If so, walking through a grieving process is essential in their treatment of depression. Furthermore, many people – especially those in the church – feel guilty when they are grieving and/or are not always feeling happy, upbeat, and victorious. Christians need to have permission to grieve!

Death, divorce, and unemployment are common losses, but there are many other loss experiences that can freeze us emotionally.

Grief, the <u>normal</u> emotion one feels when suffering a loss of any kind:

- Can be real, anticipated, and/or imagined
- Can be experienced in conjunction with:
  - Death
  - Divorce
  - Change in employment / dreams
  - Health changes or issues
  - Trust violations
  - Injury to one's sense of self, security, or innocence

It is never "if" we will experience loss but "when."

Loss can occur in many circumstances; sometimes in situations that we tend to overlook. It is common and appropriate to grieve when a loved one dies. However, there are many variables that affect a person's level of grief when a loved one passes away. For example, how close the grieving person was to the deceased person makes a difference. A beloved grandparent, a spouse, a sibling, a close and devoted parent, and even a best friend are special relationships that can be especially difficult to lose. And tragic losses like a suicide, a car accident, or the death of a child can overwhelm a grieving person simply because of the nature of the loss. In these situations, what is referred to as *complicated grief* can occur.

Complicated grief occurs when a person becomes stuck and struggles to break free from the powerful grip of traumatic circumstances. It can often mimic these symptoms of Post-Traumatic Stress Disorder (PTSD).

- **Trauma.** Intense fear, loss of control, helplessness, and the threat of annihilation; something that overwhelms a person's normal adapting or coping skills; an event or situation that lingers and influences a person's life; something that shakes a person to the core.
- **Abuse.** The wrong use of another person (or animal); being touched by evil!
- **Violation.** Having one's boundaries broken through by force, betrayal, or deception.

Complicated grief can be felt in survivor's guilt, extreme agitation, self-destructive behaviors, suicidal ideation, sleep and appetite disturbances,

215

strong reactions to triggers in normal events, and intrusive thoughts. Some dynamics that contribute to complicated grief include the nature of the loss having been incomprehensible, the loss itself being considered exceptionally untimely, and the culture or environment not allowing the grief process to transpire.

Unseen loss is often overlooked, as well. The loss of significance, security, identity, direction, and/or purpose can occur when someone loses their job through layoffs, being fired, or even a typically positive retirement experience. Or, when a youngster or an adult experiences sexual trauma, such as abuse, assault, or rape, they often feel a loss of innocence, safety, and security, as well as the loss of a sense of wholeness and purity, among others. For example, it is estimated that one in four girls and one in six boys are sexually assaulted by the time they turn eighteen years old (Centers for Disease Control and Prevention, 2012). The sense of loss in these and many other situations are underestimated and can define us, re-define us, or alter our belief systems. Many people have experienced, or will experience, similar losses in their lifetimes, and they may need to walk through a grieving process.

In the death of a loved one, a child may not be able to process the loss, and the experience may remain with them into adulthood. "A child takes the loss of a parent, whether through death, divorce, or however, as a personal rejection. Unhealed rejections become seedbeds of diseased "matter" such as bitterness, envy, rage, fear of rejection, and a sense of inferiority" (Payne, 2001, p. 36). Young people are not developmentally able to recognize that they need to grieve their losses. Victims of rape, physical abuse, and other trauma also experience similar effects which can linger for many years without being grieved. Part of the healing process is to grieve our losses in order to regain stability and re-establish our personhood, identity, and significance.

For adult survivors of childhood trauma, I have found that it is necessary to encourage them to identify losses in their lives that they may not have considered or faced before, and to then process them together. I assign a loss timeline for homework, asking them to briefly list the loss they experienced and their approximate age when the loss occurred. It is important to have the individual list every experience they can remember which they consider a loss. It could be of a loved one, innocence (such as from abuse or rape), stability (such as from parental divorce), or any similar situation. I then have the person describe each loss separately, ask what they remember feeling about the loss at the time and how they may feel about it in the present moment, and I invite them to grieve the loss in their own way. I also have them nail the loss to a homemade wooden cross I use in my counseling office, as a symbolic way of leaving the loss at the cross.

In her classic 1969 book, *On Death and Dying*, Dr. Elizabeth Kubler-Ross presented what she called the stages of grief. These stages may actually be more a set of reactions to grief rather than stages of grief, since they do not always occur in the same order for all people. They are as follows:

- Denial and Isolation
- Anger
- Bargaining
- Depression
- Acceptance

Kubler-Ross identified these human emotional reactions to loss as normal responses within the emotion of grief. Many times, one who is grieving experiences a sense of numbness, guilt, yearning, sorrow, or anguish, and even physical manifestations such as migraine headaches, body aches, and sleep dysfunctions, among others, can also occur. In the denial stage, emotions can be absent, delayed, or flat, or, in contrast, they can be demonstrative and uncontrollable. The anger stage may appear as prolonged anger, short temper, raging outbursts, looking to blame someone, and seeking revenge. The bargaining stage may manifest itself through statements like, "I wish…" or "If only…" Perhaps the most recognizable stage is depression. While one's experience of depression is totally understandable in grieving, a growing and prolonged sense of anguish, pain, and sorrow can be problematic. Finally, as a person travels through the grieving process, eventually they arrive at acceptance. With this stage comes a sense of relief, peace, release, and even a degree of understanding. The loss cannot be reversed, but the emotional pain can subside with treatment.

It is natural for anyone to grieve when a loss is suffered. If we do not grieve, we often become "stuck" emotionally and mentally, essentially "freezing" our identity and our life. But the reverse can also be true; a person can be "stuck" by choosing to stay in constant "grief mode," and grief can become his or her identity, how he or she is known and recognized by others. A person who is "stuck" may experience such cognitive distortions as:

- **Arbitrary Inferences.** Coming to conclusions without the facts.
- **Emotional Reasoning.** Thinking based on assumptions, perceptions, and what they *feel* is true.
- **Over Generalizations.** Taking one situation and making a blanket judgment (all teens; all men; all churches; always; etc.).
- **Personalization.** Making external events personal, as if such events were their fault.
- **Dichotomous Thinking.** All or nothing, black and white.
- **Mind Reading.** Thinking that they *know* what is going on in the mind of another person; dealing in intentions and assumptions.

Everyone the world over experiences grief and a sense of loss in certain situations; for example, the death of a loved one, the loss of a job, when going through a divorce, etc., but the way these feelings are experienced and expressed differs across cultures. In America, we do not have any particular cultural norm for grieving. Christianity, in particular, does not have a set response to grief. Even if grief is accepted initially, bereavement and mourning are only expected to be short-lived. Here are the definitions of some pertinent terms:

- **Grief** – keen mental and emotional suffering or distress over affliction or loss; sharp sorrow; painful regret; grief also has physical, behavioral, social, and philosophical dimensions.
- **Bereavement** – the state or fact of being sad over the loss or deprivation of something or someone.
- **Mourning** – an outward indication of grief over a loss; a period of time during which signs of grief are shown.

Unfortunately, the result is often an expectation that a grieving person needs to "get over it," and very quickly, I might add. In other cultures, death is surrounded by rituals and customs that help people grieve and mourn. For example:

- **Hinduism** provides 30 days of mourning.
- **Buddhism** provides 49-100 days of mourning.
- **Judaism** provides seven days of intense mourning; after that, generally 30 more days of mourning, or in the death of a parent, up to one year.
- **Islam** provides three days of mourning; for widows, four months and 10 days of mourning.
- **Christianity** has no standard custom for the period of mourning after death.

Rituals offer people ways to express their grief and provide opportunities for community members to support those who are grieving. People adapt the beliefs and values of their culture to meet their own unique experiences, needs, and situations. As a result, grief responses within a culture vary from person to person, especially in societies made up of people from a variety of cultural backgrounds, such as the United States.

There is not just one way to grieve or mourn. The length of time to mourn also varies individually, but in our American society especially, it seems that often we neither have permission to grieve, nor do we give others permission to others to grieve. This may be because grieving is believed to be a sign of weakness. For many people, it is difficult for them to witness others' expressed emotions, but the truth is that grieving is not a sign of being weak; it is a sign of being human! Grieving is a timely release of emotions that are linked to loss of any kind.

Another reason we don't receive permission to grieve is because our lifestyle is fast-paced and involves constant stimuli. Therefore, our grieving has to be completed quickly, lest we be perceived as weird or flawed. While it certainly is important to move forward through our grief, getting to the other side often requires someone (or a few individuals) to walk with us through the valley of the shadow of death. In order to move forward, we often need to grieve what has been lost. We all need to have permission to grieve!

I have written previously on the core longings of the human soul (see end of chapter for references), and I have found that grief affects the core elements in a person's life. For example, here are some typical human core longings that are impacted by grief:

- **Significance/Identity.** Ignoring her grief caused Tamar to become "desolate" (2 Samuel 13:1, 10-15, 19-20, NASB). Elisha's crying out essentially meant, "There goes my life and identity!" (2 Kings 2:12, 16-17, NASB).
- **Safety/Covering.** A feeling of vulnerability and insecurity.
- **Purpose.** Doubts about the future. "Can I go on with my life?"
- **Understanding.** Isolation; shame. "No one will understand or accept me."
- **Belonging.** A developing sense of disconnect. "Where can I go now?" Consider Peter's confession: "Lord, to whom shall we go? You have words of eternal life" (John 6:68, NASB). Regardless of how we feel, we are connected to Jesus no matter what occurs in life.
- **Love.** "If he/she loved me, why would they leave or do that to me?"

The essential truth is that no one needs (or deserves) to be identified by their loss. Everyone suffers loss. If we were identified by our losses, we would all be carrying some very depressing and debilitating identities. Even being "unemployed" is a label. While it is true that someone who is without work is unemployed, one must be careful about how such an identity can become a prevailing label. It is important to grieve a loss. We need to know that we have permission to grieve and that we have a safe place to grieve. Whether that safe place is with a loved one, a pastor, a counselor, a church group ministry, or a good friend, it is highly important that the grieving process takes its course. A person who allows his or her grieving to be a release of loss and sadness can also expect the Holy Spirit to restore and return their peace, contentment, joy, and equilibrium in order for them to regain their true identity.

The church has a unique position with—and role for—those who experience grief. If anyone has a message of hope, it is the church, which bears the message of Christ's rejection, betrayal, death, resurrection, and hope for our future. With some training, a local church can develop a lay ministry and small group grief recovery care ministry. Many churches often minister initially to individuals and families in times of loss by providing assistance, meals, and support during the early stages of grief. However, once the funeral or the initial aspects of loss are over, the grieving person often feels a gap in support, because there is little or no follow-up. Speaking as a pastor and a licensed counselor, I can say that neither the church alone nor a counselor alone can provide all the help a grieving person needs. It's a case of "both and," not "either or." That is, the best scenario is for a grieving person to be in individual or family counseling with a Christian counselor and concurrently be attending a church-sponsored grief care support group. This model allows for both the therapy that may be needed and a feeling of connectedness to the local church as the healing body of Christ. Such coordination of care encourages the partnership of the ministry of the church with that of a trusted and trained Christian counselor.

In establishing a grief care ministry, a church can provide a consistent and continuous presence to individuals who are still on the grief journey. The pastor or church leaders can help identify individuals who feel a calling to be a help to those who are mourning. Training these individuals is usually not very difficult, as they may already be able to relate in many ways to those who are suffering loss. Some basic thoughts for training are as follows:

What Does Not Help:

"I know exactly how you feel."
"You will feel better in a few weeks."
"He or she lived a good life. Some people die much younger."
"You need to get over it."
"Aren't you over this yet?"
"You should get on with your life."
"You can still have another child."
"It was God's will."
"It wasn't God's will."
"I know someone who felt fine in about a month or so."
"Your family will hate to see you cry."

What Does Help:

- Your presence—often your silent presence. Be more of a guide and companion through the grieving journey.
- Your understanding that it is natural to grieve.
- Whenever possible, working with the bereaved in the context of their family and culture.
- Being aware of the external conditions and the resources of the grieving person, thus enabling you to provide additional assistance as appropriate.
- Allowing time – whatever that time is.
- Assisting those who are grieving to anticipate potential difficult times, such as going through the first year of holidays and family celebrations, and helping them make plans to cope more effectively (meaningful pictures, music, making sure certain supportive people will be participating, etc.).
- Encouraging the bereaved to tell their story and share their memories ("My favorite memory of your loved one is…"), discussing the trauma and the circumstances, encouraging the bereaved to tell their story, listening.
- Avoiding over catastrophizing; acknowledging and validating the loss or event in its reality, while gently conveying the conviction that the bereaved will survive the experience; instilling hope.
- Exercising patience with the grieving person, understanding that the journey will involve several ups and downs.
- Journaling or activities in which they can express their feelings without words, such as art, music, finger painting (this may be especially helpful with children), etc.
- Engaging in physical activity.
- Finding a support group and attending it faithfully.
- Encouraging and facilitating the grieving person's re-connection with social contacts (as opposed to being isolated); helping the bereaved to re-establish healthy routines and make room for new dreams and a new life.
- Being supportive, kind, and willing to serve.

- Encouraging the person as the grieving process grows, helping them understand that they don't have to feel guilty if they seem to be getting on with their life; that beginning to enjoy life again is not a dishonor to the missing loved one.
- Empathizing with the pain of the bereaved while at the same time maintaining objectivity; a balance is essential. "Rejoice with those who rejoice, and weep with those who weep" (Romans 12:15, NASB).

I can vividly remember a supportive experience when I was thirty-two years old, shortly after my father died. A few days after the funeral, after a mid-week church meeting, a friend of mine came over to where I was sitting. As he expressed his sincere condolences, he began to cry, along with me. No other words were spoken during those few, incredibly healing moments. His support helped my grieving process, and the shared pain that I felt we experienced together exponentially helped in my grief recovery process.

Dr. David Crenshaw, a clinical psychologist who specializes in grief counseling, provides what he calls Seven Tasks of Mourning (Crenshaw, 1990):

1. Acknowledge the Reality of the Loss
2. Identify and Express the Emotions of Grief
3. Commemorate the Loss
4. Acknowledge Ambivalence – a mix of emotions, such as love for the deceased, as well as anger for the perception of desertion through death (or real desertion through divorce).
5. Resolution of the Ambivalence – a realistic balance of warm and hostile feelings needs to be addressed and discussed with the bereaved, in order to break through any blockages in resolving grief).
6. Letting Go
7. Moving On

Resilience, the ability to bounce back, overcome, and continue to show healthy development and adjustment, is a growing topic of attention in counseling, especially in military counseling and grief counseling. Elements affecting people's resiliency include previous exposure to and recovery from adverse situations or traumatic events, and how they dealt with them in the past; how successfully they adapt to the situation or circumstances; the quality of their community (family, church, work place, etc.); their degree of self-efficacy and healthy self-awareness; the effectiveness of their coping skills; their cognitive ability and their ability to regulate their emotions; their degree of social support; the maturity level of their faith; and their temperament and personality.

GriefShare is an excellent Christ-centered, lay ministry developing resource that can be purchased and utilized by the local church. The training is given by 46 Christian leaders, pastors, and counselors, all of whom have personally experienced various levels of loss and grief. It is an excellent tool for a church's lay ministry and grief recovery groups. In addition, the American Association of Christian Counselors (AACC) has training materials to help a church begin a grief recovery ministry. One resource is the Traumatic Grief, Loss, and Crisis program, which provides specific training for caring for the grieving young person and adult.

In the book of Acts 3:1-11, we read the story of a lame man who was healed. This man had lost several things, including his health; he was lame from birth. Upon his healing by the power of the Holy Spirit, he experienced restoration of much of what he had lost, leading to the recovery of his core longings. Among the things the man had lost were his physical mobility, his ability to earn income, his social status, and his independence. As Peter and John entered the temple, they gave the man their time and attention (significance, helping him overcome shame), a reason for hope (purpose), real help through practicality and involvement (understanding, love), knowledge of Jesus and his presence (love, understanding, safety), new life direction and the ability to be part of the house of God (purpose, belonging, covering), and the opportunity to glorify God and to help others receive ministry, as well (understanding, purpose).

From this account, we understand that the church has been given the responsibility to reflect Christ by carrying on his ministry of restoration and reconciliation to the hurting people with whom we come in contact. As we minister to grieving people, we have the potential of being seen as Christ in the flesh. People may know about God, but can they experience

God through us? It would be gratifying indeed if we were to hear a similar declaration as Job's: "My ears had heard of you but now my eyes have seen you" (Job 42:5, NIV).

While there are many Bible passages that can be used to encourage a grieving person, here are several verses (NASB) I would like to point out as I bring this chapter to an end.

- **Psalm 31:7** – "I will rejoice and be glad in Your lovingkindness, because You have seen my affliction; You have known the troubles of my soul,"
- **Hebrews 4:15-16** – "For we do not have a high priest who cannot sympathize with our weaknesses, but One who has been tempted in all things as we are, yet without sin. Therefore let us draw near with confidence to the throne of grace, so that we may receive mercy and find grace to help in time of need."
- **1 Peter 5:10** – "After you have suffered for a little while, the God of all grace, who called you to His eternal glory in Christ, will Himself perfect, confirm, strengthen and establish you."

Finally, referring to himself, Jesus himself quoted a passage from the book of Isaiah during his earthly ministry. He also charged his disciples and the church to remain steadfast to the Father, for as they did so, "greater works than these shall he do" (John 14:9-21, NASB). Through the grace and power of the Holy Spirit, we have the privilege of bringing grieving people to the Father, bringing light to their places of darkness, bringing comfort and freedom to their souls, and restoring the peace of Jesus in their lives. The passage Jesus quoted is Isaiah 61:1-3, and we can glean from this passage a clarion call to help those who mourn and are hurting.

We can bring good news and hope.
We can ask God to heal the brokenhearted.
We can proclaim liberty and freedom.
We can declare that God will vindicate and comfort.
We can help those who mourn discover rest and peace.
We can help wounded people recover their praise.
We can rejoice in God again, as he restores.

References

Centers for Disease Control and Prevention (2012). *Sexual violence facts at a glance.* Accessed September, 2016 from http://www.cdc.gov/ViolencePrevention/pdf/SV-DataSheet-a.pdf

Crenshaw, D. A. (1990). *Bereavement: Counseling the grieving throughout the life cycle.* New York: The Continuum Publishing Company.

Kubler-Ross, E. (1969). *On death and dying.* New York: Simon and Schuster.

Payne, L. (2001). *Restoring the Christian soul.* Grand Rapids, MI: Baker Books.

Kay Lyn Carlson, LSW

Kay Lyn Carlson is a social worker specializing in reproductive loss healing and recovery. Her story is featured in the book *Planned from the Start: A Healing Devotional* written in conjunction with the recent movie *Unplanned*. As the founder and director of Choose Grace International, Kay Lyn provides professional and lay counseling, education, training, and consultation services and shares her redemptive story of grace after an abortion. She is also the division leader for the American Association of Christian Counselor's (AACC) Reproductive Loss and Sexual Trauma Network.

As a speaker, Kay Lyn has been a featured presenter at the United Nations, various American Association of Christian Counseling conferences, Heartbeat International, National Right to Life, and assorted women's conferences, churches, and pregnancy care centers. Her passion is to educate others on both the moral injuries incurred after an abortion and the critical importance of a holistic treatment approach. Kay Lyn believes that abortion is—through moral injury—the root cause of many mental illnesses, addictions, and suicides.

Recognizing that abortion is not the only reproductive loss suffered, Choose Grace International is committed to offering services to those dealing with infertility, miscarriage, still birth, adoption, and early infant death, helping them to grow and mature.

Kay Lyn earned her undergraduate and graduate social work degrees at Washburn University in Topeka, Kansas and is currently working on her Doctorate in Faith Learning Integration at Omega Graduate School in Dayton, Tennessee.

CHAPTER 15

How to Develop an Effective Reproductive Loss Recovery Ministry

Kay Lyn Carlson, LSW

"It is a silent place of tears in the hollow of sorrow."
~ Margaret Bauman White

Sarah sits in the pew listening to a passionate sermon about the value of human life and how God hates the shedding of innocent blood. The pastor is on fire today and believes he's connecting well with his congregation whom he loves, cares deeply about, and would never knowingly wound.

But because Sarah is buried beneath a pile of shame, his words are like daggers piercing her battered and sickened soul. What the pastor doesn't realize is that Sarah's well-being (psychological, social, and spiritual) has been shattered and is paralyzed with fear and shame. She shares her anguish and grief with no one. She wants to run out of the service (and run away from herself) as her internal, unseen battle rages on – in silence and isolation.

Her eyes remaining fixed on the pastor, Sarah emotionally disconnects. Self-deprecating thoughts run rampant and take over: *"If the church only knew, they wouldn't want you here. You don't belong here. They wouldn't want you teaching their kids in Sunday School. Look at you: you're a fake, a fraud, a phony! You're a murderer. YOU should die! You killed an innocent child, your own precious child. Look at you. God can't stand the sight of you..."*

Sarah jolts back into reality to escape her thoughts. Her earnest prayer is for God to take her life because she cannot deal with her tormented soul. Yet she sits in the pew next to her husband and three children, falsely portraying that she's got it all together with her perfect, happy family.

The characters and stories included in this chapter are fictional. Any resemblance to actual persons or events is purely coincidental.

229

As a Christian social worker who specializes in reproductive loss, I am amazed at how many women (and men) are suffering from the loss of a baby or babies through miscarriage, abortion, stillbirth, early infant death, adoption placement, and infertility. Tragically, the heart-breaking aftermath of these losses often remains hidden. Untold numbers of men and women grieve the empty, childless womb, and that grief is often causative to—or interrelated with—the heavy burdens of depression, anxiety, suicidal ideation, addictions, fear, anger, and/or self-punishing behavior(s) that they carry with them; many for the rest of their lives.

It is important for pastors, church leaders, and congregational members to realize that they can unknowingly be unhelpful to—or even an obstacle to—those struggling to cope with and heal from reproductive loss. Through the power of story, the initial part of this chapter briefly highlights the personal impact on those who have experienced a specific type of reproductive loss. The remainder of the chapter explores five key components of developing an effective reproductive loss ministry. It will take time, trust, courage, humility, forgiveness, patience, understanding, and grace for the church and the image-bearer/sufferer to effectively navigate this area of ministry.

Infertility [one of every six couples]

Excerpts from Margaret's reflection:

> Every month, what is longed for in the warmth of the womb—life—is shed, without ceremony, without acknowledgement. The deeply hoped-for possibility of life, a baby, is shed and gone. A childless mother's heart breaks again, but due to feelings of shame, soul-numbing sadness, and depression, she doesn't talk about it.
>
> Often silently, the longing parents begin the trek through lonely barrenness once more. Such is the life, defined by perpetual grief, of those who desperately yearn for a child. The intricacy and intimacy of the couple's relationship become burdened with ongoing loss, as hope

and anticipation struggle once again to not fall victim to grief and hopelessness. Countless appointments with medical professionals, intrusive, expensive, embarrassing, and painful procedures and injections and incessant waiting mixed with dread—define their lives. They unwillingly ride a proverbial emotional roller coaster every month. Their pain is exacerbated by their friends' baby showers, birth announcements, and discussions about their children—all of which serve as constant reminders of their sorrow and shame.

The journey through infertility eventually resolves one way or another: either a baby is conceived and born, a little one is lovingly adopted, or a woman or couple decides that life will be lived, but that love will be given in ways other than through parenthood. No matter the outcome, life is forever different, and we are changed. We either grow, or we continue living in the heartache and pain of what might have been.

The people of God can help those in the throes of infertility by acknowledging their own times of loss, powerlessness, and grief. Those yearning for a child need to know that they are "not alone in their aloneness." The most important gift that the church can offer the individual or couple waiting for a child is the willingness to compassionately hold that sense of unfulfilled longing with them. Words of hope and encouragement are helpful, but the message, "We will stand with you in this storm, knowing that God will get us through it together as the vulnerable human beings that we are," reminds the childless woman or couple that all of us share in being human. All of us have experienced loss, and relying on God to be the conduit for our anger and hurt—and ultimately our Father of love and miracles—is the only way we can retreat to a place of safety and comfort.

Miscarriage [one of every six pregnancies]

Excerpts related to Laura's two miscarriages:

> When I learned of my pregnancy, I was overjoyed and thrilled at the prospect of becoming a mother. A week later, I was going through a miscarriage. It was both emotionally and physically painful. After two months we decided to try again. I experienced intense fear during this time, thinking, "What if I cannot conceive, or even worse, what if I have another miscarriage?"

Laura conceived again, this time with twins, and miscarried one of them. She writes:

> There was fear of losing the pregnancies, fear of never having a healthy baby (ever), and wondering what I had done wrong and blaming myself for causing the previous miscarriage—and now this one. There was anger at God for letting this happen and doubt that he would grant me a new life. I feel like I'm invisible; that I'm the only one who has ever had to go through this, and that no one could understand my feelings of helplessness, inadequacy, and frustration. There was despair with my losses, and I regret that I never gave myself permission or time to process them. I feel shameful and inadequate because somehow my body couldn't do what it was supposed to. I was secretive; not wanting to burden others with something "so minor."

Another woman, Amber, shares what she wishes every pastor and congregational member who hasn't experienced a miscarriage knew:

> Platitudes such as "Your baby is in Jesus' care" or "You can try again" are not helpful; they are more hurtful. They don't acknowledge the loss: the loss of life, loss of future, and loss of hope. And there is no guarantee that

trying again will be successful. It's scary to try again, because what if miscarriage happens again? That's the battle within a woman's heart and mind: "I want to be a mother (or have another), but I'm not sure I can bear another loss."

Early Infant Death [over 22,000 babies each year in the United States]

Jordan and Leah tell about their baby's brief life:

> The fragility of life can teach us many things. It shows us who we truly are, what we're made of, and mostly, how little control we have over our own lives. When my wife and I lost our first child, our world came crashing down. I was so looking forward to being Sophia Joy's dad. When the day came to deliver her, mommy and I were both so excited! The anticipation of new life was palpable, and the uncertainties of our shared responsibility were exciting. When she was born and the cord tethering her life to her mom's was severed, she was free to experience her life on her own breaths and strength.
>
> Little did we know that an unknown, undiagnosed congenital heart defect (CHD) would claim her short, precious life a mere four hours later. The rush to save her life from lack of oxygenation filled us with adrenaline, causing us to forget everything around us. "Save our baby" was the only thought in our heads, and the only prayers our souls could muster. Surely the medical team could think of something. Surely we could take our sweet baby girl home to her crib. After all… God is good, right?
>
> Holding our little girl while she took her last breath on this earth, never having gotten to eat, or see the sun, or laugh, or partake of any of the achievements, pleasures,

or enjoyments this world can offer was soul-crushing. My wife had all but forgotten needing to recover from childbirth, and in a surge of instinctive maternal strength, was up walking and at her newborn's side. When you watch a soul slip away from the mortal coil and be taken up from this earth, it changes you.

My faith in God took a major blow, and in the anger stage of my grieving process (which isn't a step-by-step, organized pattern), I took out my heartbreak and wrath on the one person I'd believed could save her – God. I was broken, crushed, shaken, and enraged. The ongoing agony and nightmares kept us awake constantly. I had no hope of ever returning to normalcy, and the experience of other "Christians" chastising our pain like Job's friends only drove me further away from my childhood faith.

But that's not where the story ends. I'd like to say there is a neat, tidy, and trite answer for the problem of pain. There isn't, and that's ok. Pain teaches us many lessons, and some of those are quite unpleasant in our personal growth and journey. I've learned and am continuing to learn just how good God is. We have an adversary who steals, kills, and destroys, and I've been so close numerous times to becoming yet another victim, but God has made me a victor. I wish I could say that five years later I've healed and didn't cry writing this, but that's not the case. What I do know is that life, while fragile, is also beautiful in all of its mess, and that you'll never be more alone than if you allow pain to cause you to reject the love of God. It was there for me all along, even if I refused to acknowledge it. We've met so many people with similar heartbreaking stories, and have been able to share this experience to be used of God to show love and compassion to those who are hurting where we couldn't have otherwise. Turn your sorrow into strength, because joy often can come in the mourning.

Stillbirth [over 24,000 babies each year in the United States]

A father's wound shared by Earl:

> We knew our baby had died 24 hours before she was born. After the delivery, the hospital staff gave us some time alone, and my wife and I took turns holding her. She was so cute, wearing a little pink beanie on her head. When the doctor returned, he stated that it was better if we don't worry about it. That the baby's going to be fine. I didn't have time to think about it. Still in shock, I allowed the hospital to take care of her remains.
>
> To find some sense of relief, I numbingly walked to the waiting room to find my dad. When I saw him, I clutched onto him and began to weep. Immediately, he pushed back and exclaimed in front of everyone, "You gotta be a man!" I felt like I was falling. I was so taken aback by his response!
>
> Out of nowhere, my sister-in-law (also a hospital pediatrician) caught me. She grabbed me and held tight. "I've got you!" she said. It was like God being right there in the room assuring me, "I've got you, Earl, and I will never let go!"
>
> My sister-in-law took me to another room and just let me cry. We regret not having a funeral and allowing the doctor to take and dispose of her remains in such an unorthodox way. She was fully developed, and my wife and I needed time to grieve and have some sense of closure. Our church, where I was employed, didn't say or do anything for us—except for a card taped to my door from the district superintendent. It's been over 30 years now, and we still talk, and sometimes cry, about our irretrievable loss.

Adoption Placement [approximately 20,000 women place their child for adoption each year in the United States]

There are multiple reasons pregnant women choose adoption for their baby. An adoption decision can be made coercively (particularly for younger girls) in an unplanned or crisis pregnancy. Although circumstances vary greatly, factors such as age, economics, family dynamics, and/or relationship issues are often involved in the decision for a mother to place her child with someone who can hopefully provide better than she can in her present life situation. It is common for the mother to experience grief and loss; she feels abandoned with empty arms and an aching heart, wondering about—and often longing for—her baby for the rest of her life.

Christine shares her story:

> I was 18 when I got pregnant. I was barely into college. I was holding down an internship and had a million hopes and dreams for myself. I knew for sure that I did not want to terminate the pregnancy out of respect for this little person inside me. I needed to consider the baby's life as I was making decisions for my life.

> I did consider keeping the baby, but the more I thought about what I wanted to provide the baby with, the more I realized I just didn't have access to the right resources. I was a college student scraping by and still had a lot of growing up to do emotionally. Looking back, I don't think it's what the baby's father wanted, but neither of us was in a position to be responsible for a baby. The baby's father and I have been able to stay in contact all these years and thankfully he was supportive during that time.

> The more I heard about the family I placed my son with and how close we were in terms of hobbies, skills, and background, the more comfortable I got. I also felt a good

connection with the adoption agency staff. They were caring and genuine.

I was exhausted after giving birth, but the next day I spent some time with him. I remember him being wheeled into my room in a baby cart. He was all swaddled up with a cute cap on. I could only see his little face, and the poor thing was crying. I put one finger gently near his cheek and said it was okay; we would always be close. And he stopped crying. I will never forget that. That will be our moment forever.

I also held him when I was saying good bye. Holding him felt awkward, but I wanted to be able to tell him that I loved him and hug and kiss him so that he would know how much I loved him. I felt heartbroken. It's overwhelming to spend so much time with someone, even if you can't see him, and then walk away from a place knowing you are leaving him behind. But in my heart I knew he was in amazing care and going to a place where he could be so happy. A place where he would have everything he could possibly want. A place where he would have two loving and dedicated parents.

Abortion [one in four women—and men—have had an abortion in the United States]

Excerpts related to Julie's surgical abortion:

I had no idea the physical pain that would rack my body after the anesthesia wore off. Nobody told me that I would think of myself as the most inhumane of murderers in that I murdered my first child. I believed the loss of my second pregnancy to miscarriage was my penalty for aborting my baby. The scars that I carry on a mental, spiritual, and emotional level are permanent. My children live with the fact that their mother killed their sibling. The fact is that this choice kills an innocent child and also kills a portion of the soul of the mother. She is never the same because the burden of this horrific act is a weight that can never be lifted.

Paul shares his experience:

> We didn't start out intending to have an abortion… We went to Planned Parenthood thinking we would obtain information on how to plan for our role as parents. The decision we made to obtain an abortion was a decision we made together after being convinced that it was our best option, or a better option than having the baby. We were persuaded to have an abortion because we were told by the nurse that it was probably our best option because of our age… We initially planned and hoped we would parent the baby together.

> I hated myself for years and had a hard time looking at myself in the mirror, especially after entering adulthood and realizing what we really did in taking the life of our unborn child. I have suffered from bouts of depression, alcoholism, and drug abuse.

> Even now, more than thirty years later, I still have a hard time living with it… I had a very hard time getting close to my other children. When they were born I didn't feel as though I deserved them and feared something horrible would happen to them as punishment for the abortion.

Abortion is often misunderstood and mischaracterized. The political controversies surrounding pro-life and pro-choice viewpoints can overshadow the multilayered therapeutic and spiritual needs of a wounded client, couple, and/or family. Often, the church doesn't know how to respond, what to say, what to believe, what to do, and how to care for abortion-wounded souls.

The mother's womb is a sacred and holy place where God is at work creating one of his great masterpieces: an image-bearer of himself! One may wonder how anyone could ever have an abortion and allow something so horrific to happen—to their own child. Even worse, how can women continue to have more abortions? Did they not learn from the first one? Many times, the parents who've aborted a child wonder the same thing. *How could I?* They are often traumatized, perplexed, and haunted by their abortion decision.

Abortion is a very complex and delicate subject. So delicate, in fact, that often the wounded individual can barely utter the word; much less confront their involvement with it. Whereas other types of reproductive losses (excepting adoption placement) are *biological – beyond human control,* abortion is *volitional – intentionally terminating a pregnancy.* One man writes: "For nearly two decades, I never spoke about the abortion. Not a word… In reality, I simply suffered in silence from the deep wounds unseen and numbed, hidden and unresolved, even though my lifestyle and attitude screamed of them" (Burke, T., et. al. 2002, p. 93).

Indeed, it is essential to understand that the issues surrounding an abortion are not usually simplistic or clearly black and white. Research indicates that the majority of abortions are actually coerced or forced against the woman's will, sometimes violently! From deceptive or coercive so-called "counseling" at abortion facilities, to blackmail and/or threats of violence by manipulative parents or partners, according to recent reports [Rue, et. al. (2004), www.theunchoice.com] the majority (64%) of women felt pressured to have their abortion. Pressure for a woman to abort often comes from her husband, boyfriend, parents, employer, physician, landlord, college or university (most athletes lose their scholarship if pregnant), friends, family, and from the abortion industry itself.

> Many—perhaps even most—women choose abortion not according to their conscience, but in violation of the conscience…Many of the women I have treated knowingly violated their conscience or betrayed their maternal desires because of the pressures they faced. Those pressures were many: abandonment by their partner, poverty, homelessness, violence, lack of education, unemployment,

emotional problems, incest, rape, and fetal abnormalities, to name just a few. Many women felt they had "no choice" but to submit to an unwanted abortion (Burke, T., et. al. 2002, p. xx).

Drawing from my personal experience, listening to hundreds of other accounts, and after extensive education and research, here are a few key points to consider regarding abortion.

People don't always make the best decisions during a crisis situation. Fearing the future consequences of having a baby, there is, for whatever reason(s), a heightened sense of urgency to take care of the "problem," in this case needing to be *un-pregnant,* as quickly as possible. Time is an enemy because life continues to grow second-by-second. Not slowing down, you quickly schedule an appointment for an abortion; something you never saw yourself doing. Replaying the reasons why you need to do this, you have second thoughts but don't allow yourself to go there because you must stay focused on the task at hand. It seems less outrageous to get *It* over with quickly while *It* is still very small. You don't allow yourself to think about *It* while waiting for your scheduled day. In other words, you don't allow yourself to emotionally attach to *It.*

At 17, I arrive at the abortion facility and pay first. Sobbing, I ask the "counselor" if *It* is a baby. "No," I'm told, *"It* is a cluster of cells, a product of conception, a blob of tissue." Somewhat relieved, and although the decision is extremely difficult, that information is enough for me to ambivalently consent. Given kind, soothing words of assurance that I'm doing the right thing, that my parents will never have to know, that I can go home and not ever have to think about *It* again… I go through with the "procedure."

Crying throughout the abortion that you feel you must get, you lie there and endure the most unnatural act of being female. *How did I get here?* you wonder, while the beauty of—and within—your womb is being callously brutalized and savagely ransacked. Nothing prepares you for the nightmarish aftermath. But, crisis over, you can go home and never have to think about *It* again. Forever changed, a different person than when you went in with *It,* you walk out without *It,* permanently scarred, traumatized, and numb.

For many, like me, it's seeing an ultrasound of a subsequent pregnancy that shocks and ousts the inescapable truth. Tragically, *It* was NOT a blob of tissue, a cluster of cells, or a product of conception, but a baby – with arms, legs, hands, feet, head, eyes, and heart. Denial is unearthed, and the lines are distinctly drawn between what God calls very good (his creation of humankind) and what is very evil (abortion, the calloused and intentional destruction of humankind).

Allowing the sacred womb and its innermost parts to be desecrated is devastating to our femaleness (our motherhood), and there is no turning back. The great deceit is that one can go unscathed by the experience. Virtue and beauty are overtaken by shame and disgust.

And what about maleness? Fatherhood? C. T. Coyle asserts, "Most people have heard the expression, 'maternal instinct.' I would argue that there is an equally powerful 'paternal instinct' which motivates men to protect and care for their families" (1999, p. 92).

> I was in the middle of another sleepless night ruminating on how my life had fallen apart. I played judge and jury in this courtroom in my head and kept coming up with the same sentence… Death! I was a completely abject father. I couldn't stand the thought of waking up to face another day in my own tortured skin. I hated what my life had become, I hated my weakness and fear, and I hated myself. I told myself with deadly self-pity that everyone I knew would be better off if I was out of the picture (Burke, K., et. al. 2007, pg. 13).

The abortion industry is a commercial profiteering business with goals to meet, quotas to make, and specific time allowances to complete every procedure. An abortion facility is a well-oiled machine, its staff is highly crafted at what they do, and once you're inside the building, it's nearly impossible to leave there pregnant, especially when employees work on commission or bonus structure and strongly believe in their work.

Fortunately, God's grace covers all sin, and recovery is possible. But the challenge is two-fold: first earning the trust of a wounded soul and giving them an opportunity to heal, and then the wounded soul choosing to step out in faith and trust again—in themselves and in others.

While some people do adjust to their reproductive loss(es), many remain in isolation and lack the social and spiritual connection they need to help guide them through the healing process. To get started in meeting these needs in a local church, consider the following guidelines.

Five Critically Essential Processes Pastors Can Facilitate to Develop an Effective Reproductive Loss Ministry

1. Create Understanding and Awareness...

- **... of the tremendous need for reproductive loss healing,** emphasizing that a one-size-fits-all approach is not effective when dealing with the different kinds of reproductive losses. Many women and men feel ignored or neglected when their needs are not met and when their pain and grief are not acknowledged, validated, and ministered to.

- **... about the need to follow Jesus Christ's leadership and utilize emotional intelligence** when dealing with matters of the heart. Being unable or unwilling to follow Christ's example of unconditional love and acceptance should be a warning sign that a given person will not make a great shepherd leader to these types of sheep. Those who minister to people who have suffered reproductive loss must understand that when someone shares their story they are entrusting the listener with a special gift: their vulnerable and fragmented heart. The recipient of this gift can either squeeze the life out of that fragile heart through further shame and condemnation or nourish it by displaying God's grace and love.

Before I met with our pastor, I was extremely nervous and having second thoughts about talking with him, but my husband remarked that talking to him would be just like talking to Jesus. I agreed. Crying and telling him my story was such a relief. Desperate for help, it felt as though I were ripping out my very heart and handing it to him on a silver platter. After I finished speaking, he said the kindest thing to me. He started his first sentence by saying, "My dear Christian friend...," and years of heartache bellowed out of me. Friend?!? How could he call me friend after what I had just told him? That momentous experience was the beginning of putting the pieces of my heart back together again.

- **... that reproductive loss is not just a women's issue;** that men, families, grandparents, siblings, and others can be negatively impacted by a reproductive loss.

- **... about the social and moral pain that often exist,** perpetuate silence, shame, and stigma, and ultimately ostracize a lost sheep from its flock.

- **... of barriers which prevent openness,** including spiritual abuse, fears of judgment, condemnation, humiliation, retribution, risks of being vulnerable, and fears of loss of emotional control.

- **... about the need to take responsibility for harm willingly and unwillingly committed** by the church and/or congregation. In the case of abortion, hypocrisy can run rampant and the secrets may be deep. For example:

> A minister and his spouse, to save his job and reputation, drive their pregnant teenage daughter to an abortion facility, instructing her, "Don't come out pregnant," even though she wants to keep her baby. To save face, they sacrifice their daughter's physical and emotional wellbeing, her opportunity and desire to have a family, and their own grandchild. Worse, he preaches about the sanctity of human life!

We all need to seek God's forgiveness and grace to be free from the bondages of our sin and moral depravity.

- **... of the need for education about reproductive loss** and the effects it has on one's overall well-being—biological, psychological, social, and spiritual—and the various ways defense mechanisms and coping strategies are at work both interpersonally and intrapersonally.

- **... of the urgent need to equip others** with the tools and skills they need, both to effectively lead support and recovery groups and to know when to refer someone to a mental health professional [see Chapter 8].

2. Create Opportunities for Openness and Change:

- **Share from the pulpit previous mistakes you have made and misconceptions you have had** related to any type of reproductive loss. Pastor Jack Hayford writes,

> There was a time when I was not unlike many Christians who wrestle against bitterness, self-righteousness and even condemnation toward the parents of aborted children. I was not only angry that lives were being taken, but I also felt superior. And that was the hateful blindness I had to deal with – the cocksureness of my self-righteous opinion.
>
> In that state, I couldn't even begin to gain perspective on the fear, pain, hurt, agony and embarrassment of so many who needed something else from me... I now see a place where life, light and love are desperately needed – a place in our world where truth not only can shine like a beacon light discerning good and evil but where that same truth can also shed the light of healing warmth and hopefulness (2003, pp. 9-10).

- **Sincerely apologize and ask for forgiveness** if you already know, or become aware, that your words or actions may have caused further harm.

- **Invite outside speakers to share** their reproductive loss story (from brokenness to restoration), instilling hope in the hopeless.

- **Find educational workshops and seminars** for you and your congregation to attend. This demonstrates that you care and are serious about tending to the needs of those suffering reproductive loss. Time is a precious gift; it will be noticed and valued.

3. Create Connectedness:

- **Be vulnerable to share your own reproductive loss story** or a loss that was difficult to walk through, realizing that vulnerability begets vulnerability.

- **Reach out to families when there has been a loss**, remembering that your presence means more than your words. Simply saying, "I'm saddened about your loss," and being with them in the moment demonstrates love and empathy.

- **Provide a safe place for support and recovery groups** where people feel most at ease sharing. Consider holding such meetings somewhere other than at the church. Reproductive losses are very personal and intimate, so extreme care should be taken to respect grievers' anonymity and confidentiality. Being gripped with the fear of being discovered can prevent people from participating and thwart your best ministry efforts.

4. Create Community:

- **Normalize the individual and relational pain and suffering** involved in each area of reproductive loss by preaching and teaching about them. For abortion, it's not necessary to focus on the sin as much as it is to focus on God's love for ALL and his grace, forgiveness, and earnest desire to see his children restored.

- **Consider hosting an annual event to memorialize pregnancy losses**—either born, unborn, or never born—by planting a tree. Everyone can participate by planting a tree in honor of someone they know who has experienced a loss. It is not important to know which kind of pregnancy loss or why anyone is planting a tree (unless the person wants to share that information without any outside pressure to do so). It is an acknowledgment that there has been a loss and that a child is remembered and loved. For infertility loss, the act recognizes the deep longing and love of the parents whose child hasn't been born. Commemoration facilitates the grief process.

- **Encourage networking** with hospitals, doctor's offices (especially obstetricians), infertility clinics, pregnancy care centers, adoption agencies, mental health professionals, and other churches so that they can make referrals to your program.

5. Create a Support System:

- **Network with local Christian licensed mental health professionals**, preferably those with reproductive loss training and expertise.

- **Maintain a referral list of outside supportive resources** such as local pregnancy centers, adoption agencies, and nationwide ministries specializing in reproductive loss.

This by no means is an exhaustive list on how to create an effective reproductive loss ministry, but it is a starting place. For questions, referrals, and further information, please email info@choosegrace.com or phone (804) 835-6505, and we will be happy to assist you.

References

Burke, K., Wemhoff, D., Stockwell, M. (2007). *Redeeming a father's heart: Men share powerful stories of abortion loss and recovery.* Bloomington, IN: AuthorHouse.

Burke, T. (2002). *Forbidden grief: The unspoken pain of abortion.* Springfield, IL: Acorn Books.

Coyle, C. T. (1999). *Men and Abortion: A Path to Healing.* Toronto, ON; Lewiston, NY: Life Cycle Books, Ltd.

Hayford, Jack (2003). *I'll hold you in heaven.* Ada, MI: Chosen Books.

Rue, V.M., et. al. (2004). "Induced abortion and traumatic stress: A preliminary comparison of American and Russian women," *Medical Science Monitor,* 10(10): SR5-16.

www.theunchoice.com (which see for further information and cases)

David Mikkelson, Ph.D, M.Div.

David P. Mikkelson grew up in a Marine Corps family and later served as a Marine Corps artillery officer for 10 years and, after seminary, as an Army chaplain for 18 years. As the director of a pastoral counseling training center at Ft. Bragg, NC, he counseled hundreds of soldiers and families affected by combat, and clinically supervised dozens of pastoral counselors in the same ministry. He has presented at many conferences on helping civilian counselors better understand and more effectively counsel and care for military families. He is currently in private practice in Forest, VA as a marriage and family therapist, clinical supervisor, and a consultant on military counseling, church-based counseling, and combat trauma. Dr. Mikkelson earned his Ph.D. from Regent University in Counselor Education and Supervision, an M.Div. from Reformed Theological Seminary with emphasis in Counseling, an M.S. in Counseling Psychology from Tarleton State University, and a B.A. from Duke University.

Suzanne Mikkelson, Ph.D.

Suzanne Mikkelson is a former military spouse with nearly 20 years of Christian counseling experience with military members and their families. She is a Licensed Marriage and Family Therapist, an American Association for Marriage and Family Therapy (AAMFT) Approved Supervisor, and an Approved Consultant with Eye Movement Desensitization Reprocessing International Association (EMDRIA). Her clinical specialties include trauma, adultery recovery, marital issues, and parenting. As a pastor's wife, she has also experienced the dynamics of counseling and mental health care in the church. She is currently an Assistant Professor at Liberty University and prepares counseling students for effective Christian counseling. Dr. Mikkelson earned her Ph.D. from Regent University in Counselor Education and Supervision, an M.A. in Marriage and Family Counseling from Reformed Theological Seminary, and a B.A. from Duke University. She and David are blessed with three adult sons and three grandsons.

CHAPTER 16

How to Develop an Effective Military Family Support Ministry

David Mikkelson, Ph.D., M.Div. and
Suzanne Mikkelson, Ph.D.

Pastors and churches are in a strategic position to bring hope and healing to the millions of military service members, veterans, and their families. These men and women are America's greatest treasure, and their families have sacrificed immeasurably, often without recognition or compensation. They live and work in every corner of America, not just the areas surrounding major military installations, and some of them likely attend your church. As of 2014, there were 6.6 million Vietnam veterans living in America, with about 30% under the age of 65 and 93% under the age of 75 (US Department of Veterans Affairs (VA), 2016). In addition, 2.6 million Americans have served in the wars on terror since 2001, a number expected to grow to just under 3.5 million by 2019 (VA, 2016).

The large-scale deployment of our nation's Reserve and National Guard units since 2001 has placed combat veterans in nearly every community in America. These special citizens are volunteers who accepted the call to fight our nation's battles on behalf of every American. They are a resilient, resourceful, strong, experienced, tough, committed, and loyal group who willingly accept hardship to sacrificially serve others. Reading that line again, many pastors may wish that more of their parishioners matched that description. Their service, however, has not been without cost, and mixed in with their strengths are a variety of challenging issues that pastors are uniquely and strategically positioned to address with both immediate and eternal consequences. These veterans and their families are in need of care, perhaps from a trained mental health professional, but also from caring Christians who are equipped and committed to help.

This chapter will begin with an overview of the challenges of living in the military culture. These challenges strengthen the majority of service members and their families, but for some, the challenges result in mental health and relational issues that require outside help. Next we will examine the nature and scope of military mental health and relational issues, followed by some suggestions for how pastors and church-based counselors can effectively engage these veterans and their families. Finally, the chapter will provide a number of practical ideas for pastors and churches to reach out to veterans and their families.

The Challenges of Military Culture

Those who join the military mirror the diversity of America across a number of demographic variables. In addition to coming from a variety of cultures and sub-cultures in America, a number of U.S. service members are non-citizens from a wide variety of foreign countries. Since 2001, the U.S. has naturalized 109,321 service members who served in the armed forces, and an additional 2,650 spouses from dozens of foreign countries (U.S. Citizenship and Immigration Services, 2016).

The military is not so much a melting pot of diverse cultures as it is the introduction of a new culture that overlays and in some ways supersedes the cultural values brought by the new recruit. In the crucible of basic training for both officers and enlisted personnel, it no longer matters whether one is black, white, Asian, Hispanic, rich, poor, well-educated, accomplished, or a former gang member. Every behavior and attitude is now subject to a new standard: the military culture. While service members are not stripped of their cultural heritage, it becomes clear that a new culture is overlaid onto the original one, and at any point where the cultures collide, the military values, standards, and behavior are expected to take precedence. In this sense, all veterans and their families are second-culture people, sometimes to the extent that returning to civilian life after military service results in veterans feeling out of place, strangers who no longer fit in the country they served and protected (Hall, 2016). If a service member is assigned to a foreign country or marries a foreign citizen, the cultural complexity only grows.

Pastors might recognize the parallel process they strive to produce in their churches. While people from every nation, tribe, people, and tongue

(Revelation 7:9) comprise the people of God, there is a single cultural standard and ethic expected of every person who claims Christianity – to be conformed to the image of Jesus (Romans 8:29). Regardless of color, culture, language, age, gender, economic status, or any other variable one might use to describe themselves, faith in Christ calls forth a transformation from the old self to a new life (Ephesians 4:22-24). Just as there are no cultural exceptions in the Bible whereby one is exempt from desiring and actively pursuing Christ-likeness, so the military imposes its culture on every veteran.

The following is a brief summary of seven cultural influences that shape military members and should be considered by those who seek to help veterans and their families. While this list is not exhaustive, it focuses on those aspects that present the most risk for the development of mental health and relational issues.

Mission Comes First

The military is, first and foremost, the institution that organizes and trains to fight and win our nation's wars. While educational benefits, new housing, and better dental care for family members may impact service member retention and improve quality of life, the military is not a social service agency. Combat is a strenuous and dangerous occupation where mistakes cost lives, and discipline, loyalty, teamwork, and realistic training provide a foundation for success in battle. This mission-first mentality is not only present on the battlefield; it also influences the daily schedule of service members who are often pressured to work into the evenings and on weekends in order to accomplish the mission.

In one of the brigades in which I (David) served, the unit motto was "Duty First." It was the customary greeting between any two members of the unit and was recited many times each day. While it represented a sense of warrior pride, it also served as a daily reminder that our duty and mission came before self and family. It is true that some commanders help create a more family-friendly atmosphere and a better work/life balance, but in any crisis, combat-related training, or actual deployment, everyone knows that mission comes first.

While this approach is not only effective but necessary to train and develop a winning military, the impact on family relationships is painfully obvious. Many military families have service members who affirm that God and family are more important than their work, but functionally that is not always supported when long hours on the job are required, including training on Sundays. The result is the formation of close-knit relationships at work – much like a 'second family' – which, when coupled with high levels of dedication to the mission and love of country, often creates serious relational conflicts over loyalty (Hall, 2016). Thus, many spouses give their service member partner an ultimatum: it's either me or the military. In our experience, about 80-90% of service members at that point chose the military and pursued divorce, a powerful indicator of the strength of the warrior bond.

Warrior Ethos

A related concept to the importance of mission is the warrior ethos or identity that is instilled during basic training and reinforced throughout one's career. Many who join the military have a desire to "merge their identity with that of the warrior" (Wertsch, 1991, p. 17). Being a warrior is an ancient and noble profession, worthy of honor and respect from society. Some view it as a test of manhood and a rite of passage, historically among males (Nash, 2007; Tick, 2005). The American warrior is disciplined, trained, and ready to give his or her life to protect what so many others take for granted: the exercise of freedom and American values. A quote attributed to Ronald Reagan in 1985 sums up the pride one has as a warrior, regardless of branch of service: "Some people spend an entire lifetime wondering if they made a difference in the world. Marines don't have that problem." This warrior ethos and *esprit de corps* is an integral part of what has made America's military so dominant for over two centuries. This ethos is a double-edge sword, however, as the very attitude and toughness that promotes success on the battlefield creates risk for relationships at home.

Rigid Authoritarian Structure

Across the branches of service, the military is a rigid organization that operates with a strict authoritarian structure. Except for the most junior ranks, all service members are accustomed to both receiving and giving orders that are expected to be obeyed in a timely and accurate manner. It is an arrangement that lends itself to success in combat where quick decisions must be made by leaders and obeyed by followers, even when death is both likely and imminent. The risk at home is that many military parents employ an authoritarian parenting style, overseeing their homes as a miniature military unit. This arrangement works for some, but especially when children reach adolescence, it tends to break down and result in daily power struggles, rebellion, and loss of family closeness. I (David) have counseled senior Special Forces warriors who make a regular habit of doing heroic deeds in battle, but they admit near incompetence when it comes to maintaining close relationships with their spouse and children.

Frequent Moves

The military has a stubborn habit of moving its members every 2-3 years. Referred to as a permanent change of station (PCS) move, it is anything but permanent. Our family experienced greater stability than most of our peers, and we still had 10 PCS moves in our 29-year career. In addition, due to local moves among rental units and delayed assignment to on-post quarters, we lived in 18 different homes in our 29-year career. Our three sons attended an average of eight different schools before high school graduation and spent five to seven years living in foreign countries. One effect of such a mobile lifestyle is being removed from extended family, the familiarity of hometown, and the safety of long-term close friends. The resilient response to such forces is often that members of military families develop the ability to make quick and lasting friendships, but their level of personal investment and vulnerability may be low. This could be a psychological defense against the inevitable loss of friends each year, and the result of atrophied long-term relationship skills. Frequent moves can instill both a fierce independence and can-do attitude that welcome any challenges, but also a sense that asking for help is a weakness. Veterans and their families who join a church may find being stable and having the same friends for many years to be a strange and awkward experience.

Deployments and Separations

Whether for training in another state, another country, or a deployment around the world, separations have been a part of the military culture long before the wars in Iraq and Afghanistan. Those recent wars have, however, increased the number of service members deployed and raised the probability of multiple deployments. These separations place significant strains on service members and families alike. Parents are often absent for birthdays, proms, football games, drama productions, the first day of school, a baby's first steps, or a child's first lost tooth (Hall, 2011). While most families adjust and spouses accept the role of parenting alone, the risk is that family functioning can be upset and not easily recovered. Family roles often shift in order to compensate for the missing parent, and both parents and children gain new skills and strategies in life (Armstrong, Best, & Domenici, 2006). While such resilience can be a valuable strength, conflict over family roles and rules can leave a family confused and operating by a superficial truce.

Isolation

Ironically, the military culture is also characterized by isolation from the civilian society it protects (Hall, 2011). Families often live on gated installations, attend Department of Defense schools, and shop for food and clothes, get their cars fixed, and engage in a variety of recreation activities on the installation—separated from civilian society. While this often builds a sense of camaraderie and loyalty within the military community, there is a risk that in later years it may be more difficult for veterans and their families to connect with civilians (Wertsch, 1991). The authors have both felt this dynamic recently in our own lives, having retired just three years ago after 29 years of active duty and reserve service, including living on post for nearly half those years. Now, when visiting churches or attending social engagements, we are keenly aware that most people have no idea the lifestyle we have lived or the extent to which our life experiences have been so dramatically different from theirs.

Secrecy and Stoicism

These are two common psychological and relational effects of living within the military culture, and especially when living on the installation. As Hall (2016) states, "The one imperative for family members is not to get the service member in trouble or do anything that will reflect badly on him or her" (p. 52). This easily creates an acceptable level of secrecy within the family, and when combined with the classified information security clearance held by many service members today, an entire information economy is dominated by secrecy. Not only can unhealthy family dynamics such as domestic violence or substance abuse go undetected and untreated, the service member learns to build a wall around what is done at work that shuts out the spouse. Moreover, many combat veterans are coached by peers not to speak of the harsh realities or unglamorous deeds of war, and spouses often accept this silence that unwittingly drives a wedge between the couple, eroding trust and hindering intimacy in their marriage.

In addition to a pervasive climate of secrecy, service members are socialized to respond to the hardships, hostilities, and horrors of combat with stoicism (Wertsch, 1991). Again, the relentless pace of modern combat often dictates that a squad or platoon that attends a memorial ceremony for a fallen comrade today will almost certainly be back in the thick of combat tomorrow. There is little or no time for expressions, much less healthy processing, of grief. When combined with a complex array of powerful emotions such as rage, loneliness, despair, pride, and resignation, the only reliable strategy to avoid being overwhelmed and losing control is to remain ruthlessly stoic and focused on mission accomplishment from day to day. Again, such a strategy is both reasonable and adaptive in combat, but when it is brought home, it is both unhelpful to and corrosive of marital and family trust when the veteran is persistently emotionally unavailable to loved ones.

Nature and Scope of Mental Health Issues for Service Members and Their Families

The ongoing war on terrorism, formally beginning in 2001 and with no end in sight, has taken a toll on our nation's warriors and their families. The repetitive deployments into complex and unrelenting war zones, the lack of front lines or safe places for rest, the seeming randomness of injury and death, and the complex rules of engagement are some hallmarks of the current combat experience that contribute to the nature and scope of mental health and relational issues for service members and families (Mikkelson, 2015).

Mental Health Among Service Members

We begin by emphasizing that most service members and their families experience increased resilience, flexibility, and overall mental health benefits from their time in the military. According to the Veterans Administration, post-9/11 veterans are more likely to be insured, have higher levels of personal income, and are less likely to live below the poverty line than non-veterans (VA, 2016). Additionally, post-9/11 veterans are more racially diverse than all other veterans, have lower divorce rates, and have a higher rate of service-connected disabilities, yet they are less likely to use their VA medical benefits than all other veterans (VA, 2016). We hope pastors are encouraged that military members and their families are likely to be mentally strong members of a congregation who bring a wealth of knowledge, resiliency, and experience to a local church family.

However, a significant minority of veteran families develop a variety of mental health issues both during and after their time of service. In 2016, researchers found that service members with combat deployments had higher rates of PTSD, depression, panic/anxiety, and other mental disorders, as well as higher rates of maladaptive behavioral disorders than non-deployers (Crum-Cianflone, Powell, LeardMann, Russell, & Boyko, 2016). Overall, 12% of combat deployers had some mental health condition while over 60% had maladaptive behavioral problems with either alcohol or tobacco (Crum-Cianflone, et al., 2016). The relentless demands of 24-hour operations in today's combat environment have resulted in extended sleep disruptions for combat personnel, creating a substantially higher risk of developing PTSD, anxiety, and depression (Taylor et al., 2014).

There is little difference between the mental health issues of active duty personnel and those from the reserve components. Reservists had similar rates of PTSD and depression to their active duty counterparts but a higher prevalence of alcohol use disorders (Cohen, Fink, Sampson, & Galea, 2015). Overall, the most common mental health issues for veterans are PTSD, depression, anxiety, and substance use problems (Cohen et al, 2015; Crum-Cianflone, 2016; Lazar, 2014; Negrusa & Sebastian, 2014; Pickett et al., 2015). These psychiatric and behavioral issues were strong predictors for homelessness, compromised parenting skills, sexual risk-taking behaviors, intimate-partner violence, and obesity (Lazar, 2014). There is also an increase in the risk of death from homicide, unintentional injury, cancer, cardiovascular disease, and suicide for veterans with PTSD and depression (Lazar, 2014). Clearly military service, and particularly combat exposure, can have a debilitating effect on many people.

PTSD, Depression, and Suicide

Not surprisingly, PTSD and depression often go hand in hand. In fact, 73% of those with PTSD will also concurrently develop at least one other mental health or behavioral condition (Crum-Cianflone et al., 2016). In 2014, 6% of active duty Army personnel reported suicidality within the past year (Ramsawh et al., 2014). Soldiers who had both PTSD and major depressive disorder were nearly three times more likely to be suicidal than those with either diagnosis by itself (Ramsawh et al., 2014). As of 2015, there had been nearly 163,000 psychiatric hospitalizations since the onset of the post-9/11 conflicts (Pickett et al., 2015). From 2010 to 2012 researchers reported 2553 suicide attempts and 812 deaths from suicide (Pickett et al., 2015). Pastors who minister to service members struggling with PTSD and depression should remain vigilant and regularly assess the risk of suicidal thoughts and actions for these struggling veterans.

PTSD and Moral (or Spiritual) Injury

We believe that PTSD involves more than just a traumatized brain with long-term altered neurobiological functioning. There is often also a debilitating moral (or spiritual) injury that is both real and powerful (Berg, 2011; Tick, 2005). A moral injury is a wound or injury to the soul, a fundamental disruption of identity, meaning, or justice (Tick, 2005). Moral injury may be due to perceived transgressions by self or others we trusted, or due to perceived betrayals by self or others we trusted. Killing or harming others in certain situations, failing to protect others, failing to prevent the immoral acts of others, and being abandoned by a team member or leader are all potential moral injuries. Moral injury is the wound we suffer when our actions do not measure up to our ideal morals and expectations, especially when someone else is hurt because of our action or inaction (Nash, 2007). Moral injuries do not just happen in combat; they can result from other violent or injurious personal encounters such as rape, torture, or kidnapping. These moral injuries create [or result in] serious spiritual quandaries, leaving the sufferer grappling with often profound spiritual damage.

In a study of Vietnam veterans, spiritual injuries were highly associated with both PTSD and depression (Berg, 2011). Combat veterans often blamed themselves for immoral actions or failures to act on the battlefield. Spiritual injury symptoms of guilt, anger, sadness, meaninglessness, despair, unfairness, and religious doubt were all positively correlated with the severity of both PTSD and depression (Berg, 2011).

Conversely, PTSD and depression were inversely related to intrinsic religious faith. Vietnam veterans who had intrinsic faith in God and regularly worshiped with a faith community had significantly lower levels of both PTSD and depression (Berg, 2011). If that same situation holds true for our post-9/11 veterans, churches and pastors serve a crucial role in improving the mental health of combat veterans. Indeed, churches and pastors are uniquely equipped to address the spiritual injury that often accompanies combat experiences.

The symptoms of moral injury have significant overlap with PTSD: extreme shame or guilt, anxiety about consequences, feelings of condemnation, rage over perceived betrayal, alienation, purposelessness, self-condemnation, and self-harming or self-handicapping behaviors. Not only does this make PTSD and moral injury highly associated, it also can make them hard to distinguish. However, the difference in assessment is crucial, since the treatments are very different. PTSD is most often treated with prolonged exposure therapy, cognitive processing therapy, or eye movement desensitization and reprocessing (EMDR), all of which require licensed clinicians with specialized training. However, moral injury can be addressed by pastors and other church-based counselors who address issues of guilt, sin, forgiveness, grief, evil, the nature of man, and the reality and significance of one's identity in Christ.

Pastors are excellent resources to address the moral injuries that often accompany traumatic events. Veterans who show symptoms of PTSD and depression are often "experiencing significant levels of spiritual distress as measured by guilt, anger, grief, lack of meaning and purpose in life, despair, and religious doubt" (Berg, 2011, p. 6). Indeed, such symptoms have been the purview of pastors for two millennia, long before the modern mental health profession was established (Jones, 2012).

Mental Health Issues and Marriage

Service members' mental health and behavioral issues can have a detrimental impact on families. Those diagnosed with PTSD are more likely to also have depression and/or anxiety, which collectively exert tremendous strain on loved ones. In several studies, divorce rates for those with PTSD were significantly higher than for those without PTSD and higher than the divorce rate for their civilian counterparts (Lundquist, 2007; Negrusa & Sebastian, 2014). Within those statistics, officers with PTSD divorced at an even higher rate than enlisted personnel (Negrusa & Sebastian, 2014). Spouses also struggled with increased anxiety and depression as deployment duration increased (Rodriquez & Margolin, 2015). Not surprisingly, longer and more frequent deployments increased the risk for divorce (Negrusa & Sebastian, 2014).

Mental Health Issues and Children

Military life greatly impacts children. In general, military children's well-being is correlated with parental adjustment; when parents do better, children do better. When parents are satisfied with their military experience and feel supported by their unit structure, children tend to follow suit (DeGraff, O'Neal, & Mancini, 2016). Parent-child interactions have been the key to the well-being and adjustment of children, particularly adolescents. Parent adjustment and mental health is associated with both parent-child attachment and parental satisfaction levels (DeGraff, O'Neal, & Mancini, 2016). For some youth, frequent contact with the absent parent during deployment buffers the negative effects of extended absences (Rodriguez & Margolin, 2015). However, when service members miss important family events such as birthdays, graduations, sporting events, moves, illnesses, or deaths, children often respond with increased anxiety and depression (Rodriguez & Margolin, 2015). Finally, children of veterans with PTSD often have behavioral problems, academic difficulties, and they have a 23% rate of receiving psychiatric treatment (Lazar, 2014).

Pastoral Counseling Strategies for Military Personnel

Despite the complex impact that military service can have on veterans' mental health, spiritual values, and family relationships, we are fully convinced that pastors and church-based counselors can make a big difference in their lives. While there are treatment methods and protocols that only mental health professionals can provide, here are six helpful ways that pastors and church-based counselors can provide effective ministry for veterans and their families.

Have Them Tell their Stories

Quite often we find that veterans are not really looking for our pastoral advice or admonition, they are looking for us to listen to their story and offer assurance that they are still loveable by God (Blaisure, Saathoff-Wells, Pereira, Wadsworth, & Dombro, 2012). Through telling our stories we define our place in life, we discover and assign meaning to our experiences, and we connect with others in the community. Combat veterans often carry around images and memories of unspeakable cruelty and human tragedy, but they also know of the triumph of faithfulness, sacrifice, and courage. We can validate their story and honor them, especially when their story includes the need to repent and experience forgiveness.

Veterans often withhold their stories not because they are painful to tell (they are), but more so because they don't believe their story will be heard and valued, and/or that no one will understand or care (Armstrong, Best, & Domenici, 2006). Stay calm when they share terrible experiences or use rough language, as they may well be testing you to see if you can handle their life experience. Their default presumption is often that you cannot, so it may take intentional calmness to convince them otherwise.

Share the Amazing Forgiveness of God

Many veterans carry a heavy burden of wartime deeds of which they are not proud, and are perhaps even profoundly ashamed (Mikkelson, 2016b). How does one shake off the guilt of shooting a civilian who was mistaken for a combatant? Logical arguments about being within the rules of engagement and that others would have done the same thing ring hollow, and combat veterans often feel convinced they must carry their heavy burden of guilt to the grave as a kind of self-imposed penance. Persistent and genuine assurances that God still loves them and is both willing and able to forgive every deed and make them clean in their soul can be a life-changer.

Identify Losses and Help them Grieve

Combat is a long accumulation of loss, yet few in the military frame it as such. Their warrior training tells them to bottle up emotions and pursue mission success, even when buddies die at their side. The need to "bottle it up" and keep moving is perhaps a necessary strategy for success in battle, but it is the opposite of what leads to success at home. Help them embrace the tragedy they bring, weep with them, and help them grieve their losses. Now that they are past their war-fighting days they have the time, space, and permission to explore their losses and travel grief's journey (Armstrong, Best, & Domenici, 2006). The old, pre-war person is gone; help them discover the new person they are becoming. We can bring them to God who alone can bring back to life those parts of their heart that have been walled off for many years. We help them speak truth about what happened, and how they feel about it. Avoiding stressors and using meds to mask symptoms leaves the debilitating memories buried in the mind, continuing to burden the soul. We want to help them recover their own soul (Tick, 2005). A healthy soul can carry even big wounds.

Provide Safety

Strive to provide a safe environment and be a safe person for veterans. Their world was often fundamentally unsafe, but you can help them experience something different. Start with little things, like a quiet counseling office away from loud distractions. Being on time and reliable for appointments communicates value and respect. Maintain a non-anxious presence no matter what they say to you. You are modeling that their problems do not have to be overwhelming and that God does not pull back and shudder when they disclose a troubling memory or story.

Be an Agent of Hope

It is wisely said in combat that hope is not a course of action; leaders want more concrete plans for success. Be an agent of hope; be confident and optimistic about recovery and healing. Remind veterans that, with God, they *can* overcome their current struggles; they *can* find peace in life, because God offers hope in daily life. In counseling, hope *is* a valuable and effective course of action! Despite the attitudes of some mental health professionals, PTSD does not have to be a life-long condition to manage. It is a very treatable condition, and healing is very possible. Loan them your hope, if needed.

Make Good Referrals

As previously noted, PTSD is often combined with other mental health issues, most commonly depression, anxiety, and substance abuse. At the appropriate time and with pastoral sensitivity, refer the client to a psychologist or psychiatrist for depression or anxiety screening and possible medication as a helpful part of the recovery process. Make an effort to personally know those to whom you may refer military clients for alcohol or drug abuse, anger classes, domestic violence counseling, PTSD treatment, etc. Know if these providers take Tricare insurance or if they are willing to donate time to veterans and their families. Veterans are often cynical about the military and VA healthcare systems that overpromise and underperform, often giving them the runaround in an effort to obtain care. Pastors who can make one referral to a competent Christian provider who has the background to treat military personnel and who takes Tricare insurance can be an immensely valuable gift to your military clients.

Helpful Pastoral Strategies to Honor Veterans and Their Families

In addition to counseling strategies offered by a pastor or church-based counselor, the pastor can provide leadership to help his or her church provide a number of responses to veterans and their families.

Relentlessly Show Appreciation

Tell veterans that you appreciate and admire them and that what they did or are doing is honorable and really matters. They are agents of peace for our country, standing on point against our adversaries on behalf of every American. Make your appreciation personal: instead of a generic "thank you for your service" or "thanks for what you do," consider saying "thank you for serving my family and protecting our country." Honor them in church as courageous protectors at every opportunity, including Memorial Day, Independence Day, Patriots Day, and Veterans Day. This helps add meaning, purpose, and social acceptance to what they have done and are doing.

Preach on Restraining Evil

Include relevant biblical teaching on the righteous use of force to restrain and defeat evil (Mikkelson, 2016a). The Bible repeatedly portrays God as a mighty warrior strong in battle. There is good and evil in this world, and the military has a God-given responsibility to preserve life and defeat evil. Many of them wonder how they can follow orders and kill the enemy without condemnation and guilt. Help them with a biblical view that honors what they do, within legal and moral boundaries. So many veterans struggle with whether the killing they did was murder or not, and if they can be forgiven.

Preach a Theology of Suffering

It is vital that all believers have a sound theology of suffering in order to deal with modern life. So many combat veterans we have talked to believe that the presence of suffering indicates that God does not exist, does not care, or is powerless to act. "Why do bad things happen to good people?" is one of the most common and distressing questions people ask, but it is especially present for many veterans. You will be reaching out to them in deep ways by preaching and teaching on this topic.

Host Special Events

Provide a special dinner and evening session for military members and their families. It would be an opportunity for military people to meet each other in your church, and for them to be shown honor and appreciation. The session could be a special recognition ceremony for family members, a marriage or relationship enhancement program, or just a fun night with a motivational speaker.

Reach Out Quickly

Many veterans and military families feel like they don't really belong in the mainstream of civilian life (Hall, 2011). If they visit your church and are not quickly welcomed and personally engaged, it may only reinforce their notion of awkwardness and isolation. Ensuring that your church has a good method for greeting and welcoming all visitors will have the secondary effect of welcoming veterans and their families into your church. If you have identified their military connection, consider having another military member or small group visit them to establish a further connection. Identify some veterans in your church who are willing to be a contact team; veterans are often motivated to reach out to other veterans (Blaisure et. al., 2012).

Be the Church

Finally, just be the church. In a world full of hypocrisy, superficial relationships, and empty promises, we must not minimize the powerful witness of a healthy church. We ascribe to an "if you build it they will come" approach to evangelism. Suzanne and I both volunteer as a chaplain couple to provide ministry, counseling, and marriage education to wounded warrior couples in the Operation Heal Our Patriots program in Alaska. One of the most common responses we hear from the couples each week is the impact of so many Christians loving on them throughout the week. They are not used to being surrounded by loving, caring, genuine servants who are complete strangers. "Why would these people come all the way up to rural Alaska and volunteer without pay, just to serve me and help me learn more about a biblical marriage?" Be the body of Christ by loving them, respecting them, and helping them; it may well be more effective than even the best of sermons.

Conclusion

Pastors and church-based counselors are in a strategic position to help warriors and their families. Other mental health professionals may be needed to address certain issues whose treatment lies beyond the training and expertise of pastors and church-based counselors. However, there is much you can do, and there are things *only* you can do. Be prepared to engage the military families in your community. Honor them, support them in tangible ways, and hear their stories. Look for the gifts they bring to your congregation and give them a new place of service. Help them find the resources they need. Most importantly, show them and tell them of the good news of salvation offered only through a relationship with Jesus Christ. Recovering a sense of personal worth, experiencing forgiveness, and finding new meaning in life are at the very center of what veterans and their families need, and what you and your church can provide.

References

Armstrong, K., Best, S., & Domenici, P. (2006). *Courage after fire: Coping strategies for troops returning from Iraq and Afghanistan and their families.* Berkeley, CA: Ulysses Press.

Berg, G. (2011). The relationship between spiritual distress, PTSD, and depression in Vietnam combat veterans. *Journal of Pastoral Care & Counseling, 65*(1), 1-11.

Blaisure, K. R., Saathoff-Wells, T., Pereira, A., Wadsworth, S. M., & Dombro, A. L. (2012). *Serving military families in the 21ˢᵗ century.* New York, NY: Routledge.

Cohen, G.H., Fink, D. S., Sampson, L., & Galea.S. (2015). Mental health among reserve component military service members and veterans. *Epidemiologic Reviews, 37,* 7-22. doi: 10.1093/epirev/mxu007

Crum-Cianflone, N.F., Powell, T.M., LeardMann, C.A., Russell, D.W., & Boyko, E.J. (2016). Mental health and comorbidities in U.S. military members. *Military Medicine, 181*(6), 537-545.

DeGraff, A.N., O'Neal, C.W., & Mancini, J.A. (2016). The significance of military contexts and culture for understanding family well-being: Parent life satisfaction and adolescent outcomes. *Journal of Child and Family Studies, 25,* 3022-3033. doi: 10.1007/s10826-016-0471-0

Hall, L. K. (2011). The military culture, language, and lifestyle. In R. B. Everson, & C. Figley (Eds.), *Families under fire: Systemic therapy with military families* (pp. 31-52). New York, NY: Routledge.

Hall, L. K. (2016). *Counseling military families: What mental health professionals need to know.* New York, NY: Routledge.

Jones, I. F. (2012). *Counselor preparation in evangelical seminaries: Reclaiming the pastoral counseling identity.* Unpublished manuscript,

Department of Psychology and Counseling, New Orleans Baptist Theological Seminary, New Orleans, LA.

Lazar. S. G. (2014). The mental health needs of military service members and veterans. *Psychodynamic Psychiatry, 42*(3), 459-478.

Lundquist, J. H. (2007). A comparison of civilian and enlisted divorce rates during the early all volunteer force era. *Journal of Political and Military Sociology, 35*(2), 199-217.

Mikkelson, D. P. (2016a). God and guns: Christian faith and bearing arms. *Christian Counseling Today, 21*(4), 16-20.

Mikkelson, D. P. (2016b). Helping combat vets deal with guilt. *AACC Military Counseling Initiative, 3*(1), 3-4.

Mikkelson, D. P. (2015). The modern warfare experience: What counselors should know. *AACC Military Counseling Initiative, 2*(4), 1-2.

Nash, W. P. (2007). The stressor of war. In C. R. Figley & W. P. Nash (Eds.), *Combat stress injury: Theory, research, and management* (pp. 11-32). New York, NY: Routledge.

Negrusa, B. & Sebastian, N. (2014). Home front: Post-deployment mental health and divorces. *Demography, 51*, 895-916. doi: 10.1007/s13524-014-0294-9

Pickett, T., Rothman, D., Crawford, E.F., Brancu, M., Fairbank, J.A., & Kudler, H.S. (2015). Mental health among military personnel and veterans. *North Carolina Medical Journal, 76*(5), 299-306.

Ramsawh, H. J., Fullerton, C. S., Herberman Mash, H. B., Ng, T. H., Kessler, R. C., Stein, M. B., & Ursano, R. J. (2014). Risk for suicidal behaviors associated with PTSD, depression, and their comorbidity in the U.S. Army. *Journal of Affective Disorders, 161*, 116-122.

Rodriguez, A.J., & Margolin, G. (2015). Military service absences and family members' mental health: A timeline followback assessment. *Journal of Family Psychology, 29*(4), 642-648.

Tick. E. (2005). *War and the soul: Healing our nation's veterans from post-traumatic stress disorder.* Wheaton, IL: Quest Books.

U.S. Citizenship and Immigration Services. (2016). *Naturalization through military service: Fact sheet.* Retrieved from https://www.uscis.gov/news/fact-sheets/naturalization-through-military-service-fact-sheet

US Department of Veterans Affairs. (2016). Profile of post-9/11 veterans: 2014. Retrieved from: http://www.va.gov/vetdata/docs/SpecialReports/Post_911_Veterans_Profile_2014.pdf

Wertsch, M. E. (1991). *Military brats: Legacies of childhood inside the fortress.* St. Louis, MO: Brightwell.

Diane Langberg, Ph.D.

Dr. Diane Langberg is a practicing psychologist whose clinical expertise includes over 35 years of working with trauma survivors and clergy. She speaks internationally on topics related to women, trauma, ministry, and the Christian life.

She is the director of Diane Langberg, Ph.D. & Associates, a group practice in suburban Philadelphia, Pennsylvania, staffed by Christian psychologists, social workers, and counselors. Their expertise includes sexual and domestic abuse, addictions, depression, and eating disorders. They work with adults, children and adolescents, and couples.

Dr. Langberg is a faculty member of Westminster Theological Seminary. She is the author of *Suffering and the Heart of God: How Trauma Destroys and Christ Restores* (New Growth Press), *In Our Lives First: Mediations for Counselors* (CreateSpace), *Counsel for Pastors' Wives* (Zondervan), *Counseling Survivors of Sexual Abuse* (Xulon Press), *Counseling Women* (with Dr. Tim Clinton, Baker Books), *Bringing Christ to Abused Women: Learning to See and Respond* (New Growth Press), and *On the Threshold of Hope: Opening the Door to Healing for Survivors of Sexual Abuse* (Tyndale House). Diane is a columnist for *Christian Counseling Today* and contributes to many other publications.

Dr. Langberg is Chair of the Executive Board of the American Association of Christian Counselors, serves on the boards of GRACE (Godly Response to Abuse in a Christian Environment), the Society of Christian Psychology, and World Reformed Fellowship. Diane is also co-founder of The Place of Refuge, an inner-city, non-profit trauma and training center. Dr. Langberg is the recipient of the Distinguished Alumna for Professional Achievement Award from Taylor University, the American Association of Christian Counselors' Caregiver Award, and the Philadelphia Council of Clergy's Christian Service Award. She is married and has two sons.

CHAPTER 17

How to Develop an Effective Trauma Recovery Ministry

Diane Langberg, Ph.D.

Our God describes a good shepherd when he says, "I will feed my flock and...lead them to rest... I will seek the lost, bring back the scattered, bind up the broken and strengthen the sick..." (Ezekiel 34:15-16, NAS). As pastors and church leaders, you are shepherds of God's sheep. You have an eternally significant task that is often fraught with difficulties, and in order to do your work well, one factor is crucial: You must know your sheep. You cannot care for or guide those whom you do not know. In this chapter, I would like to help you understand some of the people in your churches in a new and deeper way in order to be redemptive instruments of healing to them.

I have spent over forty years as a Christian psychologist who has worked with victims of trauma of all kinds—sexual abuse, rape, domestic abuse, war, trafficking, and genocide. Given the statistics for sexual abuse alone (one in four girls and one in six boys are sexually abused before they turn eighteen), it seems safe to conclude that all churches have trauma victims sitting in their pews. Most are silent about what they have endured. Some have tried to tell and were not believed. Most of them never hear a word about the subject from the pulpit. They have never heard what God has to say about such life-shaping evil. Some of them have experienced abuse within the confines of a church, and their presence in our pews is one of desperation and great courage.

The word *trauma* means "wound," so trauma is a wound to the mind, the heart, and the soul. Similarly, the word *abuse*, which comes from the Latin word *abutor*, means "to use wrongly." It also means "to insult, violate, tarnish, or walk on." So then, abuse occurs when someone uses another wrongly. And abuse always leaves traumatic effects on the mind, heart, and soul of the person wounded. Sometimes it's a wound to the body as well, but it is a wound to the whole person, and it happens when suffering overwhelms what we would consider normal human coping. The memories of trauma infect victims' sleep, destroy their relationships and capacity to work, and torment their emotions. The wounds of trauma are not visible; the effects are. And mental/emotional/relational/spiritual wounds, like physical wounds, can fester if not properly cared for.

Trauma is not forgotten, and it continues to have a profound impact. Trauma raises questions about who God is; his character, his faithfulness, his purposes, and his capacity to keep us. It mutilates hope; it shatters faith; it turns the world upside down. Some of you are pastors, and you stand up to preach and deliver to those in the pews the words of our God about who he is and about his great love for us as demonstrated at the cross. But what do these victims hear? What do they think? You teach the truth about God's greatness and power. Many wonder why it was so absent in their lives. You teach about the love of our God as seen in Christ. They may believe you and yet be certain that his love is for others and not for them. You say God is our refuge in trouble. What do they think? You say God does not abandon us… ever. What do they think? You say that Jesus told the little children to come to him and not stop them. What do they think? You teach that our God hates evil. Many will assume that God's definition of evil does not include sexual abuse or rape or domestic violence, because no one ever speaks about such subjects in church.

It is important that we understand these struggles and do not silence them or treat them as a failure of faith. When we silence victims of trauma and their questions, we do further damage and, in fact, become an obstacle to the work that God can and wants to do in a life battered by trauma and evil. Thus, it is imperative that we give them a voice, and a safe, trusted context (i.e., a literal and figurative sanctuary) in which to share their pain, anguish, and turmoil.

People who have suffered trauma and abuse have had their personal walls broken down, their borders overrun, and their boundaries violated. Be ever mindful of and sensitive to these historical realities in their lives. Recent neuroscience research enlightens us that a trauma survivor's brain chemistry is literally and dramatically altered as a result of their painful experience(s). In order to recover fully, they require compassionate, sensitive, and accurately informed support and assistance.

People who are suffering long for help and comfort. Their pain is an open door for the church to bend down, like our Lord bent down for us, and enter into their traumatized lives with real help, companionship, and comfort. As we do, we will begin to see, like Israel of old, the trauma wilderness, the "valley of Trouble" in which many dwell, become a door of hope (Hosea 2:14-15). The church of Jesus Christ is called to bring light to dark places, love to damaged souls, and truth to people in pain; truth about who our God is—he who entered in so that we might know him and become like him.

How to Enter into Traumatized Lives

How can you as shepherds enter into traumatized lives and lead your people to do the same? Most importantly, you must first of all clearly understand what suffering does to humans. If you live with someone full of cancer or battling chronic pain, you know that suffering reduces people. It lessens all of their capacities, not just physically but also mentally, emotionally, relationally, and spiritually. They become less themselves. And that is just as true for unseen wounds as it is for physical diseases. It is true for a combat veteran, a rape victim, an incest survivor, a domestic violence victim, or a survivor of war. Such persons may look fine, but the wounds to their mind and heart run deep and affect them profoundly.

In order to attempt to enter into the life of someone who is reduced, limited, and altered by suffering, we must reduce ourselves as well. That is why we are quiet in a hospital room. For those suffering trauma, fewer words, quiet voices, patience, and pausing so they are not overwhelmed are all vital to our entering in without bringing further harm. In doing so, we are following our Savior who was made flesh, greatly reduced from his eternal glory, so he could enter in and become like us. It is, in fact, Christlike to reduce ourselves in the face of another's suffering. And then, when sufferers are slow to speak, slow to listen, or slow to change, our responses are also to be like our incarnate savior's response toward us. This gives those who are suffering a glimpse, a small example in the flesh, of who our God truly is with his creatures when they are reduced, overwhelmed, helpless, or slow. We bring him to them by who we are with them in their worst and/or most painful places. They learn over time, through us, that our God patiently bends toward and protects the vulnerable. He *never* abuses them or discards them.

At the same time, a truth I did not see for some time became stunningly clear to me as the years went by. God is always working both sides. I am not just present to sufferers so that they can receive comfort or grow. I am there because God is exposing to me where I am unlike him, so that I can run to him and have him teach me where I am wrong and what he would do in me to make me more like himself. This principle is applicable to all of life. All God's people are called to Christlikeness. Our failures in that area, which are many, teach lies about who he is and damage both us and those with whom we interact. In truth, you yourself will inevitably be transformed into a more sensitive, compassionate, and effective minister to hurting people as you allow the Holy Spirit to speak to you and through you while serving this challenging population within your congregation.

In painful situations, we humans typically react by attempting to change the other person and/or the circumstances. This can be particularly true when hearing a story of overwhelming evil and suffering. We want the other person to get better so we will feel better. But God uses ministry to the traumatized to change caregivers and the rest of the church as much as victims. Thus, the powerfully profound principle embedded in 2 Corinthians 1:3-7 of comforting those who are afflicted breathes resurrection life into the miraculous transformation of that which was meant for evil, ultimately resulting in the saving of many lives (cf. Genesis 50:20). God is truly a Redeemer!

Following a traumatic experience, every human being must make the heartbreaking adjustment to a new world full of losses. Human beings who experience trauma feel alone, helpless, humiliated, and hopeless. Following trauma, people turn inward, away from actual life, because the memories and the feelings are all they can handle. This is not wrong; it is necessary for a while. However, if life is to go on, eventually they must return to the outside world. How can you help people face what is inside—to help them remember well and yet still be able to return to life in a way that is good?

Why Some People Don't Share Their Story

Numerous things keep people from talking about what has happened to them; things such as shame, others in the church not speaking openly, and an overwhelming lack of a sense of safety. Oftentimes the church doesn't know how to respond to these sorts of trauma and abuse issues, so church leaders or other people in the church remain silent, making it even more difficult for victims to feel they can open up. Because of this, the trauma stays with the victims, and they can feel ashamed, broken and helpless, or flawed and unworthy, all of which make them hesitant to tell their story.

Many trauma wounds carry a great deal of shame, particularly in relation to experiences like rape, childhood abuses, trafficking, and domestic violence. Because of this feeling of shame, people carry their trauma wounds privately, and they often don't get the care they need.

Additionally, their sense of security has been damaged by the trauma, and they feel increasingly vulnerable to danger, which changes the way they think and live and the way they do relationships. So the wound of their trauma festers and begins to infect every area of their life. They live in a constant state of feeling unsafe, always scrambling for a sense of safety and security.

They Don't Trust God Anymore

One major reason some people don't share their story after a trauma is because of the magnitude with which it can impact even solid faith. When we encounter personal evil or disaster in life, it rocks us. It can turn faith upside down. People begin to wonder where God was when the trauma happened or ask why he wasn't there to protect them or their loved ones. I once had a client ask, "What was God thinking when my daddy raped me?" These sorts of questions come up.

People who are dealing with trauma are struggling with what seem to be two irreconcilable realities. On the one hand, we can understand a loving God and no sexual abuse of a child. Or, we can understand sexual abuse and no loving God. But it can be hard to reconcile in our minds the reality of a loving God while maintaining the reality of sexual abuse of a child. It's the age-old "problem of evil" question, how we reconcile evil with a good and loving God. Intense questions regarding theodicy abound.

When trauma happens, then, this "problem of evil" question becomes extremely personal and no longer theoretical. So many people who have been traumatized feel like they've lost the God they knew and trusted. He doesn't feel safe anymore. *As a result, opening up to a pastor, minister, or other spiritual leader, someone who is a representative of God to them, may not feel safe anymore, either.*

When individuals tell you as a pastor, church leader, or other spiritual authority figure that they were traumatized, sexually abused, or raped, they are often terrified, full of shame, and sure that you are going to think less of them. However, they have also given you great honor and privilege because they have taken the enormous risk of deciding that you may be a safe person (thereby imparting to you a most sacred trust) to welcome into their most unsafe, pain-filled place.

But ministering to men and women who are victims of trauma and sexual abuse can be puzzling; there are several common mistakes that pastors and church leaders often make. By being aware of these pitfalls, you can be better prepared to minister effectively to those within your church who have trauma wounds.

Mistake #1: Failing to Understand the Weight of What They are Telling You

First and foremost, we need to recognize the experience of survivors of trauma and sexual abuse and affirm their courage in sharing about their experiences. To do so, we should be gathering information. What do they mean by "sexual abuse?" Was it one time or ongoing? For adults who share that they were sexually abused as a child, it may be that over the course of a decade or more, they were victims of that abuse. Or it may have been a one-time occurrence. Those marinated in abuse throughout childhood have been shaped by that abuse. In gathering information, we are beginning to understand the weight of what they have been through, and we can be better prepared to minister to them.

Mistake #2: Assuming They are Safe

We often make the assumption that because sexual abuse happened when someone was a child, it no longer happens to that person as an adult. Or we assume that it will never happen again. But these are wrong assumptions. Just because people are "adults" doesn't mean they are safe where they are. This is more obvious when the problem is domestic violence, but it is also true for those abused many years ago.

Pastors and other church leaders should be asking questions about their current safety, such as, "Are you safe where you are now, and if not, can I help you find a safe place?" You should ask these questions regardless of their age. Spiritual leaders should be asking questions about the victim's current safety.

As an example, a twenty-year-old may share that an uncle who used to abuse her is now coming to visit for the weekend. That should be a red flag for us; it may be that this young woman does not have the strength to keep the abuse from happening again. Because of this, we may need to find a place for her to stay, or we may need to call the police to help keep her safe. We cannot assume that the abuse has ended or that she is strong enough to keep it from happening again.

Mistake #3: Underreacting

A third mistake that church leaders may make is underreacting to hearing about sexual abuse. This presents itself primarily in two ways. First, a pastor or church may fail to report the abuse. By law, in all fifty states we are required to report the abuse (or neglect) of a minor. It is a felony to fail to report any instance of child abuse that we hear about. Sometimes this is passed off as wanting to gather more information. However, we are not forensic investigators. Even with forty-five years of experience in counseling the sexually abused, I am still not the expert in that area. Our duty is to report and to let the forensic investigators take it from there.

The other way that pastors and churches frequently underreact is that they try to cover up the abuse. Perhaps the accused abuser is a church member or a friend. I have seen churches try to cover up for those accused, either to protect their church's reputation or out of pure disbelief. However, covering up abuse is also a felony.

Mistake #4: Failing to be the Church

A fourth common mistake spiritual leaders and churches make when ministering to victims of trauma and sexual abuse is simply failing to be the church to them. The role of the church is to care for the brokenhearted: to listen well, bear witness, and walk alongside them. But sometimes I see churches fail in these things. It is also the role of the church to model healthy relationships, which may mean engaging mentors or people who can demonstrate what it means to love one another properly.

As an example, when I work with a woman who has experienced a severe trauma like sexual abuse, it may be that she's never known what a safe or healthy relationship looks like. With her permission, I have oftentimes had women close to her come meet with me. I give them resources to read, and I talk about what it might look like to be helpful to the victim on a practical, day-to-day level. This may mean having dinner in their homes and seeing how family members are supposed to treat one another. Or it may be demonstrating how to show respect to one's spouse. There are all sorts of healthy ways of interacting to which a survivor of sexual abuse, especially ongoing abuse, may have never been exposed; examples that church members close to them can help model..

Mistake #5: Forgetting to Lament

Finally, one of the other vital functions of the church, and one that I think we've forgotten, is the art and necessity of lamenting. People who have suffered severe traumas, such as sexual abuse or violence, need to lament. I help them find words from Scripture (often in the Psalms or the Prophets) to express their pain, their fear, their doubts, and sometimes even their anger at God. We see often in Scripture where the psalmist or the prophets call out to God, "Where are you?" or "Why don't you hear me?"

As the church, we need to come alongside those victims and help them find those words. But we also need to be saying those words with them.

We need to lament with them, to weep with those who weep. We need to be like the friends of Job in Job 2:11-13 (ESV):

> Now when Job's three friends heard of all this evil that had come upon him, they came each from his own place… They made an appointment together to come to show him sympathy and comfort him. And when they saw him from a distance, they did not recognize him. And they raised their voices and wept, and they tore their robes and sprinkled dust on their heads toward heaven. And they sat with him on the ground seven days and seven nights, and no one spoke a word to him, for they saw that his suffering was very great.

We need to be like these friends, weeping and crying out to the Lord on their behalf.

As pastors, church leaders, and churches in general seek to minister to victims of trauma and sexual abuse, they should recognize the gravity of what is being shared with them. In doing so, they can walk alongside the survivors and lament with them. While that may also mean reporting cases of abuse as required by law, supporting victims of all kinds of trauma demonstrates Christ-like love toward them and ultimately leads to their healing.

What Does Healing Look Like?

Recovery involves a reversal of the experience of trauma. Trauma brings silence because it feels like there are no words to describe what happened. Trauma brings emotional darkness and aloneness because it feels like no one cares and no one could possibly understand. Trauma makes time stand still because we get so lost in what happened that we cannot see forward and we have lost hope. Three essential components are required in order to reverse the experience of trauma and bring about recovery. All three take place within the redemptive context of caring, safe relationships. All three must happen for "victims" to be transformed into "survivors." Becoming a survivor means the person's identity is no longer defined by having been victimized by the trauma they suffered.

First, survivors need to talk, to tell their story. They may be afraid to do so, slow to speak, uncertain of their words. But as we listen and bear witness to their trauma, we grant them dignity, safety, and comfort.

Second, survivors need to grieve. Trauma always includes loss. The survivors' sense of self is altered, as is their way of living in this world. Trauma shatters faith and mutilates hope. There is much to grieve, so talking eventually must include tears.

Third, survivors need time. Both you and trauma survivors will want a quick recovery. Such significant and deep wounds do not recover quickly. The more life-threatening the wound, the slower the recovery (obviously this is true physically as well). Talking, tears, and time are all necessary for healing.

Here are the words of a genocide survivor in Rwanda who lived through unspeakable atrocities and trauma.

> I saw only evil. I no longer believed God to be good. The church was not a sanctuary for my family; it was a cemetery. But then you came, you listened, and you heard my broken heart. And now I think I can believe that God too is listening and hears my pain and will be my sanctuary because I have gotten a taste of him through you.

Four Ways to Encourage Survivors to Tell Their Story

When we think about the personal nature of the problem of evil that presents itself in the midst of trauma, the answer must first and foremost be in the person of Jesus Christ. At the Cross, the reality of evil and the goodness of God met. He was assaulted by evil; he bore our sorrows. While we can certainly share scripture with those victimized by trauma, we must also bring those persons to an encounter with Christ. We have to first incarnate the love and mercy of God through Christ to them. When we do so, little by little his presence is sensed and is known by the survivors. His carrying of their suffering becomes a more believable reality because we have carried it with them.

So ultimately, it is the place of the Cross that provides answers for their questions, but the path to it is through the people of God caring for, bearing witness to, and walking alongside a traumatized life. In reaching out to persons in your church who are experiencing—or who have experienced— trauma, consider the following guidelines as you formulate specific, formalized ways to minister to them.

1. **Exercise patience in your response.** When it comes to dealing with trauma, we oftentimes have an inclination to rush in and talk a lot in an effort to help them and give them answers. In these cases, though, all we are doing is adding to their sense of being overwhelmed. We don't want to overwhelm them in the way we respond. If we speak too quickly, they are likely to withdraw again. As long as they are telling their story, ask questions only for understanding, not for correction. Eventually, we can come back and start to draw them into the truth, but still not confront them. It has to be done gently, and we want victims to come to understanding, rather than it being forced on them. The latter can ironically be experienced by the survivor as abusive, not because we are not speaking the truth, but because we speak unlovingly when we are forceful with the truth. Instead, we want the survivor to wrestle with the truth and apply it to themselves. That's the source of deep change.

2. **Allow the survivor to speak.** Talking is so important to healing, partly because the process of speaking teaches us truth, even truth that has been hidden or is unbearably painful. Trauma is evil in nature, and evil teaches us lies. For instance, prolonged childhood sexual assault teaches survivors that they are worthless, and regardless of how many scripture passages they read that say otherwise, they still believe they are worthless. These lies must

come out into the light in front of someone who speaks truth and also treats them in accordance with truth. The lies must come out to someone who listens patiently and responds safely and quietly. Then the bondage of those lies is released when the lies are spoken in the light and in the presence of someone who is aiming to be a representative of who Christ is and who speaks truth to them. Furthermore, we typically interact with suffering people, or pain, by talking. But sometimes we don't know how to stop, or we want to tell them how they need to change or act. Trauma needs a great deal of talking in order to heal, but the talking is not ours, it's the survivor's. We need to be present and gentle and inviting and safe, so that over time they may find their own voice and their own words to express what is oftentimes unspeakable.

3. **Understand suffering.** We also need to understand what suffering does to people. As mentioned earlier, suffering reduces people. It lessens their capacities— not just physically, but also mentally, emotionally, relationally, and spiritually. They become less of themselves. And these effects occur with unseen wounds just as they do with physical illnesses that are more obvious. While the people may look fine outwardly, wounds to their mind and heart run deep and affect them profoundly. Words are slow to come. How do you articulate a rape at age seven? And in the bigger scheme of things, remember that suffering people struggle mightily with questions of theodicy—why did God allow this to happen?

4. **Become little.** If we want to enter into the life of somebody who is limited by his or her suffering, we must bend down. For those people suffering traumas, we want to use fewer words, quiet voices, and lots of patience and pausing, so they are not overwhelmed. The trauma overwhelmed them, and we do not want to replicate that in our helping. This "becoming little" is vital to our entering in so we don't bring further harm. The beauty of it is that in doing so, we are following Christ, who was incomprehensibly reduced from his eternal glory so as to enter in and become like us. We are privileged to likewise enter into the fellowship of a trauma survivor's sufferings.

The Word was made flesh for you and for me. Now you and I are called to do the same for the world. When you, as a shepherd of the sheep, name the unspeakable things for your people and gently call them to begin to speak the truth about their lives and the wounds they bear, you invite them out of the darkness of trauma and abuse. As you study and learn, you can teach your people to go with you into the dark places of great suffering in your pews and around the world.

Jesus went through villages and cities, teaching, preaching, and healing. And *seeing* the people, he was moved with compassion. They were distressed, wounded, bleeding sheep. He saw what others did not see. They were fainting, fleeced by wolves, and without a shepherd's care. In response he said, "The harvest..." These seem to be contradictory figures, mixed metaphors. A flock of sheep wounded and fainting, and harvest? Harvest is usually about a robust, healthy, flourishing crop. But here is the deep truth about Jesus's mission: Human need, distress, and trauma constitute harvest for him and his workers. Where the day is darkest and the need is sorest, *there* the fields are white to harvest. Trauma—a mission field of the twenty-first century; he did not say it was hopeless, but that it was a plenteous harvest.

It is my prayer that you will lead his people to follow him into the dark and difficult places, throwing the shadow of his great glory over the suffering of this earth. There are a multitude of trauma and abuse survivors to minister to, not only in the "uttermost" parts of the earth, but right in your own "Jerusalem."

Jennifer Cisney Ellers, M.A.

Jennifer Cisney Ellers is a Professional Counselor, life coach, crisis response trainer, author, and speaker. She conducts training, counseling, and coaching in the field of grief, crisis, and trauma through the Institute for Compassionate Care. Jennifer is an approved instructor for the International Critical Incident Stress Foundation, teaching several CISM courses. Also, Jennifer provides divorce coaching, training, and speaking through Emerge Victorious, a ministry for women rebuilding their lives after divorce. With her husband, Dr. Kevin Ellers, she is the co-author of *The First 48 Hours: Spiritual Caregivers as First Responders.* In addition, Jennifer co-authored *Emerge Victorious: A Woman's Transformational Guide After Her Divorce* with Sandra Dopf Lee.

Kevin Ellers, D.Min.

Kevin Ellers is the Territorial Disaster Services Coordinator for The Salvation Army in the U.S.A. Central Territory. He is also president of the Institute for Compassionate Care, which is dedicated to education, training, and direct care. Dr. Ellers is an associate chaplain with the Illinois Fraternal Order of Police, serves as faculty for the International Critical Incident Stress Foundation, is an adjunct professor at Olivet Nazarene University, and is a member of the American Association of Christian Counselors Crisis Response Training Team. He has extensive training and experience in the fields of crisis response, grief, trauma, disaster management, chaplaincy, pastoral ministries, marriage and family therapy, and social services. As an author and speaker, he teaches broadly in these related topics.

CHAPTER 18

How to Develop an Effective Suicide Awareness and Crisis Response Ministry

Jennifer Cisney Ellers, M.A. and
Kevin Ellers, D.Min.

Should the local church have a central and leading role in crisis response? We think Scripture clearly answers this question, and we outlined this discussion in the introduction to our book, *The first 48 hours: Spiritual caregivers as first responders* (Cisney & Ellers, 2009).

"And who is my neighbor?" This pointed question, posed by an expert in the law in Luke 10:29 (NIV), alludes to what one must do to inherit eternal life and prompts a widely-recognized story told by Jesus and known as the parable of the good Samaritan. This parable aptly illustrates a number of key principles that relate to how we care for others in times of crisis, which will be explored throughout this chapter. The research field of crisis response is still relatively new, having only come into existence in the last century and only prominently in the last three decades, but the principles of caring for individuals in crisis date back to biblical times, and through the centuries the church has played a crucial role in providing front-line crisis response care. Let's look at this familiar parable in Luke 10:25-37 (NIV).

> On one occasion an expert in the law stood up to test Jesus. "Teacher," he asked, "what must I do to inherit eternal life?"
>
> "What is written in the Law?" he replied. "How do you read it?"
>
> He answered: "'Love the Lord your God with all your heart and with all your soul and with all your strength

and with all your mind'; and, 'Love your neighbor as yourself.'"

"You have answered correctly," Jesus replied. "Do this and you will live."

But he wanted to justify himself, so he asked Jesus, "And who is my neighbor?" In reply Jesus said: "A man was going down from Jerusalem to Jericho, when he fell into the hands of robbers. They stripped him of his clothes, beat him and went away, leaving him half dead. A priest happened to be going down the same road, and when he saw the man, he passed by on the other side. So too, a Levite, when he came to the place and saw him, passed by on the other side. But a Samaritan, as he traveled, came where the man was; and when he saw him, he took pity on him. He went to him and bandaged his wounds, pouring on oil and wine. Then he put the man on his own donkey, took him to an inn and took care of him. The next day he took out two silver coins and gave them to the innkeeper. 'Look after him,' he said, 'and when I return, I will reimburse you for any extra expense you may have.' Which of these three do you think was a neighbor to the man who fell into the hands of robbers?"

The expert in the law replied, "The one who had mercy on him."

Jesus told him, "Go and do likewise."

This parable is launched as an expert in the law strategically poses a question to Jesus about what he must do to inherit eternal life and then follows up with an inquiry as to just who is his neighbor. It should be noted that in the sociological context in which Jesus gives this parable, a "good Samaritan" would have been a contradiction in terms for most Jews of that day, because for centuries Jews and Samaritans had mutually hated each other.

This same "Who is my neighbor?" question is still being asked almost daily and in many forms by those of us who are Christians in the 21st century. Exactly whom should I help in a world that is full of hurting people? How much should I help? Is it really my responsibility? Which charitable organization should I contribute to this year?

This passage of scripture demonstrates that we are to care for all people; not just our families, our friends, or those in our church, but even those from different races, cultures, and religions. The church is called to respond to all in society who are disenfranchised. By "church" we mean the church universal, the body of believers throughout the world who are followers of Christ. It is not a building, an organization, or a denomination; the church of which we speak and to which we will refer throughout this chapter references an active, driving force which, when empowered by the Holy Spirit, has the potential to accomplish tremendous change and bring healing to a hurting world.

Many organizations that provide services to the homeless find it difficult to secure a location for this type of outreach due to a pervasive "not in my back yard" mentality, commonly known as NIMBY. But the parable of the good Samaritan indicates that there is a correlation between our love for God and our social responsibility to put that love into action with those around us. There is a call to care for those who are in crisis; those who have been traumatized physically, emotionally, and/or spiritually by violence or disaster of any kind. A pattern for modern day crisis response can be found in the good Samaritan's care of the man who fell among thieves. Jesus's command to love our neighbor as ourselves is just as applicable to those who are in the midst of crisis today as it was two thousand years ago (Cisney & Ellers, 2009).

Crisis Response/Crisis Intervention

We clearly live in a time when crisis events will be a part of the life of any church community. Whether widespread natural disasters like hurricanes, floods, fires, tornados, and earthquakes or the more common daily crises that impact smaller numbers of people, all churches will face the challenge of knowing how to assist those in their care who face traumatic and potentially life-altering unexpected events. Most will agree that these types of events are increasing in our society. It is our hearts' desire to see the church step purposefully into crisis ministry on the front lines. Many governmental and social agencies offer crisis and disaster response services, but in our opinion, the finest work in crisis and disaster intervention is currently being done by faith-based organizations. That said, there is still a need for more services, especially from the local church.

While churches have many opportunities and options for providing assistance, the most common way for a local church to support those in crisis is through a lay counseling or support group ministry. Such ministries can be extremely helpful for individuals going through specific types of situations (grief support groups for those who lose loved ones, divorce support groups for those who have a marital crisis, etc.), but there are limits to the scope of these ministries. We strongly support church-based crisis response teams which can involve either a single church creating and supporting a community-based team or a number of churches within a community coming together to form a multi-church support team to serve their larger community. In this chapter, we will offer some thoughts for churches considering a crisis response ministry or for those seeking to enhance or grow an existing ministry.

Formation and Management of a Crisis Response Ministry/Team

Any crisis response team should start with experienced leadership, and its primary team leaders should have as much experience with actual crisis response/crisis intervention as possible. Most often, this involves experience on a Critical Incident Stress Management (CISM) or related type of community response team. It is also ideal to include members who have, for example, been deployed with local and/or national disaster response agencies. But it is also critical that some of their training and experience involve the emotional and spiritual care aspect, in addition to general disaster support.

The most essential component in the formation of a church-based team is for pastoral staff and key church leaders to be fully supportive and to understand the advantages and challenges of this type of ministry. Sadly, some churches' desire to start a crisis response ministry has been thwarted by leadership concerns about liability. Of course, any outreach ministry carries some risk, but following the appropriate training and supervision guidelines outlined in this chapter should minimize those risks. Like any successful ministry, passionate individuals who are deeply committed and called (in this case to crisis response) will be the key to an effective long-term program.

It is also essential for all teams to have mental health supervision. Therefore, at least one team member should have a master's degree or higher in a mental health field, but it is not necessary for this individual to be in current practice as a mental health professional. Recently graduated students and retired mental health professionals are ideal to serve on teams. It is also important for the team to include ordained clergy.

When possible, recruiting retired or former first responders to serve provides depth and dimension to your team and helps tremendously in networking with local law enforcement agencies and fire departments. Although active first responders often do not have the time to serve on a church-based team or may be prohibited from doing so by their employment policies, making them consultants or assistant trainers for the team is a wise option.

It may go without saying, but do choose team members who have good people skills. Optimal team members possess a high level of emotional intelligence, strong empathy, and keen sensitivity. Most people who are effective at crisis response and psychological first aid have gone through difficult times in their own lives. While there is no one experience that qualifies a person to be an effective crisis responder, painful life situations of loss or trauma can leave people with the sensitivity and understanding that help them be "present" with others who are suffering. (cf. 2 Corinthians 1:3-7.) You will likely find that people drawn to this type of helping ministry will have experienced pain and personal challenges in their own lives. That being said, it is also important for team members to have enough distance from their own painful experiences to be able to be fully available to those they are serving.

Training and Supervision

It is essential for all team members to undergo basic training in crisis intervention, psychological first aid, or Critical Incident Stress Management. This requirement can be one of the biggest roadblocks to the formation of a church-based team because specialized training can be costly. There are also low-cost or free options available for training team members, but getting team members adequately trained usually takes time and patience. Don't be tempted to compromise by allowing untrained people to serve. Doing so can undermine the integrity of the ministry and put the entire program at risk. A comprehensive list of appropriate training curricula is beyond the scope of this chapter, but we will highlight the most recognized and readily available classes that can prepare your team members.

Critical Incident Stress Management Courses

CISM courses are offered through the International Critical Incident Stress Foundation. This organization is based in Baltimore, MD, but classes are frequently offered across the country. Many faith-based organizations, including the American Association of Christian Counselors (AACC), the Billy Graham Evangelistic Association, and The Salvation Army offer these classes. AACC also offers online (and DVD-based) curricula in crisis response and provides certification in Christian Crisis Response. This certification is not required, but it is highly recommended for team leaders and supervisors.

Each team member should have a minimum of two core courses totaling approximately 25-30 hours of training in crisis intervention. Leaders should also, over time, acquire additional hours of training, including completing advanced and specialized training classes. If you have enough individuals in your church or community who are seeking this training, it can be cost-effective to host group training at your church (more information on training and certification is available at the AACC website in the references list at the end of this chapter). You should consider specialized training for at least some of your team members in the following key areas:

- Intervention with children and teens
- Grief and loss
- Emotional and spiritual care in disasters
- Crisis response with senior adults (or gerontology)
- Suicide intervention and prevention

Scope and Policies

It is important to clearly define who, how, when, and where your team will serve. There are many crisis events occurring daily, even in small communities, so care should be taken to define the parameters of service. Generally, teams start by serving individuals and families within their own church congregations when a crisis event occurs. This certainly includes any type of injury, death, violence, or threat to those in the church or their loved ones or family members, but it is important for a crisis response ministry to be open to serving the larger community as well.

Team leadership should carefully consider the service parameters for their team. Such considerations should include the size of your team and the experience, training, and qualifications of your team members. You must also take into consideration other crisis response services available in your community. This often involves a great deal of research and networking.

Your ministry will be most effective if you fill unmet needs and underserved populations. Major metropolitan areas will often have many crisis response services available, including CISM teams that service the first responder community, Community Emergency Response Teams (CERT), and other groups of chaplains and trained community volunteers who serve specific groups or types of critical incidents. Being aware of and networking with these other services will insure that your team focuses its efforts in the areas most needed and will facilitate preparation for larger-scale events that impact the entire community. When these relationships have been established, your team will be able to work cooperatively within the community and alongside other teams when natural disasters or major critical incidents hit your region.

It will be essential to create a policies and procedures manual for your team prior to or soon after formation. Of course, you can add to such a manual as needed, but the following guidelines will serve as the foundation both for how the team operates and for heading off potential problems. Minimally, policies addressing these specific areas should be included:

- Definition of leadership positions, including requirements and responsibilities;
- Supervision of the team and its placement within the organizational structure of the church, including which department will govern and supervise the team;
- Funding and budget requirements;
- Parameters for team selection and training, including training requirements;
- Ethical policies for team members, including confidentiality, supervision, and suicide protocols, among others;
- Ethical policies and procedures for discipline or dismissal from the team;
- Procedures for addressing complaints or concerns; and
- Reporting and documentation procedures.

We recommend regular (monthly or quarterly) team meetings that include some sessions for ongoing training. As previously mentioned, all teams should have mental health supervision, which should always include a mental health professional who is "on call" for any team deployment. It is not always possible to have a mental health professional who is physically onsite for all team deployments, but care should be taken to have a mental health professional available to the team at all times. This generally involves an on-call schedule such that a mental health professional is accessible by phone or text should the team have a high-level crisis situation which requires mental health consultation. These situations should be outlined in training and procedural manuals and should always address the following:

- Suicidal or homicidal ideation;
- Violent behavior requiring emergency intervention; and
- Any indication of psychosis or mental instability indicating a need for medical or mental health screening.

All team members should always have access to team leadership when faced with any situation they do not feel equipped to handle.

Connection with Community and National Crisis Response Organizations

As previously mentioned, networking with other local groups and crisis response agencies will help position your team to be most effective within the scope of other services offered in the community. It is also important for your team leaders to network with national organizations in crisis response. These organizations may include associations such as the American Association of Christian Counselors, (specifically the Grief, Crisis and Disaster Network division), the International Critical Incident Stress Foundation, and the National Voluntary Organization Active in Disaster. As most major denominations also offer disaster response services, a church team may also have access to specific services within its denomination. In addition, there are many faith-based organizations offering disaster and crisis response that work across denominations; for example, The Salvation Army, Convoy of Hope, and the Billy Graham Evangelistic Association's Rapid Response Team. Your team may want to network with these organizations and consider working cooperatively with them, thus enabling you to send your team members to deploy with these organizations during larger-scale national or international situations.

Suicide Awareness and Intervention

One issue of vital importance related to crisis response is suicide awareness and intervention. Any crisis response team or ministry of the church should have leaders and some members who have received specialized training in suicide intervention. And even if a church does not have a designated crisis response team, it should have a clear protocol for suicide intervention, and all pastoral staff and ministry leaders should be trained in this basic protocol, with at least a few key leaders having completed a suicide training program.

Suicide is a major and growing problem in our current society that will inevitably impact even the smallest church congregations. Suicide is the 10th leading cause of death in the U.S. Each year, an average of 44,193 Americans die by suicide, and for every completed suicide, there are at least 25 suicide attempts (American Foundation for Suicide Prevention). The suicide rate in the U.S. has risen steadily since 2006, and it is still rising. These numbers do not include the many, many Americans of all ages who silently battle with thoughts of suicide, but have not yet made an attempt. The issue of suicide will touch every congregation in some way. This makes it critically important for every church to address the issue in a way that is appropriate to their congregation. Here are some basic steps that may help in addressing this very significant mental health issue:

1. Consider recognizing the National Suicide Prevention Week (or World Suicide Prevention Day); these generally occur in September each year. You could offer guest speakers, prevention education, or even mental health screenings during the month of September.

2. Provide training in suicide intervention for staff and ministry leaders. AACC offers the Suicide PAIR Program (Prevention, Assessment, Intervention and Recovery; see link in the references list) that is appropriate for ministry leaders, mental health professionals, or lay volunteers. There are also many widely-offered face-to-face trainings, including "Understanding Suicide," a two-day course by the authors of this chapter.

3. Locate and publish local and national resources on suicide, to help both those struggling with suicidal ideation and survivors who have lost loved ones to suicide. The National Suicide Hotline is available 24 hours a day, 7 days a week, 365 days a year by calling 800-273-TALK (8255). Most major communities also have suicide survivors support groups that meet either weekly or monthly and are free of charge. Such local groups can be located through the American Foundation for Suicide Prevention. Its website and those for two other wonderfully supportive organizations, Alliance of Hope for Suicide Survivors and Survivors of Suicide can be found in the references list.

4. Identify local counselor resources through professional Christian counseling centers and county mental health programs. Develop and maintain a list of local Christian mental health professionals to whom you can refer those members of your congregation or community who are dealing with suicidal thoughts. These should be professionals you have carefully vetted and personally met with

prior to referral. If you are not aware of such professionals in your community, the AACC's Christian Care Coalition can provide a list of professionals to interview. This list can be accessed through the website in the references list or by calling 800-COUNSEL.

Of course, the first step in suicide prevention is building a greater awareness about mental health issues within your congregation. The fact that you are reading this book indicates your desire to do this. It is estimated that 90% of people who complete suicide have a diagnosable mental illness at the time of their death (National Alliance on Mental Illness). People who die by suicide are often experiencing undiagnosed, untreated, or undertreated mental illness(es). If churches can build awareness of mental health issues and increase access to good mental health care, they will make significant progress in suicide prevention.

It is crucial for us to make the church a safe place to discuss issues related to mental health, including mental illness and the often taboo topic of suicide. The truth is that many believers who love and follow Christ suffer from mental illness and become suicidal. We will conclude this chapter with a letter from one of those people. She is a beautiful, loving woman who bravely battles mental illness every day of her life and who wants to share a message with the church.

Dear family and friends of the church,

I am writing to you because I want you to understand better what it is like to be suicidal and to be so distraught that you actually attempt suicide. I have suffered for over 20 years with severe depression and Bipolar 2 disorder. People who attempt to take their own lives are not selfish, as most people tend to believe. They are just in so much agony and pain that they cannot even think about or see the effect their actions will have on their loved ones. They do not attempt to hurt themselves in order to punish or hurt their families and friends. The pain is quite literally blinding to the person, so they do not know what they are doing to others. They only know that the pain has become so unbearable that they do not want to live. Oftentimes, they honestly feel like ending their lives will lift a great burden off of everyone whom they feel they already hurt by just existing. This is especially true if they have loved ones who are also their caretakers.

If someone has attempted, but not completed their suicide attempt, then the best and most helpful thing you can do is to be understanding and not be judgmental or blame them for their attempt. Just "being" there for the person, without a lot of talking or questions is the best thing you can do as a church family.

I can only hope and pray that this small insight can help people to understand where "we" are coming from. Please don't judge or condemn, whether the attempt was completed or not. This is all I can ask of you for all of us that suffer so tremendously, often on a daily basis.

Sincerely,
A Sister in Christ

If the church goes even further to become a place of caring and compassion where suicidal people can turn for help and hope without fear of judgment or condemnation, then we will truly begin to see a change in the suicide rates, and we will also fulfill God's call to love our neighbor as ourselves. Don't just stand by or "pass by." Reach out in love. As a result, many will be saved, both emotionally and spiritually.

References

Alliance of Hope for Suicide Loss Survivors. http://www.allianceofhope.org/

American Association of Christian Counselors. aacc.net

American Foundation for Suicide Prevention. https://afsp.org/about-suicide/
    suicide-statistics/

Christian Care Connect. American Association of Christian Counselors. http://www.aacc.net/resources/find-a-counselor/

Cisney, J. and Ellers, K. (2009). *The first 48 hours: Spiritual caregivers as first responders.* Nashville: Abingdon Press.

National Alliance on Mental Illness. https://www.nami.org/Learn-More/Mental-Health-Conditions/Related-Conditions/Suicide

Substance Abuse and Mental Health Administration. https://www.samhsa.gov/suicide-prevention

Suicide PAIR program. American Association of Christian Counselors. http://www.aacc.net/courses/suicide-pair/

Survivors of Suicide. survivorsofsuicide.com

Douglas Rosenau, Ed.D.

Doug Rosenau is a Licensed Clinical Psychologist (LCP) and a Licensed Marriage & Family Therapist (LMFT), specializing in sex therapy. He is a nationally known speaker and author of *A Celebration of Sex, A Celebration of Sex for Newlyweds, A Celebration of Sex After 50*, and *Slaying the Marriage Dragons*.

In addition to maintaining a private practice, Dr. Rosenau is also co-founder of Sexual Wholeness, Inc. He serves as Professor for the Institute for Sexual Wholeness in conjunction with the Psychological Studies Institute in Atlanta, GA and is a Certified Sex Therapist and a Diplomat of the American Board of Sexology. Doug currently serves as an adjunct professor at Reformed Theological Seminary in Orlando, FL and Jackson, MI. He is a Full Clinical Member of the Society for Sex Therapy and Research (SSTAR) and has written numerous articles on healthy sexuality for such publications as *Christian Counseling Today* and *New Man*.

CHAPTER 19

How to Develop an Effective Sexual Integrity Ministry

Doug Rosenau, Ed.D.

Introduction

Jesus was the only person to ever walk this earth with a life and lifestyle of sinless love and total sexual integrity. We can't wisely achieve sexual integrity (reliability, wholeness) on our own. As Christians, we realize that "True North," our foundational cornerstone, will always be that person who told us boldly that he was "the Way, the Truth, and the Life." Jesus has gone ahead of us and modeled for us how to sexually treat our sisters and brothers with respect, love, and honor.

So the quest for sexual integrity begins by allowing the Intimate Trinity to create a personal love relationship with us through Jesus Christ and give us the empowering Holy Spirit. Our masculinity or femininity and our sexuality were created to flourish within intimate relationships that begin with being rightly related to our Creator. The Holy Spirit gives us the capacity to understand and focus on the sexual compass of truth that God gives us in scripture. We can then, with the help of our Christian brothers and sisters, follow our Lord Jesus's "True North" and become people who live out their sexuality as God intended.

> *"But the Counselor, the Holy Spirit, whom the Father will send in my name, will teach you all things and will remind you of everything I have said to you" (John 14:26, NIV).*

This chapter will be divided into two sets of building blocks for establishing and maintaining a godly sexual integrity. Jesus Christ will always be the cornerstone in our building. Our first set of building blocks will focus on foundational concepts for understanding and working out a personal and communal sexual integrity. The second set of building blocks will detail practical ways to embrace and fight for sexual integrity as part of a godly lifestyle. Each of these sets of building blocks is crucial to the development of a healthy ministry in the church, and when they are taught in a clear and systematic way, they can provide the structure and basis for healthy gender-based support groups in a church community.

Set One Building Blocks

The foundation of sexual integrity. Certain concepts and practices create a foundation for a healthy and God-reflective sexuality. This first set of building blocks will develop four important ideas that are central to establishing long-lasting sexual integrity and wholeness. Remember that God created our sexuality so that we could reflect the loving Trinity with deeply intimate love relationships. Our masculinity or femininity adds depth and a rich texture to all of our human interactions.

> *"So God created man(kind) in his own image,… male and female he created them" (Genesis 1:27, NIV).*

Each of us has been innately wired to be sexually and romantically attracted and aroused. Like Christ and his Bride, we desire that exclusive love relationship of marriage and becoming one flesh. Along with his precious gift of sexuality, God also gave us his guidelines, so that the gift would glorify him. That is where we begin our quest to achieve sexual holiness and integrity.

A. Start with God-Centered Sexuality: Work Inside Out

> *"…to be made new in the **attitude of your minds**; and to put on the new self, created to be like God in true righteousness and holiness" (Ephesians 4:23-24, NIV, emphasis added).*

*"All the ways of a man are pure in his own eyes, but the LORD weighs the **spirit**" (Proverbs 16:2, ESV, emphasis added).*

*"Don't become so well-adjusted to your culture that you fit into it without even thinking. Instead, fix your attention on God. **You'll be changed from the inside out**. Readily recognize what he wants from you, and quickly respond to it. Unlike the culture around you, always dragging you down to its level of immaturity, God brings the best out of you, develops well-formed maturity in you" (Romans 12:2, MSG, emphasis added).*

Many of us who grew up with conservative Christian backgrounds tried to become like Christ by making sure all our behaviors and actions were right. Sexual integrity was based on what we *did not do* sexually, the idea being that by refraining from engaging in certain behaviors we would start to more closely emulate God in our thoughts and attitudes. As a result, our hearts would be changed, and we would start to understand God and what he wanted for us. This was a legalistic, "outside-in" approach. It managed to keep us sexually pure when the sex police (parents, pastors, dorm monitors) were on duty to insure right behavior, but eventually it broke down. We were often reminded about the importance of chastity and that "True Love Waits" until marriage to have sexual intercourse, but no one ever really explained "why" and "how" true love waited.

In our present culture, this outside-in approach has so broken down that most Christian dating couples are getting naked or creating mutual orgasms—while thinking they are sexually pure as long as they don't engage in the one sexual behavior of sexual intercourse. So chastity is now defined by one behavior and not by God's character… or by scripture, or by the moving of the Holy Spirit.

How can we recapture a true sexual integrity? By starting with an "inside-out" approach to living out our sexuality in relationships. Loving and meaningful sexual behaviors can only begin after we have a personal love relationship with God through Jesus Christ. This is the very inside of our God circle. With redemption, Jesus brings the Holy Spirit into our lives, and he guides us into his truth. God's Word, applied to our hearts by the Holy Spirit, becomes the centering foundation for both our sexual integrity and, even more foundationally, our right heart attitudes about sexuality. This personal transformation begins in our hearts, renews our minds (attitudes), and then shapes our behaviors.

> *"But this is the new covenant... says the Lord: I will put my laws in their minds, and I will write them on their hearts. I will be their God, and they will be my people" (Hebrews 8:10, NLT).*

> *"Above all else guard your heart, for everything you do flows from it" (Proverbs 4:23, NIV).*

For example, 1 Corinthians 13:4-5 describes God's love as patient and kind, never rude or self-serving. Think what will happen in our sexual relating when we incorporate into our heart these attitudes of patience, kindness, and selflessness. What if we were trying to make those we are in relationship with the most confident and Christ-like sexual people possible, rather than selfishly trying to get something? What if the Holy Spirit was giving us the motivation and power to overcome our sinful, insecure selves and help us experience our true sexual purity and integrity?

> *"Put on your new nature, and be renewed as you learn to know your Creator and become like him" (Colossians 3:10, NLT).*

Our hearts and attitudes are what shape our behaviors. Your Christ-like heart attitudes allow you to value, celebrate, and protect God's design for sexuality—spirit, mind, and body— in yourself and in others. With the empowerment of Jesus Christ and the Holy Spirit, redemption allows God to work "inside-out" as he takes over lives, develops Christ-likeness in hearts, and builds sexual attitudes which dramatically change our behaviors and transform the way we live our lives sexually.

B. Create Sexual Conversations that Reflect Godly Character Traits

> *"Do not let any **unwholesome talk** come out of your mouths, but only what is helpful in building others up according to their needs, that it may benefit those who listen" (Ephesians 4:29, NIV, emphasis added).*

> *"But among you there must not be even a hint of sexual immorality, or of any kind of impurity... because these are improper for God's holy people. Nor should there be **obscenity, foolish talk** or course joking..." (Ephesians 5:3-4a, NIV, emphasis added).*

In creating healthy sexual conversations, Christians face a double whammy. First, much of the sexual language and information we learned in middle school and as teenagers did not reflect godly values. Television, the locker room, YouTube, and our peers were hardly fountains of wise sexual knowledge. The sexual terminology we learned conveyed cultural values, the slang words for sexual anatomy often reflected disparaging attitudes toward women and men, and the slang words for sexual activities were—and are—frequently silly, crude, or demeaning.

A second obstacle to healthy sexual conversations is the church's reluctance to even deal with sexual topics. Not only does coarse language sinfully demean God's gift of sexuality, but our Intimate Creator also views the way the church often treats sex ("Sex can be hurtful and distorting; don't be sexual." "Those sexual desires are scary; you'd better repress them.") as "unwholesome and foolish obscenity."

If we want sexual integrity in the church, we have to create helpful and healthy conversations about sex! We need sermons and workshops and an attitude within our Christian communities that sex is a wonderful, God-given topic. We must help each other value, celebrate, and protect each other's sexuality and sexual relating. And one key to this is creating a better vocabulary and bringing the character traits of the Almighty Trinity into our sexual conversations.

The church can view sexuality through God's lens. We can grow up and elevate our sexual language and our ability to deal with sexual topics in mature healthy ways. God designed our sexuality to reflect who he is, and as his image-bearers, our sexual vocabulary, conversations, and marital lovemaking emulate him and his transforming, elevating character.

God is:

Creative. The Trinity are creative geniuses, always inventing or producing something wonderfully generous and intimate. In each divine encounter, we walk away with something added to us, and our sexuality should have the same result: unselfish *addition* as we nurture and steward our own and each other's sexuality. Our contact with others should add something to their lives. *"… His compassions never fail. They are new every morning…" (Lamentations 3:22-23, NIV).*

Beautiful. The Almighty Creator is startlingly beautiful, and he only creates things of beauty. Our bodies and our sexuality are glories of God's creation and reveal his matchless beauty. What lovely insights and stunning feelings he reveals to us sexually. He is also *good*—wholesome and helpful. Our language—including our language about our sexuality—should reflect beauty and goodness! *"He has made everything beautiful in its time. He has also set eternity in the hearts of men…" (Ecclesiastes 3:11, NIV).*

Loving. God deeply loves and creates every person special (thus not to be objectified!). We can love through our total three-dimensional person: through our bodies, our minds and emotions, and our hearts. Our sexuality should always be about intimacy and expressing love and affection. *"God is love. Whoever lives in love lives in God, and God in him. … if we love one another, God lives in us and his love is made complete in us" (1 John 4:16b, 12, NIV).*

Holy. God's holiness creates protective boundaries that enable us to live out our sexuality in true freedom. The Holy Spirit within us helps us elevate our vocabulary so we can become creatively intimate and treat our brothers and sisters with *honor. "It is God's will… that each of you should learn to control his own body in a way that is holy and honorable, not in passionate lust like the heathen, who do not know God: and that in this matter no one* *should wrong [defraud] his brother or take advantage of him… For God did not call us to be impure, but to live a holy life" (1 Thessalonians 4:3-7, NIV).*

Passionate. The Trinity interacts with playfulness and passion. God desires our sexuality to be full of good feelings that we learn to discipline. *"… I was filled with delight day after day, rejoicing [Hebrew word for "playing" and "laughing"] always in his presence, rejoicing… delighting in mankind" (Proverbs 8:30-31, NIV).*

As you think through God's character, work to make your sexual vocabulary and conversations reflect unselfishness, intimacy, beautiful feelings, and a sacred purity. Sexual integrity can flourish as we reflect our amazing Creator.

C. Embrace Your Sexuality and Your Body, God's Temple

> *"He wants each of you to control your own body in a way that is holy and honorable. Don't use your body for sexual sin like the people who do not know God. Also, do not wrong or cheat another Christian in this way…" (1 Thessalonians 4:4-6, NCV).*

> *"Do you not know that your body is a temple of the Holy Spirit…" (1 Corinthians 6:19, NIV).*

God gave each of us our bodies and our sexual responses. Some Christians may feel sex is somehow dirty or wrong, but our Creator wants us to embrace his precious gift of sexuality. Although we may think our physical bodies may be inherently unholy and that only the spiritual part of us can be holy (reminiscent of the ancient heresy of Gnosticism), God made us three-dimensional beings with a body, a mind, and a heart that all work together for his glory and help us live out our sexuality with integrity.

Our bodies, which include our genitals and our sex drive, give us humans the ability to enjoy sexual attractions and create sexual intimacy in a way that animals cannot. Our bodies are also the dwelling place of the Holy Spirit who enables us to express ourselves sexually within godly guidelines. Why do you think God gave humans a sex drive that—unlike animals—allows us to mate for life and become "one flesh" with meaningful lovemaking? Even if you think God gave you a much stronger sex drive than you need, be assured that God is always intimate and intentional. He created us with a physical body with a sex drive for several reasons:

1. **Our sex drive teaches us about God.** The eternal Trinity places a high value on intimate relating, and sexual intimacy is one of the most powerful examples of intimacy God has provided. Maleness and femaleness reflect his very image, so our sex drive and sexual attractions reveal important characteristics of the Almighty who pursues and delights in us. Our intense sexual hunger mirrors God's desire for pursuing us and having an intimate relationship with us.

2. **It drives us to God.** A high sex drive (a characteristic of most men) can make us despair at times. But it also pushes us to humbly rely on God's power to help us discipline that enormous libido.

3. **Hormones and sexual cravings prompt a desire to fulfill God's call for us to reflect him in oneness.** They push us to get married and build a deeply intimate relationship. If, like women, men only had a gentle wave of estrogen, they might never seek out a lifetime mate.

4. **Our sex drive can be a catalyst within marriage for us to pursue our own Eve or Adam and create intense pleasure, excitement, and intimacy.**

Our sex drive and sexual attractions are not sinful; we sin when we misuse this gift from God. He wants us to embrace and wisely steward our libido and enjoy our bodies which he has designed for us to use to express intimacy.

D. Practice a Three-Dimensional Chastity and Sexual Integrity

"… let us purify ourselves from everything that contaminates body and spirit, perfecting holiness out of reverence for God" (2 Corinthians 7:1, NIV).

"This is the covenant I will make with them after that time, says the Lord. I will put my laws in their hearts, and I will write them on their minds" (Hebrews 10:16, NIV).

"… may you rejoice in the wife of your youth. A loving doe, a graceful deer—may her breasts satisfy you always, may you be ever captivated by her love" (Proverbs 5:18-19, NIV).

In Scripture, the word "soul" often means a three-dimensional person with a body, mind, and spirit. These are not separate parts but interacting dimensions of being human. Our bodies are beautiful and attractive. They let us physically express affection and feelings. Our mind is the organizing function in us that thinks and imagines. It is also the center of feelings and the place where we make choices about what is important to us. Our heart is that deepest place in us where we love and spiritually connect with God himself. First Corinthians 6 emphasizes this three-dimensional nature of our humanity and states that our bodies are the temple of the Holy Spirit. Paul tells the Corinthians that when they have relations with temple prostitutes, they become united with them not only in body, but in mind and spirit as well.

Men, the Creator wants us to notice and enjoy his female creation in all three of her dimensions. Yes, Eve is attractive sexually, but we ought not to reduce her to sexy female parts and make her an impersonal, dehumanized sexual object. We can look beyond her body to enjoy a woman's mind and emotions, along with her deep need for spiritual fulfillment and a committed love relationship.

We Christians can give our mates a three-dimensional sexiness. We will, of course, be attracted visually to their bodies. We will also notice and be drawn in by the mysterious ways they think and operate. Beyond her body, I like the fact that just by winking or grinning at me, my wife can communicate her special femininity. I am also deeply attracted to her love for Jesus and the way it permeates her feminine life and interactions.

What's the advantage of treating the people in our lives in a three-dimensional manner? One of my clients who struggled with sexual addiction told me that I had ruined lust for him. He said it had become difficult for him to lust when he was at the mall and saw a shapely woman, because he would begin to think, "I wonder if she knows Jesus?" When he gave her a life and a spirit, along with her breasts and gorgeous legs, he couldn't lust in the same way.

Our sexual integrity will benefit greatly from our using this building block of making our sisters and brothers three-dimensionally sexy by giving them a life with minds and emotions and a deep desire to be intimately known.

Set Two Building Blocks

A lifestyle of sexual integrity. How fascinating that God never instantly gives us character (maturity) with an automatic sexual integrity. Character is something that has to be grown! With the help of the Holy Spirit, we "grow up" our sexuality into a healthy, mature condition by *disciplining* ourselves and making daily choices to follow God's sexual guidelines.

> *"No discipline seems pleasant at the time, but painful. Later on, however, it produces a harvest of righteousness and peace for those who have been trained by it" (Hebrews 12:11, NIV).*

This set of sexual integrity building blocks involves practical ways Christians can build sexual character and live out a life of sexual integrity.

A. Discipline Your Eyes and Thoughts

> *"I made a covenant with my eyes, not to look lustfully at a young woman" (Job 31:1, NIV).*

"The eye is the lamp of the body. If your eyes are healthy, your whole body will be full of light" (Matthew 6:22, NIV).

"… take captive every thought to make it obedient to Christ" (2 Corinthians 10:5, NIV).

Sexual integrity requires daily decisions and ongoing discipline. Nowhere is this more evident than in how we choose to direct our vision and our thought life in today's sexually saturated culture. Here are three practical ways Christians can discipline their seeing and thinking to help achieve consistent sexual integrity:

1. **Practice the "half-second rule" and keep your vision moving by bouncing your eyes from one cue to another.** When you see a visual cue (a tight tank top at the mall, a great figure), *keep your eyes moving.* I have heard it said that, "The first look is on God, the second look is on you, and the third look is becoming lust." The word "ogle" means to stare or rubberneck. Men especially have the propensity to ogle every woman in their line of sight. The discipline of not zooming in on and focusing our attention on female parts really honors our wives, daughters, and other women. When men objectify and do not view sexuality deeply and through God's eyes, they cheat themselves and the women in their lives. Men, we sexually objectify in many ways the women God calls us to honor as sisters and daughters when we don't practice the "bouncing the eyes" discipline. Ladies, you can also make men uncomfortable and feel like an object with your looks. All of us as Christians are called to see others as three-dimensional beings and not just sexual objects. Disciplining our vision can help us see the whole person, not just body parts.

2. **Don't run with cues.** So often the male mind runs with cues until we are more and more sexually aroused. When you see a cute woman at the neighborhood pool, direct your vision *and your mind* in a different direction. If you focus your gaze on her, you may begin to undress her and let your thought life go in lustful

directions. One of my pastor friends likes to exclaim, "Thank you, Lord, for feminine beauty, but that's not my woman." He then focuses his attention on something else. This can apply to Christian women as well as men. Each of us can choose how we take in sexual cues, and when we choose not to run with those cues, we can keep ourselves from being triggered or becoming increasingly aroused.

3. **Make immediate decisions to discipline thoughts and behaviors, because "immediately" is when you will make your best decisions.** One of my clients was angry with God because he said the Lord had promised in scripture to not let him be tempted above what he was able to resist (1 Corinthians 10:13), and God had let him down. We explored his situation, and he quickly realized that if he imagined his thought life as an expressway, he had ignored at least three exits God had provided for him before he "crashed." The sooner you make the decision to flee temptation, the better choices you will make. Pay attention to that catch in your spirit. Know your boundaries and keep them. Immediately take the very first exit from sinful thoughts and behaviors.

I really like the Genesis 39 story of Joseph fleeing from Potiphar's seductive wife, leaving so quickly that he left his cloak in her hands. We can do the same when Satan throws unexpected temptations into our lives. We can also greatly minimize our triggers to misbehave sexually by making immediate decisions to guard what we take in (television, movies, websites), and we can avoid what the movie "Top Gun" called "target-rich environments."

B. Meet Nonsexual Needs Non-sexually

"Put to death, therefore, whatever belongs to your earthly nature: sexual immorality, impurity, lust, evil desire and greed, which is idolatry" (Colossians 3:5, NIV).

"Pay careful attention to your own work [actions], for then you will get the satisfaction of a job well done, and you won't need to compare yourself to anyone else. For we are each responsible for our own conduct" (Galatians 6:4-5, NLT).

Sexual wholeness depends on our meeting our nonsexual needs in appropriate nonsexual ways; when we don't, everything gets out of whack. In order to develop true sexual integrity, we have to be self-aware enough to distinguish between our sexual and nonsexual needs. Here are some common nonsexual needs that we may mistakenly try to meet sexually, thus falling into life-distorting relationships and/or sinful behavior patterns.

Ego-boosting and affirmation. Men, in particular, desire to feel significant, and a woman's affirmation can do that incredibly effectively, especially sexually. Many husbands are drawn into affairs, and many single guys get involved in destructive hook-ups because a woman makes them feel sexy, like a real "stud." A man's ego can make him very vulnerable. We all—both men and women—need to create healthy avenues to receive daily affirmation from healthy relationships in our lives. We can also learn to practice self-affirmation, as we personally accept and build up our masculine or feminine worth and appeal.

Adventures. Masculine competiveness and the thrill of the chase can lead to a desire for sexual conquests. Men (and women) need adventures, but chasing "skirt" is not God's way to meet this need. I often ask men, "Are you really horny, or are you just bored?" We can meet boredom in much healthier ways than sexual adventures; with everything from work challenges, to tackling a new hobby, to creating surprises in our life and relationships.

Acceptance and friendship. All of us want to be chosen and accepted just for being our real selves, but this God-given need for recognition and love can easily shift comfortable friendships into sexual relationships. Clear and firm boundaries must be placed around opposite-sex friendships and even around work relationships that involve bonding around work projects, mutual enjoyment of the relationship, and the intimacy of many hours spent together.

Physical touch. God created all humans with "skin hunger" and a need for physical touch and affection. In marriage, touch needs can be met sexually, but even married couples need to engage in nonsexual physical touch, as well. This need may explain why men roughhouse and are comfortable with fist-butting and hugs.

Recreation. All of us need time to relax and recreate, but porn and illicit sexual relationships are not God's plan for our recreation. We must learn other ways to fill our recreational needs, like visiting Home Depot, golfing, dancing, or relaxing with mindless activities like sports, video games, or music. Of course, we should recreate in ways that maintain a balance in our lives and don't keep us from bonding with friends.

Intimacy. Although we may hope that instant sexual connecting will create instant intimacy, God's design is for us to create an intimate and committed relationship first; then amazing sexual intimacy can flow through our marriage. Instant intimacy is *false intimacy*. Porn, singles' hook-ups, or extramarital affairs will never meet our deepest needs and hungers; they are unfulfilling fantasies, cheap imitations that will ultimately leave us wounded, disappointed, and insecure.

Within these various nonsexual yearnings, each of us will have unique vulnerabilities based on our personalities, experiences, and relationships. For some of us, certain ones of these nonsexual needs are more important than others, and they are the ones that are most likely to trip us up, especially if we attempt to meet them in wrongful ways. Let the Holy Spirit guide you as you carefully think through how you can better meet your nonsexual needs non-sexually, and follow him as you take specific steps to build and protect your sexual integrity.

C. Fight Pornography and All Sexual Distortions

> *"God wants you to be holy and to stay away from sexual sins. He wants each of you to learn to control your own body in a way that is holy and honorable. Don't use your body for sexual sin like people who do not know God"* (1 Thessalonians 4:3-5, NCV).

*"What benefit did you reap at that time from the things you
are now ashamed of? Those things result in death! But now
that you have been set free from sin and have become slaves
of God, the benefit you reap leads to holiness, and the result
is eternal life" (Romans 6:21-22, NIV).*

Pornography is an epidemic, and it can permeate our lives so easily. Most
men and many women have watched porn at some time. Pornography is
pervasive—from internet spam to television and movies, romantic novels,
soap operas, and actual porn sites. If we are ever to be people of sexual
integrity, this is a battle we must fight and win together.

Satan cannot create; instead, he distorts the sexual beauty and passion
that God meant for good. And pornography does this powerfully. Guys,
most of the time Satan doesn't suddenly put a naked woman in your
path. Instead, he starts with your poorly disciplined vision and tendency
to objectify women in your environment. He uses things like looking at
women who are not completely naked (wearing bathing suits or other
revealing attire) and making inappropriate comments to or about a woman
at work (creating your own mental porn around her). The only things the
Forces of Evil really need to do with many Christians is to gently nudge
them in the wrong direction; then Satan will escalate their downward,
destructive process.

Romans 6: 21-22 explains one of the false ideas about sinful behaviors:
at the time we are engaging in them, we think there is great gain, but when
we live by God's sexual guidelines instead of Satan's lies, we can clearly see
that when we watch porn and commit other sexual sins, something—often
God's best—actually dies. But the truth is that we have been set free to a
more creative and loving use of our sexual drives! The Holy Spirit helps
us see the great gain of sexual maturity and good choices. *"… God is
faithful; he will not let you be tempted beyond what you can bear. But when
you are tempted, he will also provide a way out so you can stand up under it"
(1 Corinthians 10:13, NIV).*

Keep in mind what we said earlier: the more quickly you make godly
choices, the easier it will be to conquer temptations and avoid costly
mistakes. And keep remembering that Satan just wants to get you moving
in the wrong direction. He starts small, by leading you to make little,

seemingly inconsequential, wrong choices, but then, before long you are doing things and crossing lines you never thought possible. He is the Master of Lies, and he wants to distort everything that God created for beauty and intimacy. Satan hates sexual integrity!

D. Forgive and Redeem the Sexual Past

> *"The Lord is compassionate and gracious, slow to anger, abounding in love... he does not treat us as our sins deserve or repay us according to our iniquities... for he knows how we are formed, he remembers that we are dust [human]" (Psalm 103:8,10,14, NIV).*

> *"Have mercy on me, O God, according to your unfailing love; according to your great compassion blot out my transgressions" (Psalm 53:1, NIV).*

We all have a sexual history with some mistakes and baggage. We all have sinned, but our sins and bad choices do not have to haunt us forever or define who we are. Satan would love for us to believe that our sins sideline us from ever having sexual wholeness. But God trumps Satan. He not only readily forgives us, he also turns our mistakes and sins into blessings as he uses them to transform us and create change in our lives. God's grace is more than sufficient to cover our sins and mistakes.

As we endeavor to mature into people with genuine sexual integrity, the forgiving and healing process becomes critical. But it is not an easy journey, and guilt often robs us of the freedom God wishes to give and makes us more vulnerable to further sexual mistakes and distortions. Here are some guidelines for forgiving and redeeming the past:

1. **God's grace is more than sufficient to cover all our sins and mistakes.** We must accept and believe this fact. Often the hardest person to forgive is ourselves. We must trust that God wants to bestow grace and mercy on us personally, specifically, and individually and heal us of all our sexual mistakes and sins. He wants to free us from crippling guilt and shame.

2. **We must forgive others as he has forgiven us.** Not only can his grace cover our sins, it can also help us forgive others. Many of us have been sexually offended or harmed, and our Savior wants to remove that load from us. Forgiveness is not about justice being served, but about God allowing you to pardon someone else so that their evil behaviors won't haunt you and can't control you.

3. **God trumps Satan.** This is worth saying again! God takes our mistakes and sins and turns them into blessings as he uses them to motivate and create change in our lives. What a comforting privilege it is to serve a Creator who can take a world full of broken people and work in us—even through our mistakes and immaturity—to bring us to a better place.

Forgiveness means being able to *live fully in the present without being haunted by the past.* Our loving Father wants to lift distorting guilt off our shoulders as we accept grace and forgiveness. Confession is an important component of working toward the heart-deep understanding that we've been forgiven, as well as the practical experience of "feeling" forgiven. Guilt gives way to freedom when we choose an appropriate, safe, and confidential Christian brother or sister and bring our secrets to the light.

> *"Therefore confess your sins to each other and pray for each other so that you may be healed" (James 5:16, NIV).*

> *"… Forgetting what is behind and straining toward what is ahead, I press on toward the goal…" (Philippians 3:13-14, NIV).*

Let God transform your life through confession and forgiveness. Seek out, lean into, and fully utilize your community for accountability and healing. Jesus came to "heal the broken and set the captives free" (Isaiah 61:1, NIV). He wants to help you press on into new goals and incredible intimacy as you heal and grow. We can learn to live fully in the present with a wonderful, satisfying sexual integrity.

Please create those sexual conversations in your personal relationships and in your congregation as you praise God for his gift of sexuality. Practice the building blocks. Embrace your sexual feelings and allow the Holy Spirit to guide you "inside-out" into a life of sexual wholeness and intimacy. Your church community will be transformed.

Les Parrott, Ph.D. and Leslie Parrott, Ed.D.

Drs. Les and Leslie Parrott work as a husband-and-wife team who share not only the same name, but also the same passion for helping others build healthy relationships. In 1991, the Parrotts founded the Center for Relationship Development on the campus of Seattle Pacific University—a groundbreaking program dedicated to teaching the basics of good relationships. Les is a clinical psychologist who delivers presentations that are grounded, insightful, and cutting-edge.

Each year, Les and Leslie speak to audiences in more than 40 cities, in venues ranging from churches to Fortune 500 company board rooms. The Governor of Oklahoma appointed the Parrotts as the first-ever statewide Marriage Ambassadors. The Parrotts have been featured in *USA Today* and the *New York Times*. Their television appearances include *CNN, The View, The O'Reilly Factor, The Today Show* and *Oprah*. As #1 *New York Times* best-selling authors, their books, including their Gold-medallion winner, *Saving Your Marriage Before It Starts*, have sold over two million copies in more than two dozen languages. Other popular titles include *Real Relationships, L.O.V.E., The Parent You Want To Be, Trading Places, The Complete Guide to Marriage Mentoring,* and *Love Talk*. Les and Leslie are also founders of two acclaimed marital assessments: the SYMBIS Assessment (especially for pre-marriage couples) and the Deep Love Assessment (for couples at any age or stage). More information about their resources, as well as the Marriage Mentoring Academy, is available at LesAndLeslie.com.

CHAPTER 20

How to Develop an Effective Marriage Mentoring Ministry

Les Parrott, Ph.D. and
Leslie Parrot, Ed.D.

Jack and Rose. Two simple names that, to recent movie-goers, are as synonymous with love as Romeo and Juliet. Perhaps even more so. Writer and director James Cameron dreamed them up (as well as their steamy love story), for his impressive cinematic retelling of the fateful voyage of the Titanic, which became one of the highest grossing movies of all time. Despite the fact that the film opens with eerie footage of the actual drowned liner and closes with gruesome reconstructed scenes of some of its passengers plummeting down the ship's listing decks while others are freezing to death in the icy Atlantic, viewers of the film hardly gave the historical event an ounce of emotional attention. For most people who watched the movie, the disaster itself was peripheral to the "real" story on the screen, the story of Jack and Rose.

Jack is the quintessential charming American boy-man, played by Leonardo DiCaprio. Rose is the impetuous beauty, played by Kate Winslet and faced with an impending marriage to a villainous character who will surely to make her future life miserable. When Winslet's Rose gazes at DiCaprio's Jack, fascination quickly turns into longing into love, the kind of love movies are made of. It's a love in which neither lover ever discovers, much less has to tolerate, anything seriously objectionable in the other. It's the kind of love that doesn't occur in real life.

In a superb irony, this most romantic of fantasies is played out against one of history's most famous calamities. In the midst of dire peril—not only because their ship is sinking, but also because a jilted lover is chasing them with a loaded gun—Jack and Rose still love. Perhaps that's one of the reasons so many people were drawn en masse to this story. Perhaps that's the main reason some people paid to see it a second and third time and then bought the collector's edition video to watch at home. And perhaps that's the reason the cruise ship business boomed as never before following the release of *Titanic* in theaters. Because of Jack and Rose, couples everywhere began searching for love on the high seas—without seeming to care or even notice that the ship carrying that fictional couple... sank. Like all of us, couples everywhere are looking for the kind of love that runs into something really bad – dare we say even an iceberg? – and survives.

But alas, even in this cinematic fairytale, their love does not survive. It's cut short by Jack's death. And at the end of the movie, Rose, reminiscing in her old age, asks the same searching question we all face: Why?

A Question Every Couple Needs to Ask

The question of why love was cut short for this fictional couple is actually quite clear to anyone who studies literature. Almost all enduring love stories end the same way. Of course, the tragic twosome of Romeo and Juliet is a classic. So are Lancelot and Guinevere. Rhett and Scarlett. And now add to this list Jack and Rose. Each snuffed out their powerful love while the heat of passion was turned up full blast. Why? Because it couldn't last. The heat of storybook passion was never meant to last indefinitely, much less permanently. Can you imagine Romeo and Juliet as a married couple... going off to work... paying bills... grocery shopping? How about Jack and Rose? It's almost incongruous; at least it takes a lot of the luster off their love story.

Far more difficult to answer is the question that matters most. Why do some couples manage to enjoy lasting love, despite facing the same circumstances that defeat others? Have you thought about this? It's apparent to most observers that some couples run head-first into a crisis and come out on the other side stronger than they started, while others hit similar problems and end up barely holding it together—or having their marriage destroyed. But why? Are the ones who thrive despite adversity just lucky? Not according to the couples we've surveyed. These couples never counted on luck to see them through anything.

So what's the difference? The answer begins to unfold when we take a closer look at the question. Why do bad things interfere with something as good as love and marriage? It's a question we've asked ourselves countless times in recent years. Too many couples too close to us have hit rock bottom – often as a result of contending with a mental health issue. As professionals, we are used to facing such situations in a counseling office, but it's quite another thing when marriages of our own friends and family are rocked to the core. We've seen firsthand how a secret addiction to alcohol can shatter a couple's trust in each other. We've seen how a person's sheer self-centeredness emanating from full-blown narcissism can erode the feelings that once glued a couple together. We've seen, on at least two occasions, how an exposed affair and addictions to pornography can explode a family to smithereens. And we've seen marriages self-destruct for reasons that are not even discernible. Each time we are left with little more than the questions "Why?" and "How could something like this happen to them?" And in times of quiet soul searching, we may ask the same question of ourselves.

You see, the misfortunes of good people are not only a problem for the people who suffer; they are also problems to all who wonder if the same thing could happen to them. When a marriage breaks up, we watch in horror like gawkers at a traffic accident, because we want to find some sign, some justification for it happening to "them" and not to "us." But after seeing too many good couples suffer bad things, the question still remains: Why? It is perhaps the most important question couples these days can ask, so we will pose it again: Why do bad things happen to good marriages?

Our research points to at least five possibilities: 1) some idealistic couples hold onto unfulfilled expectations; 2) some restless couples have not studied their unexamined selves; 3) some contented couples have not tapped into their unskilled potential; 4) some unwitting couples continue to make unhealthy choices; and 5) some unfortunate couples run into unpredictable circumstances like mental health issues. This last situation is the focus of this chapter.

The Jolt of a Mental Health Issue on Marriage

A couple may have resolved all their unrealistic expectations. Each spouse may have invited feedback and opened themselves up to their partner to increase self-awareness. They may have learned the skills required for overcoming their marital deficiencies. And, by the grace of God, they may have steered clear of making unhealthy choices. They may have done everything right, but this does not protect their good marriage from everything bad. Why not? Some bad things strike a good marriage like a lightening bolt at high noon. When you least expect it, something can happen that turns your marriage, not to mention your world, inside out and upside down. That something can be schizophrenia, severe anxiety, major depression, and the list goes on. Not only that, the mental health issue may not even involve a condition with which the husband or wife is personally diagnosed; it may be affecting a child or close relative.

I'll never forget the look on Ray's (not this family's real names) face the day he poked his head in my doorway at work and asked to talk. As colleagues at the same university, we'd known each other long enough for me to immediately see that something was wrong. He walked in, shut the door, and told me his sixteen-year-old daughter, Liz, had run away from home after being caught abusing alcohol. Ray was so ashamed that it had taken him nearly two days before he called the police. "Nancy and I are numb," he confided. "We don't know how to feel… enraged? depressed? frantic?" His lower lip started to quiver as my heart sank in anguish.

"How are you and Nancy holding up?" I asked.

"She won't even talk to me," Ray broke down, shoulders shuddering, tears flowing. "The night before Lizzy left, we had a run-in because Nancy didn't like me setting Lizzy's new curfew so much earlier. I was so upset I moved it up an hour just to spite her." Ray was trying to control his crying as I handed him a box of tissues.

"So Nancy thinks you caused Liz to run away?" I asked.

Ray defended his wife's reaction and berated himself with unflinching guilt. I tried my best to console my friend and colleague that day, but I felt about as helpful as a Band-Aid on a gaping wound.

Another day passed before Liz returned safely home after hiding out with a friend whose parents were out of town. Ray and Nancy were, to say the least, relieved. They hoped life would soon get back to normal, but it didn't. As weeks turned into months, although Liz's acting out subsided, Ray and Nancy, who had always been very close, began drifting apart; so much so that it scared them. That's when Ray stopped by my office again, this time for a counseling referral to a marriage therapist. I'm happy to say that they got the help they needed and worked through the issues between them that their family crisis had stirred up, but not all couples who run into ugly, unpredictable circumstances are so fortunate. We all know couples whose good marriages have been jolted by bad things, sometimes with the result that their marriages were shattered forever.

Life is filled with more than enough circumstances that test a couple's strength: an employment crisis, a serious injury, the divorce of a close friend, a natural disaster, a community tragedy caused by crime, substance abuse, infertility, a rebellious son or daughter, a financial loss, a life-threatening illness, a burglary or theft, a drunk driving accident, an unfaithful spouse, and the list goes on. But one situation that is often left un-addressed is the jolt of a mental health issue. It sometimes feels like a sucker punch to the gut that knocks the wind right out of a marriage, but it's a strike we often don't want to even acknowledge, much less bring into public view with our pastor.

The Sometimes Unspoken Agony in Marriage

Greg, a high school basketball coach, blacked out and lost consciousness during a routine practice with his team. When he came to at the hospital later that evening, a dark secret began to unravel. Nobody knew that Greg was an alcoholic. For 11 years he had been secretly drinking vodka, an odorless libation, from a secret stash in his garage. That night at the hospital Connie, his wife of ten years, sat in shock while Greg laid open his long-standing secret.

A basketball star in college, Greg had never taken an alcoholic drink in his life until he joined some teammates one evening after a game. "The next morning when I woke up," he later said, "all I thought about was getting another drink." He did. By the time he married Connie later that year he was already well into his private addiction, and she didn't have a clue.

Eleven years later, when Greg's alcoholism was exposed, Connie came unglued. She called us from the hospital halfway across the country: "Did you have any idea this was happening?" But we were as helpless as she was. It had to be the loneliest night of Connie's life—and her life would never be the same.

Few things divide a couple more painfully than a hidden addiction. Whatever the specific "drug of choice" may be, whether alcohol, drugs, overeating, pornography, or something else, addiction is as divisive in marriage as an international border. It creates a quiet chasm that grows increasingly wider with each compulsive behavior. If your marriage has been assaulted by the damage of addiction, we want to make one fundamental point that may help you keep this jolt from ruining your relationship: like grief, addiction involves denial.

Grief is a normal emotional response to loss, and the loss of a stable marriage because of addictive behavior generates despair, anger, and loneliness. And because such loss is not as tangible as some other losses (the addict is still present), losing a loved one to addiction has the potential of keeping one stuck indefinitely in the early stages of grief. This kind of emotional "stuckness" can be the undoing of any relationship, and therein lies the bind of the "co-addict" spouse; he or she wants to mend the broken relationship but winds up unwittingly participating in the same impaired mental processes as the addict. By definition, an addict replaces normal human relationships with compulsive behavior that is out of control. If you are married to an addict, you feel the loss, you try to deny its existence and the pain it causes, and you become hurt and angry. In spite of your despair—or perhaps because of it—you go to extreme lengths to preserve the exterior world of your addicted spouse and your once happy home.

That's exactly what happened to Ruth, the daughter of an alcoholic. She married James, who had also grown up in an alcoholic home. In fact, part of their initial attraction was that they agreed they would never do what their parents did. Even though James drank, Ruth felt secure that he would not become an addict, but that all changed the night he was arrested on a drunk and disorderly charge. Embarrassed, Ruth told no one. James gave excuses for his behavior, and although Ruth didn't believe him, she acted as if she did. Deep inside, she also believed she was partly to blame. In short, Ruth was in almost as much denial about her husband's addiction as he was. Each promise he made to abstain from alcohol made Ruth all the more certain that their problem would be resolved. But it wasn't.

With the help of a counselor, Ruth eventually realized that she was sacrificing her own identity, giving up a part of herself, in order to stay in a relationship with James. She was overlooking and covering up behavior which hurt her deeply and which she despised. She appeared cheerful when she was hurting, and most of all, she blamed herself for a problem she didn't start and which wasn't her responsibility. Her reactions were only making their situation worse.

Ruth was a co-addict; she was classically codependent. The result? More isolation and distance form James. The reason? When there was a chance for real intimacy, it was evaded by silence or fighting. Sadly, this led Ruth, like all co-addicts, to continue her martyrdom in an effort to make herself indispensable to her poor husband. Meanwhile, James' failure to provide the love and care for which she was longing resulted in Ruth's continuing codependent (and subconscious) solo efforts to reform her husband. And the cycle went on.

For some couples this sad cycle goes on for years and years, and, not surprisingly in such relationships, addictions of all kinds thrive. Alcoholism and compulsive overeating may even mingle with sexual addiction or other addictive behaviors in such an environment. The husband who justifies his sexual addiction because "she is always drunk" is doing something his wife can't control. The wife who gains fifty pounds as an expression of her rage, fear, or insecurity is doing something her husband can't control. Each specific addiction may involve different behaviors, but every addiction cries out for the same remedy: personal responsibility. The key to overcoming and recovering from any major problem, including an addiction, is a shift from blaming circumstances and other people to taking ownership for feelings and behaviors. The positive energy this change produces creates a new environment of trust in a marriage.

What Can a Pastor Do?

My (Les') father, a pastor, often says that every person will have their own private Gethsemane, and it will usually happen in a familiar place. For Jesus, it was in the place where he routinely prayed and where Judas knew he could find him. Our own personal Gethsemane will probably also include a Judas; someone—maybe even our spouse—who will let us down in ways we never dreamed (because unlike Jesus, we mere mortals are not omniscient and can't always see a betrayal coming!). And in our private Gethsemane, we may also have close friends who suddenly "go to sleep" emotionally or relationally when we need them the most—our own versions of Peter, James, and John.

No matter the specifics of how people have fallen into the abyss, whether it is due to addiction, depression, anxiety, or some other mental health challenge, they probably didn't see it coming. No amount of planning can completely prevent all jolts from striking a marriage; some still will. So, as a pastor, what can you do to help the couples in your care who are battling a mental health issue? The answer? More than you might think.

When President Ronald Reagan was a teenager in Dixon, Illinois, he had a summer job as a lifeguard on the treacherous Rock River. One day, from his elevated perch at Lowell Park, he noticed one of Dixon's most popular girls waving at him from the water. "At least I thought she was waving," Reagan recalls. "My chest puffed out a little, and I waved back. Then I turned away for a moment. When I looked again, she was going down. She had tried to signal for help."

Ever felt the same way young Ronald Reagan felt in that moment? Whether you know it or not, Pastor, some people in your congregation may not look particularly needy or desperate for help, but many of them are. On any given weekend, countless couples file into churches across the country, looking their "Sunday best" and quietly keeping a marriage problem to themselves. The stigma of counseling may be keeping them from seeking help. Or they may feel all alone and assume that nobody else would understand. Or they may simply have nobody to talk to. But truth be told, some of these couples are going down. Their marriages are hurting because of mental health issues, and nobody has recognized their signal for help. Or even if someone else has, they don't feel it's their place to step in.

But what if these hurting couples in your congregation could be linked with other couples who are more seasoned and have experienced what these couples are going through; couples who have lived a similar path of pain and anguish and are now on the other side of it, living a vibrant married life together? Would such couple-to-couple relationships make any difference? You bet. How do we know? Because for more than two decades we've been recruiting, screening, and training couples to become marriage mentors. We've heard their stories. We've done the research. Marriage mentoring works.

What is marriage mentoring? Simply put, marriage mentoring is two-on-two discipleship. It happens when a veteran couple commits to share life experience, a listening ear, ongoing care, and prayerful support with a rookie couple in a safe, casual, nonthreatening relationship. Of course, the mentor couple should be carefully screened in terms of their spiritual maturity, marital commitment, and general willingness and availability to nurture a younger couple. Most marriage mentor couples commit to meet and share for a couple of hours one or two times a month for six months to a year. The structure and format is informal, generally meeting casually over coffee and dessert. Surprisingly, it's that simple!

And perhaps not surprisingly, our research reports a frequent and powerful boomerang effect on the mentor couple—assisting another couple to form and live out their dreams often reawakens and fulfills their dreams for their own relationship. One mentor wife reported, "I don't know how much we helped them, but we sure got a lot of out it!"

Her husband added, "Helping a young couple seemed to spark a lot of things in our own marriage that we had neglected." Having another set of eyes watching their marriage can often bring inspiration, motivation, and accountability in unexpected, yet welcomed ways—ironically helping both couples grow.

The truth is that all young couples struggle. The unmet expectations, unfamiliar stressors, and unexpected disappointments typical for newlyweds can range from a disastrous honeymoon to the multiple pressures of making budgets work (including trying to pay off huge student loans); from attempting to please and set boundaries with in-laws to dealing with and adjusting to the "surprises" their spouse neglected to inform them about while dating; all frequently compounded by the needs and demands of babies crying in the night. And even if couples obtain good premarital counseling, navigating the rapids, currents, and unforeseeable waves of life together can cause many young marital vessels to capsize.

Actually, marriage may be the very hardest thing there is to do well. Is it any wonder that the highest rate of divorce in our culture occurs within the first two to three years of marriage? Lack of preparation, few healthy role models, separation from customary support systems, and shame-filled disillusionment all combine and contribute to our national epidemic of divorce. Additionally, because this epidemic has created mass skepticism, pessimism, and fear of divorce, many younger adults now choose to just cohabit, foregoing marriage completely. Indeed, mentoring young couples may be one of the most important contemporary mission fields of all.

Whether you are already aware of the power of marriage mentoring or you're just now learning about it, our online Marriage Mentoring Academy (see MarriageMentoring.com) will provide you with everything you need to begin a ministry that doesn't add a single minute to your workload and may be one of the most compassionate moves you ever make in your ministry.

We each grew up in pastors' homes. We've been involved in church work our entire lives. Les is an ordained minister, and we also speak to hundreds of ministers annually, so we understand that you may have some reticence. You may be saying, "I don't need another program to administer." You're right. That's why marriage mentoring is low-maintenance. It belongs to the laity.

Or maybe you're saying, "I can't get volunteers to teach classes, let alone mentor other couples." We understand, but we'll show you how recruiting mentor couples is easier than you think.

Perhaps you're saying, "I don't want to detract from the marriage counseling program we've built up." It won't. In fact, it will augment it.

And you may say, "For now, we're putting our energies and resources into children's ministry and youth work." Worthy indeed, but marriage mentoring may be the most important thing you ever do for the young people in your church. They desperately need good examples of how to be married well. Future generations will be benefited and blessed by seeing healthy role models of discipled, mature, godly marriages lived out in front of them. Growing and nurturing healthy marriages can literally increase the spiritual vitality of your entire congregation. It can also be the first line of defense in identifying mental health concerns and offering safe relational support for the couple experiencing them. It is obviously not the mentor couple's responsibility to diagnose and treat those issues, but they can, without taking sides, provide a compassionate listening ear, emotional safety, relational support, and objective accountability while the hurting couple is seeking and obtaining help.

The truth is, we can't think of a legitimate excuse for not having a marriage mentoring ministry in every local church, large or small.

Why? Because couples of every age and stage can benefit from marriage mentoring, and it's an easy ministry for a local church to implement. Not only that, but the Bible calls us to this kind of action. Marriage mentoring is a means by which you can fulfill Paul's injunction that one of the jobs of a pastor is "to prepare God's people for works of service" (Ephesians 4:12, NIV). In the American church today, the divorce rate remains high, cohabitation is rampant and escalating, and marriage is in more trouble than ever before in history. What "works of service" could be of more value to the couples in your care than marriage mentoring—especially for couples who are suffering with the silent agony of mental health issues?

Ron Deal, M.MFT.

 Ron L. Deal, M.MFT, LMFT, LPC is one of the most widely read and viewed experts in the country on blended families. He is founder of Smart Stepfamilies™, Director of FamilyLife Blended® for FamilyLife®, the author of over a dozen books and video resources on stepfamily living, including the bestselling book *The Smart Stepfamily*, and is Consulting Editor of the Smart Stepfamily Series of books for Bethany House Publishers. His podcast *FamilyLife Blended with Ron Deal* and his one-minute radio feature are heard around the world, and his work has been quoted/referenced by multiple news outlets such as The New York Times, The Wall Street Journal, and USA Today. Ron is a licensed marriage and family therapist who frequently appears in the national media and conducts marriage and family seminars around the country. He and his wife, Nan, have three sons and live in Little Rock, Arkansas. Learn more at RonDeal.org.

CHAPTER 21

How to Develop an Effective Blended Family Support Ministry

Ron Deal, M.MFT.

Stepfamily ministry represents the next big challenge for American churches. Blended families are a field ripe for harvest, but the workers are few. Consider this email:

> Please respond if you can help. I'm not sure what to do. I have been married two times and have one son by each marriage. My current wife has been growing increasingly hostile toward my first son. Just yesterday she complained that I am spending too much time with him and not enough with our son. She's bitter, jealous, and possessive (she even wants him written out of my will), and I'm caught in the middle. No matter what I do, somebody loses. I know it doesn't help that my first son's mother shows up my current wife (they're always competing)— and once again, I'm stuck in the middle. Any suggestions you might have would be greatly appreciated.

Ministering to stepfamilies will be one of the greatest challenges of the new millennium. Clearly, the relational and spiritual issues of stepfamily members are opportunities for the church to touch people's lives with the power of the gospel. However, the church is far behind in its understanding of stepfamily life and has been slow to offer assistance. As a result, Satan and his forces are having their way with generations of people. Adults and children are discouraged, disillusioned, and therefore distracted from active service in God's kingdom, and divorce and *redivorce* are having their way with generations of families.

Satan's best line of attack is – and has always been – against the home.

For example, if he can prevent a stepfamily from integrating successfully, he can take captive multiple generations. Depression, anxiety, drug use, and other unhealthy attachments (to food, to work, to porn, etc.) become temporary coping mechanisms for adults and adolescents who suffer from unhealthy family circumstances. Unhealthy behaviors then sabotage someone's walk with the Lord and take the place of healthy, intimate family relationships. In addition, children experience conditional love as they witness their parents engaging in serial Velcro marriages (stick and peel, repeat). What results for children, as evidenced by the high cohabitation rate in America, is a cynical view of marriage and a tendency toward distrust of committed relationships.

Before continuing let me remind you that Satan's efforts to hamstring families and stepfamilies are not new. I do receive countless emails from stepfamilies throughout the world, but the "email" at the beginning of this chapter is not an email at all. It is, in fact, a fictional retelling of the story of Abraham, Sarah, and Hagar found in Genesis 16 and 21. In contrast to the modern day stepfamily, their "expanded family" included a man with two wives instead of a wife and ex-wife, but the dynamics of their home, including jealousy between insiders and outsiders, competing attachments, and a biological parent caught between his wife and son by another woman, are very similar to those in many modern-day stepfamilies. Truly, unless the church finds a way to help complex families, the next generation will unnecessarily repeat the same mistakes as their parents and the generations before them. (Please note that I am not suggesting that stepfamilies are mistakes; they are not. The mistakes come in how people manage stepfamily dynamics.)

Family Life Ministry

Churches have long supported the family as the primary vehicle for spiritual formation in children (see Psalm 78; Deuteronomy 6) and spiritual maturity in adults, but our ministry of discipleship through families has not kept up with the changing structure of families. More specifically, stepfamilies, while encompassing a large number of children and adults in America, continue to be overlooked by most church family ministries.

I believe the church must always hold up God's design that one man and one woman married for life is the standard for marriage. This is what we should call people to, but we must also recognize that divorce is not the source of all stepfamilies; many are a result of death or "disobedience," i.e., nonmarital birth. Whichever the pathway, for those who find themselves in a stepfamily, the church must provide healing from brokenness or loss and equipping so that the family is a place of grace and discipleship. Said another way, *we must be just as serious about preventing divorce in second and third marriages as we are in preventing a first marriage divorce; otherwise the cycle of divorce and brokenness will continue.*

The antidote, of course, to this generational curse is God's redemptive power. A strong, stable blended family can actually be a redemptive tool that stops the generational cycle of divorce and moves future generations back toward God's design for the family. In other words, one of the ways to prevent divorce in the next generation is by preventing *redivorce* in this generation. Giving children whose biological family has been truncated by death or divorce a healthy marriage model within a strong stepfamily environment increases the odds that they will have more successful marriages when they grow up, and that they will be more available for the Kingdom. The church is perfectly positioned to aid millions of people in this process, but we have to recognize the need. Consider these compelling statistics about American stepfamilies:

- Stepfamilies, sometimes called blended families, are quickly becoming the new traditional family in America. According to 2002 data only 23% of all U.S. households consist of a first marriage couple with their biological children, what is commonly referred to as the "traditional family." Of households with children, 40% are stepfamilies, whether formed after the death of a spouse, a divorce, or a non-marital birth (Karney, Garvan, & Thomas, 2003).[5] The percentage in many other countries (e.g., Canada,

---

[5] These findings were replicated in two other state representative samples. In Karney's findings, at least one partner had a child from a previous relationship before marriage. (His research includes full and part-time residential stepfamilies and those with children under and/or over the age of 18.) The percentage of all married couple households is 35%.

United Kingdom, New Zealand, and Australia) is approaching this same rate.

- At least 30% of all weddings create stepfamilies, and many believe this is a conservative estimate.[6]

- As of this writing, 100 million Americans have a steprelationship of some kind (a stepparent, stepsibling, or stepchild), and it is predicted that one in two Americans will have a steprelationship at some point in their lifetime (Parker, 2011).

- 40% of children are born out of wedlock; nearly 60% of these couples already have at least one child from a previous relationship. In other words, the majority of children being born out of wedlock are entering functional (nonmarital) stepfamilies (Carlson & Furstenburg, 2006).

- The rate of divorce for remarriages with stepchildren is 50% higher than the rate of divorce for remarriages without children. Many estimate that the divorce rate for stepcouples is nearly 60% (Hetherington & Kelly, 2002).

- 29% of U.S. children have experienced two or more mother breakups… by age 15. For perspective, children in the U.S. are more likely to experience the divorce of their married parents than are Swedish children the breakup of their cohabiting parents. Most importantly, the more parental partnerships (transitions in and out of couple relationships) children experience, the lower their overall emotional, psychological, and academic well-being (Cherlin, 2009).

Up-to-date statistics regarding marriage, family, divorce, and stepfamilies can be found at smartstepfamilies.com.

Despite the prevalence of stepfamilies and the remarriage divorce rate, stepfamilies remain one of the most neglected people groups in churches today. I'm thankful, however, that churches and faith-based organizational

---

[6] This is a composite approximation considering the remarriage rate (38% of all weddings) and the number of post-divorce remarriages that include children from previous relationships (75%), widows who remarry, and the out-of-wedlock rate (40% of all children are born out of wedlock) resulting in first marriages that form stepfamilies if the mother marries someone other than the biological father.

"sleeping giants" are beginning to awaken to the incredible opportunities for stepfamily ministry and community outreach. Stepfamilies lack a clear, coherent Christ-centered blueprint of the 3-D family puzzle they find themselves trying to assemble, but today more than ever, churches have available to them resources that integrate scriptural principles with valuable research and give blended families the answers they need. However, even though resources are available, many barriers to effective local ministry still exist.

Barriers to Stepfamily Ministry

Church Leaders Don't Perceive the Need

The first barrier is that most church leaders (and some counselors) don't perceive the need. We can't begin to address stepfamily concerns until we realize and acknowledge that stepfamilies exist. Despite the vast number of stepfamilies in the general population, they remain invisible to many church leaders for a number of reasons.

For one thing, churches often have fewer stepfamilies than the society at large. While good research on the number of stepfamilies in the average U.S. church is not available, close to 20 years of church consulting tells me that the number is lower than the 40% of families in the general population. The problem, then, is that church leaders sometimes do not interact with the congregational or community stepfamilies enough to notice their increasing numbers or experience their struggles. And even when they do, finding practical, biblically centered resources to aid in pastoral care or small group education has been difficult – until now. Further, stepfamily couples often do not assertively ask their leaders for help. In other words, we may have more stepfamilies in churches than the numbers suggest due to an underreporting by the stepfamily couples themselves.

"Closet stepfamilies," as I have come to call them, sit in our pews every Sunday, afraid to be identified as stepfamilies. They fear judgment for their past and reminders of their differentness. Many years ago, the leader of our blended family support group and I attended a conference on stepfamilies. I asked him how many stepfamilies he knew of in our church. In addition to those well known to me, he listed six couples that I had no idea were stepcouples. I was stunned. Even in a church that openly welcomed and ministered to stepfamilies, we had stepfamily couples who feared their pasts becoming known. Truly, feelings of shame and a sense of unworthiness are among our greatest barriers to effective stepfamily ministry. Churches must begin to program stepfamily educational opportunities, but even more important, we must convey a message of acceptance and grace, or else few will take advantage of the programs we do offer.

Stepfamilies Can Be Spiritually Marginalized

A second barrier to stepfamily ministry, and incidentally, another reason there are fewer stepfamilies in local congregations, is spiritual marginalization. This happens for a variety of reasons. The first is personal spiritual shame and guilt from divorce or past sin. The same shame that drives some into the closet drives others away from God and the church altogether. One person said, "I am not sure if I am accepted by God in regard to remarriage. I am almost afraid to read the Bible because I'm not sure what I might find."

In addition, some divorced and remarried persons are marginalized due to being socially shunned or spiritually judged by the church. One sad example is a couple who were told straight out by a minister, "I'm sorry. Your background and past might infect everyone else, so we can't have you at our church." Obviously this was a direct message; other families experience marginalization that is more subtle but just as insidious. One friend told me she shared during a women's Bible study that she struggled with loving her stepdaughter. The women looked at her with harsh disbelief at her honest confession. She felt completely rejected and awkward and made a clear decision never again to entrust her stepfamily struggles to the women of her church.

Even more subtle are the inadvertent messages in church language and programming that make stepfamilies feel like unclean outsiders or second-class Christians. For example, the advice given in parent education courses often doesn't come close to addressing the daily struggles of stepparents; they are left wondering what's wrong with them. In addition, for years I've heard stepcouples give feedback about marriage enrichment classes and conferences they attend. It goes something like this, "The material and speaker were wonderful, but I kept having to translate the material into our language." For pre-stepfamily couples it goes like this, "We went to our pastor for premarital counseling. I think he went through the same things with us that he does with a young first-time marriage couple. We didn't need to talk about not borrowing money from our parents; we needed help with parenting our kids." As I'll explain in more detail later, stepfamilies swim in a different ocean. They need help learning to swim together in their own blended family ocean, not the ocean of a first marriage. General marriage and family training is helpful, but if it doesn't in some way speak to the unique dynamics of stepfamilies, we send inadvertent and unfortunate messages like, "It's your fault your life is complicated," or "You're on your own," or even worse, "You don't belong here." As one woman said, "I got so discouraged going to my church, because no one could help us. It was as if my family was unimportant."

The antidote to this internal and externally imposed shame and fear that marginalizes stepfamilies is, of course, grace. Churches must communicate messages of grace in order to build bridges of hope that stepfamilies can then cross to come out of their shame. After attending my *Building a Successful Stepfamily* conference, a stepfather told one of his elders, "I'm so glad I came this weekend. I never thought I could step foot in a church again." He obviously felt unworthy and unacceptable. By hosting the conference, that church made a statement: "God's grace is available here; even if you feel unworthy, come join our club." Churches who have vibrant stepfamily ministries work hard at communicating these messages throughout the year— from the pulpit, in Bible classes and small groups, and in personal dialogue with couples—and it attracts nontraditional families.

Pastoral Time Demands

A third barrier is the practical time demands on pastors. I know from 20 years of local church ministry that ministers are busy; there is always something or someone demanding their time. Taking the time to get educated about another people group or provide leadership for another ministry can be challenging. Thankfully, however, I and others have created practical resources to help ministers and counselors learn the basics of working with blended families (see the suggested resources in the Practical Ministry Suggestions section below). It doesn't take much to get started, but you do have to make it a priority or it will never make it onto your to-do list. Such initiative on the part of the pastor can also provide strong encouragement to lay leaders in the church.

Theological Barriers

The fourth key barrier to stepfamily ministry pertains to *theological struggles with marriage and divorce.* Of course, not all blended families are the result of divorce, but many are. It is beyond the scope of this chapter to address marriage, divorce, and remarriage from a scriptural standpoint. Suffice it to say that each minister and church needs to study carefully the biblical text in order to arrive at a doctrinal position. I have not answered all of my own questions. Just when I think I've got it figured out, another question arises that is not easily answered. But I have determined that divorce is not the "unforgivable sin," and once remarried, no matter what their background, every couple should work to honor their vows.

And something else is very clear to me. Ministering to stepfamilies does not mean we are pro-divorce any more than believing in hospitals makes one pro-illness.[7] Stepfamily ministry is not about condoning someone's past or lowering God's standard for marriage. God's standard is that people honor their marriage covenants.

The "married for life" nuclear family *is* God's design for the home. It's Plan A, and it truly is the most optimal environment for a healthy marriage and child-rearing. Therefore, we should encourage reconciliation of a first marriage whenever possible. But the reality of God's people throughout time has included plenty of Plan B homes. Abraham's home did not meet God's ideal. He had multiple wives who were stepparents to the other's children, as did Jacob, David, and many other heroes of the faith. Their homes were not "as they should be," but God extended grace to these less-than-ideal people and families. He even used them for his purposes. When Jesus met the woman at the well in John 4, she was cohabiting with a man

---

[7] I am grateful to Dr. Susan Gamache for sharing this analogy with me.

and likely was a five-time divorcée,[8] but in a matter of minutes, Jesus not only affirmed her acceptability to God and her value, he turned her into an evangelist. After receiving living water, she returned to town and told everyone that grace is available no matter what your family story. And people came to Jesus!

Grace has the audacity to grab you where you are and then nurture you back to a relationship with God. First it redeems, and then it transforms. But smart churches have known this for years and have designed ministries to facilitate and communicate God's redemptive power to people from a variety of backgrounds. They offer divorce recovery programs without condoning divorce. They offer post-abortion and ex-gay ministries and walk people out of darkness into light and hope. And churches across America are celebrating recovery on a weekly basis without ever believing they are celebrating addiction! Can't we have the same attitude about ministry to stepfamilies, especially for those formed after sinful divorce? As I said earlier, not all stepfamilies are formed by personal transgression— many are formed after the death of a spouse—but for those born from sinful choices, stepfamily ministry offers healing, grace, redemptive hope for the future, and practical tools for faithful living.

Stepfamily ministry, then, is about *preventing divorce and strengthening blended family homes.* It is also about reducing the pressures of stepfamily life; pressures that hold people back from serving in God's kingdom and prevent parents from raising children to know the Lord. Furthermore, when the body of Christ extends itself as a supportive community, stepfamilies will find direction and courage to continue through their wilderness wanderings toward the Promised Land (Townsend, 2000). The church has a message that can crush Satan's attack on the stepfamily home: First, *God forgives the imperfect people in stepfamilies just as he does the imperfect people in traditional, biological families;* and second, *God's strength and healing are available to any who come to him in faithfulness.* It is time for the church to articulate that message of redemption and hope and to become a spiritual extended family for stepfamilies.

---

[8] Though the text doesn't explicitly tell us why she was married five times, the implied shame in the passage suggests at least one divorce, if not five.

How Do We Help?

Once we have opened our eyes and noticed the prevalence of stepfamilies in both our church and larger community, worked through any theological questions that may have arisen, and decided to overcome any marginalization that may be taking place, what is the church supposed to do? What do we teach, how do we teach it, and how do we structure ministry to stepfamilies in a local church? One ministry leader shared their personal experience and how it illustrates the need for churches to address these concerns. They stated,

> We have programs to deal with first time marriages but nothing to address the needs of second marriages. So many couples are so ill prepared to handle the unique issues of stepfamilies. We went into our marriage knowing we were doing things right in God's eyes but were, and still can be, totally overwhelmed by the issues that arise. I have seen so many friends not make it the second time around because we, the church, have not had the tools to help them.

Here are a few practical suggestions to help you think through and begin taking steps to develop a local stepfamily ministry.

1. **Become educated about the unique dynamics of stepfamily living and learn the essential elements of blended family ministry.**
    Suggested resources (available at Familylife.com/blended): *Ministering to stepfamilies* DVD by Ron Deal and a variety of free tip sheets on marriage ministry, student ministry, and military stepfamilies.

2. **Maintain an outreach (evangelistic) mentality.** Even if you only have a few stepfamilies in your congregation, you have many surrounding it. Educate your leadership and staff to consider

stepfamily ministry as an outreach effort. Design your classes (titles, meeting times, etc.) with the unchurched in mind.

3. **Start a small group or Bible class for stepfamilies.** Recruit one or two stepfamily couples, and perhaps a non-stepfamily ministry couple, to co-lead the group. Add your ministry to our "Find a Ministry" registry at FamilyLife.com/blended so we can refer local couples to your group.

   Suggested resources: *The smart stepfamily (Revised and expanded edition)* book and DVD small group resource (Ron Deal, 8 sessions) and *The smart stepfamily marriage* book and small group curriculum (Ron Deal & David Olson, 13 weeks).

   Can stepcouples benefit from attending your standard marriage enrichment and parenting classes or events? Yes, they can. But a few unique factors necessitate specific training opportunities designed just for stepfamilies.

   First, stepcouples have a high need for fellowship with others "who get their story." Even with other married couples, stepcouples occasionally report feeling like outsiders; getting them together with others who share a similar experience and have similar challenges bolsters their courage.

   Second, a typical marriage enrichment course or series of premarital counseling sessions, for example, is about *half* of what they need. Why? *Because stepcouples swim in a different ocean from first-marriage couples.* Their ocean has a cooler water temperature (trusting a partner can be a challenge after you've nearly been drowned before), different undercurrents (most everyone in the stepfamily has experienced a loss that is always just under the surface and influences everyday interactions), a few more sharks (ex-spouses, co-parenting issues, and the stress of integrating often fit in that category), and the water is less clear (stepfamily life can be murky: What is the role of a stepparent? Do we combine our assets or leave them separate? How do we combine traditions and holidays? How do I balance my children's needs with those of my new spouse? Do we take the kids to my ex-in-laws for Christmas or don't we?). Clearly, stepcouples swim in a different ocean.

   To successfully swim in these waters, stepcouples must

understand what's going on and how it impacts their couple relationship. There are two parts: what happens *between* the couple and what happens *around* them. Research that David Olson and I conducted for our book, *The smart stepfamily marriage*, revealed that:

- Before marriage, couple satisfaction is closely tied to dyadic factors, that is, couple interaction.
- However, after the wedding, couple satisfaction is increasingly tied to triadic factors, that is, the stepfamily ocean around them.

Most couples just can't see this coming until they're already swimming in the ocean. That's when disillusionment and discouragement set in. To facilitate their beating the odds, we have to help them become stepfamily smart; this makes the swim manageable initially and eventually quite enjoyable.

4. **Sensitize your Bible class teachers to stepfamily complexities and acknowledge them from the pulpit.** For example, during Father's Day activities, give children the option (but not the requirement) of making two cards, one for dad and one for stepdad. On Mother's Day, encourage stepmoms in their role and sympathize with their struggles. Most stepmoms will tell you that Mother's Day is the worst day of the year for them to attend church because of the anxiety that surrounds their role. To be honest, most stepmoms skip church that day! On special days like this, use language from the pulpit that acknowledges stepmothers. For example, say something like, "Of course today is Mother's Day and we welcome all our moms. If you are a mom, a stepmom, a foster mother, an adoptive mother, a grandmother, or a woman who is mentoring a child not her own, please stand so we can thank you for all you do." This goes a long way in acknowledging the presence of different family types and affirms the role these people play in the lives of children. Finally, because some parents coordinate visitation exchange at church, find out who is authorized to pick

up the kids after Bible class and who is not. The custodial parent should put this in writing for the teachers.

5. **Structure student ministries with sensitivity to stepfamilies.**

   • Medical releases should be signed by biological parents; stepparents generally do not have the legal right to provide consent for medical treatment.

   • If traveling with youth, chaperones should carry phone numbers of both sets of parents (i.e., both households) in case of emergency, not just the church member parent.

   • Since students in single parent and stepfamily homes frequently can't attend church each week, avoid using sequential Bible class curricula, which can make kids feel lost and peripheral to the group. In addition, help kids find social connections within your group even when they aren't in attendance, and make a special effort to reach out to students who will be part of your program only in the summer while spending time with a noncustodial parent. Remember, kids who feel "lost" or "left out" find it hard to belong and often drift away from the youth program, especially as teenagers. And when kids drift, their parents may drift as well.

   • Learning activities should include case studies that deal with adolescent struggles common to blended family; struggles like how to "honor" one's stepparents, handling conflicts with stepsiblings, and coping with an uninvolved biological parent. Teens need a place to talk about such matters with youth leaders who understand their experiences.

   • Youth staff should develop counseling skills and tips to help co-parents wrestling with both the potential negative influence of their child's other home and the many other possible between-home frustrations (see *The smart stepfamily, revised & expanded edition*).

6. **Discuss stepparenting and remarriage pressures when presenting general marriage and family enrichment classes**

or sermons. I've found that "verbal sidebars" are an effective method of speaking to diverse family situations. A sidebar is when you pause your general presentation and speak for a few brief moments to a particular subgroup within your audience, usually to point out how the principle you just shared applies differently to them. For example, when speaking to couples about how a strong marital commitment helps to stabilize their home and provides a backbone for parenting, you might say, "Now, for those of you in stepfamilies, please know that in the early years of your marriage, expressing marital commitment to your spouse—like hugging them in front of the children or going on a date—actually increases insecurity in your own biological children because they may feel pushed out. They've already had a number of losses in their life, and your emotional attachment to a new spouse may feel like another loss to them. Besides, at least in the beginning, they aren't as invested in the success of your new marriage as you are. Despite these reactions in your children, however, a strong commitment to your marriage is very important. You just need to expect some resistance to it." This quick sidebar to stepcouples recalibrates the principle you just taught and lets them know that you care specifically about their marriages. It might also encourage them to speak with you directly after the class about how they can learn more.

7. **Pre-stepfamily counseling should educate couples and children about stepfamily dynamics.** Notice that I included children. To educate just the couple and not the children is to short-change the effectiveness of your premarital training/counseling. The man and woman need to learn how to be a family, not just a couple. These are two separate dynamics with two separate trajectories that must each be attended to. Plus, children need perspective on how life will change when a stepparent (and perhaps stepsiblings) moves into the house. Some of the topics to address include:
   - Dealing with Losses (children and adults)
   - Realistic and Unrealistic Expectations
   - "How To Cook A Stepfamily" (how bonding takes place)
   - Establishing the Couple Relationship After Remarriage

- Parenting and Stepparenting Roles
- "The eX-FILES: Co-Parenting Issues After Divorce"
- Loyalty Issues
- Establishing Traditions and Rituals

Sessions might include:

- Multiple sessions with adults and children separately and together to discuss expectations, roles, authority, and how children will refer to their stepparent;
- An ex-spouse session to negotiate co-parenting responsibilities;
- Scheduling six-month and twelve-month follow-up sessions to gauge their progress and coach them through difficulties.

Suggested resources:

Books: *Dating and the single parent* and *The smartstepfamily (Revised & expanded edition)* both by Ron Deal.

Website: *smartstepfamilies.com/view/counselor* (includes a complete discussion of pre-stepfamily counseling).

8. **Sponsor a community event.** Host a stepfamily conference, sponsor a stepfamily retreat, or offer a short-course for stepfamily adults. This communicates your awareness of stepfamilies in the community and extends a welcome to them.
9. **Offer competent pastoral counseling.** When couples are hurting they will seek out help from their local church. For years I have had to undo a lot of poor counsel from well-intentioned pastors and licensed counselors who didn't do their homework on stepfamily dynamics. In order to be helpful, you must be able to provide good information related to their presenting problems. At a minimum, this requires a basic understanding of stepfamily dynamics. Take the next few months to read a book on stepfamily living.

   If you are not a counselor, find a competent marriage and family therapist in your area to refer couples to. Keep in mind that most therapists have no specific training in stepfamily therapy and may cause more harm than good. Ask a few questions to see if they have had any training in stepfamily therapy before adding them to your referral list.

A Call to Ministry

What would you say to someone who suggested that you could not minister to or evangelize half of your community's population? Let's just say someone told you to be insensitive to the needs of all the women in your community (approximately half the population). Would you embrace that restriction? Or perhaps you would feel better if you were told to ignore the men. But my guess is that you would not feel good about either.

Half of all people in America will have a steprelationship at some point in their lifetime. It may be a stepparent, stepchild, stepsibling, or stepgrandparent relationship, but 50 percent of us will swim in the stepfamily ocean to some degree. Stepfamily ministry is a tremendous opportunity for churches across America and throughout the world, but it must begin with a willingness to re-tool yourself and expand your understanding of complex families. The only question is, when will you begin?

To learn more, visit FamilyLife.com/blended and SmartStepfamilies.com.

References

Carlson, M. and Furstenberg, F. (2006). The prevalence and correlates of multipartnered fertility among urban U.S. parents. *Journal of Marriage and Family, 68,* 718-732.

Cherlin, A. (2009).*The marriage-go-round: The state of marriage and the family in America today.* New York: Vintage Books.

Deal, R. (2002, 2006). *The smart stepfamily: Seven steps to a healthy family.* Bloomington, MN: Bethany House Publishers.

Deal, R. and Chapman, G. (2014). *The smart stepfamily: Seven steps to a healthy family, revised and expanded edition*. Bloomington, MN: Bethany House Publishers.

Hetherington, E. and Kelly, J. (2002). *For better or for worse: Divorce reconsidered*. New York: W.W. Norton Co.

Karney, B., Garvan, C., and Thomas, M. (2003). Published report by the University of Florida: Family formation in Florida: 2003 Baseline survey of attitudes, beliefs, and demographics relating to marriage and family formation.

Parker, K. (2011, January 13). *A Portrait of Stepfamilies*. Pew Research Center report. Retrieved May 2013 http://pewsocialtrends.org/2011/01/13/a-portrait-of-stepfamilies/

Townsend, L. (2000). *Pastoral care with stepfamilies: Mapping the wilderness*. St. Louis: Chalice Press.

Robert Burns, Ph.D., D.Min.

Robert Burns has been involved in ministry since 1971. His experience includes congregational positions ranging from youth and singles ministry to worship and arts, as well as church planter and senior pastor. He also served as Director of the Center for Ministry Leadership, Director of the Doctor of Ministry, and Associate Professor of Educational Ministries at Covenant Theological Seminary. Dr. Burns currently serves as Pastor of Spiritual Formation at Seven Hills Fellowship in Rome, Georgia and is an adjunct professor at both Covenant and Reformed Theological Seminaries. He was the founder of Fresh Start Seminars and participated as a speaker and writer in the area of divorce recovery for over fifteen years.

Bob holds degrees from the University of Maryland (B.A.), Covenant Theological Seminary (M.Div), Westminster Theological Seminary (D.Min.), and the University of Georgia (Ph.D.). He is the author of numerous articles and books, including *Recovery From Divorce* (Nelson, 1992), *The Adult Child of Divorce* (with Michael Brissett) (Nelson, 1991), *The Fresh Start Divorce Recovery Workbook* (with Thomas Whiteman) (Nelson, 1998), and *Resilient Ministry* (with Tasha Chapman and Donald Guthrie) (InterVarsity, 2013).

Bob and his wife Janet, a Licensed Professional Counselor, have been married since 1978. They have two married sons and eight grandchildren.

CHAPTER 22

How to Develop an Effective Divorce Recovery Ministry

Robert Burns, Ph.D., D.Min.

Natalie had first met Jill when they served in the church nursery together many years ago. They had sons who were the same age, and over the years Natalie and Jill shared carpool duty, attended baseball games, and went through several Bible studies together. Their sons, who were entering the eighth grade, were best friends. Even though they hadn't done much together as couples, Natalie always assumed that Jill's marriage was healthy and stable. After all, Jill and Tom were members of the church, they participated in Sunday school, and Tom occasionally served as an usher.

Two days ago Jill called Natalie with sad news. "Natalie," she said, "Tom just told me he is going to file for divorce…what should I do?" Suddenly, all of the statistics about divorce became very personal to Natalie. Jill wasn't a statistic; she was a friend. In her heart Natalie cried out, "Lord, help me. What should I say? What should I do?" She decided to call her pastor for help.

In my own experience as a pastor, as well as in many conversations I've had with pastors over the years, we often feel unprepared to know how to respond when we receive calls from people like Natalie. How should we counsel her? What are we as a church going to do about our members facing marital disruption?

When the Bible addresses the issue of divorce, it approaches the topic from two mutually dependent perspectives. The first is the relational side of divorce: How are believers in Christ to care for those who are facing the wrenching death of a relationship? The second side is what the scriptures teach about marital separation. The Bible is our final rule on how we live our faith, and when we talk to someone about divorce, we must frame our understanding around its truth.

Express Empathy

One of the first and most important responses pastors or laypersons can have to people in pain is an expression of genuine empathy. In Romans 12:15 (ESV) Paul says, "Rejoice with those who rejoice; weep with those who weep." When people share their raw emotions, they have placed a deep trust in us. This is not a time to present simplistic solutions, but to slow down and listen. We should take the time to re-state in our own words what we are hearing them say. And we should ask how they are coping with this mess right now. It is a very healing thing just to be heard by others and to know they are relating to you. Consider Jesus talking with the woman at the well in John 4. There he asked caring and probing questions; he was a model of empathy.

At the same time, when someone is telling us things that are surprising, embarrassing, or shocking, we need to pray that God will give us an attitude that is discerning but not judgmental. When, in Matthew 7:1 (ESV), Jesus says, "Judge not, that you be not judged," he is not saying we should have a valueless, undiscerning perspective. Rather, we should have a grace-filled attitude that seeks to be supportive, while maintaining a commitment to biblical norms. When people share about their separation or divorce, we must remember that we aren't hearing the whole story. Proverbs 18:17 (ESV) states, "The one who states his case first seems right, until the other comes and examines him." Unfortunately, we often jump to conclusions before we know what is really going on.

During initial conversations about a possible divorce, it is not necessarily helpful to address whether there are biblical grounds for the action. There is a time for that discussion, but in the initial shock, the persons involved are looking for understanding. I remember when a close friend told me he was leaving his wife. While I knew this couple faced problems, I questioned whether there were biblical grounds for such an action. But at that moment he was in no condition to hear my arguments, so I delayed that conversation in order to care about him in the immediacy of his pain.

Understand the Dynamics of Divorce Trauma

Divorce is a devastating experience. Regardless of how long a couple has been married or how bad their marriage has been, over the years it becomes the norm of their life. The disruption of this steady state is not unlike the death of a spouse. However, in the case of divorce there are few accepted means of bereavement: no funeral, no cards, no flowers, and few visits from concerned friends. People who divorce tend to face this experience alone. It is helpful to know that there are three basic elements in divorce trauma: the roles people play, the time frame of their experience, and the emotional stages of divorce.

In most divorce situations, a person takes the role of either the active agent or the passive agent. Active agents generally leave the marriage and file for divorce. Passive agents often know there are problems, but do not anticipate divorce. While partners usually take one role or the other, occasionally they switch. I know of a case where the wife left her husband. He pleaded with her to reconcile. After two sessions of counseling, the husband filed for divorce. We should seek to understand what role a person is taking, and why. This will help us shape our response.

Active and passive agents usually experience emotional trauma in different time frames. The most difficult time for active agents occurs prior to separating and filing for divorce. During this time they often feel a mixture of confusion, sadness, and resolve. After taking these actions, they often view the marriage as a past event. And though they may continue to struggle with guilt, they feel the need to get on with life. They have already worked through their grief; they've become emotionally detached from their marriage, and regardless of shared history, family, friends, or even what the church might say, active agents can be reluctant to review or revise their decision.

While active agents are acting out the decision to divorce, passive agents are only beginning to experience grief. Hearing of a spouse's decision to divorce, a passive agent feels that the foundations of life are crumbling. They often work frantically to hold things together and will do almost anything to prevent the divorce. Or they might blindly assume that the marriage will come back together. When the passive agent is sharing with us, the matter is still raw; their grieving has just begun.

Divorced persons go through emotional stages of shock and denial, anger, bargaining, depression, and acceptance. Shock and denial is the "Oh, no, not me; this happens to other people" phase. Anger comes when denial is broken by the reality that "Yes, it really is me." Bargaining is a time of seeking simple solutions to complex issues. And depression results when bargaining fails. People can swing back and forth between these stages for weeks, months, or years. Acceptance comes slowly over time as they stop blaming their former spouse, take responsibility for their lives, and look to the future rather than the past.

Recognize Our Biblical Responsibility to Care for the Separated and Divorced

The prophet Malachi says that God hates divorce (Malachi 2:16). But does that mean God calls his people to treat with hatred those shattered by marital separation? Let's look at what both the Old and New Testaments say about this question.

The Old Testament. Passages from the Old Testament that are often cited on the topic of divorce include Genesis 3, Leviticus 18, Deuteronomy 24, Jeremiah 3, and Malachi 2. They state the moral context of divorce, describing it as the breaking of a marriage covenant, and also provide the legal context of divorce, with the steps of litigation for proper regulation. However, these passages do not provide a full understanding of the care and concern that God required his people to give to those facing divorce. This understanding becomes clearer when we study the use of the Hebrew word for widow, *almanah*.

This Hebrew word refers to a woman who has been divested of her male protector through death or abandonment. For example, when God forsook his people and their land, they were characterized as *almanah*, "widow" (Isaiah 47:8). But Israel's "husband" (God) had not passed away! Rather, he had written her a certificate of divorce (Jeremiah 3:8)! Similarly, when King David returned to Jerusalem after his son Absalom's revolt, "the king took the ten women [David's concubines with whom Absalom had committed adultery]… and put them in seclusion and supported them, but did not go in to [have sexual relations with] them. So they were shut up to the day of their death, *living in widowhood*" (2 Samuel 20:3, NKJV, emphasis added). All of this is to say the Old Testament taught that the forsaken spouse was considered as a widow.

The implications of this connection between the forsaken and the widow are powerful because the Old Testament is full of God's commands to care for widows.[9] God was clearly on the side of the widow (Psalm 68:5, 146:9), and he expected his people to be as well. Similarly, God took a firm stand for justice toward the oppressed and expected his people to administer justice in a meaningful way. While the law described the proper legal procedure people were to take in order to obtain a divorce, it also provided for legal discipline within the community directed toward those who had abandoned their covenant responsibility to their spouse.

The New Testament. Regarding the treatment of divorced persons, the New Testament carried on the tradition of the Old, but it went further, clarifying how God's people were to deal with all parties in the divorce.

First, consider again Jesus's attitude toward the woman at the well (John 4). We find a balance in Jesus's ministry with this woman. On the one hand, he understood her circumstances and feelings. He knew of her previous marriages and her present adultery, but he did not use these against her. Rather, Jesus's honest and open handling of her situation broke through her emotional and religious smoke screens, preparing her to hear the truth.

Further, Jesus demonstrated an honest concern for this woman by breaking significant cultural taboos in order to care for her. He spoke in open with a woman whose husband was not present (a questionable act in the Middle East to this day). She was also a "despised Samaritan," and to make matters worse, she was a flagrant sinner! But Jesus did not allow these social matters to keep him from sharing with her the good news.

On the other hand, Jesus never condoned the woman's sin. He initiated the topic of her loose morality. Perhaps he delved into more of her past than we read in the narrative, for she later reported, "He told me everything I ever did." According to John 1:14, Jesus ministered with grace and truth. Revealing his understanding of her circumstances, he spoke with candor. Yet this truth was couched in the grace of his power to forgive and restore her to wholeness.

---

[9] Deuteronomy 10:18, 14:28-29, 24:19-22; Proverbs 15:25; Isaiah 1:17, 23-25; Jeremiah 7:5-6, 22:3; Zechariah 7:10; Malachi 3:5.

The response of this woman to Jesus's caring acceptance and honest confrontation is phenomenal. She returned to town and owned up to her past. Then she urged everyone to come and see this man named Jesus. It is obvious that significant healing had taken place in her life.

This entire scene happened because our Savior extended himself to one who had been divorced. He initiated the conversation. He disclosed the truth of her situation. He led her to an understanding of life fulfillment beyond the disappointment of a broken marriage or a new sexual liaison.

A similar pattern of ministry to the rejected took place in the early church. In 1 Corinthians 6, Paul said that some of the new believers had come out of a variety of backgrounds including sexual immorality, adultery, thievery, and other disreputable lifestyles. He did not include divorce in this list, but his obvious concern with such circumstances in the next chapter must mean that many in this situation were within the fellowship.

Other New Testament writers highlight the same theme: Spiritual rebirth extends hope to the rejected, healing to the brokenhearted, and opportunities for meaningful service to those who once thought their lives had little significance.

While the New Testament described the gospel as a source of renewal, it also provided for a specific framework for persons involved in divorce. It addressed the problem of mixed marriages between believer and nonbeliever (1 Corinthians 7). It presented the restorative role that church discipline should take in the life of God's people.[10] It required the appointment of church leaders who were expected to provide a supportive context where difficult issues would be handled before God with objectivity and compassion.[11]

Although the church was never to tolerate sin, it was to provide a place where the conditions preceding and following divorce would be handled. And it was responsible to follow the lead of the Lord Jesus, who actively sought out and ministered to divorced persons.

---

[10] Matthew 18:15-20; 1 Corinthians 5:1-5; 2 Corinthians 2:5-11.

[11] Matthew 18:15-20; Acts 20:28; 1 Corinthians 6:1-6; Hebrews 13:17; 1 Peter 5:2-4.

Talk About the Bible

Whether it is with the leadership of the church, with persons facing divorce like Jill and Tom, or with friends like Natalie who are trying to figure out how to help, the time will come when we will need to talk about the Bible. As I said above, the Bible is the final rule on how we practice our faith, and we must frame our understanding of separation, divorce, and remarriage around its truth.

Depending on the circumstances, there are things we can share to reassure people dealing with marital disruption. For example, we can say that God loves them, that he is concerned about them and their children, and that he will help them deal with all of this as they sincerely seek his will.

Though it is beyond the scope of this chapter to present the biblical data on separation, divorce, and remarriage, it is important for everyone in ministry to know what we believe.[12] It is important for the pastor(s) and leadership of any church to establish their convictions on this topic. Some churches even have written position papers and make them available to their congregations.[13] If your congregational leadership has not grappled with this issue, I would urge you to clarify your views before a crisis requires you to present your convictions.

It is important for an individual Christian, be it a pastor, an officer, a therapist, or a church member, not to assume the authority to determine God's will in any given divorce situation. It is the collective leadership of the local congregation (often called "elders") who are responsible before

---

[12] There is a spectrum of interpretations on what the Bible teaches regarding marriage, divorce, and remarriage. Some of the studies I often recommend are: David Instone-Brewer's *Divorce and remarriage in the church* (2003, Downers Grove: IVP) and his more scholarly *Divorce and remarriage in the Bible* (2002, Grand Rapids: Eerdmans); David Jones' *Biblical Christian ethics* (1994, Grand Rapids: Baker); John Murray's classic *Divorce* (1978, Phillipsburg: Presbyterian and Reformed); and chapter three of my book co-authored by Tom Whiteman, *The fresh start divorce recovery workbook* (1998, Nashville: Nelson).

[13] For an example, see the Fresh Start Position Paper on Marriage and Divorce found in Appendix C of my book co-authored by Tom Whiteman, *The fresh start divorce recovery workbook* (1998, Nashville: Nelson). To see how one major denomination has studied and presented its views, see http://www.pcahistory.org/pca/1979-AdInterim-Divorce.pdf.

God for the welfare of God's people (Hebrews 13:17; 1 Peter 5:1-4). If we are working with persons who are the active agent, and we deeply believe they do not have biblical grounds, this is all the more reason to give them time to talk. People are more likely to receive what we have to say if they feel we have heard and understood them. Then, when the time comes for us to share, we must prayerfully speak the truth in love (Ephesians 4:15).

Church Involvement

According to Scripture, the church is responsible to provide oversight and shepherding for God's people, and we should encourage Christians facing divorce to contact their church. As we have already seen, God calls elders to this responsibility as his leaders for the church. It is common for persons going through marital separation to assume they know God's will regarding their divorce. However, as previously stated, it is never the place of any one individual to determine if there are valid biblical grounds for such action. God has given the keys of the kingdom to the leaders of the church to make these decisions.

The idea of going to the church is scary for many people. They feel that the leadership will not understand their circumstances or may use church discipline as a means of punishment. Unfortunately, there are enough stories of bad process to keep these tales alive. But the Bible teaches that church leaders are appointed to provide a supportive context where issues can be handled with objectivity and compassion.[14] This requires an attitude of humility among those in leadership, recognizing that every believer stands before God in need of mercy (Galatians 6:1-3).

In separation and divorce there is rarely, if ever, a case where one party is beyond reproach and the other should receive total blame. Marriage is a shared responsibility, and those involved in shepherding and church discipline must labor to maintain joint accountability. At the same time, in most divorce cases only one partner seeks the aid of the church. For this person, the process should not create deeper guilt but should provide a healthy context for restoration so that the person can maintain the status of a fully functioning member of Christ's church.

---

14 Matthew 18:15-20; Acts 20:28; 1 Corinthians 6:1-6.

What is the role of shepherding and discipline toward those who lack any desire for the church's involvement? It is to win them back through a prolonged and concerned call to the promises they made in church membership and marriage. Jesus came to give life, and his church must be part of this life-giving and life-restoring process.

How should pastors and leaders shepherd the congregation in their attitude toward people experiencing separation and divorce? Christians in marital turmoil often feel abandoned by God's people. In the church, marriage is the socially acceptable status, even if the marriage is in shambles. When those who are single-again enter the church, they often feel like the odd ones out.

At the same time, over the last few decades there have been marked attitudinal changes among Christians concerning separation and divorce. Some believers have developed a tolerance of divorce for any reason. However, such "liberation" is not the attitudinal change needed among believers today. Neither is there a need for hardened insensitivity that writes off all persons going through divorce as sinners who no longer hold an equal position in the church. Rather, the mindset necessary toward the divorced individual should be one of practical grace. Practical grace is the humility of recognizing that every believer stands before God in need of mercy. No one person is better than another at the foot of the cross.

While most Christians would affirm this concept of grace in theory, the practical side means applying the truth of God's acceptance of us in our relationships with others. Developing an attitude of practical grace means we must beware lest we take on the attitude of the boasting Pharisee in Luke 18:10-14 (NIV) who said, "God, I thank you that I am not like other people." It also requires that we treat divorced persons in the same way Jesus Christ has treated us: redeeming us from our past failures, forgiving us for our present sin, and challenging us to live and relate on the basis of the truth revealed in Scripture.

Acceptance can never be based on anything less than our mutual submission to Jesus Christ. When this is the standard, a caring attitude toward the divorced should follow. Were divorced persons to experience rejection simply on the basis of their single-again status, a church and its leaders should examine themselves as to their understanding of justification in practical terms.

Provide Ongoing Ministry

Divorce is a devastating experience in all aspects of life. It usually creates financial havoc that can take years to stabilize. Divorce can also impact one's mental condition. Those affected often become disoriented ("How could this be happening to me?"), questioning both their discernment ("How could I be so stupid?") and their decision-making ability ("How could I let him/her do that?"). They may become vulnerable to quick solutions and rebound relationships. It can take a minimum of two to five years for them to regain social and emotional stability.

Where will a battered spouse turn when they desire to remain faithful, yet fear for their life? Where will a spouse receive counsel when they are struggling with a decision to contest their divorce? Christians in these situations need the support offered by God's church.

We can offer practical care. Perhaps divorcing persons are being forced back into the work force. Counsel regarding professional choices would be helpful. The church could also arrange for meals and childcare options during this time of transition. Pastors could connect them with resources such as books, seminars, and podcasts. They could also refer them to Christian counselors who agree with the church's convictions on marriage, separation, and divorce. Most of all, the church can provide friends who can simply be there to listen, support, pray, and understand.

It is rare, if not impossible, to find a church which does not need to minister to the divorced. However, it is another thing for a church to commit itself to establish and maintain a divorce recovery ministry. A church must count the cost of capacity and resources if it plans to develop an ongoing outreach to the separated and divorced. Far too often congregations with good intentions start such ministries only to see them fizzle out due to a lack of leadership or commitment. Even worse is the impact such failures have on single-again persons where such programs begin with great enthusiasm but fail to be sustained.

For churches that desire to establish and support a divorce recovery program, there are many formats and options available. These include weekend intensives as well as programs varying from six to sixteen weeks, usually meeting once a week. Program formats include options using live speakers, employing video programs,[15] or involving small groups utilizing workbooks.[16] Regardless of the program format, smaller process groups for discussion of content and personal experience are essential. Each church needs to identify its own goals and resource capacities. But regardless of the format and content delivery method, it is strongly recommended that the program be organized and facilitated by local people. As Andy Morgan has stated, "By not making it another thing done for you but something you do for yourselves, you benefit from knowing that you have helped build the kingdom in your own community" (Morgan, 1997).

What topics ought to be presented and discussed in a divorce recovery seminar? Four core themes are vital. The first is understanding the grief process as it applies to marital separation. As presented above, the grief stages include shock and denial, anger, bargaining, depression, and acceptance.[17]

The second theme is re-entry into single life. Topics under this theme include facing the shock of living alone, building a network of supportive friends, navigating the challenges of single-parenting, and dealing with single-again sexuality.[18]

The third theme that needs to be discussed is what the Bible teaches on separation, divorce, and remarriage. Sometimes churches are reluctant to address this issue, but I have found that both Christians and non-Christians are vitally interested in understanding what the Bible says about

---

[15] One popular video program is DivorceCare. For more information, see www. divorcecare.org.

[16] This author's book written with Dr. Tom Whiteman, is a well-researched and practical guide that can be easily adapted to a small group context. See *The fresh start divorce recovery workbook* (1998, Nashville: Thomas Nelson). Another helpful ministry tool is the classic book by Jim Smoke, *Growing through divorce* (2007, Eugene: Harvest House). Note that there are any number of helpful workbooks available. Be sure to explore the biblical and philosophical basis for any resource before using it.

[17] For a helpful study on the stages of grief see either *Recovery from divorce* by Bob Burns (1992, Nashville: Nelson), or Chapter 1, "Hitting the slope: The stages of divorce recovery" in *The fresh start divorce recovery workbook*, Bob Burns and Tom Whiteman (1998, Nashville: Nelson).

[18] See *The single again handbook* by Thomas Jones (1993, Nashville: Nelson).

their situation, as well as how God can bring any good from experiencing such pain.

Finally, divorce recovery seminars must address the dynamics of working through bitterness and learning to forgive[19]. Divorced persons often feel that their lives have been shattered, perhaps beyond repair. The anger, disappointment, and pain of divorce remain long after the ink of the documents has dried. Bitterness can actually shape their personality so that their approach to life becomes hardened and negative. At the same time, some of the very best things we ever learn come through hardship and difficulty. Forgiveness begins with an understanding of how God has forgiven us. And the way God forgives us forms a pattern for the way we can forgive others.

After these four core themes, there are multiple options for additional areas of discussion. These can either build on ideas found in the "core four" or can be stand-alone topics. Ideas include children and divorce, communication and conflict, separation and reconciliation, legal issues, finances, and handling the holidays.

Minister to All Who Are Impacted by Divorce

Divorce is not an isolated event. Children, parents of adult children, grandparents, friends, and neighbors are all impacted when a marriage ends. Pastors and church leaders need to be aware of the broader systemic effects of separation and divorce. And they need to prepare to address these needs in their congregations.

Every family requires coverage in at least three areas: Someone who provides income for the household; someone who oversees the care and upkeep of the home, including laundry, food preparation, and cleaning; and someone who is responsible for child care. It can be hard enough for an intact family to cover these bases! Normally when a couple separates, one or more of these areas suffer (usually beginning with home upkeep). It

---

[19] See Chapter 9, "Pardon me: Working through bitterness and learning to forgive" in my book co-authored by Tom Whiteman, *The fresh start divorce recovery workbook* (1998, Nashville: Nelson) and Chapter 6, The process of forgiveness" in my book co-authored by Michael Brissett, *The adult child of divorce: A recovery handbook* (1991, Nashville: Nelson).

is important for all those who wish to help divorcing persons to understand how stretched the lives of single-again persons can become.

Children. When parents go through divorce, be aware that their children are facing a myriad of changes. First, they experience the collapse of their family structure. This can create tremendous feelings of fear, vulnerability, stress, and loneliness. Second, children must deal with the potential loss of access to their non-custodial parent, which may create feelings of rejection and abandonment. Third, the demands of life mentioned above may bring decreased attention from their custodial parent. Then there are worries about finances, worries about the welfare of their parents, and worries about the possible loss of home, school, friends, church, and neighborhood. Add to this children's concerns about how they are to cope with the reactions of friends, teachers, and neighbors, plus loyalty issues with parents who are expressing anger and resentment toward one another. Pastors, Sunday school teachers, youth workers, and others in ministry need to be made aware of these concerns.

Parents whose children are divorcing. Similarly, parents of divorcing children can expect to face an intense grieving reaction similar to the one their children are going through. Their family will never be the same. An understanding of how the stages of grief described above apply to their unique situation is important in order to provide the empathy and support parents need during this time. The fellowship and encouragement of the church will be needed as these seniors face a myriad of changes in their family system. It is not unusual for this transition process to mirror that of a divorcing person, lasting from two to five years.

Practical suggestions. A few practical suggestions for anyone who has friends or family going through divorce should be stressed:

- Don't be one more source of stress for those going through a marital breakup. Recognize that these people need you for stability, objectivity, wisdom, and support.
- Understand that if your adult child or friend is now a single parent, she or he might be much busier and less available.

- When it is possible to continue to love and befriend both parties going through the divorce without betraying loyalties, getting pulled into the middle of unresolved disputes, or taking up one or both party's offenses, this can be one of the healthiest post-divorce arrangements.
- If a separated or divorced person asks for either financial or emotional support, give what you can without allowing dependency to develop. While you want to help your adult child or friend stabilize, extended dependence only prolongs a sense of despair and hopelessness.
- Do not encourage or support unbiblical behavior by your friend or adult child. For example, do not provide financial support to someone who is abandoning spouse and family.
- Grandparents must not be allowed to be shut out of the lives of their grandchildren. If necessary, ask that their visitation rights be included in any custody arrangement.
- Finally, if you have a specific issue with one member of a divorcing couple, take it directly to that person. Don't put others in the middle by asking them to express your concerns.

Bottom Line: Genuine Care in Jesus's Name

The divorce experience is a complex process. Old lifestyle patterns and goals that were once assumed are challenged during this time of life transition. In the midst of such upheaval the church can provide nurture, support, encouragement, and discipleship. During this time, people will be evaluating their own values and commitments. This provides an exceptional context for thoughtful consideration of the gospel's implications for life if the church is prepared to connect with persons at their point of need. The divorced person needs unconditional acceptance without fear of judgment or condemnation. The shame and stigma of divorce in our Christian subculture is still pervasive, problematic, and pejorative.

The form that any particular church would decide to use in a ministry to single-again persons is not at issue here. Rather, the concern is for the divorced and separated persons in the congregation and the surrounding community to sense that a redemptive fellowship is prepared to take action on their behalf. When this Christ-like concern is present and expressed, the details, structure, and format of specific programs will work themselves out accordingly.

References

Burns, R. (1992). *Recovery from divorce.* Nashville: Nelson.

Burns, R. & Brissett, M. (1991). *The adult child of divorce: A recovery handbook.* Nashville: Nelson.

Burns, R. & Whiteman, T. (1998). *The fresh start divorce recovery workbook.* Nashville: Nelson.

DivorceCare video curriculum. www.divorcecare.org

Instone-Brewer, D. (2002). *Divorce and remarriage in the Bible.* Grand Rapids: Eerdmans.

Instone-Brewer, D. (2003). *Divorce and remarriage in the church.* Downers Grove: IVP.

Jones, D. (1994). *Biblical Christian ethics.* Grand Rapids: Baker.

Jones, T. (1993) *The single again handbook.* Nashville: Nelson.

Morgan, A. (1997). Organizing a divorce recovery workshop. *Baker handbook of single adult ministry* (D. L. Fagerstrom. Ed.). Grand Rapids: Baker Books.

Murray, J. (1978). *Divorce.* Phillipsburg: Presbyterian and Reformed.

Report of the ad interim theological committee on divorce (1979). General Assembly of the Presbyterian Church in America. Retrieved November 2, 2016 from http://www.pcahistory.org/pca/1979-AdInterim-Divorce.pdf

Smoke, J. (2007) *Growing through divorce.* Eugene: Harvest House.

Joneal Kirby, Ph.D.

Joneal Kirby earned a Ph.D. in Marriage and Family Therapy and immediately began a private counseling practice. She also developed a counseling center within her church which provided services for clients from a four-state region. Prior to this, she served as an educator, school administrator, and family counselor for over 20 years. In 2003, she created Heartfelt Ministries, which focuses on discipling programs for women. Dr. Kirby has spoken at conferences and workshops and on radio and television all over the country. Her own conference, *The Heartfelt Experience,* is attended by thousands of women. Dr. Kirby hosts a daily radio program with a current audience of over 100,000 listeners. She also co-wrote and co-hosted a television Bible study and Christian lifestyle program for Legacy Network.

Dr. Kirby is the author of *Heartfelt: A Woman's Guide to Creating Meaningful Friendships, The Heartfelt Friends Training Manual, Heart of a Family for Mom: Common Sense Parenting with Wisdom from the Word,* and *Hope for Your Family: A Parent's Guide,* as well as numerous articles for a variety of publications. She has written Bible studies for women's ministry, including *Be the Woman, A Study of Proverbs 31, Living the Gospel,* and *Parables of Purpose: Nine Stories Jesus Told.*

Joneal and her husband, Randy, have been married more than 40 years. They met while in college, and began their newlywed life teaching in the same school. They have three children who have blessed them with their spouses and five grandboys. Both of their mothers have been an active part of their families. They worked in children's and youth ministries for years before creating a marriage ministry for their local church which has had national success. Through this work, they became close friends with Alan and Lisa Robertson of A & E's *Duck Dynasty.* The two couples have worked together in marriage ministry for over 15 years and are currently doing marriage retreats including The Marriage Cruise by Premiere Productions. The Kirbys live in West Monroe, Louisiana on 130 acres of wooded land where their five grandsons often run and play.

CHAPTER 23

How to Develop an Effective Women's Mentoring Ministry

Joneal Kirby, Ph.D.

Mindy has spent a lot of time in prisons. She goes behind locked, guarded doors for hours. Although she is not a prisoner, Mindy knows a lot about prison life, so she ministers to women who are there. This is work which is out of her comfort zone; although not as far out as it may be for you or for me. Mindy's father has been a prisoner for most of her life, serving a life sentence, jailed in one of the most infamous prisons in our country. He is there because he was found guilty of killing Mindy's mother.

When Mindy was a young teenager, she lost her mother and then her father within a few, brief, anguishing hours. Can you imagine what it would be like to have your routine of family and home, school and friends totally shot to pieces, never to be put back together again? Can you imagine how alone and frightened a 15-year-old girl would feel, knowing her mother was murdered and her father was accused of being the one who shot her? Here's Mindy's description of her life as it disintegrated: "A week after my mother's death my father was arrested for that crime, and a year later he was convicted by a jury. Within a matter of a few months, my sister and I were orphaned. Our lives were turned upside down" (Kirby, 2015).

While her remaining teen years were somewhat peaceful thanks to her grandparents' care and attention, her early adult years were chaotic. Mindy's life became one disaster after another. She married twice, unwisely and hastily. The first was a disaster, very abusive, and it soon ended in divorce. She became deeply ashamed, and resentment and bitterness took over. Struggling to find attachment and security, she married again and this dysfunctional relationship ended too. It appeared that disaster and crisis would be her life's normal.

But then she discovered a long-lost relationship with Jesus. And a relationship with a church family who took her in, loved her, accepted her, and helped her to turn it all around. This is not an unusual testimony for someone who comes out of the world and finds salvation and a healthy church attachment. What is different—what is unique—is the people she became close to and the impact they made on her future. She experienced significant relationships with older, godly women who became her lifeline to building a new way of living. She became close friends with women in her church who were mother figures to her and who finally provided the love, the nurturing, and the guidance she had been searching for.

Mindy shared what this meant to her.

It changed everything in my life. These incredible women taught me from the ground up how to be a wife and mother, how to study the Bible and Biblical truths, how to be open with others. I didn't really know how to have relationships with women, so I even learned that. I did that by being in small groups where I could talk about things and about my feelings. Without these women, without my mentors, I probably never would have done that. They challenged me to step up and to move forward and build a close relationship with my own daughter. They modeled what it looked like so I could live it out with her. They showed me practical things like how to fix my daughter's hair and how to sew. I've been mentored by, and have friendships with elders' wives and Bible teachers and godly homemakers. They are women with amazing abilities and women I stand in awe of. We were all seeking the same goal: to become godly women to the best of our abilities (Kirby, 2015).

As her life improved and her decisions were wiser, Mindy met a wonderful Christian man, and with the blessing of their church family, they married. Recently they celebrated their fourteen-year anniversary. Mindy's daughter is now eleven and she enjoys a close relationship with her. Her son is in his second year of college and is active in the church's student ministry. Although Mindy had been taken to church by her grandparents, her spiritual growth didn't begin until she became connected with and was mentored and cared for by selfless, wise, godly women. They made such a difference in her life that their friendships became the catalyst for changing the faith legacy of Mindy's family.

She went from a life struggling alone to a richly blessed, full life surrounded by a caring church family. These loving folks shepherded her from chaos and confusion to stability. Devoted to Christ and his church, Mindy now spends many hours each week ministering to families, children, and women prisoners. She is one of my closest friends and ministry partners, now serving alongside me in women's ministry.

In 2003, I began Heartfelt Ministries, a women's mentoring program. When Mindy needed help, Heartfelt was there to help her, but before we began Heartfelt, our church had nothing like it available for young women who needed continuous, specific care; we had no programs to teach and train someone who was motherless and needing the resources of an ongoing church family effort. But at the right time, Heartfelt was there to help Mindy find God's way.

Not all the women I have worked with through Heartfelt have such a devastating story. As mentors in our program, we reach out regularly to younger women who have familiar, routine struggles. Woman who are in the middle of raising babies and demanding preschoolers. Women who are balancing work life with family time. Women who desire to have more time with God and need specific carved-out time to do so. Wives who are thriving in strong marriages and some who are constantly struggling in weaker ones. Some have stories as crazy as Mindy's, but most do not. It's been interesting to learn that many of them, until they became involved with Heartfelt, had not had meaningful relationships with women who were called by God to do real life with and intentionally disciple and mentor younger women toward spiritual growth. For most ladies, women's Bible classes and church fellowships were the extent of their experiences with women's ministry.

Over my many years in women's ministry, I have talked to hundreds of women who crave close spiritually-meaningful relationships. They also desire authentic friendships with godly, older women. I have learned of this desire and need mainly through the hours I have spent knee-to-knee with clients in my counseling practice. Over my years in practice I have worked with and taught thousands of women, and I have also heard this yearning for deeper relationships from students in my Bible classes and family workshops as I listen to their questions and see their eagerness for advice, direction, and instruction. My experience has taught me that without a doubt, younger women are hungry for attention, guidance, and wisdom from healthy, older women in our churches.

Most of us have a few folks we are close to. Some are family. Some are friends. But not many are intentionally influencing our spiritual walk.

When I think about my own spiritual journey, I imagine the course of a marathon race. I see myself running down the middle of a street flanked by thousands who are cheering me on and others who are running along beside me. I have been exceptionally well-mentored in my spiritual walk. Perhaps you have been also. In the crowd are faces of those who have discipled me; wise church leaders, gifted Bible study teachers, caring co-workers, loving friends, and loyal family members. These precious friends have all been spiritual mentors, guides, encouragers, and lifelines in my spiritual journey. I have learned that no one matures well on their own. Teachers are fundamental. Influencers are vital. Examples are necessary. Encouragement is essential. Life is hard and complicated and messy, and while walking the path of the Lord without prayer partners and fellow journeymen may be possible, it is difficult.

I've noticed this about church life: many churchgoers are fine in the foyer. We're fine with the chitchat of "Hello" and "How are you?" This small talk is safe... and empty. It camouflages us. It's only when we get past what I call the foyer-façades that women can really connect and get to know one another. Only then are we able to share with one another our hurts, habits, and hang-ups, as well as our needs, desires, passions, and purpose.

I don't know about you, but my hurts, habits, and hang-ups don't go away when I enter the church building. I'd rather not carry them back out the door with me. But living a real life for Christ can be an almost daily challenge. What I need, and maybe what you need, is to have people in our lives that are there when we need a smile of encouragement, a shoulder to cry on, a prayer of petition, a blessing for support, and often a nudge to be better than we are.

I felt this when I was a young wife and mother and for the first time moved away from my home base; away from my familiar church, my parents, and my closest friends. My husband was changing jobs, and of course, my mind understood the reason and the need for our relocation, but those raw answers still left my heart hurting. In just a few weeks' time, we uprooted our three children and moved them away from their grandparents, all the schools they had ever known, and the church they had been born into.

We did have family in the new place, so that provided some comfort, and on our previous visits to see them, we had also met several couples, but everything else was a new experience, from choosing a dry cleaner to finding a pediatrician. After a dozen years of marriage and putting down our family roots in one place, this unfamiliarity led to some uncomfortable feelings. Being a stranger was a new phenomenon for me. Of course, we immediately joined a church, but although our new town was much smaller than the former one, the church was much larger both in physical size and member count than what we were used to. It was full of families and friends who had longtime ties to each other and who were all deeply rooted in their community. I soon realized that our new church was made up of a very close community of folks who either were related to each other and/or had been members there for years, and I knew it would take me a while to make close friends, especially friends as close as those I had known in my previous church. Predictably, I began by getting as involved with the church as time would allow, including participating in and teaching women's Bible studies.

In 2003, I was in a Bible study going through the book of Titus, and as I heard, read, and studied the book deeply, I saw a distinct blueprint. Right there in Titus 2 was a list of concrete and explicit instructions on a woman's role in the church, and those instructions were overt and unambiguous. Women were told to disciple one another, woman to woman and women to women. This has been called mentoring. Or training. Or teaching. And it was exceedingly clear to me—especially in light of the many women with whom I was working on life and spiritual issues—that this kind of discipling was essential in our church. I also realized that although we were following these instructions at least informally, we weren't doing so in a routine, regularly occurring manner. A few of us were involved this way with just a few other women, but there was no structured program or formalized plan for reaching the hundreds of women, wives, and mothers in our church in the way that Titus 2 teaches.

As I travel and teach the principles of the Heartfelt program, I have found that our congregation was only one of many (actually most) that did not have women specifically, intentionally, and routinely fulfilling this clear ministry role:

> Teach the older women to be reverent in the way that they live... to teach what is good. Then they can train the younger women to love their husbands and children, to be self-controlled and pure, to be busy at home, to be kind, and to be subject to their husbands, so that no one will malign the word of God (Titus 2:3-5, NIV).

One of the refreshing blessings that comes from this ministry is that it increases the spiritual health of women, and this impacts their marriages and their families. The constant, caring interactions of close friendships are playing an essential role in improving the mental and relational health of women in the church. As a mental health therapist, I saw that many of my clients' struggles were the result of inadequate, dysfunctional, absent, or severed relationships, but as women began to understand and experience the true nature of God's love and grace, as they began praying more, learning God's Word, and then practicing spiritual disciplines, their interactions with others were transformed.

They were learning not just to cope with loss or tragedy or harm; they were rising above those situations with a triumphant, courageous spirit. Their hope was being restored, and they were seeking peace not just within themselves but with others. Through our women's programs, those who were lonely or depressed, grieving or suffering found safe spaces in other ladies' homes where they could share their burdens, hurts, problems, and troubles. Instead of being overwhelmed by their life issues, they were prayed for and with, and the burdens of their lives were shared between sisters in Christ. As trite as the saying may seem, it is true: a burden shared is a burden lightened.

In addition to strengthening the spiritual and mental well-being of the women, families were growing and becoming healthier and stronger. Customarily, the heart of a home is connected to the emotional presence of the woman living there. Having spiritually strong, mentally sound, and more content wives and mothers benefits husbands and children. The sanctuary of home and family is amplified when a woman becomes more knowledgeable of and secure in God's Word. Her faith life and her trust in God directly impact the spiritual health of her children, and that can influence her husband immensely.

A women's ministry which focuses on strengthening the community of women in a church should always encourage the biblical view of marriage and family. Heartfelt has successfully taught thousands of women what the Bible says about living as godly wives; reading, understanding, and respecting the Word of God; and teaching their children to love and honor God and respect his plan for a husband and wife in a covenant marriage for life. In Heartfelt, we also believe the welfare of a healthy family is dependent on the mother's understanding of her God-designed role, regardless of her marital status. Whether she is a single mother, a married mother, a divorced mother, or a mother who has never been married, the teachings of Titus 2, Ephesians 6, and Proverbs 31, as well as numerous other passages which we have taught, provide clear instructions on living well spiritually.

Let me stretch this concept. If the heart of a family is intricately connected to the woman of the family—if this woman is commanded to be wise, loving, and respectful to God, and if her obedience leads her household well—then in like ways the same is also true in a church. The hearts of the women in a church family set the tone for the emotional and spiritual connections made there, and they contribute useful, unique gifts to the various ministry works. Can you imagine a church where the women are so loving, supportive, giving, and encouraging of each other that women of all ages and stages of life feel loved, connected, needed, and wanted? Can you imagine what would happen if a large number of the women in your church were consistently in God's word with one another? Can you imagine a church where the elderly, especially the widows, remain a necessary and vital part of the church's community and service? Can you imagine a church where the older Christian women are in such close relationship with the younger women, wives, and mothers that these wise women are sought out for spiritual answers and guidance on personal and family matters?

If you are a pastor or ministry leader perhaps you can answer the following question for me, as it is one I think about a lot. Why do so many churches not follow any consistent or organized plan based on the Titus 2 teaching? Do church leaders not see the need? I invite conversations (not defenses) about this because I am still learning, and I want to know the reasons for—and hopefully better understand—the barriers that hinder women's discipling/mentoring programs. As a therapist, women's ministry leader, woman, wife, mother, and grandmother who has seen the dramatic moral and spiritual changes and decline in American society during my sixty-plus years, I have to ask this: Don't we need the Titus 2 model today more than ever before in our country and in our churches?

Our Heartfelt ministry is designed as a women-to-women mentoring program to build opportunities for community between older and younger women in churches, whether they are single women, single mothers, divorced women, or young wives and mothers. The church needs a way to bridge the gap so as to increase the older generation's influence on the younger generation. Heartfelt has found a key that works for building relationships between thousands of women in God's church. It facilitates forming influential friendships that are used for mentoring, teaching, guiding, nurturing, supporting, and blessing God's women. Through Heartfelt, women are learning to build deeply significant, spiritually meaningful relationships. And many lives are being changed—seriously transformed—because of this intentional interaction.

This is a unique time for Christians in our country. Perhaps there has never been a time in the church in the United States when God's women have been more consistently confronted by a culture so unfriendly to believers. Regularly, women of faith are confronted with a public stance which is increasingly unsupportive and often hostile toward Bible-centered lifestyles. Paul's writing to Titus strongly emphasized the need for God's people to return to holy living. He wrote of the corrupt, pagan Cretan culture and the impact it would have on the church. Titus's mission there on the island of Crete was to establish Christ-centered church leadership, instructing and inspiring the churches to rise above the culture and honor God with their lifestyles.

Certainly, this is what we as God's people face today in America. And the women of the church now, much as the women of the church then, are being called on for such a time as this. Now is the time for women of faith to become the light that reflects God's goodness. The darkness that surrounds us does not have to invade or overcome our homes and families. We can speak out graciously, courageously, and certainly as we seek righteousness, strengthen our faith, live out his grace, and show mercy and love. "One generation [will] commend your works to another; they [will] tell of your mighty acts" (Psalm 145:4, NIV).

A real concern, however, is this: if women older in the faith are not teaching younger women to build strong families, to love their husbands, and to combat worldliness, then what will happen to our children, our grandchildren, and our great-grandchildren's faith and families? Judges 2 tells us exactly what will happen. There will come a generation that does not know the Lord. The saying is true; we are but one generation away from losing the faith of our own families.

According to much of the Bible, it is the responsibility of the older generations to consistently and clearly teach the younger generations and train them in the ways of faith. Although older women may see themselves as neither wise nor mature, all their prior experiences in their relationships with others and with the Lord give them the faith and wisdom necessary to influence those who come behind them in age and stage. The lessons of God's consistency sustaining them are messages of faith that speak to all. Women are encouraged to use these faith experiences to mentor, instruct, teach, train, and certainly to inspire the younger generation. First though, in order for an older woman to influence a younger one, she must build a relationship by cultivating a friendship.

Heartfelt's program is designed in such a way that a woman who mentors need only be willing to serve and willing to share; to share all that God has done, is doing, and will do in her life. Such a "simple" pre-requisite for serving in women's ministry is rare in that there are actually no other requirements for participating; no educational qualification, no specific talent, no particular skill set. This ministry is for every woman in every church. It is pure, basic discipleship: simply equipping and encouraging.

Another aspect of our program is its strong evangelical thrust. Our small home group meetings provide a safe place for women to invite their non-Christian associates and those looking for a church identity. Women are encouraged to invite their friends—and even family members—who are searching for spiritual relationships to come and meet comfortably with their faith friends. While the invited friend may not have a salvation experience as her goal, that is a natural result of becoming good friends with believing women who openly share their journey of faith.

This women's ministry works, and it has provided multiple benefits for churches in which it is implemented. One of these is a return to biblical hospitality. Younger women are experiencing firsthand the spiritual gifts of hospitality, and the more examples they have, the more it becomes second nature for them to respond in kind. Many are now opening their own homes and cooking and sharing meals with friends and neighbors like they never have before. As they build confidence in their skills, they are generously taking meals to new moms and serving others. It's been amazing to see how through Heartfelt we are changing the course of a generation who otherwise may not have learned hospitality. And as a result of mothers now preparing meals in their homes, more families are now sitting down around the dinner table together on a regular basis.

One of the strongest messages of our hospitality focus is that by thinking of others and fostering relationships, women are building a base of support for themselves. They are arming themselves with very practical skills that help them to be a support for their family and friends. We all need women we can call on when a need arises in our lives. We want someone who loves God, respects the Lord's Word, and will stand beside us. These women, through our Titus 2 discipline, build a network of caring support.

In any contemporary town or city today, it is normal for young women, wives, and mothers to be separated from meaningful connections with their own "first" families. They are disconnected for multiple reasons: geography, broken homes, or painful pasts. These women, detached from their biological families, and perhaps from their former spiritual families, need healthy, godly people to help them live life successfully God's way. But many do not have a godly person in their lives to remind them that Jesus loves them and to show them how to live life in a God-honoring way. Many of them need help to do life differently than their families of origin did, if they grew up in situations that were spiritually and/or emotionally unhealthy. Many families did not model or even teach faith, and their adult children, as first-in-the-family Christians, are looking for living examples of biblical faith.

Through our Titus 2 ministry, we're giving them that model, and we're creating bonds between women of faith to help facilitate the process of spiritual growth. Some of these younger women may never otherwise share even a meal—much less share life—with anyone in the family of God. Many of them will remain lonely, disconnected, frightened, anxious, and cut off from spiritually influential people.

Through sharing homes and hospitality, struggles and triumphs, real life and spiritual lessons, we move beyond shallow, surface conversations and deepen our interactions. When genuine relationships are built in the family of God, they never go away. Such friends are eternally linked as "forever family" with deep emotional and spiritual bonds that will last. They are relationships which will continue to bless friends of faith for years to come.

In the end, what we've done through this Titus 2 ministry has been great for the women who are taught and loved, and it is equally wonderful for those older women who serve them. God instructs us to teach the young so they can live faith-centered, meaningful lives, and doing this also builds and strengthens the mature Christian women's faith. As mentors, we gain greatly from the experience, as well. The Bible lessons, the prayers, and the personal sharing times are as important and necessary for the older women, many of whom are now widows, as they are to their younger friends.

Several years ago, I received this note from Ruth M., one of our Heartfelt mentors. (We call them Heart Moms.)

What an exciting time in our lives to have such an opportunity to help others see what we have found in following Jesus. Being one of the chiefest of sinners, I truly know that my dysfunctions in my journey and the lessons I've learned are ones that my young friends are currently learning. I want to give them the opportunity to see one, so tarnished with bad choices, traumatic losses, and a lot of sinning, who overcame with trusting and obeying and accepting the gift of the Cross. I feel blessed to have made the choice to be a Heart Mom and share my journey of faith.

Healthy churches are continuously seeking out programs to help church members grow stronger and become more committed to their faith and to their families. Heartfelt's experience in women's ministry is that churches grow numerically and spiritually when the church community is designed to be supportive of women, their faith, and their families.

Our plan and our mission is to help women of God develop meaningful, intentional relationships among and across the generations in order to encourage deeper spiritual growth, stronger faith in God, and healthier families.

So I am reminded that it is truly a blessing and a gracious gift from God that during her painful and pitiful days, dear Mindy was connected with a church that had women who were willing to spend hours, weeks, and even years investing in her life and in the lives of her husband and children. How incredibly gracious God was to insure that Mindy was surrounded by a life-giving ministry of women who were prepared to pour into her life large quantities of the spiritual, emotional, and physical resources she so desperately needed.

There are lots of "Mindys" out there who need to experience God's love expressed to them through the lives of godly "mothers." What if a group of women from your church were to purposely declare that they would spend time each month coordinating and developing ways to respond to the needs of younger families in your church? What if this group of older women were to spend focused time praying each month for the younger women who need care and attention? What if this group of mature, caring Christian women were determined to bond tightly with the younger wives and mothers in your church? And what if they met together regularly to build bonds of friendship that focused on mentoring and spiritual growth? What would be different in your church as a result?

Does your church need more spiritually healthy women practicing the principles of Titus 2:3-5?

For more information or to learn how your church can begin a women's Titus 2 program, go to www.heartfeltministries.org.

Reference

Kirby, J. (2015). *Heartfelt*. Nashville: Worthy Books.

Roy Smith, Ph.D., M.Div.

Dr. Roy Smith has worked for more than 35 years as a psychologist and counselor to men and their families. Pennsylvania Counseling Services (pacounseling.com), which he began out of his home, offers a variety of services in 10 counties in south central Pennsylvania. Roy is also an ordained minister with the Evangelical Church Alliance. He developed LiveUp Resources (liveupresources.com), a ministry that produces books and video series to guide men, women, and youth toward their God-given potential, contributing to the overarching goal of positively changing our culture. Roy has also written several books in the area of men's issues, including *Bull*, *Being God's Man*, *Basic Warrior Training*, *Manhood Journey* (Volumes 1-5), *Why Not Try To Hit The Real Target—Men*, and *You're Not Dead Yet*. He recently began writing *The Campfire Gang* series, which now includes eight published volumes, to teach young boys biblical leadership and character-building skills through an engaging storyline. Roy has a master of divinity degree and a master's and a doctorate degree in clinical psychology. He is married to Jan, who is also a psychologist; they have two children, a son-in-law, and two grandsons.

CHAPTER 24

How to Develop an Effective Men's Mentoring Ministry

Roy Smith, Ph.D., M.Div.

She sat down in my office, crossed her arms, and leaned back.

"He's just turned into a different man since we got married. Back then he promised to be a loving husband to me, a dad to our kids, and a leader at home, but now all I see is an irrational, lazy child. He hates his job but won't do anything about it, and he brings that anger out on me and the kids every day. Or even worse than his outbursts, he just ignores us and watches TV all night. He pretty much just sleeps, works, sits on the couch, sleeps, works... you get the picture. He never wants to spend time with me—unless he wants sex. Actually, he doesn't spend time with anyone anymore."

In my experience counseling couples, I have heard these same disappointments spill out of the mouths of hundreds of wives. Women recognize their husbands' dissatisfaction and passivity. Children sense their father's emotional distance. They feel disconnected, unwanted, and lonely as he withdraws into his fears and anxieties. If unaddressed, these symptoms and behaviors often lead to more serious mental health concerns for the whole family. Most churches underestimate the effect men have on the wellbeing of an entire family or community, and the resulting importance of effectively guiding the men in their congregation. A child may spend several hours at church on Sunday learning that God is their Father, but their experience with their earthly father over the following six days often skews, discounts, or even erases that message. A wife wants to communicate intimately with her husband, yet he responds with "I don't know," "fine," or gives her a blank look. A son senses his father's unwillingness to connect with him, contributing to his eventual exodus from the church as a young adult. Because of their lack of godly male role models, young men often conclude that church is for women. Supportive relationships between men diminish, leaving them to face job challenges, relationship problems, sinful impulses, physical diseases, and other life difficulties alone.

These issues typically occur because the church lacks a clear plan and suitable funds to invest in the development of men and their role as leaders. Fatherless boys need mentors. Young girls need godly examples of how a healthy man should treat them. Women look for trustworthy male friends and supportive husbands. The elderly need physical support. Investing in the men of the church can create a resource on which the rest of the congregation can rely.

In my book *Why Not Try to Hit the Real Target—Men*, I set forth the case that one of the chief goals of a pastor should be to help the men in his church experience complete spiritual growth. This includes walking intimately with Jesus, understanding God's Word, consistently applying their faith to all of their relationships, and addressing spiritual or emotional issues in their life. A church's work to develop and strengthen manly leaders—to increase their relational influence within the church, build up the families they represent, and expand their impact in their community— enhances all other areas of the church's mission. When males exchange their aimlessness and passivity for a grounded identity in God, the church gains a powerful resource to help effectively carry out its mission.

One study (CDPO, 1999) found that in families with a mother who regularly practiced religion and a non-practicing father, only 1.5 percent of children continued to practice religion regularly; however, if the father regularly practiced religion, 44.2 percent of those children adopted the same practice. This chapter will look at several areas the church can focus on to help its men live spiritually strong, addiction free, relationally healthy, satisfying, and productive lives—while subsequently increasing the effectiveness of the whole church.

Many of the mental health issues that challenge men begin as a result of a male's inability to cope with and adapt to the common struggles all men face. Without access to positive mentorship, males allow destructive influences to guide their decision-making, often causing them to develop negative symptoms that further impede their ability to make good choices. Experiencing "the peace of God, which surpasses all understanding"

(Philippians 4:7, NKJV) as well as the fruit of a Spirit-led life (Galatians 5:13-26) becomes difficult for males who struggle with managing their emotions, recognizing their offensive style of communication, listening to their conscience, behaving compulsively, sinning impulsively, abusing substances, dwelling on negative thoughts and fears, relying on problematic relationships, or dealing with an unbalanced biological chemistry. As Christ's representative, the church is responsible for portraying Jesus's message of redemption and positive change to men, along with teaching them to become Jesus's best. Helping men become more whole occurs when an effective men's ministry offers specific forms of guidance and counseling for the entrenched issues mentioned above.

When we recognize and understand the areas of life that are difficult for men, we can begin to guide them through these challenges. Every man will encounter five specific struggles throughout his life: the search for manhood, male isolation, emotional disconnect, cultural attacks, and pursuing manly action. These struggles result from a sin-filled world colliding with an imperfect male. Understanding these challenges will help the church effectively deal with the emotional, cognitive, relational, physical, and spiritual needs of its men. Jesus calls us to be fully functioning men of God; his mission of making disciples (Matthew 28:16-20) demands that we fully develop the potential and skills he has given us. Studying our possible areas of weakness can also help us prepare for the constant spiritual war around us (Ephesians 6:12).

Struggle 1: Searching for Manhood

Despite a male's strong desire to achieve manhood, he is often inhibited by an inability to figure out what manhood is. Unfortunately, in a world that groans under the stress of separation from God (Romans 8:22), cultural changes and distorted thinking have skewed the true definition of manhood. When manhood is defined by external achievements such as war and work, men overlook their responsibility to be present as positive role models to their family. When manhood is defined by a specific occupation rather than internal character, men find themselves angry and lost as the definition of men's and women's roles blur and change. When manhood is defined by immediate gratification, fathers ignore their need to sacrifice for the benefit of their child.

Other inadequate definitions of manhood rely on age, driving ability, aggression, sexual prowess, money, and fashion. Our culture rarely teaches or expects men to display mature, Christ-like character traits such as integrity, perseverance, courage, toughness, sacrifice, contribution, wise risk-taking, protection, respect, or honor. Jesus, the Ultimate Man, cried over Jerusalem (Luke 19:41-44) and the death of Lazarus (John 11:32-36). He recognized the internal pain of the Samaritan woman (John 4:1-26), intellectually sparred with the hypocritical Pharisees (Matthew 22:15-40), and physically demonstrated his respect for and protection of the temple and what it stood for (Matthew 21:12-13). Unfortunately, this emotional expressiveness has been cast aside as aimless, and passive males fail to become mature men who uphold structure and leadership. As a result of this great loss, our culture continues to move toward darkness.

Some research suggests that by age three-and-a-half boys develop beliefs of what males do and what females do (Brizendine, 2010). Once these beliefs are established, the hormone MIS (Müllerian inhibiting substance) causes them to avoid behaviors they perceive as feminine. These early beliefs are deeply engrained and serve as a code of conduct. I believe this tendency has contributed to the current exodus of males between age 17 and 27 from the church. These young males observe how the different genders involve themselves in church and notice that the majority of church programming is geared toward women and children. This conclusion leads many males to define church as a stereotypic feminine interest.

The church can change this disastrous pattern by focusing on men's ministry and establishing a men's program that associates the church with manhood through emphasizing the characteristics of Jesus Christ, the Ultimate Man. Although it requires intentionality and involves a considerable investment of energy, the challenge of manhood and its virtues can be taught and seized upon. I have seen males of all ages and cultural backgrounds respond positively when a church's intervention meets their inherent drive to achieve manhood. Men over 80 years old have had tears in their eyes as their lifetime goal of achieving manhood has been affirmed within a church setting.

Our culture implicitly encourages men to live with an attitude of complacency. When manhood is defined as a series of positive behaviors or a regular confrontation with our self-destructive actions, males tend to respond to life differently. Instead of abstractly viewing sin as inevitable, a male can learn to judge his own actions as either manly or unmanly. Abstract theological concepts become relatable beliefs when a man learns that taking his wife out on a date is a manly act, while involving himself in pornography is not. In this way, manhood becomes a synonym for sanctification.

Struggle 2: The Isolation of Males

Many men struggle with the tendency to isolate themselves, often accepting the myth that living disconnected from a support system is manly. Territorial, aggressive, and competitive tendencies influence them to ignore their need for others. Many men have not been involved in a community of males striving with, confronting, and encouraging each other since their teenage years in high school sports. They now describe their close friendships with other men as non-existent. Studies show that most males claim not to have any close male friendships. Many rely on a series of acquaintances in order to avoid what they perceive as more "sticky" intimate relationships. Males often act on an underlying fear that close relationships bring with them an emotional obligation or responsibility that may limit their freedom.

The male tendency to avoid close relationships is usually manifested in an aversion toward change, meeting new people, and interacting in social environments. Instead of approaching new situations with courage, many men resort to unhealthy coping methods like social withdrawal or alcohol use. The symptoms that isolation can generate pave the way for future destructive relationships, an ongoing sense of loneliness, long-term depression, and addiction. Although essentially negative, feelings like depression and loneliness serve as unwanted consequences that can compel an isolated man to pursue the healthy companionship and mutual support experienced in interpersonal relationships (Brizendine, 2010). Maturing into manhood is demonstrated by a male's development of social skills, awareness of the needs of others, and ability to manage the emotional responses of both himself and others. Jesus serves as an excellent example

389

of how to deal with a wide range of people, opinions, and viewpoints while maintaining focus on God's will. It is important for the church to spend time developing the social skills of its men so they can better follow Jesus's command to love others.

Spiritually speaking, we know that the predators of life attack us when we are lonely, discouraged, or living with secret sin. This fact highlights the importance of developing a strong community of men within the church setting. Such a community gives men the opportunity to work on the relationship skills they need in their homes and workplaces. Through the continual dynamics of confrontation, encouragement, mutual sharing, celebration, and accountability, men effectively sharpen each other's identity and character (Proverbs 27:17). This environment allows men to process the important decisions and challenges they face daily. By speaking into each other's lives, these men act as representatives of Jesus. Prayer, biblically-based discussion, and conversations about their personal journey help men develop their spirituality.

Jesus's example demonstrated the importance of relationships. He expressed a wide range of social skills, maintained mutually-supportive friendships, and contributed to the life of each individual he met. He modeled humanity's need for a diverse group of people to serve as a support system. Jesus had over 12 individuals in his support system; shouldn't we have at least six?

When speaking at different conferences, I often ask males the following question: "If life were to suddenly crash in on you, could you name six men you could call on and know they would be there for you?" Most men have trouble naming one non-relative; most women can name six fairly quickly. A church, sports team, club, military unit, or bar can each help a man build a support team—I wonder which one God views as the best source?

As a brief aside, I want to mention two ways many churches unknowingly limit their effectiveness by overlooking the importance of male involvement. First, while couples' groups can aid a man's development, they cannot meet his need for a band of brothers. Mixed gender groups can limit a man's growth because of the differences in how males and females communicate. The male tendency to put up a false front and the sensitive nature of certain topics make it less likely for a male to be completely honest in mixed gender groups. When a church focuses its energy solely on couples' groups, it often overlooks the need to address vital issues that are specific to men.

Second, having counseled numerous pastors over the years, I have found that even they often struggle with the male tendency to want to isolate themselves. This fact may contribute to the statistical improbability of pastors initiating and leading men's groups. As men themselves, they often have difficulty recognizing or wanting to meet their own basic need for support. Most women will wholeheartedly support their church's decision to create opportunities for men to meet and grow spiritually together. Wives know that they cannot meet all of their husband's relational and social needs, even though their husbands often expect them to. This leaves many women frustrated as they try to cope with issues that only a group of men can properly address.

Struggle 3: Being Emotionally Disconnected

Our culture works to destroy men by encouraging them not to feel. Basic emotional responses like crying are defined as childish. Males are expected to overcome the natural fears of life by denying the healthy anxiety they experience. Our culture teaches young boys to be tough above all else, suppressing other emotional responses that conflict with this image. With all these factors working against them, males often struggle with managing their emotional responses and expressing their feelings to others.

God created humans with a smorgasbord of emotional capabilities, but life and cultural and parental influences often limit people's emotional expression. Males learn that anger is the chief acceptable feeling, which appeals to their aggressive hormone testosterone. As a result, males often learn to express emotions, especially anxiety or sadness, through anger. No one can get through life without being hurt in some way. We all experience pain because of our own choices, the negative acts of others, and life circumstances that are beyond our control. A man must learn to recognize his feelings, put them into words, and talk about them with others so that he can gain emotional support and do "grief work." This process allows a man to move beyond his disappointment. Many mental health issues are linked to a negative life event that has never been emotionally digested. One painful experience can overshadow a man's self-definition *for the rest of his life.* Rather than dealing with their issues head-on, men tend to hold their emotional freedom hostage, sowing the bitter seeds of unforgiveness, self-condemnation, and stunted emotional growth.

Another problem that men run into is treating their feelings the same way they treat their thoughts. Thoughts contain timelines; they are linear and can be neatly organized and compartmentalized. Emotions, on the other hand, are usually blended together. When a father has unprocessed emotions that result in frequent flashbacks to his time at war, they affect his ability to be vulnerable and love his family well. When a man experiences a life loss, he must work through his grief and process his feelings within an emotionally supportive relationship. Jesus expressed grief and connected to his emotional makeup. As the time of his death approached, he drew on his closest relationships for prayer and support (Matthew 26:36-38). An effective church ministry acts as a catalyst for men to build these types of relationships and find mutual support during the natural griefs of life.

When a male remains stuck in an emotionally disconnected or dysfunctional state, he limits the level of intimacy he can experience with others. Without processing his own feelings, he cannot feel or express empathy for others. In this way, a husband's lack of emotional development harms his wife. This factor alone causes many women to support church activities that equip their husbands to strengthen their relationships. Developing emotional intelligence can also improve a man's work life. Leadership requires a man to help everyone around him be more productive. This type of motivation happens most often through his interpersonal interactions. A man can limit the prevalence of sexual harassment, hostile work environments, and other negative work experiences simply by expressing all of who God created him to be within the workplace.

By providing programming that teaches men to express their God-given emotions, the church can help limit some of the mental health and addiction issues males would otherwise experience. God created us to be relational with him and with each other, saying, "It is not good for the man to be alone" (Genesis 2:18, NIV). Emotions serve as the social "grease" within these relationships. As stated in the book *Why Not Try to Hit the Real Target—Men*:

By providing a forum for encouraging men's relationships with each other, the church provides a support structure for talking about and grieving the losses of life. Developing the ability to love God, others and oneself in Christ-like ways is a significant manhood achievement (Mark 12:30). Men must be encouraged to talk to each other in ways that build emotional bonds and stimulate spiritual growth (p. 61).

Struggle 4: The Culture—Always in Attack Mode

Modern media constantly reinforces our culture's negative perceptions of manhood. Commercials manipulate men by stimulating their sex drive in order to sell products. Sitcoms portray fathers who speak and act in inappropriate ways while their wives and children attempt to make up for their inadequacies. Our culture also discounts a man's responsibility to act respectfully. It attempts to suppress natural male aggression by neutering, domesticating, and encouraging passivity in men. There is a difference between violence and violating others (which, appropriately, is rarely condoned) and limiting the male process of wrestling with others so that they can discover and develop their full potential. Men are aggressive, but many males accept our current culture of low expectations and live down to it.

God calls each man to fulfill a specific purpose (Jeremiah 1:5); ignoring this call will only lead to further mental and relational health struggles. Victor Frankl, who wrote about his concentration camp experiences, reinforced the idea that everyone must have a sense of meaning in their life in order to be whole (Frankl, 2006). When a man does not build his life on a meaningful relationship with God, he may misunderstand his designed purpose. God's purpose for an individual can only be fully developed within his plan. God created each man to be his artist by reflecting his identity and soul through some type of expressive action or accomplishment (Romans 1:20). God's plan is expressed when a mechanic accurately diagnoses a car's defect, or when a teacher guides a student to recognize truth through paying attention to multiple levels of an experience. Untapped or underdeveloped potential haunts many men, and the disease of male passivity has become an epidemic. Individuals who sit around complaining or fail to get off the couch of life put themselves at risk when they do not ask God for his empowerment to be cultural change agents.

Our culture also harms males by suppressing their natural curiosity and desire to learn. Much of our current educational system is verbally-based rather than action-oriented. Since only a small percentage of males possess high verbal skills, few succeed in this type of setting. Young boys often believe something is wrong with them because they do not want to sit quietly. When boys equate school and learning with boredom and frustration, they stifle their curious tendencies and potential skills. God has given each man unique interests that, when developed, can aid the entire community. The church can guide men toward their natural gifts by understanding the wide diversity of masculine skills. This focus encourages each man to contribute his own unique interests to the body of Christ (1 Corinthians 12). Whether a man volunteers as a greeter or cooks eggs for a prayer breakfast, he is sharing and exercising his faith and becoming spiritually stronger as a result. The Christian culture often harms its mission by attempting to draw men in through teaching abstract theological concepts and rules. Instead, the church must first meet a man where he is by addressing his specific needs and skills, simultaneously showing him how to apply biblical teaching to his everyday life. This approach allows men to express and celebrate each other's gifts.

Additionally, by establishing an effective men's ministry, churches can help men share their faith with others. Many males feel inadequate discussing their faith, just like they do when they share any of their abstract thoughts. Instead, these men can invite a friend to an organized church program that reflects their own beliefs. Unfulfilled potential leads to depression, anxiety, and general life dissatisfaction. Helping each man fulfill the Great Commission within his own skill set blesses both the man and the church community.

An effective men's ministry confronts the culture's constant attack by challenging men to live according to Christ-like standards. It expects men to follow their God-given dreams, and it creates church events that help men express their specific ministry calling while at the same time meeting their own spiritual needs. Men often experience spiritual growth by participating in projects that contribute to the community. Encouraging men to take action in this way confronts their negative thoughts and behaviors, challenges them to understand their complexity (Psalm 139), and motivates them to use all of who they are for God's glory. God's message of redemption and purpose contradicts the culture's message that men are simple, sexual, aimless, and angry. The church can uphold a code of honor and a standard of behavior that will inspire men to say to the world, "I am not like how you define me to be—I am God's."

It should be noted that those who attempt to create a positive spiritual environment for men will become the focus of cultural attack. Satan knows that by attacking men he can simultaneously oppress and discourage the women and distort the thinking of the children who look up to them. The process of leading men will challenge you to test the authenticity of your faith. I believe Satan is a strong opponent who knows well the positive domino effect that happens when formerly passive males sacrifice themselves for a greater cause and use their gifts for God's glory. An immature, ungodly male lies at the root of many of our culture's problems. For permanent cultural change to occur, the church must unleash the power that godly men bring, which is certainly a force to be reckoned with.

Struggle 5: What Does a Real Man Do?

The first struggle we discussed addressed the need to define manhood from a godly perspective, which can then be positively reinforced by a church men's group that guides men to define manhood through an understanding of Jesus's character. Struggle 5 steps further into this definition of manhood by addressing the need to translate a Christ-like identity into Christ-like action. God designed men to move. The hormone testosterone compels men to pursue territorial conquests, master their physical environment, physically protect what they love, climb the social ladder, and compete with other men for status. It draws men toward challenges that measure their strength, test their limits, and stretch their personal boundaries (especially in adolescence). Men possess a natural attraction to action. This instinct was keenly displayed when Peter attempted to walk on water to show his faith in Christ (Matthew 14:25-29).

Just like God gave Adam a specific job to do in the Garden of Eden (Genesis 2:15), God also gives each man today a specific job to complete.

When asked to describe himself, most men will include what they do for a living. The kinesthetic results of finishing work-related tasks help a man develop himself and understand who he is. Men often lose their sense of wellbeing and experience mental and relational health issues when their work is disrupted for an extended period of time; in fact, it takes longer for a man to recover from the loss of a job than from the loss of a loved one (Rath & Harter, 2010). Several mental and emotional needs are met through a man's job. Beyond financial compensation, a man's job challenges him to reach his full potential and provides him with a sense of meaning, self-respect, connection, and contribution.

Men need a safe space to be able to talk about work issues and learn how to live out their faith at their job. The women's movement left many males confused, angry, and withdrawn because their sense of identity and manhood relied too much on what they did for a living. This existential crisis points to the problems that occur when an individual or culture overemphasizes external achievements. If a man does not address his internal emotions and thoughts, his behaviors will remain unchanged. The church can help men adjust to life by teaching them to measure their actions by the integrity of their character rather than by their occupation and job performance. The Bible highlights the importance of a man's walk with Jesus Christ and how it is reflected in his everyday life (1 Corinthians 3:1-3). As his relationship with Jesus matures, he becomes less dependent on finding his identity in upholding his external status, accomplishments, or occupation. Men will move toward this mindset when the church teaches them how to live out the fruit of the Spirit in their daily lives (James 1:22).

It is important that men take into consideration how their genetic predispositions and physical self-care can affect every area of their life. Men must learn to appreciate the way God crafted their physical bodies and ask for his help in achieving their body's full potential. Furthermore, it is imperative that men recognize their role as a servant leader in their home. They must strive to be present for their loved ones and make their lives better. A godly man chooses friends who will build him up rather than derail his manly efforts. He involves himself in ministry to fulfill his eternal purpose. He builds his life on God's Word so that he can accurately distinguish between Christ-like and immature behaviors.

Although God created men for action and challenge, many give in to passivity. Their skills and mental dexterity atrophy as they choose addictive behaviors and mindless distractions to numb their need for action. Life becomes a monotonous series of routines as men overlook the miraculousness of God's Spirit and instead choose a life of ease. Males become observers rather than responsible participants in their experiences. They suppress their instinct to sacrifice themselves for the greater good by allowing self-centered comfort to take precedence.

Jesus demonstrated manly action by balancing his time between prayer and actively meeting the needs of others. The church can guide men to do the same by providing opportunities for men to participate in godly action, while simultaneously growing closer to Jesus, forming bonds with each other, and learning about their God-given design. Like an unused car that slowly crumbles, a man who gives in to passivity wastes his potential. Men are most satisfied when their actions are inspired by God. When churches focus on motivating men toward godly action, they will simultaneously meet the spiritual and practical needs of the community and provide a way to alleviate some of the existential concerns that affect the mental and relational health of men.

A church with a strong men's program not only provides its attendees with an opportunity to grow spiritually, but also helps prevent mental and relational health issues by encouraging men to build personal support systems. Jesus Christ exemplified the type of support system that is essential to a man's success and life satisfaction. For these types of relationships to grow, a men's program must give participants enough time to talk about how they think and feel about life. Meeting times must be regular and consistent so that their natural defensiveness has time to develop into trust. Many churches unintentionally harm their males through the intermittent nature of their men's programs. Meetings scheduled with long periods of time between them inhibit strong, long-term relational connections between men. Irregular group meetings limit men from becoming as supportive and intimate as possible.

God calls the church to minister to all of its members. By focusing on the men of the congregation, churches will simultaneously benefit their families, friends, and communities. This process starts by addressing the five struggles of manhood and tackling the connected mental health and addiction issues head-on. Through an effective, Christ-centered church program, a male who is struggling with such issues can learn to rely on the support of a group of men working together. Jesus ministered to others on several levels while also maintaining a focused relationship with God. In the same way, the church can offer an opportunity for men to experience holistic growth through learning, praying, and talking with one another. It is this leadership response that will maximize the church's effectiveness within the community it is called to serve.

References

Brizendine, L. *The Male Brain*. New York: Broadway Books, 119, 19.

European Population Committee (CDPO). (1999). The demographic characteristics of linguistic and religious groups in Switzerland. *Council of Europe.* Retrieved from https://rm.coe.int/CoERMPublic CommonSearchServices/DisplayDCTMContent?documentId= 09000016804fb7b1

Frankl, V. (2006). *Man's Search for Meaning*. Boston: Beacon Press.

Rath, T., & Harter, J. (2010). *Wellbeing*. New York: Gallup Press, 17.

Smith, R. (2015). *Why not try to hit the real target: Men*. Pennsylvania Counseling Services.

Stephanie Holmes, M.A.

Rev. Stephanie C. Holmes, MA, Board Certified Christian Counselor, is a professional counselor, ordained minister, and certified autism specialist, but her credentials come from being the mother to an amazing Aspie (AS) teenage daughter. Stephanie's career focus changed when her eldest daughter was diagnosed with Asperger's in 2004. Her book, *Confessions of a Christian Counselor: How Infertility and Autism Grew My Faith,* was released fall of 2015.

Stephanie counsels/consults/coaches (AS) Aspie-NT couples from all over the world and consults with families to help their marriages move beyond surviving to thriving with an AS/ASD child. She can be contacted at www.counselorstephanieholmes.com.

CHAPTER 25

How to Develop an Effective Support Ministry for Parents of Autistic and Special Needs Children

Stephanie Holmes, M.A.

Many families who visit your church may have children, teens, or young adults with special needs or disabilities such as Autism Spectrum Disorder (ASD), Attention Deficit Hyperactivity Disorder (ADHD), anxiety disorders, learning differences, intellectual challenges, or communication delays that are not obvious when you are greeting the family at the door. This class of disabilities is often referred to as "hidden disabilities," and collectively represents a huge segment of the population.

When presenting in conferences, I often begin with a picture of my family and say, "Look at this great-looking family. They are picture perfect. Surely, they have no major issues, and this family would be a great asset to serve in your local church body." The problem with a picture is that it is a pose of one moment in time. The question is, "What does this family deal with when they are not posing? What are the issues, challenges, and stressors that are associated with hidden disabilities such as autism spectrum disorder/Asperger's Syndrome (ASD/AS)?"

In the past decade, there has been an explosion of information concerning autism awareness which has led to an international World Autism Awareness Day held in April each year. Many families in the autism community and persons on the autism spectrum are excited about this increase in overall public awareness. They are also ready for more understanding and acceptance of their often very private and painful struggles. They need people in the community to move from awareness to advocacy and then to action – which will lead them to more completely embrace persons and families with ASD/AS in various communities, including the church. We will explore and assess church culture, the prevalence of "hidden disabilities" (there are many kinds of special needs), family support needs, and finally practical strategies that can help more families experience church life in a way that more closely fits who they are and addresses the unique needs of their souls.

Assessment of Church Culture

It is wise to find persons who are already involved in ministering to the autism and special needs community and seek their guidance. Pastor Lamar Hardwick of New Community Church in LaGrange, Georgia, who is also a person on the autism spectrum, believes that before ministries begin intentional action toward the autism community, a church culture assessment is a crucial first step. His thoughts on ministering to the autism community include the following:

> When discussing the role of the local church ministering to the autism community, an important area to assess is the health of the church. This requires the pastor and church leaders to assess church culture. Church culture is most often the key to understanding the barriers to accomplishing the goals and vision of the church. To fully include the autism community, the church and its leaders must have a laser focus on caring for those in the autism community. Inconsistent vision is a thorn that crowds out the message of the gospel and the method of the local church to reach all groups with the power of the gospel. If the autism community is to be served, they must be part of the church's expressed vision.

Pastor Lamar gives three steps to help a church minister intentionally to the autism community:

Step 1: Create understanding. The first priority of this ministry in the church is to provide a safe space for the autism community by creating a culture of understanding. By creating an intentional culture of ongoing education, churches can empower their members and their community to move from autism awareness to autism acceptance to autism advocacy with action. Likewise, the church must understand the differences between the way neurodiverse brains process information and the way neurotypical brains process information.

Step 2: Create community. Most churches struggle to provide ministry for the autism community because they fear they will be unable to accommodate all of their unique needs. However, the number one thing the autism community needs is acceptance and compassionate understanding. Churches must have an attitude that seeks to help these families be rooted in the DNA and functional life of the church. The easiest way to accomplish this is by creating support groups for families impacted by autism. Every family—including those affected by autism—craves a sense of community.

Step 3: Create opportunities. This will look different in different churches, depending on the size of the church and resources available, but with training and intentionality, there are ways to better serve the family of a special needs child. There are also ways for persons on the spectrum and those having other special needs to be able to serve in the church, thus helping to create a sense of belonging, value, and community for the individual.

Awareness: Prevalence

Many times when I speak with pastors they tell me, "Stephanie, I do not think we have anybody like that at our church." Recently, I read an article in *USA Today* that spoke of the millions of persons with various disabilities unable to find a church that could meet their needs and the fact that they therefore felt excluded by the church. How prevalent are these hidden disabilities? According to the federal Centers for Disease Control and Prevention (CDC), one in six children have some form of developmental disability. The CDC website says, "These disabilities range from a mild disability such as speech or language impairment to serious developmental disorders such as intellectual disabilities that include cerebral palsy or autism." The CDC states the prevalence of autism in America as 1 child in 68. However, a National Health Statistics Report in November 2015 stated that the number could be as high as 1 in 45 children ages 3 through 17. Whether the official number is 1 in 45 or 1 in 68, autism (ASD/AS) affects hundreds of thousands of American families. Although you may not be aware of it, there is likely someone in your church who is on the autism spectrum, and the hidden disabilities in your church are likely to be more prevalent than you realize:

- Autism Spectrum Disorder: 1 in 68 or 1 in 45 children
- ADHD: 5.4 million children or 1 in 10 children
- Anxiety Disorders such as Obsessive Compulsive Disorder (now anxiety cluster disorders): 1 in 100 children
- Intellectual Disabilities: 7 out of 1,000 children
- Sensory Processing Disorder: 1 out of 20 children
- Cerebral Palsy: 1 out of 250 children
- Learning Differences (formerly Learning Disabilities): 1 out of 6 children

Acceptance: Ministering to the Family; Levels of Support at Different Stages

The Kubler-Ross stages of grief have been utilized for many years for understanding grief and loss due to death (Kubler-Ross, 1969). As grief expert H. Norman Wright has said, "Loss is loss. Grief is grief." Dr. Wright expounded on grief extending from loss through death, but loss of dreams, hope, and plans can also cause grief. These same stages of grief can occur in families when a child is diagnosed with special needs (Parent Companion, 2016). Though sequential, the stages of grief are not necessarily linear, nor do they manifest in the same way for each griever. The stages include periods of:

1. Denial and Isolation
2. Anger
3. Bargaining (sometimes accompanied by guilt)
4. Depression
5. Acceptance

My perspective regarding ASD/AS is twofold: as a counselor/minister and as a parent. My oldest daughter was diagnosed with Asperger's Syndrome/ AS (now called ASD level 1) in 2004. At that time I was a Licensed Professional Counselor (LPC) in private practice, and although my educational training had introduced me to the term Asperger's, it did not prepare me for the ensuing personal journey our family embarked on. Each family will approach their journey a little differently, and some may be offended if you suggest they need to grieve. My family's journey is outlined in *Confessions of a Christian counselor: How infertility and autism grew my faith.* I have included here my own journey with grieving (reprinted with permission from *Autism Asperger's Digest*).

> My type A personality was not going to let this diagnosis alter my life- DENIAL. I was right on track with Kubler-Ross' stages of grief. Denial can take the form of being in denial about the diagnosis, the prognosis of the diagnosis, or how the diagnosis will impact the life of the family unit. At this stage in the game, without knowing it my faith was in ME. I am smart and educated and I will do everything in my power to "help" her or "cure her" or make other people understand her. I spent a lot of time demanding answers from God and demanding He "fix this" so I could get on with my life plan. I became a little disillusioned with God that He was not "helping." As I attended every Autism conference I could find, and read every book on the shelf I could find about Asperger's, my disillusionment grew to anger. Even my grieving is Type A. I was right on schedule.

> The "Whys" with God became "Well God, if you don't handle this, I will!" There were many things to be angry with. The first anger was directed at the almighty public school system that was supposed to be helping her and helping me. It seems like they would WANT her to be successful in school and they would WANT to carry out the Individualized Educational Plan (IEP) and assist her,

but many did not. There were some beacons of hope in this time of trial by fire, but few who actually helped. Most teachers, special education teachers, administrators and county officials were ignorant about Asperger's in general and even more ignorant about Aspie girls. It was becoming obvious to me that my family was not always accepted at some church or community functions. Some would invite us but say "Well, we don't know if we can handle her." I grew angry at God because instead of growing a private practice I was spending every spare moment rescuing a teacher or school who was mishandling my daughter's ASD or reading up on preparing for an IEP meeting or learning more about Asperger's and finding nothing about Aspie girls. I knew something was wrong inside when often I was angry with my daughter for having this syndrome that was altering our life.

One cannot stay angry forever so I moved on to bargaining. "Ok God, if you will find her the right school or take this away from her I will...." "Ok God I will homeschool one year, but that is it; one year then You need to......" Bargaining did not go so well with me. I was still not in control of my situation no matter how hard I tried.

For some people the next stage is the hardest; thankfully for me my Type A personality wouldn't let me stay depressed very long. As I had to pull her from public school, give up my career, homeschool her, and turn my life to the world of learning about the spectrum, I was depressed. For some people this can lead to clinical depression and a professional counselor is needed, but it was here I began to wrestle with my faith. Apparently believing in ME and doing things MY way was not working. The focus of "helping her" was really more about "How can we get this under control so I can move about my life more freely." It was the homeschool year I truly got to know HER:

who she is, her unique personality, what set off reactions, what she liked and disliked, and how sensory issues come into play. As I finally began to understand HER, I finally made it to acceptance. That was my personal journey to acceptance as a mother. Her journey was a separate, longer journey to acceptance on different terms as the person on the spectrum living with the challenges and giftings of her AS diagnosis.

I am not of the mind that autism in and of itself is a gift. However, the PERSON with autism is a gift, and the PERSON with autism has dreams and challenges just like everyone else. It just so happens that the challenges are a little more pronounced. Autism represents a broad spectrum and the way it affects each family is different. Some may see autism as a gift while for others the diagnosis is the start of a long-term season of grief. It is also important to remember that each parent may be at a different grief stage.

What is very painful for a family struggling toward acceptance is either not being allowed to grieve or having their grief over-spiritualized. Many of my own clients have found it difficult to go to church. This can be especially true in some stereotypic charismatic/Pentecostal churches. When unrealized, the doctrine of divine healing can create a stigma for not having a "miraculous" story. These clients are still challenged by the trials of each day. As a Pentecostal believer I also felt this stigma and had often been told that my daughter's condition was demonic or spiritual and that through spiritual warfare – if I prayed hard enough or in a certain way – I would see my daughter delivered from the autism spirit. I absolutely believe in divine healing, but divine healing is not everyone's story. Many people's story is adjusting to and accepting the diagnosis; the miracle is relying on God every day to renew one's strength and trust in him when you do not understand the "whys." Let me urge you that being a good listener and admitting to what you do not know or understand is actually helpful.

For my fellow Pentecostal believers I include this statement from the official stance of the Assemblies of God doctrinal paper, entitled "Ministry to people with disabilities: A biblical perspective" (reprinted with permission).

Pentecostal evangelicals, believing that miracles still happen today, sometimes have difficulty dealing with people with permanent disabilities and with those who are not healed after much prayer. But does our theology include, along with our belief in supernatural miracles today, a biblical explanation for those who are not immediately healed or made whole? We accept death by old age, and even by accident; but constant reminders of many with mental and physical disabilities, who are not restored to full health and activity, seem to suggest that our belief or our faith is faulty. Our theology makes place for pain and suffering, because we have hope for healing and an end to pain. But how does our theology, our faith, and our practice handle the person who may never walk again or the mentally challenged child who may never participate in normal social interaction? A proper understanding of the gospel must boldly proclaim, even though we do not have all the answers, that the God who created the universe and all human life in it is aware of the tension His children feel. He expects us to be people of compassion as well as people of power.

To me, the most powerful phrase in this ministry statement is that we are to be people of compassion as well as people of power. Many times compassion, understanding, and following the command of Romans 12:15 (NIV) to "Rejoice with those who rejoice, and weep with those who weep" can comfort and encourage more than you realize.

Understanding the Family's Journey

In order to minister to the family of a child with special needs such as autism, it is important to understand some of the challenges and stressors with which the family may be struggling after receiving the diagnosis. These include:

- An often grueling diagnosis process
- Medical issues; frequent therapeutic appointments
- Financial struggles. Many therapies for autism or sensory issues are not covered by insurance. Often, the educational system cannot help the child fully, so a parent is forced to quit work to homeschool or the family must pay private school tuition.
- Strained extended family relationships. Many families do not live near extended family that can help; also some family members exclude themselves from the member with special needs.
- Isolation. Although autism and special needs are prevalent, many families do not have local support systems or groups to rely on for strength. Outings are exhausting, and many venues (including churches) do not or cannot support families with special needs. This is getting better, but there is a long way to go.
- Physical, mental, emotional, and spiritual exhaustion. Families are frequently going through this journey alone, and continuous caring for a member with special needs usually does not allow for self-care or respite.
- The education system. Many families are fighting or advocating each school year to get the resources their child needs to have equal rights at school. There are issues in gaining the resources, attending meetings, educating the educators, and in dealing with bullying issues that the child with special needs may encounter.
- Time management. Often families with a child who has special needs also have other neurotypical (NT) children. There is a tension in the home of broadening the world of the NT child while making the world of the special needs child smaller and more controllable.
- Ignorant people. Those people who see a child acting out without knowing or caring that the child may have a neurological problem may subsequently judge or demean the family for not managing the child's behavior "properly."

These factors often contribute to the growing rate of divorce in families with persons on the autism spectrum. Depending on the study you read, families with a special needs child encounter a higher divorce rate which can create secondary issues as blended family challenges overlay the already complex layer of autism. Empirical data are lacking on the actual divorce rate, but a study in the Journal of Autism Developmental Disorders from 2011 observed, "Despite the little research dedicated to ASD and divorce/separation, the marital relationship has been found to be negatively impacted by raising a child with ASD. Previous studies of parents of children with ASD have shown decreased marital satisfaction when compared to parents of typically developing children and parents with children of other disabilities." Much emerging research confirms that if a marriage/family has a strong support group and there is a strong marital unit, the family can actually become more resilient against divorce. Should not the church be leading the way in supporting and building resilient marriages?

Action: Practical Ways to Minister to the Family

Families with special needs may be exhausted, so permission to rest and be served is a gift. However, I am by no means saying that having a special needs family member disqualifies one from serving. Depending on where that person is in their journey, he or she may be ready to serve in their local church, but when a new family with a special needs member comes to the church, permission to rest and have a place to receive self-care and grow spiritually is very important. This is not the family to ask to be in the 20% who do 80% of the work.

We certainly cannot neglect spiritual strength. Often, children's ministries not being equipped to help a special needs child keeps families from being able to attend church. Parents may solve this by alternating weekly; one parent attends service while the other stays with the child. However, having trained workers available that help in that capacity is a huge support. Specialized child care becomes a major issue for parents attending any church function.

Depending on where the parent(s) are in their acceptance process, they may be struggling in their faith or having difficulty trusting in God and his goodness. Helping them find their faith or hope again in a loving, nonjudgmental manner can aid in their journey of acceptance.

Often there are children without special needs in this family who may be limited in opportunities because they have a special needs sibling. Pairing families who may partner with this family will help broaden the world and experience of the typically developing sibling. Parents may carry false guilt because they are not able to do certain activities or go places with the neurotypical sibling. This is an opportunity for the body of Christ to function as an extended family to serve the siblings of the special needs child.

With the stressors and challenges mentioned previously, date nights or short getaways together as a couple can be nearly impossible due to time, finances, or lack of childcare options. Churches in a community may need to break denominational barriers and fears of "sheep swapping" to host a joint "Parent's Night Out" in order to strengthen marital ties and provide time and opportunity for such couples to have self-care.

Apathy: Ramifications of Isolation

We have discussed the fact that parents of special needs children tend to express lower marital satisfaction and have a higher divorce rate than parents of neurotypical children. Without support and resources for marriage and family, isolation can lead not only to divorce but also to disillusionment with church, the body of Christ, and even faith in God. More people leave the church because of how they were treated in the church by the people of God than because of personal issues with God.

What about the person on the spectrum who may feel excluded or even abandoned by the church? Feelings of isolation and rejection are leading to higher rates of suicide in spectrum teens. Voluminous research indicates that many persons on the spectrum feel abandoned or rejected by the church. Although people on the spectrum struggle interpersonally with making and keeping friendships, this does not mean that they do not want to have friends or that they somehow lack the God-created desire to experience a sense of belonging. We were created to be with people and to be part of a fellowship of believers. Spectrum teens are known to be literal, black-and-white thinkers who often need evidence or proof, and faith is a subject that, by definition, does not involve proof. Many spectrum teens have average to above average intelligence and they value knowledge. But spectrum teens who reject faith generally do so not solely because there was a lack of science to prove various principles.

The reason most spectrum teens leave the church is a lack of connection to—or outright rejection by—peers and adults. Regarding spectrum teens and adults who have left the church, the biggest issue is usually what they refer to as the hypocrisy of the church members; not so much that they are "caught" in the "big sins," but that they do not feel loved and accepted for who they are. It seems these spectrum individuals do pay attention to the Bible lessons and sermons about Christians being called to love, but the biggest hypocrisy to them is how believers treat them. A common stumbling block for them is dealing with so-called Christian peers at school or having negative experiences with Christians at church. Many individuals on the spectrum believe that although their school, job, or peers may have rejected them, the church will be a safe refuge; sadly, that is not the experience they report. Research shows that being rejected is the main reason that by the age of 13 nearly 50-60% of spectrum teens have contemplated suicide; this is double the norm for neurotypical teens. When asked why they attempted suicide, the most common answer given is isolation or rejection.

Creating an Atmosphere of Agape Love

As a church we need to model for – and train – our children and teens how to show Christ's love to those who are different from us, whether those differences involve a fairly obvious physical or mental disability or a hidden disability such as autism. We need to do a better job of equipping our youngest congregants with examples and tools to help them demonstrate love and acceptance to others. My own daughter's biggest bullies have been Christian teens from the most prestigious churches in our area. Even in trying to attend FCA or other Christian-based events in the community, she was rejected because of social skill deficits. We can start by teaching our youth John 13:35 (NIV): "By this everyone will know that you are my disciples, if you love one another." Love and acceptance are the most valuable gifts we can give to persons on the spectrum. The best way to teach acceptance is to model it and be intentional about it. Many local schools are trying to bridge the gap of awareness between neurotypical teens and those with special needs by building opportunities to interact with those who are neurologically different or differently abled. Not only can Christian students be involved in these school-based programs, but church youth groups can also build a bridge by reaching out in "buddy" programs that pair Christian neurotypical youth with those special needs students who are craving community, love, acceptance, and friendship.

Ministering to Children on the Autism Spectrum

The following practical tips for ministering to persons on the spectrum come from author Ron Sandison, who is also a person on the autism spectrum. Ron provided these tips for churches/ministries:

> Ask the family what they need in support or what their child may need in order to feel comfortable in the children's program or to remain in service. Do not assume. Ask. Even if you cannot provide everything they need, being asked is a gift. This can range from places they can take the child to watch the service if the child becomes disruptive to supports the child may need in the children's program.
>
> If the child is able to attend Sunday School or the children's group, it is best to have an additional volunteer who is knowledgeable of autism and who can provide extra help for the children's worker. It is important to discuss a safety plan with the parents, to understand what may trigger the child to have a meltdown, and to have strategies in place to deal with the meltdown.
>
> Structure and visual presentations are very important to the child with autism. Providing more structure and communication to the child about the order of events and how things will occur is helpful for meltdown prevention because it can reduce anxiety.

Think of all the symbolic and abstract religious phrases that are part of our Christian services, such as under the blood of Jesus, fishers of men, born again, second birth, Jesus is in your heart, take up your cross, and others. Children with autism are literal thinkers and may not understand this language. Allow them to ask questions, and be prepared to explain these concepts in a way the child can understand and that will have meaning to them.

Children with autism tend to be visual learners, so illustrating concepts with pictures and other visual aids is very helpful. Many have sensory issues to sound. If there will be loud parts of the story or loud music, be prepared with headphones to help the child be able to manage the sounds.

Autistic children do not like surprises in the schedule. Cue them when things are about to change or transition.

If the child is fidgety or needs to stim, requiring them to sit in a chair and be still is not possible. Having fidget toys or a wiggle seat can help them stay connected to the group and engaged in learning. If a child hates a certain activity, do not force the child to participate; allow them to watch or observe without guilt or shame for not participating.

Ron reminds us that as the body of Christ we should care for each other's needs and reach out to help children on the spectrum understand God's love for them and that he has a purpose for their lives. The church should be a place where every child and teen feels accepted and loved. As the church, we need to be equipped to serve even the littlest (or "least of these") in our congregations.

My concluding question is: will we *be* the church? Will we reach out to families and persons on the autism spectrum or with other special needs? Or will they feel rejection because they cannot serve the way we may need people to serve or because they are socially awkward or have various personal quirks? As Christians, we must take the lead in being proactive in loving and serving this population. We need to offer hope and acceptance and be a safe space for those who may be wired differently from us. Each body of believers has different resources and challenges, but we are all equipped at some level to give the greatest gifts of love and acceptance.

Suggested Readings for More Information/Training

From a Mother's View:

Colson, Emily. (2010). *Dancing with Max.* Zondervan Publishing.

Holmes, Stephanie. (2015). *Confessions of a Christian counselor: How autism and infertility grew my faith.* Highway 51 Publishing. Website: www.counselorstephanieholmes.com

From a Person on the Spectrum and Father's view:

Sandison, Ron. (2016). *A parent's guide to autism: Practical advice, biblical wisdom.* Charisma House Publishing. Website: https://www.spectruminclusion.com/author/ronsandison/

Hardwick, Lamar. [Author, speaker, pastor, and person on the autism spectrum.] Resources for the church and families at www.themighty.com

For Further Disability Inclusion Training:

Joni and Friends: Website: http://www.joniandfriends.org/education-and-training/

Accessibility summit and conferences for churches: Website: http://accessibilitysummit.org/

Tips for churches on how to include those with special needs: Website: https://theinclusivechurch.wordpress.com/

References

Autism Speaks. *New government survey pegs autism prevalence at 1 in 45.* Retrieved from: https://www.autismspeaks.org/science/science-news/new-government-survey-pegs-autism-prevalence-1-45

Assemblies of God Belief Positions (2000). *Ministry to people with disabilities: A biblical perspective.* Retrieved from: http://ag.org/top/beliefs/position_papers/pp_downloads/pp_disabilities.pdf

CDC ASD Data and Statistics. Website: http://www.cdc.gov/ncbddd/autism/data.html

Freedman, B., Kalb, L., Zablotsky, B., & Stuart, E. (2011). Relationship status among parents of children with autism spectrum disorders: A population-based study. *Journal of Autism Developmental Disorders.* Published online at: http://fathersnetwork.org/wp-content/uploads/2013/11/Freedman-JADD-marriage-study.pdf

Hardwick, L. Email interview with the author. August 12, 2016.

Holmes, S. (2013). How autism grew my faith. *Autism Asperger's Digest.* Retrieved from: http://autismdigest.com/autism-grew-faith/

Kubler-Ross, E. (1969). *On death and dying.* New York: Macmillan.

Parent Companion (2016). Understanding the stages of grief. Retrieved from: http://www.parentcompanion.org/article/understanding-the-stages-of-grief

Pinsky, M. (2011). Churches mustn't neglect the disabled. *USA Today.* Retrieved from: http://usatoday30.usatoday.com/news/opinion/forum/2011-01-10-column10_ST_N.htm

Soraya, L. (2010). The pain of isolation: Asperger's and suicide: Why would a person with Asperger's feel driven to suicide? *Psychology*

Today. Retrieved from: https://www.psychologytoday.com/blog/aspergers-diary/201011/the-pain-isolation-asperger-s-and-suicide

Soraya, L. (2009). Bullying, hypocrisy, and church: An Asperger perspective on religion. *Psychology Today*. Retrieved from: https://www.psychologytoday.com/blog/aspergers-diary/200909/bullying-hypocrisy-and-church-asperger-perspective-religion

Wright, H. (2009, 2011). Seminar on grief at AACC world conferences.

Daniel Nehrbass, Ph.D.

Daniel Nehrbass is the President of Nightlight Christian Adoptions, home of the Snowflakes® Embryo Adoption program. He has worked as a pastor, professional counselor, and adjunct professor of biblical studies at Biola University. His articles have been published in numerous adoption and religious magazines, and he is the author of four books: *Praying Curses: The Therapeutic and Preaching Value of the Imprecatory Psalms; Who's Using You?: Making Yourself Available for God's Use; A Biblical Model of Church Decision Making: Guidelines for Leadership, Decisions, and Governance* and *Beyond Kum Ba Ya*.

Dr. Nehrbass earned a Ph.D. in Practical Theology (emphasis in pastoral counseling) at Fuller Seminary. He completed his Th.M. from Talbot School of Theology, his M.Div. at the Southern Baptist Theological Seminary, and his M.A. in Ministerial Education at Indiana Wesleyan University. Daniel and his wife, Kristina (his best friend since they were thirteen years old) have six children and live in southern California. His hobbies include rock climbing, off-roading, hiking, skiing, and reading.

CHAPTER 26

How to Develop an Effective Support Ministry for Adoptive and Foster Parents

Daniel Nehrbass, Ph.D.

Spiritual Battle

We adopted Aidana from Kyrgyzstan when she was five years old. Her first two weeks were the some of the most difficult weeks of our lives. Frustrated with so many changes in her life over which she had no control, and angry that she didn't speak our language, she bit, spit, kicked, and screamed. One particular night my wife was holding her in bed with her, trying to get her to fall asleep, but Aidana was inconsolable. My wife said, "It was like a scene straight out of Poltergeist. She mustered a deep voice, and while spitting on me she cursed at me repeatedly, 'Suka! Suka! Suka!' I prayed for her aloud, and when I began saying, 'Dear God,' she said 'Niet God! Niet God!'" Aidana didn't even know what "God" meant in English, but her spirit knew! Pastors and counselors should be mindful of Paul's words in Ephesians 6:12 (NIV), "For our struggle is not against flesh and blood, but against the rulers, against the authorities, against the powers of this dark world and against the spiritual forces of evil in the heavenly realms."

When we say, "The struggle is real," we recognize that there is a real spiritual struggle as we wrestle over the eternal life and earthly joy of these precious adopted children. After a couple weeks, Aidana reached a very normal place with our family and learned to communicate. A year later it was clear the spiritual battle had been won. She was in the car with my wife, and she said something disrespectful. My wife ignored the comment, but about ten minutes later Aidana said, "Why did I say that? I'm sorry, Mommy." The voice of the Holy Spirit was victoriously able to reach into this six-year-old girl's heart.

The remainder of this chapter will address many of the other struggles which accompany adoption.

Rearranged Lives

I met Diane in the Denver airport. As we were waiting for our flights, I mentioned that I worked for an adoption agency, and she was eager to tell her story. She was a single 40-year-old woman when she decided to adopt a four-year-old boy named Alex from Ukraine. Alex struggled in school, first in learning, and later also in his behavior. This had all occurred fifteen years earlier, before education about bonding and connection was commonplace within the field of adoption. But she knew that Alex was not bonding and that they were not connecting. Because Diane was committed to her son's success, she changed jobs to one that would allow her to work from home over the internet. She moved from California to a secluded area of the Rockies, homeschooled Alex, worked from home, and gave a 100% effort at bonding. She rearranged her entire life around her new son. He is now 19 years old, and they have a good relationship. Alex is likely to succeed in life, although he continues to struggle socially.

Diane was able to rearrange her entire life. She was fortunate enough to have the emotional strength to make these changes, especially as a single parent. And she was fortunate to have the professional experience to enable her to find a job that would support this lifestyle change. Not every person is so fortunate. Not everyone can rearrange their entire life around an adopted child, but you can help members of your congregation by:

- Understanding that adoption sometimes results in a completely re-arranged life;
- Being non-judgmental;
- Accepting that the solution one family implements may not be what you would choose; and
- Realizing that they are doing their best to navigate this journey.

Extraordinary Circumstances

Competent, caring pastors will understand that many adoptive parents are normal people facing normal problems, but they are living in extraordinary circumstances. My wife and I became parents at the age of twenty-five; not unusually young, but on the younger side. However, we became parents of a seven-year-old, who was adopted from foster care, and we were about to learn how to parent from him! Many of the challenges he presented were typical, but our experience of parenting was out of the ordinary because we went from not being parents to being parents of a seven-year-old... overnight.

Other adoptive families have several children. Again, not completely unheard of. But these several children may have entered their home as a complete sibling set, all on the same day! Compassionate counselors and pastors should recognize that while a certain family situation may not on the surface seem out of the ordinary, the circumstances that led to that adoption may be extraordinary.

Unmet Expectations

Ted is an adoptive parent of four children. He posed a question whose answer seemed extremely obvious to him, but which I almost never hear articulated. He asked, "What is the greatest barrier to people adopting?" And then he answered his own question as if everyone already knows the answer: "change in lifestyle." Ted is absolutely right, even if people don't express it or think of it that way. People are afraid that adoption will present a change of lifestyle beyond what they can (or even want to) handle. Ironically, Ted then asked, "What is the main reason people adopt?" And he offered the equally obvious answer: "change in lifestyle." He was right again. People adopt because they desire to have a change in their current life situation. They desire to become parents, or parents of additional children, or parents of particular children in need. There is a hole in their life that can only be filled by an adopted child.

Both of Ted's questions illustrate the most significant struggle adoptive parents face: unmet expectations. When we say, "The struggle is real," please understand that the primary struggle adoptive parents are facing is that their adoption did not meet the expectations they had hoped for. As we counsel adoptive parents in our agency, the recurring theme for those couples is unmet expectations. As we work with adoptions that are dissolving and resulting in replacement adoptive families, the recurring theme is unmet expectations. Social workers do all they can to help adoptive parents have realistic expectations, but some couples think they will defy the odds. Some are simply not paying attention. Some overestimate their ability to handle the dashing of their expectations. But every couple will have disappointment. Realistic expectations will include knowing, understanding, and accepting the fact that marriage is hard, parenting is harder, and parenting adopted children is harder still. A realistic expectation is that the first year of an adoption of a child over two years of age will be the most difficult year in their lives. Ready with this expectation, adoptive parents have less room to be disappointed! Pastors can help struggling families by:

- Normalizing the pain resulting from unmet expectations;
- Identifying those unmet expectations, naming them, giving them over to God, and maybe even repenting of them; and
- Offering hope that the disillusionment is temporary and will improve.

Infertility

Before my wife and I got married, we talked about having ten children. We were somewhat serious; that was shorthand for "lots of kids." After we were married for five years, and had been trying to conceive for about a year, we started getting concerned that there may be a fertility problem. Like many couples, we people put off going to specialists, so instead of having clear answers, every month was met with grief, confusion, vain optimism, and fear of "worst case scenarios." Choosing the right time to see a specialist is difficult for many reasons: you don't want to hear terrible news, specialists want you to attempt conceiving for an entire year before seeing them, and worried want-to-be parents are often too quick to convince themselves there is a problem. When we did see fertility specialists, they determined that our likelihood of conception was nearly zero; the diagnosis was sterility. That diagnosis actually came by a phone call on the very day that my twin brother's first son was born. That day we genuinely welcomed our new nephew at the hospital, but when we returned home my wife collected everything she had been saving since childhood for her own children, put it all in trash bags, and threw them into storage. We did eventually—miraculously—have three biological children and three adopted children. But we became very familiar with the seemingly endless grief of infertility, with its painful reminders every month, every Mother's Day, and even daily when you see children, toys, preschools, and a multitude of other images.

Compassionate pastors will be mindful that one out of six couples has difficulty conceiving. These couples may have put dreams of having children behind them; perhaps now they are beyond child-rearing age, but they often think about the grief and loss. It never goes away. That grief may not be as acute as the years go on, but reminders of the pain persist. It is a God-given part of our nature to desire children, and the grief when we can't is a ubiquitous biblical theme (Sarah, Hannah, Elizabeth). It may seem to pastors, counselors, friends, and family that the remedies for infertility are simple and abundant: "Why don't you adopt?" "You can try IVF (In Vitro Fertilization)." "It was God's will." "You just need to keep trying." "Have you prayed with faith?" Pastors competent to counsel will offer an empathic ear. They can connect couples with others who have had similar struggles. And they can understand that adoption is a separate issue from infertility. Adoption is a calling... it is not right for everyone. Adoption professionals help prospective adoptive couples wrestle with the reality that adoption sometimes feels like "plan B" or "second best." For many couples, instead of the initial call to an adoption agency being filled with excitement and expectation, it feels like "giving up" or settling for something they didn't intend.

Embryo Guilt

Cameron and Beth were like many of the one out of six couples who struggle with infertility. They pursued In Vitro Fertilization (IVF) to conceive their two babies, as do one out of ten American couples nowadays. In the IVF process, embryos are created and implanted. About one-third of frozen embryo transfers result in a live birth. Since doctors and patients want to make the process successful and cost-effective, they often create as many embryos as possible. Cameron and Beth's doctor was able to create twenty embryos. Nowadays, women under forty years of age typically have only two embryos implanted at a time, so at the time of Beth's first embryo transfer, the remaining eighteen were frozen and stored. One of the embryos successfully implanted, and Beth had her first baby from that process. Two years later they thawed four more embryos, since half of those were expected not to survive the thaw. The two which did survive were implanted. One survived the implantation process, and she gave birth to her second baby boy. Now Cameron and Beth have fourteen frozen embryos remaining, but they have decided they are done building their family.

Beth said, "I realized that I have fourteen tiny human beings, my children, waiting in frozen storage for an opportunity at life. I felt extremely guilty about not giving these embryos a chance at life, and I worried about the future. My husband and I couldn't agree about what to do. All of the options seemed difficult. We knew we couldn't destroy the embryos or donate them to researchers, because this goes against our pro-life convictions. When we looked at our boys, we sometimes were reminded that their siblings were in the freezer. So my husband and I talked about donating the embryos to another couple, but the idea of someone else raising our biological children terrified us. So for twelve years, we decided to do nothing (which is what 86% of couples do). But the guilt remained."

If you are a pastor, couples in your congregation have embryos in frozen storage. If you have 1000 church members, a good guess is that twenty of the couples in your church currently have embryos in frozen storage, left over from their In Vitro Fertilization attempts. Pastors need to understand that these couples are filled with guilt, grief, and uncertainty. Like adoption, pastors should understand the complexity of saying, "You should donate them to another couple."

Beth continued her story. "The phone call to donate our frozen embryos was the most difficult decision we ever made. We wrestled with the thought that there is someone out there raising my biological children."

Pastors and counselors can encourage couples who have embryos in frozen storage that the fear of donating their embryos to another couple can be mitigated by choosing to donate through an adoption agency with an open adoption and a home studied (vetted) and matched family (such as the Snowflakes® program we pioneered at Nightlight Christian Adoptions).

Birthmother Grief

Vivian told me, "I was thinking about adoption every day; ever since the moment I heard I was pregnant I thought about nothing else... how it is the best option for me and my baby." But when she gave birth in the hospital, two nurses waited until the adoptive parents left the room and then they pleaded (with tears) for her to not go through with the adoption plan.

Before *Roe v. Wade* (1973), about 8% of births resulted in adoption. Since the legalization of abortion, the number of births resulting in adoption has dropped to only 1%. However, that means that if you have 200 people in your church, there is a strong chance you have a parent (birthmother or birthfather) who voluntarily relinquished their child for adoption. But you may never know it. In fact, they may never have told anyone in their entire life. In the 1950s, American culture stigmatized all three members of the adoption triad: it was degrading to be an adopted child, embarrassing to be an adoptive parent, and shameful to be a birthparent. Since that time, the stigma has disappeared for two members of that triad, but the stigma for birthparents is as great as ever. In fact, it has increased. In the 1950s women were EXPECTED to place children born out of wedlock for adoption. Nowadays, any woman who chooses to place for adoption is met with INTENSE criticism from parents, medical professionals, and even pro-life church members. Everywhere the birthmother goes, she hears, "You can do this yourself. You don't need to place for adoption. You shouldn't do it!"

The stigma of being a birthmother is specifically and inversely related to the stigma of being a single mother. When it was taboo to have a child out of wedlock, it was acceptable to place for adoption. Now that the stigma of having children out of wedlock is practically nonexistent, the stigma of placing for adoption is intense.

Pastors should recognize that when they speak they are speaking to birthmothers and birthfathers. On Mother's Day and Father's Day, there is someone out there in your congregation who made a decision to place their child for adoption. You can help birthparents in your midst by:

- Acknowledging their presence, and keeping this in mind as you speak sensitively;
- Being aware of birthmother/father counseling resources, books, and websites; and
- Helping them work through the grief of the lost relationship with their child.

Not On the Same Page

Jerri is a second grade teacher who works with my wife. She is now forty-eight years old, has been married for twenty years, and does not have children. People who know that my wife, Kristina, has adopted several children sometimes blurt out over the lunch table something like, "Jerri, when are you going to adopt? Why don't you adopt? You could always adopt." Jerri doesn't like to talk about it so publicly, but she has already had this conversation with my wife privately. She thought about adoption a dozen years ago. She talked about it with her husband, and he made it extremely clear that would never love an adopted child as much as he would a biological one. He couldn't adopt. Rather than argue whether her husband could love an adopted child as much as a biological one, she opted to trust his judgment... after all, it was his vow that he could not do so! As that conversation recurred over the next few years, she also realized that she would have to make a choice: stay married without children, or be a divorced parent by adoption. She could not have both. She decided to stick with her marriage.

Competent pastors and counselors must understand that couples are not always on the same page. In fact, they rarely approach adoption identically. One desires to adopt sooner than the other. One desires to adopt again (and again and again). One is open to children with special needs. One is open to children of other ethnicity. One is open to a sibling group. If a couple proceeds when they are not on the same page, they may successfully adopt, but whenever they struggle in the future, the "losing" spouse will likely recall the conflict."I told you not to adopt two kids!" "I said I didn't want a teenager."

Exceptional Physical or Psychological Issues

Anastasia told her adoption story to her high school class. "When I was seven years old, I was living with my mother in St. Petersburg, Russia. Both of my parents were alcoholics, but I actually never met my father. I just heard from my mother that he was a drunk, which I thought ironic because of her drinking problem. She had a lot of boyfriends who came in and out of the house. I couldn't stand it when these guys came and stayed the night so I just decided to leave when I was ten years old. I would go out on the streets and find friends to keep company. Most of them were older and they gave me cigarettes and liquor. One time when I was eleven the police found me drunk and passed out on the street. They took me back home, but the second time they found me drunk they took me to the Detsky Dom (an orphanage). I was there until I was fourteen and a family from California met me and adopted me. I still cannot believe they adopted a girl on the other side of the world who got drunk. Sometimes I have to pinch myself to see if this is real life."

Think of the enduring issues that Anastasia has to deal with. Though she has fared well, she falls into a spectrum of multiple disorders:

- **Attachment disorder**, due to not having healthy relationships in her entire childhood experience;
- **A drinking problem**, which may lead to a drug problem in the future;
- **Exposure to sexual conduct and pornography**, which could lead to future acting out or sexual disorders;
- **Trauma**, as we might assume some of the "boyfriends" were either physically, emotionally, or sexually abusive to her;
- **Possible Fetal Alcohol Syndrome/Spectrum disorder (FAS)**, if her mother was drinking when she was in utero;
- **Emotional disturbance, Attention Deficit Hyperactivity Disorder (ADHD), or Attention Deficit Disorder (ADD)**, one or more of which often accompany children raised in institutional settings; and
- **Depression**, due to her lack of relational connection.

Anastasia graduated high school, and the effects listed above have seemed minimal but not absent. Each of the disorders above is visible in a small degree in her. None of those disorders is immediately identifiable. No single one of them appears to be consuming her life, but each has left its mark, and the mark will be lifelong. At our adoption agency, we require parents to take a course called "Lifelong Issues of Adoption" because the issues surrounding and related to adoption are indeed lifelong. We also require families to take a course called "Medical Issues in Adoption" because there are always medical issues in adoption (some of which are listed above), as well as the frequent lack of knowledge regarding potential genetic or inherited conditions or disease tendencies. As a pastor, you can help these families by:

- Having a list of referral resources (books, movies, websites) to deal with the topics above;
- Having a list of referral sources for Christian counselors who specialize in those areas above;
- Being familiar with the signs and presence of the above disorders and their link to adoption;
- Assuming that the issues above and others are often present in children who have been institutionalized; and
- Being familiar with Trust Based Relational Intervention® (TBRI)[20] as a commonly accepted means of helping children who come from difficult places.

Parents Unprepared for the Task

Since 1973, as the number of voluntary placements of children into adoptive families has plummeted to 1%, the number of children placed in foster care has skyrocketed. So the phenomenon we are experiencing is that, due to the stigma of being a birthmother, while women are still placing for adoption in high numbers, they're just not doing it voluntarily. Instead, the state is removing their children for cause. If you are a pastor, it is very likely you have a couple in your church whose child was removed by the state for cause of neglect or abuse. And if you were unlikely to know about the birthparent(s) in your midst, you are surely not going to know about the couple who lost custody! The relevance here is that the compassionate pastor will recognize that adoption is not a positive word for everyone. Please remember that when you celebrate an adoption, someone else silently grieves, and when you speak of adoptive couples as heroes, there is a couple who implicitly hears they are villains.

Audrey attended our church off and on for several years, and none of

---

[20] See https://child.tcu.edu/about-us/tbri/

the pastors realized the private horror her family was experiencing. Her husband had a drinking problem and was at times abusive to her and her six-year-old son. A teacher called CPS (Child Protective Services), and the social worker told Audrey she was at risk of her son being placed in foster care if she stayed in the home with her husband. Essentially, she was being forced to choose between her husband and her child. Paralyzed by this decision, she did nothing. But she didn't realize at the time that "doing nothing" was, in fact, choosing.

Pastors can help families in their church who are at risk of losing custody, or who have lost custody, in a variety of ways: parenting classes, support groups, implementing a SAFE Families model,[21] personal coaching and counseling, and treatment support for drug, alcohol, or other addiction(s).

Anxiety with Child and Birthparents

Foster parents in your midst are likely navigating the largest challenge of their lives. A typical foster family will have some sort of atypical event every day of the week. On Monday, they will have an appointment at a psychologist's office with the birth family and child for re-unification therapy. They'll have an IEP (Individualized Educational Plan) meeting with the child's teacher on Tuesday. On Wednesday, they will have a monitored two-hour therapy visit with the birth mother at the department of social services. Thursday, they'll take her to speech therapy. On Friday, there will be a home visit with the social worker. Add these atypical events to all the "normal" events involving children—school, sports, friends, medical appointments, etc.—and you can't imagine how busy foster parents are. Even if everything is going well, life is brimming with stress due to these atypical demands and expenditures of time, money, and energy.

But often things don't go well. Let's revisit that schedule. On Monday, after being with her birth family, Sasha was very disturbed. In fact, every week it takes her 24 hours to recover from the bio-family visit, and after each session with them, she is defiant to her foster parents. It takes them

---

[21] See http://safe-families.org/

a few months to figure out why, but eventually her foster parents discover that the birthfather has been telling Sasha that she will be coming to live with them in just a couple weeks, so she shouldn't forget that they are her actual parents. The IEP with the teacher on Tuesday revealed that Sasha's behavior is nearly unmanageable in school. She waffles between being totally disengaged to being disrespectful and defiant. The Wednesday therapy visit was a waste of time because the foster mom had to drive 45 minutes each way, and the birthmother didn't show up. The speech therapist on Thursday said that Sasha will likely need two additional surgeries, both requiring in-patient overnight hospital stays, to repair her cleft palate so that her speech can be improved. When the social worker came to visit on Friday, she left the foster parents with a completely ambiguous outlook… the family that abused Sasha is likely to regain custody once they complete their case-plan, but since her birthparents have been falling just barely short of their requirements, her foster parents may be able to adopt her, after all. That was, in fact, the most difficult of all the week's events.

Children who are adopted from voluntary placements (normally called private, or domestic adoptions) often have a relationship with their biological parents, even if they were placed with the adoptive family at birth. This is called an open adoption. Open adoptions avoid much of the stress and anxiety described above, because the birthmother made the decision to place her child, as opposed to having lost custody by court action. Nevertheless, navigating the relationship between the adoptive parents, the biological parents, and the adopted child can be difficult for some families, for the following reasons:

- Adoptive parents fear that the birthparents will cause psychological confusion;
- Adoptive parents fear the birthparents will try to regain custody legally or illegally;
- Birthparents fear the adoptive parents will not honor their openness agreement (that they won't communicate by mail, email, phone, or in person); and
- Birthparents fear the adoptive parents will sour the relationship with them or turn the children against them.

Pastors and counselors can help all members of this "triad" deal with the above concerns by noting that nearly all adoptive parents find that openness with the birthmother (and sometimes with the birthfather) is a blessing. Most birth parents are reasonable, mature, and easy to work with. They made a voluntary decision to place their child, and they expect the adoptive parent(s) to keep to their agreement. Most people stop struggling when they don't have to fight. On the other hand, most people do fight for things they don't even want when they feel like they are powerless or continually in a losing position.

The adoption is about the child, not the parents, so adoptive parents are investing in an open relationship with the birthparents because it is good for the child. Whether or not it's convenient or easy is irrelevant; what matters is whether or not it's the right thing to do. Importantly, at some point in their lives nearly all adopted children inevitably embark on a search for their birth parents. They sense there is a void in themselves that can only be filled by finding their birth family. It is wise for adoptive families to fill this void early on with the actual family, rather than allowing the child to fill the void with a fantasy one. The fantasy family is always ultimately unsatisfying, and it poses a larger threat to the adoptive parents than the real biological family!

Child Protective Services

Some of the people in your congregation have had Child Protective Services respond to calls or complaints about them, and some of these people are parents by adoption. It's possible that the parents themselves bear little or no responsibility for why CPS was called, but this does not negate the presence of a problem. Catherine and Chris adopted Julio from Guatemala ten years ago. When he was fifteen years old, he decided he wanted to have a completely independent lifestyle. So now he leaves the house at night whenever he sees fit. And he returns home whenever he feels like it—usually after smoking a joint or two by himself (he has trouble keeping friends). Catherine and Chris feel uncomfortable keeping the doors unlocked all night, yet they know Julio is outside. They've called the police numerous times about this situation, and the police are not interested in getting involved. One night Julio returned at 3 a.m. to a locked house and decided to sleep on the porch. Neighbors called CPS and said the parents were locking their child out of the house and making him sleep outside. CPS came to investigate, made a report, and determined no further action was needed.

Pastors and counselors should understand that this is not an atypical situation for any parent, but it might be more common for parents of children who have troubled pasts (which may be the case for some adopted children). Imagine the stress that having CPS come to the home adds to an already painful situation. Added to the "normal" stress of navigating parenthood, such a couple must also worry about appearances and even legal actions. You can help parents who are in the midst of an investigation with Child Protective Services by:

- Providing an empathic ear;
- Connecting them with other families for support and mentoring;
- Connecting them with a qualified respite family;
- Connecting them with the organization SAFE Families;[22] and
- Providing resources (books, classes, videos, websites) to assist in growing their parenting skills.

When parenting adopted children, difficulties are completely normal and to be expected. One adoptive parent pointed out to me that, "Pain in childbirth was part of God's response to Adam and Eve's sin in the Garden of Eden. Children enter the home in a variety of ways, but you can't expect to escape the curse of The Fall" (Genesis 3). Counselors and pastors can help families cope with the "adoptive birth pangs" by communicating that the difficulty is normal, to be expected, endurable, and, in the end, well worth it!

All Adoptions Involve Loss and Tragedy.

When people hear that I work for an adoption agency, they often say something like, "How wonderful! Your work must be very rewarding." While it can be rewarding, what they overlook is that all adoption involves

---

[22] See http://safe-families.org/

grief and sometimes tragedy. Every adoption is the result of loss. A child loses connection to his birth family, his past, and sometimes his culture and language. A birth parent loses a relationship with their child. An adoptive family loses "the family they had before the adoption." In other words, the adoption affects their family's status quo, or homeostasis (balance). Counselors can help adopted children and their adoptive parents deal with the following types of grief:

- Child's loss of biological parents to death;
- Child's loss of biological parents by court action (jail, incompetence, neglect, abuse);
- Child's loss of relationship with siblings;
- Child's loss of cultural heritage (language, country, food, community);
- Child's loss of extended family (grandparents, aunts and uncles);
- Child's loss of emotional or physical health, due to neglect or abuse in the past;
- Losses in the adoptive parents' history that affect their ability to have healthy, attached relationships;
- Adoptive parents' grief over infertility; and
- Adoptive parents' grief over unmet expectations.

It is, of course, strange that anyone would tell an adopted child he or she is "lucky," given the loss and tragedy that often accompanies the circumstances leading to adoption.

Identity Crisis

There are children in your congregation who were conceived by sperm or eggs donated anonymously. When Martin was 21 years old, his mother revealed to him that he was conceived by sperm from an anonymous donor. Both of Martin's parents dreaded the day they would have to tell him this news, so they put it off. They justified the delay by saying they would wait until he was old enough to understand. Then, when he was clearly old enough to understand, they were terrified he would be angry with them for waiting so long to tell him! Martin's situation isn't unlike children whose parents wait too long to reveal the news that they were adopted. Martin eventually accepted the news, and he didn't love his father any less for not being biologically related, but he did experience a great deal of preventable pain which lasted for years. Counselors can help families prevent these identity crises by:

- Having on hand books for children that explain adoption, embryo adoption, or gamete donation. There are plenty (many Christian) children's books available at amazon.com specifically for this purpose.
- Educating families that the right time to talk about a child being adopted or conceived through artificial reproductive technology (ART) is starting at birth and then frequently (at least annually) thereafter. And if they haven't already broken the news, then today is the right day to start.

Unresolved Personal Issues

Lena recognized that one of the challenges adoptive parents face is themselves and their own background. Before becoming an adoptive parent, she realized she had her own "baggage" to deal with. Her father had left the family when she was twelve years old, and after that, she was abused by one of her mother's boyfriends. In her adoption preparation, she accessed every assessment tool she could find and asked for appropriate counseling to accompany it. Lena rightly recognized that "the primary goal of adoptive parenting is to build attachment. I cannot expect my child to have more healthy attachments than I am able to build myself." Counselors should be familiar with adult attachment and skilled in helping clients develop the ability to build connected relationships. They should also be able to recommend resources (books, people, videos, websites) that help assess, model, and create better attachment for adults.

Conclusion

Isaiah 1:17 (NIV) says, "Take up the cause of the fatherless." That is what some members of your congregation have done. They have heard the cry of the orphan, and they have shared the heart of God. They have offered to a child the same things that God offers to us: a new name, a permanent inheritance, and all the benefits of belonging to a new family. The journey to becoming adoptive parents is not easy, but it is good. God did not call us to do what is convenient or simple, but what he calls us to do is right and rewarding. Look more closely at the families in your congregation, and you'll see that a great number of them have been touched in some way by adoption. A woman placed her son for adoption decades ago. An older couple adopted their granddaughter. A couple struggling with infertility is discussing adoption again tonight. In every case, they will experience the incredible joy expressed in Isaiah 43:6-7 (NIV).

> "I will say to the north, 'Give them up!' and to the south,
> 'Do not hold them back.'
> Bring my sons from afar
> and my daughters from the ends of the earth—
> everyone who is called by my name,
> whom I created for my glory,
> whom I formed and made."

God is gathering his children from far and near into earthly families and into his heavenly family (Psalm 68:6; Ephesians 1:3-13). In this, we see lived out in earthly families what is true for us all: our adoption into his family.

Matthew Stanford, Ph.D.

Dr. Matthew Stanford is CEO of the Hope and Healing Center & Institute (HHCI) in Houston, Texas and adjunct professor of psychiatry at Baylor College of Medicine and Houston Methodist Hospital Institute for Academic Medicine.

Matthew earned his doctoral degree in Behavioral Neuroscience from Baylor University and completed a post-doctoral fellowship at the University of Texas Medical Branch at Galveston. A Fellow of the Association for Psychological Science (APS), he is the author of *Grace for the Afflicted: A Clinical and Biblical Perspective on Mental Illness, Revised and Expanded* and *The Biology of Sin: Grace, Hope, and Healing for Those Who Feel Trapped*. His research on the interplay between psychology and issues of faith has been featured in such national publications as *The New York Times*, *USA Today*, and *Christianity Today*, as well as on many news websites, including Fox, MSNBC, Yahoo, and U.S. News & World Report. Dr. Stanford may be contacted at the Hope and Healing Center & Institute, 717 Sage Rd., Houston, TX 77056, 713-871-1004.

CHAPTER 27

How to Develop Effective Connections with Community Mental Health Resources

Matthew Stanford, Ph.D.

The Hope and Healing Center & Institute (HHCI) sits on the campus of a large church in Houston, Texas. Recently, the church's receptionist called and asked if I could come over because there was a suicidal woman in the front office. I walked over to the church and found Kate talking with one of the clergy. Kate, a disheveled 45 year-old woman, was obviously in distress. We spoke for about an hour.

During our conversation, she told me she was afraid to go home because she might hurt herself. She shared with me that she had struggled with depression in the past but was not presently receiving any treatment. That morning, she and her boyfriend, with whom she lived, had a heated argument about their financial difficulties. I helped her calm down and then provided connections to local resources that could help with her employment and financial problems. I also assessed her suicidality and found that while distressed, she was not actively suicidal. I scheduled an appointment for her with one of our mental health coaches at the HHCI, whom she began seeing the following week. Kate told me she did not attend a church, and this led me to ask her why she had come to this particular congregation for help. She answered, "My parents were married here 50 years ago."

Stories like this are repeated in churches across the country every day. Research shows that individuals struggling with mental health problems are more likely to go to a member of the clergy, even ones with whom they have no relationship, before consulting a mental health provider or physician (Wang, 2003). A survey of pastors conducted by author Amy Simpson for her book *Troubled minds: Mental illness and the church's mission*, found that 44.5% of pastors report being approached two to five times a year for help with mental illness, while 32.8% report being approached six or more times (Simpson, 2013). Unfortunately, the average faith community is not equipped to effectively assist or support individuals with mental health problems. A recent study found that only 28% of churches surveyed even maintained a referral list of local mental health care providers (LifeWay, 2014). How would you or your church have assisted someone like Kate?

A Divine Opportunity

Viewed through the eyes of faith, the fact that those struggling with mental health problems are first seeking assistance from the church constitutes a divine opportunity. God is sending to us those who are broken by mental illness so that they might receive hope and healing. Serving as a trusted guide to available mental health resources in the local community is one of the many important roles clergy and ministry staff play in helping individuals struggling with mental health difficulties and disorders to stabilize and recover. To be effective in this role, clergy must build relationships with local mental health care providers and seek out information on available resources in the community long before a congregant requests assistance. This chapter outlines how to connect to mental health resources that all clergy should become familiar with in their local community.

Clergy Mental Health Training

Research shows that over 70% of pastors report feeling inadequately trained to recognize mental illness (Hunter & Stanford, 2014; Farrell & Goebert, 2008). Clergy and ministry staff must be able to recognize the signs and symptoms of mental illness so that a proper referral to available mental health resources can be made. A number of organizations (e.g., National Alliance for the Mentally Ill, Mental Health America, Grace Alliance) offer mental health training that clergy and church staff can easily access. Local mental health care providers, some of whom may even attend your church, are often available to offer training on suicide, crisis intervention, and other mental health topics important to you and your staff.

Crisis Situations

Mental health problems often cause shame-filled emotional pain and disruptive chaos in the lives of families. It is important to effectively assess the nature and magnitude of a situation before you take action. The most significant distinction you must be able to make is whether you are dealing with a crisis or a problem. A crisis involves an immediate safety concern for you or another (e.g., suicidal or homicidal thoughts or actions), while a problem is an issue that can be managed or addressed over time. Emergency or crisis mental health resources that you should be familiar with include the following.

Suicide hotline. Suicide hotlines are not only for the individual who is considering harming themselves. If you need to talk to someone about a parishioner's suicidal thoughts/behavior or need guidance on how to respond to such an emergent situation, help is only a call away (800-273-TALK [8255]).

Crisis intervention teams. A crisis intervention team (CIT) goes into the community to provide emergency care to people in a mental health crisis. CITs traditionally provide crisis assessment and then link the distressed individual to psychiatric treatment and other services in the community. Follow-up after the crisis is common to make sure the individual is receiving outpatient services.

Mental health deputies/officers. Mental health deputies and officers are specially trained police officers who work with people in mental health crisis. Not all communities offer these advanced services, and you will need to determine if they exist in your area by calling your local police or sheriff's department.

Mental health crisis clinic or hospital emergency room. If an individual is in immediate danger of harming themselves or others, they need to be seen by a mental health care provider. Many communities have specialized mental health crisis clinics for situations such as this; when this is unavailable, a hospital emergency room is your best option. Making contact with the educational specialist or community liaison at your local crisis clinic or hospital to learn the process that will occur when a suicidal individual is brought there will help you to comfort and assure families when an actual crisis occurs.

Mental health warrant. A mental health warrant authorizes law enforcement to take into custody a person who shows serious need for help for a mental illness and who also is at immediate and serious risk for harm to self or others. The warrant orders a person to undergo a mental health evaluation by a doctor to determine if hospitalization is necessary. To get a mental health warrant, a family member must be able to present current, specific information that shows the prospective patient is suffering from a mental illness and constitutes an immediate danger to themselves or others. This type of extreme action is often sought by families who have a mentally ill loved one that lacks insight into their illness and refuses treatment. Most often the county attorney's office will issue a mental health warrant, although this can vary from state to state. Knowing the process for obtaining a mental health warrant will significantly aid families with a loved one who refuses treatment.

Mental Health Care Providers

It is important that you build professional relationships with mental health care providers in your local community. Referrals to a professional with whom you have a relationship are more meaningful to the person being referred than referring them to a complete stranger. A referral should not be seen as "passing the buck" but rather as a collaborative opportunity in which you and the mental health care provider work as a team to care for and support the struggling individual. You should vet a wide range of mental health professionals in the community – clinical psychologists, psychiatrists, clinical social workers, and licensed counselors – as potential referrals.

The American Association of Christian Counselors' *Christian Care Connect* is an ideal resource to help you locate such professionals. This uniquely designed, multispecialty referral and nationwide resource network will connect you with a wide variety of counselors, coaches, and clinics, all of whom have been carefully vetted both Christianly and clinically. From "Coffee Cup" coaches and pastoral counselors to professionally trained, licensed outpatient mental health clinicians to inpatient and residential treatment facilities, you will be able to find appropriate referrals along the entire continuum of care. You may access the *Christian Care Connect* at www.aacc.net or 800-5COUNSEL.

Clinical psychologists treat clients who have mental illness or struggle with psychological problems by using some form of talk therapy, generally referred to as psychotherapy. Psychotherapy can be done by many different types of mental health professionals, including clinical psychologists (those with a doctoral degree; Ph.D. or Psy.D.) or therapists such as clinical social workers (LCSW) and licensed counselors (LPC, LMFT).[23]

During treatment, the client and therapist meet regularly in private sessions to talk about concerns and issues related to the client's disorder or problems. More than just a free-flowing discussion, the therapy is guided by the theory and goals associated with the specific psychotherapeutic approach used. There are numerous approaches a psychotherapist can take. Most therapists are trained in several forms of therapy but typically concentrate on one primary approach in their daily practice.

Psychiatrists are medical doctors (M.D. or D.O) trained in the treatment of mental disorders using medication. Research has shown that in the treatment of mental disorders, the best course of action is generally a combination of medication and psychotherapy. That is why a team approach to treatment that includes both a psychiatrist and a clinical psychologist or other licensed mental health professional is important.

When building relationships in your community, seek out mental health providers who are willing to work collaboratively on cases and who are affirming of the Christian faith. Since information clients share with mental health care providers is confidential, the congregant will need to sign a release of information form for you and the provider to share information about their case.

A lack of financial resources or insurance is a significant barrier that

---

[23] Common graduate degrees related to clinical psychology include Doctor of Philosophy (Ph.D.), Doctor of Clinical Psychology (Psy.D.), Licensed Clinical Social Worker (LCSW), Licensed Professional Counselor (LPC), and Licensed Marriage and Family Therapist (LMFT).

keeps many of those most in need from being able to access mental health care. As you vet mental health care providers as potential referrals, you must also gather information on their costs and the types of insurance they accept. For those congregants without financial resources, seek out providers that charge on sliding scales or are willing to offer some limited *pro bono* services. Local universities or colleges that offer graduate programs in psychology or counseling may have clinics where students provide mental health services at a reduced fee. Most states and counties provide some system to care for the mental health of those who lack financial resources. Find out how to engage these systems in your area and what the process entails. An informed advocate is a blessing to a family struggling to care for a mentally ill loved one.

Treatment and Recovery Facilities

There are times when individuals living with mental illness may require inpatient hospitalization. Much like the selection of mental health care providers described above, you need to familiarize yourself with the residential psychiatric and addiction recovery facilities in your area. In addition to the specifically Christian programs listed in the *Christian Care Connect*, a good place to start is the Substance Abuse and Mental Health Services Administration (SAMHSA) online behavioral health treatment services locator (https://findtreatment.samhsa.gov/). By simply typing in your zip code, you will be shown all the residential mental health facilities in your area.

Trauma, Violence, and Abuse

It is likely that during your time as a minister, you will come in contact with women and children who are the victims of domestic violence, sexual assault/rape or child abuse/neglect (although some men also experience domestic violence). If these individuals have not engaged professional services in relation to their trauma, it is important that you are able to move them in the right direction. Familiarize yourself with the victim service organizations in your local community. These include domestic violence safe houses (800-799-SAFE [7233]), rape crisis centers, and women and family advocacy groups.

Veterans

Many veterans of the armed services receive their mental health care through the Veterans Administration (VA). It is important that you familiarize yourself with the VA mental health services available in your local community. A good place to direct veterans in distress and their families is to the Veterans Crisis Line, accessible by phone (800-273-8255, press 1), or online at https://www.veteranscrisisline.net/.

Support Groups

There is strong evidence for the clinical efficacy of peer-led support groups in mental health recovery. It is easy to become familiar with the organizations that offer mental health support groups (e.g., National Alliance for the Mentally Ill, Depression/Bipolar Support Alliance, Celebrate Recovery, and Alcoholics Anonymous) in your area. If your faith community is interested in being more directly involved in the delivery of support groups, partner with faith-based organizations such as Grace Alliance (www.mentalhealthgracealliance.org), Celebrate Recovery, or Fresh Hope (freshhope.us/) to have parishioners trained to lead groups. Support groups are not only beneficial to individuals living with mental illness, but are also helpful to their caregivers.

Mental Health Gateway

The Mental Health Gateway is an online resource (www. mentalhealthgateway.org) for clergy designed to provide you with the information, tools, and resources needed to effectively assist individuals with mental health difficulties who may seek your support and guidance. The website is organized by mental disorder, and includes short educational videos as well as a step-by-step guide to assist you in finding and referring an individual to mental health resources in your local community. In addition, the website gives you access (within one business day) to trained mental health coaches at the Hope and Healing Center & Institute who can answer your questions and help with referrals.

Rural Settings

For clergy in rural settings where mental health care providers and services may not be readily available, referrals to primary care physicians and the use of tele-psychiatry/psychology are important options. When no mental health care providers exist in an area, primary care physicians can be used to provide needed psychiatric medications. You should evaluate primary care physicians in your area as potential mental health referral options.

Tele-psychiatry/psychology takes advantage of technologies such as the internet or smart phones to provide mental health services directly to the client electronically. As an advocate for families struggling with mental health care problems, you should become familiar with companies that provide these services such as Doctor on Demand (www.doctorondemand.com/) or TalkSpace (www.talkspace.com/).

Children's Health Insurance

Children who don't have health insurance are very often eligible for state medical coverage. Insurance is available to children in working families, including families that include individuals with a variety of immigration statuses. To find out what your state's policies are, what's covered, and how to apply, call 877-543-7669 or find your state at www.insurekidsnow.gov/state/index.html.

Government Entitlement Programs

Individuals living with mental illness may not be able to work or may have trouble holding a job. This becomes particularly difficult when they are the primary provider in a family. Individuals with mental illness are often eligible for government assistance through entitlement programs such as Supplemental Security Income (SSI). SSI is a federal income supplement program designed to help aged, blind, and disabled people who have little or no income. It provides cash in a monthly stipend to meet basic needs for food, clothing, and shelter. Information about the program can be found on the Social Security Administration (SSA) website at www.ssa.gov/ssi/.

If an individual is eligible for Medicaid, they may be able to access mental health services through Medicaid. States vary, however, in what types of mental health services they provide under Medicaid. Use the following database to find out what Medicaid benefits are available in your state: kff.org/data-collection/medicaid-benefits/.

The Department of Housing and Urban Development (HUD) provides a number of housing assistance programs. The Housing Choice Voucher Program also known as Section 8 Housing is the federal government's program for assisting low-income families, the elderly, and the disabled. HUD also helps apartment renters by offering reduced rents to low-income residents. Under this program, a renter pays 30% of their gross adjusted income for housing and utilities. The landlord then receives a voucher from the federal government which covers the remainder of the rent.

The Supportive Housing for People with Disabilities Program also known as Section 811 is a federal program dedicated to developing and subsidizing rental housing for very or extremely low income adults with disabilities, like a chronic mental illness. The biggest difference between this program and similar ones is that it provides housing specifically for the disabled and ensures that all such housing has access to appropriate supportive services like case management and employment assistance. Information on both of these programs can be found on the HUD website at www.hud.gov.

Housing

For individuals living with mental health difficulties and disorders, finding safe and affordable housing can be difficult. You are likely to be approached by individuals and/or their families looking for two types of housing: immediate and long-term. For immediate housing needs, it is important that church leaders are familiar with local emergency shelters and missions that serve the homeless. On more than one occasion, a family has shown up at my office with their mentally ill loved one and asked me to find a place for him or her to stay that night so that they will not have to sleep on the street. Being familiar with local homeless shelters is invaluable in these situations. Long-term housing options for the mentally ill range from independent living to 24/7 assisted care. Your local National Alliance for the Mentally Ill (www.nami.org) or Mental Health America (www.mentalhealthamerica.net/) affiliate should be able to help you with housing options for those living with mental illness in your area.

Final Thoughts

People living with mental illness often behave in strange and bizarre ways. Their perception of the world and those around them can be very different from the norm. They may even perceive your attempts to help them as a threat. They may deny that they have a problem. They may refuse to be involved in treatment or cooperate with a well-designed referral. These are difficult issues—long-term, messy and requiring a steadfast commitment on your part. Don't expect appreciation; in fact, you might receive just the opposite. This is as much your trial as it is that of the person with the disorder. God wants to use it to draw you both closer to him.

There are no easy answers, and there is no quick fix. This is real life, and sometimes it will seem like you are feeling your way in the dark, but you are not alone. God is present in the midst of this storm, and he will provide sustaining grace as both of you walk toward health, hope, and healing. In so doing, you will have been used by the Comforter and Healer to ease the suffering, shame, and stigma many persons and families with mental and relational health problems experience on a daily basis.

References

Farrell, J. and Goebert, D. (2008). Collaboration between psychiatrists and clergy in recognizing and treating serious mental illness. *Psychiatric Services, 59.* 437-40.

Hunter, W. and Stanford, M. (2014). Adolescent mental health: The role of youth and college pastors. *Mental Health, Religion and Culture, 17.* 957-66

LifeWay. (2014). Study of acute mental illness and Christian faith: Research report. Retrieved from http://lifewayresearch.com/mentalillnessstudy/

Simpson, A. (2013). *Troubled minds: Mental illness and the church's mission.* Downers Grove: InterVarsity Press.

Wang, P. (2003). Patterns and correlates of contacting clergy for mental disorders in the United States. *Health Services Research, 38.* 647-73.

Gregory Jantz, Ph.D.

Dr. Gregory Jantz is founder of The Center for Counseling and Health Resources, Inc., a leading healthcare facility in Edmonds, Washington (aplaceofhope. com), a licensed psychologist, a chemical dependency professional, and a certified eating disorder specialist through IAEDP, as well as a speaker and author of over twenty books. The Center utilizes Gregg's whole-person approach to recovery, integrating emotional, relational, physical, and spiritual components into long-term healing for people across the United States and internationally.

CHAPTER 28

How to Develop an Effective Church-Based Wellness Ministry

Gregory Jantz, Ph.D.

The job of a pastor or church leader can be a lonely one. If you're in full-time ministry, you're expected to preach or teach on Sunday, open the building on Monday, redo the outdoor signage on Tuesday, attend (or lead) the mid-week class on Wednesday, visit the sick on Thursday, create the bulletin on Friday, and prep for Sunday on Saturday. If you're a lay leader, you're expected to work a full-time job for financial reasons and a part-time job for spiritual ones on whatever nights and weekends you can cram into your already busy life. Whether full-time or part-time or both, when are you supposed to find the time to effectively deal with the overwhelming mental and relational needs of the hurting, both in and out of your congregation?

Feeling the Burden

People come to you with complex, multi-faceted problems and often expect you to provide simple, one-sided answers. They believe God is a God of miracles, and so do you, creating a subtle and shared assumption that you, as God's representative, are a miracle-worker. When the miracle doesn't happen, or doesn't happen on schedule, or doesn't happen as expected, the resulting assumption can be that since God cannot fail, you have. Under-trained and overwhelmed, pastors and church leaders sacrifice professionally and personally to counsel others even when their own lives may feel just as messy. With so much at stake, is there any reason to wonder why some ministers find themselves frustrated, exhausted, and burned out?

As a professional therapist, I went through this type of burn-out, or what I've heard referred to as "compassion fatigue." My own experience with feeling stretched out, drained out, and with little or no compassion to give anyone else led me, ironically, to rekindle my compassion for fellow therapists as well as pastors and church leaders. At my counseling agency, we now incorporate a professional wellness program designed for compassion providers – from both religious and secular professions – to relax, recharge, and renew. Our professional wellness program is based on a service model I created over thirty years ago called "whole-person care."

Whole-Person Care

As a new therapist starting out, I found myself treating mental health issues with people who were self-medicating with alcohol, illegal drugs, or prescription drugs. I worked with people who experienced a wealth of physical complaints but hadn't seen a physician in years. I saw people who fueled each high stress day with large doses of sugar, carbohydrates, and caffeine. All of them wanted to feel better about themselves or their relationships but found progress toward those goals to be difficult when they felt so bad physically. Under stress and in emotional and physical pain, they were in spiritual crisis, doubting God's love and concern, and holding onto hope by the thinnest of threads.

Though I did become a chemical dependency professional as well as a mental health professional, I wasn't a pastor or a priest. I wasn't a physician or a dietitian. How was I to treat someone with so many interconnected issues when those issues kept interfering with the counseling work I was trying to do?

The answer I found was to stop treating just part of the person and start treating the whole person. Whole-person care says that people are interconnected emotionally, relationally, physically, and spiritually. This idea didn't come to me from a text book, but instead from the book of Proverbs, where I learned:

> *Do not be wise in your own eyes; fear the LORD and shun evil.*
> *This will bring health to your body and nourishment to your*
> *bones (Proverbs 3:7-8, NIV).*

Spiritual health is connected to physical health.

> *A wife of noble character is her husband's crown, but a disgraceful wife is like decay in his bones (Proverbs 12:4, NIV).*

Dysfunctional relationships can cause physical problems.

> *A heart at peace gives life to the body, but envy rots the bones (Proverbs 14:30, NIV).*

Emotional health is directly related to physical health.

> *Light in a messenger's eyes brings joy to the heart, and good news gives health to the bones (Proverbs 15:30, NIV).*

What people hear affects how they feel.

> *Gracious words are a honeycomb, sweet to the soul and healing to the bones (Proverbs 15:34, NIV).*

Words have the power to heal, but they can also break bones.

> *A cheerful heart is good medicine, but a crushed spirit dries up the bones (Proverbs 17:22, NIV).*

How you feel about yourself can determine how your body feels.

Taking these lessons from scripture, although I decided the most effective way to engage in long-term recovery was to start treating the whole person, I knew I couldn't do that on my own. I'd tried in the past and, unlike the Apostle Paul, had failed miserably. The answer wasn't for me to try to be all things to all people but to partner with a group of people, united in the recovery of one person at a time. I brought together mental health therapists, chemical dependency counselors, medical professionals, and nutritionists under a single umbrella of care. Our center's staff included therapists who were also pastors and teachers to undergird our program and provide spiritual support and guidance. Again, in Proverbs I read, "Plans fail for lack of counsel, but with many advisers they succeed (Proverbs 15:22, NIV)." I finally realized that long-term recovery from mental and relational issues required a team of "many advisors."

Equipping the Local Church

As much as I would love for our clinic to be able to help everyone, it can't. The number of hurting people outstrips our ability to help. We have helped thousands of people, but all those lives collectively are literally merely a drop in the vast bucket of suffering. There simply are not enough clinics or counseling offices. Some people harbor stigmas against getting professional help for mental and relationship issues; hurting and losing hope, they often wind up at a local church, looking for help and answers. The front line for so much of the suffering in our communities runs along the doorstep of the church.

As Christians, we are called to make a difference in the lives of people, and God has empowered us to do so. I believe there is a way for those in the local church to come together under a common purpose to create a community-based "wellness team" modeled on whole-person care. By bringing together people from the congregation along with community-based resources, the local church can address the myriad needs of the hurting. I offer the following blueprint, not as the definitive structure for all pastors and church leaders, but as a springboard for thought and prayerful consideration.

Some of you are parts of large, urban congregations with high-density populations. Others of you come from rural congregations covering many miles and multiple small communities. A few of you have congregations of over a thousand. Most of you, though, have congregations in the hundreds, with many of you shepherding churches of less than a hundred. There is no one-size-fits-all answer to equipping the local church to respond to the needs of the hurting. Instead, each of you will need to evaluate the resources you have in your congregation and in your broader community as you create a wellness team at the local church level.

Spiritual Support

Underlying this wellness team should be spiritual support. As we know from Ephesians 6:12 and 1 Samuel 17:47, the battle of the suffering is a spiritual battle, and that battle belongs to the Lord. Each person receiving help from the church for mental or relational issues needs a spiritual mentor. This spiritual mentor need not be the pastor or even a church leader, but he or she should be a spiritually mature person who has agreed to act in this capacity.

The mentor acts as a spiritual interpreter in the model of 1 Peter 3:15; someone who is "prepared to give an answer to everyone who asks" and is able to do this with "gentleness and respect." The mentor doesn't need to answer the *why* of suffering, but the mentor does need to be prepared to answer the *who* of suffering. I've found I'm not always able to explain why a certain situation has taken place; I just don't have that much insight. Yet from my own understanding and experience I can explain who God is and how he responds to suffering.

The source for providing spiritual support for mental and relationship issues is, first and foremost, the Bible. The Bible is full of practical wisdom, both in the Old and New Testaments. The words of 2 Timothy 3:16-17 (NIV) are not merely a statement of truth, they are a promise: "All Scripture is God-breathed and is useful for teaching, rebuking, correcting and training in righteousness, so that the servant of God may be thoroughly equipped for every good work." Helping people overcome and heal from their mental and relationship issues is very "good work."

In addition, there are many sound, biblically-based resource books and videos that can be used to help a person understand how spiritual concepts interface with human suffering. Over the years, I've come to use many—from the *Boundaries* books by Cloud and Townsend to the healing words of Max Lucado and Rick Warren. I've also tried to add to that pool of assistance by writing books of my own on emotional abuse, eating disorders, parenting, family issues, stress, depression, and anxiety. Along with scripture, these books can be used as a resource to guide people into spiritual discovery and healing.

Above all, the spiritual mentor should pray regularly with and for the person being mentored:

- Be specific in prayer. I believe the most effective prayer is honest and confessional.
- The prayer time should include more components than a laundry-list of the mentored person's concerns. Remember to include praise and adoration to God, as well as an acknowledgment of his power and authority; these provide encouragement and counter-balance to the issues being prayed for.
- Pray with words from scripture. Pray using the words of the Psalms. Mirror back the words, phrases, and promises God caused to be written down, for the benefit of the one being prayed for.
- Pray simply, with conversational words instead of "religious" ones. Some of those who need help for hurting do not come from a religious background and will not understand "church" words. Instead, model the style of simple prayer Jesus gave the disciples in Matthew 6.
- While I understand the convenience of texting, the Internet, and Facebook, I also believe in the power of personal touch and face-to-face interactions for prayer.

Emotional Support

Certainly, the spiritual mentor will provide emotional support, but I believe having multiple people able to provide emotional support is helpful. If the mentor is someone akin to a spiritual parent, emotional support can be provided by spiritual siblings, brothers and sisters in Christ who are able to come alongside the hurting person. This emotional support doesn't necessarily mean sitting down in a counseling type of situation. Some of the best emotional support I've experienced in my own life has come from people who have come to know me and love me through everyday activities and events at the church.

People who have been emotionally abused or bruised by people and events in their lives need to know they are valued by others. Those providing emotional support can do this through inviting the hurting person to become a part of service or ministry in the church itself. During this service or ministry activity, people often have time to talk in a natural, unstructured way while working around the church, whether caring for the grounds or helping at a food or clothing bank or in other areas of appropriate service.

Emotional support can be as simple as staying after services to talk to and encourage the hurting person. Making calls or writing notes. Inviting the person out to lunch or coffee on a regular basis. Emotional support is letting the person know you care and are willing to include that person in your life. Through these interactions, you will have opportunities to encourage, strengthen, and motivate the person to continue striving toward recovery.

Relationship Support

If I were to ask the pastors I've known over the years what area they most counsel in, I believe the number one response would be spiritual counseling, helping people understand God and the Bible. That makes perfect sense, but I believe the second most frequently addressed area for most pastors would be relationship counseling. A husband and wife come to you and beg you to "save" their marriage. Distraught parents look for a miracle to salvage a defiant teenager. Quarreling siblings expect you to take one side over the other. Spiritual pillars of the church disagree with each other and can't find a way to common ground, creating Euodia-and-Syntyche divisions and splits in the congregation (Philippians 4:2-3). Relationship issues can be landmines, waiting to blow up in a pastor's or leader's face.

The church, after all, is meant to be one big family (1 Timothy 5:1-2), and we all know what families can be like. Pastors and church leaders are not only called upon to watch over the family, they are also part of the family, bringing their own issues, problems, and inadequacies into that family mix. A pastor or church leader can feel great stress when called upon by someone else to "solve" a problem he or she is experiencing in his or her own family.

Sometimes, however, the answer to providing relationship support doesn't need to be found in a pastor or church leader providing the "right" chapter and verse. Instead, relationship support can be given by members of the congregation who have knowledge and experience in overcoming in difficult areas. Parents who have raised their children can provide support for those just starting a family. Older members of the congregation with decades of marriage can offer help and encouragement to newlyweds. Parents with difficult teenagers need a listening ear and a reassuring voice from those who know from experience that "this too shall pass." Those who have lived their lives as singles can give a needed perspective to those who despair over the lack of a romantic relationship. The combinations of those who are hurting with those who can help are multiple, depending upon the generational and experiential breadth of the congregation.

There are times, however, when the relationship issues needing support are of such a private and personal nature that the pastor or church leader must be the one involved. Pastors and church leaders, through their breadth of service, can have greater exposure to significantly difficult situations. With some issues, having multiple people to provide this support is wise and can create necessary accountability. Pastors and leaders may need to be involved, yet whenever possible, those in the local congregation can also be a divinely-gathered group of resources at a pastor's or church leader's disposal to use for the benefit of the hurting.

Physical Support

In many ways, a physician or a dietitian is like a therapist in that he or she only has so many hours in a professional day. So even if your congregation does have a medical doctor, a nurse, or a dietitian in attendance, making those people "responsible" to address the physical needs of the hurting will not be a long-term, workable strategy. However, a doctor, a nurse, or a dietitian may be able to present health classes or targeted talks that address physical issues and give general information and suggestions. Some congregations I know include a "health ministry" where volunteer nurses, doctors, or medical assistants perform simple medical procedures like blood pressure checks on a monthly basis.

Other members of the congregation can become involved in providing physical support through something as simple as becoming an activity accountability partner. Two or more people may partner together to attend a local gym or fitness class. For example, these people may also agree to meet at a designated location to walk together, either outside or at a nearby shopping mall in bad weather. Whenever possible, pairing people with similar interests, like biking or gardening, can provide support and friendship.

Once a person has worked with a healthcare professional to determine an appropriate level of physical activity, members of the congregation can help by checking in with the person and/or going with the person to appointments or outside classes, to help motivate and encourage. During these times of physical support, the potential is always there to layer on spiritual support, emotional support, and relational support.

As well as exercise, hurting people may also need help with choosing and cooking healthy, nutritious meals. With our fast-food culture, home cooking can seem like a lost art. The congregations I've been a part of over the years have all had at least one member known for her or his cooking ability. These are usually people who love food and view their culinary expression with passion. Such people may be willing to assist in giving information or helping with meal planning and preparation. Even learning how to navigate a grocery store by shopping the perimeters of the store (where the produce, meat, and dairy selections are found) and avoiding the inner aisles (where more of the processed foods are found) can be a skill passed along to others to educate and support healthy nutrition.

Addiction Support

Many churches are already sites of self-help groups, such as AA (Alcoholics Anonymous), NA (Narcotics Anonymous), GA (Gamblers Anonymous), OA (Overeaters Anonymous), SA (Sexaholics Anonymous), or CR (Celebrate Recovery). Local churches are valuable locations for groups such as these and others. Many of the participants in these groups will become members of the churches in which they are located, but even if they do not, such groups can provide important addiction support to members of those congregations.

As an addiction counselor, I understand that self-help groups are not always the best option for those seeking recovery. Recovery from alcohol and drug addiction, for example, can often require medical and professional intervention; the type of intervention lay groups are not able to give. What these self-help groups can give is ongoing accountability and peer sobriety support. In addition, the models and methods used in one group can be applicable to a variety of addictive behaviors. So, for example, a Celebrate Recovery group may have in the same group people overcoming an alcohol addiction, a gambling addiction, or a food addiction, all supporting each other.

For those hurting people who need professional intervention, the local church can still provide help and assistance by creating accountability for attending needed medical appointments, counseling sessions, or groups. This support can use the "sponsorship" model from the Alcoholics Anonymous organization, where someone who has successfully obtained sobriety acts as a "sponsor" for someone newly in recovery. The sponsor is aware of that person's schedule and checks in to make sure he or she is staying consistent with group attendance and 12-Step assignments.

Financial Support

Money, or the lack thereof, can create a cavalcade of problems. In my line of work, I've found financial stress to be a significant factor in relationship problems. Arguments that happen when people talk about money can cause stress. Problems occur when people fail to talk about money and make false assumptions about what another person should or should not do where money is concerned. Misunderstandings over money can tear couples and families apart. And financial concerns can become physical concerns when some people put off needed medical care. Handling money poorly, and poor attitudes about money, can become spiritual issues, as 1 Timothy 6:10 (NIV) so succinctly states: "For the love of money is a root of all kinds of evil. Some people, eager for money, have wandered from the faith and pierced themselves with many griefs."

The local church can contribute to a wellness team by providing targeted financial support, whenever possible. This financial support should be clearly explained as to amount and conditions. There should be markers, as part of this support, that need to be reached for financial support to continue. When providing copayment assistance for counseling appointments, for example, those markers could be as simple as a provision that the person will attend at least 90% of the appointments scheduled. Why place a number on this financial support? Because the person cannot be helped if the person does not show up.

Local churches have been in the business of benevolence since the first century (2 Corinthians 9:11-13, for example). A direct connection between those giving the help and those receiving the help is powerful. The local church should not feel badly about attaching "strings" to acts of benevolence, especially financial. Even the Apostle Paul put caveats on who should receive help from the church (2 Thessalonians 3:10; 1 Timothy 5:9-10). If at all possible, consider asking those receiving financial help to provide help around the building or grounds. Provide direction for what needs doing and praise for good effort. In such a way, a hand-out can become a hand-up.

Another way for the local church to provide financial support is through financial education. Not everyone grew up learning how to balance a checkbook or understanding how debt or compound interest works. Financial concepts can be difficult for people to grasp, leading to poor decisions and devastating consequences (or, as it were, being pierced with many griefs). Within a congregation, people with either financial training or proven financial stewardship can share their knowledge with others. This help can be individual or in a group setting. Churches can also agree to become sites of biblically-based financial trainings for the benefit of both their members and the community-at-large.

Individual and Group Support

Group support can help spread the work of the wellness team. However, group support alone is not enough. Much of the healing work is done person-to-person, with individuals reaching out to provide love, care, and support. Whether pulling weeds, or over a cup of coffee, or sorting clothes for the clothing bank, or taking a walk around the neighborhood, support can be given one interaction, one person at a time.

Groups are effective at sharing information and ideas, but some conversations need to be done in more private settings. Individual time promotes special bonding and times of safe confidences. Groups allow a person to both express his or her own thoughts, and listen to the thoughts of others (Ecclesiastes 3:7b). Yet no one—and no group—can force a person to change. A mix of individual contact and group support, based upon the person's needs, can create accountability, expectation, and a sense of personal ownership of change and recovery.

Community Support

When crafting a wellness team, I cannot emphasize enough the importance of finding that one person or several persons who are able to research and gather information on broader community resources. Some mental and relational needs are, frankly, bigger than the church; especially than smaller churches. Secular resources can be harnessed to help support these needs, under the guidance of the church-based wellness team.

God's resources are not confined to church-owned real estate (Psalm 50:10). And God's influence is not confined to only those who believe in his name. The Old Testament is filled with evidence that God can and does use those who do not know him to accomplish his purposes. Identify a person or people in your congregation who can look around your community, find out what resources are available, make calls, and do research on the Internet. From this search, a resource guide can be created that can be used by pastors, church leaders, and members to gather help and fill in any blanks that may be missing from the resources available through the local congregation.

And, while you're looking at secular resources, don't overlook spiritual ones. Even small communities can have multiple places of faith and worship. Whenever possible, partner together. One church may have classes on biblical stewardship, while another teaches parenting classes, and still another's ministry is to singles and newly marrieds. The community of faith is wider and encompasses more than many churches realize. Open your eyes and see where God is already working in your area through local faith communities. Create new opportunities to help the hurting by connecting with existing efforts where you can.

Boundaries

I would be remiss if I did not include a caution about the importance of boundaries for church-based wellness teams. As a professional therapist,

I understand the power of properly held boundaries to assist people in healing and recovery, especially from mental and relationship issues. People must be allowed to make their own choices, make their own mistakes, and enjoy their own victories. Their success should never be seen as a spiritual jewel to wear around your neck.

Boundaries are vital for the hurting person. Hurting people can be desperate, and they may cling to anything and anyone as they attempt to save themselves. The more the hurting person leans on you, the less the person relies on his or her own strength—or God's. Support from you, yes, but not dependence on you. The goal is for the person to be able to stand firm, on his or her own.

Boundaries are also vital for the helping person. The warning from Galatians 6:1 (NIV) is devastatingly true: "Brothers and sisters, if someone is caught in a sin, you who live by the Spirit should restore that person gently. But watch yourselves, or you also may be tempted." There are very clear boundaries for those of us in the counseling profession. These boundaries are necessary because of the very intimate work we do with people. We want to connect with people and their suffering but we do not want to become enmeshed or entangled.

The church-based wellness team members should, therefore, be accountable to each other. When starting such a team, make sure to determine a list of appropriate boundaries and then hold each other accountable to adhere to them. Beware the "single exception." In my experience, exceptions have an irritating propensity to become the rule. A rule broken once is still a rule broken.

Unity of Effort

The work of helping hurting people, especially those with difficult mental and relationship issues, is challenging, taxing work. For too long, as a pastor or church leader, you may have been expected by others, or by yourselves, to tackle this type of work alone. For every need that showed up on your doorstep, you may have felt obligated to answer the call like Isaiah, "Here am I. Send me (Isaiah 6:8b, NIV)!" Your operative words were "I" and "me." Yet I am witness to the sad truth that, over time and under stress, the enthusiasm of "I" and "me" can become the weariness of "I have to do this. It all depends on me."

There is something interesting about the full verse of Isaiah 6:8 (NIV): "Then I heard the voice of the Lord saying, 'Whom shall I send. And who will go for us?' And I said, 'Here am I. Send me!'" Did you notice that God said, "who will go for *us*?" God is not a solitary God; he exists in relationship and in teamwork to accomplish his purposes. Christ, likewise, when he lived upon this earth, gathered a team around him.

As a pastor or church leader, you may be a get-it-done type of person. You may be comfortable with leadership and aren't afraid to step out on your own. You may even be the type of person who finds comfort in doing the job yourself, instead of relying on others and waiting for them to help. You may be more secure with "I" and "me" instead of "we" and "us." If you're this type of person, I would ask you to consider the following. Have you ever wondered why Jesus didn't just stick around after he was resurrected, to make sure his church got off on the right foot? Wouldn't it have been better if Jesus had just stayed behind, in charge, here on earth a little bit longer? Why did he leave such an important job to people like, frankly, Peter?

Some of you may have serious questions about whether something like this wellness team could possibly work for you or your congregation. A little voice inside you may be whispering that all of this seems like a great deal of work, organization, and oversight. Wouldn't it just be easier to keep doing what you're doing, which is doing the work by yourself?

In answer to that little voice, I offer the example of the body in 1 Corinthians 12 (NIV). The operative part I'd like you to consider is verse 17: "If the whole body were an eye, where would the sense of hearing be? If the whole body were an ear, where would the sense of smell be?" Which brings me back to the beginning, when I had to admit that, unlike the Apostle Paul, I simply couldn't be all things to all people. I may be a fabulous eye, but I can't hear a single word. I may be able to hear a pin drop in a crowded room, but honestly, I can't smell a thing.

There is no "I" in teamwork, and there is no "I" in Ephesians 2:10 (NIV): "For we are God's handiwork, created in Christ Jesus to do good works, which God prepared in advance for us to do." "We" and "us," teaming together to accomplish God's good works, is a solid, biblical pattern. This is the pattern of the Triune God. This is the pattern of Jesus and his disciples. This is the pattern of the early church, and this should be the pattern of the local church today.

The blessings in store for your congregation through a wellness team are not confined to those who receive your help. The blessings are just as much for those who are called and equipped by God to provide that help. As the saying goes, don't be afraid to "share the wealth" of service. Assess your strengths. Reach out for help. Gather your team. Define your goals. Pray and expect God to empower your team. Watch for God to accomplish his will through "us."

One last verse, Ecclesiastes 4:12 (NIV): "Though one may be overpowered, two can defend themselves. A cord of three strands is not quickly broken." That's the power, protection, and promise of teamwork!

About the Editors

Tim Clinton, Ed. D., LPC, LMFT is President of the American Association of Christian Counselors, the largest and most diverse Christian counseling association in the world. He is the Executive Director of the James Dobson Family Institute and recurring co-host of "Dr. James Dobson's Family Talk." Licensed as a Professional Counselor and as a Marriage and Family Therapist, Dr. Clinton is recognized as a world leader in mental health and relationship issues and spends much of his time working with Christian leaders and professional athletes. He has authored and edited nearly 30 books, including *The Struggle is Real: How to Care for Mental and Relational Health Needs in the Church* and is the Executive Editor of *The Care and Counsel Bible* by Thomas Nelson Press.

Rev. Jared Pingleton, Psy.D., is a respected leader in the Christian Mental Health field and currently serves as the Director of Mental Health Care and Ministry of the American Association of Christian Counselors. In professional practice since 1977, he is a licensed clinical psychologist, a credentialed minister who has served on the staff of two large churches, a former professor at several Christian colleges and seminaries, and the former Director of Counseling Services at Focus on the Family. He is the author or co-author of several books, including *The Struggle is Real: How to Care for Mental and Relational Health Needs in the Church;* Making *Magnificent Marriages; Be Strong and Surrender: A 30 Day Recovery Guide; Praying With Jesus: Reset My Prayer Life; Marriage: It's Foundation, Theology, and Mission in a Changing World,* and is also the Consulting Editor of *The Care and Counsel Bible* by Thomas Nelson Press. For more about Jared, including contact information, go to www.drpingleton.com.

Printed in the United States
By Bookmasters